Literary Criticism
of Seventeenth-Century
England

The Borzoi Anthology
of 17th-Century English Literature

GENERAL EDITOR

Joseph A. Mazzeo
Columbia University

Seventeenth-Century English Poetry (Vols. I & II)
EDITED BY *MIRIAM K. STARKMAN*
Queens College of The City University of New York

Seventeenth-Century English Prose (Vol. III)
EDITED BY *DAVID NOVARR, Cornell University*

Literary Criticism of Seventeenth-Century England (Vol. IV)
EDITED BY *EDWARD W. TAYLER, Columbia University*

Religious Prose of Seventeenth-Century England (Vol. V)
EDITED BY *ANNE DAVIDSON FERRY, Harvard University*

Literary Criticism
of Seventeenth-Century
England

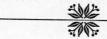

EDITED BY

Edward W. Tayler

COLUMBIA UNIVERSITY

ALFRED · A · KNOPF
NEW YORK
1967

Preface

This volume offers the materials needed for a study of the literary criticism of the seventeenth century, the century that records
the transition from the "rhetorical" criticism of the sixteenth
century to the "modern" literary criticism of Dryden: it is the
seventeenth century that gives us "critic" in its modern signification of one who does not merely judge—but judges a work of
art. It is during this period that we encounter literary biography,
editing, and criticism agitated almost for the first time by the
stirrings of the historical imagination. And, perhaps most important of all, it is during this period that we may perceive most
clearly the development of the opposed categories—scientist
and poet, prose and poetry, logic and imagination, things and
words—that still dictate the shape and direction of much of
our thinking about life and literature. If we are ever to be delivered from such antitheses, we could do worse than to look with
particular care at the century that fought its civil war in every
area of human endeavor.

Since selection was unavoidable, it was decided to concentrate
on those items that treat primarily of non-dramatic literature
and to exclude Dryden's longer works, which though interesting
and valuable command a prohibitive amount of space and are,
in any event, readily available elsewhere. Although the texts
cannot pretend to be definitive, it is hoped that they will prove
reliable for all but the most exacting ends of scholarship. A
number of the selections have never been anthologized before,
and a few have never before been edited. I have sought to offer
the selections in much the same form in which they appeared
to the critics' contemporaries: emendation occurs rarely, usually
being limited to obvious printers' errors and to the expansion of
certain abbreviations; the original orthography has been preserved, except in the case of *u* and *v*, *i* and *j*, and the long *s*;
even the original pointing has generally been retained out of

the conviction that, despite the well-known vagaries of Renaissance printers, the age of the colon and semi-colon has something to communicate to the age of the period and comma.

In accordance with the editorial practice of this series, annotation has been kept to the absolute minimum, being confined
mainly to the translation of foreign languages—except where
the writer himself offers a translation or close paraphrase—and
to the explanation of names and words not easily found in standard works of reference. Seventeenth-century English so closely
resembles modern English that a reader may be excused for not
knowing when he is not understanding. When Soames speaks of
"labour'd Sense" and Granville of "pompous" verse, they intend
to praise, and the alert reader will divine as much from context.
But of course linguistic change is not restricted to connotation:
"meer" usually denotes "pure," "still" usually denotes "always,"
and "sad" (Reynolds' "sadd weightyer true gold") can still, but
not always, mean "unchanging" or "steadfast"; in addition,
"then" doubles for "than" and "at least" for "at last." Here again
context may be expected to guide the careful, and forewarned,
reader. Unfortunately, the real problem involves our having very
nearly lost one whole dimension of seventeenth-century English.
At that time educated men lived in "divided and distinguished
worlds" of discourse, for their academic training emphasized
almost exclusively the rigorous study of Latin literature: their
use of English is often Latinate. The words of *Paradise Lost* not
only retain at times their Latin significations but also reveal puns
on their Latin stems; and when Donne tells us "how witty's
ruine," we learn that because of the Fall "we are borne ruinous"
(L. *ruina*, fall), so that children are born "headlong, and fall
upon An ominous precipitation" (L. *præ* + *caput*, head-first;
præcipitatum, headlong). "Ruine," it seems, is quite "witty" indeed, and the Introduction will suggest something of how "witty"
is Wit itself. The forewarned reader will find it easier to deal
with certain words that very nearly always recur in their Latin
significations: "sentence" (*sententia*), a statement, usually apho-
ristic, that is often italicized to draw attention to its apotheg-
matic wisdom; "rage," also "fury" (akin to *furor*, especially *furor
poeticus*), the divine madness or inspired "enthusiasm" of the
poet; "produce" (*producere*, lead out or extend in length), as in

Daniel's "taught to produce what they make short"; "translation" (*translatio*), a transferring to the figurative level, hence
"trope" or "metaphor," as well as transferring into another language; "composure" (O.F. *composer,* from L. *componere*), a
composition, as a poetic composition; "plausible" (*plausibilis,*
pleasing or deserving applause), as with Digby's "adorne with
any plausible discourses"; "conceit" (L. *conceptus,* influenced
by the Italian *concetto*), a thought, hence also a "literary concept" or "intellectual image" that may be defined, if defined at
all, by the various and conflicting uses to be found in a book
like this; and so on. I have provided notes for many such words,
but full annotation would submerge the text.

The selections are arranged insofar as possible in chrono-
logical order, usually according to the date of the earliest work
by a particular author; since much of the material circulated
in manuscript before publication, I have, wherever some kind
of plausible evidence exists, allowed myself to be guided by the
presumed date of composition. The headnotes provide brief biographical and textual information, together with briefer remarks,
supplementing the Introduction, about the historical significance
of the works reprinted. My footnotes appear in brackets to distinguish them from the notes and marginalia of the writers anthologized.

The Huntington Library (San Marino, California) has my
deep gratitude for the use of its facilities and the help of its
staff; unless otherwise noted, the selections are reprinted by permission from seventeenth-century editions held by the Library.
Although it has proven impracticable to make much direct use
of the texts provided by modern editors, I am wholly conscious
of my great debt to scholars like Herford and Simpson, whose
Ben Jonson remains a model in its kind; to those historians of
literature—most of whom appear in the Selected Bibliography—
whose findings and insights I have drawn upon to write the
Introduction; and in particular to G. Gregory Smith and Joel
Elias Spingarn, whose pioneering anthologies are also listed in
the bibliography. I am grateful for valuable suggestions or other
help in time of need to Hugh Amory, Thomas H. Blackburn,
Howard Canaan, James Clifford, French Fogle, Carolyn Gold-
berg, Joseph Anthony Mazzeo, Howard N. Porter, and Dora Odar-

enko; especially to Harry H. Boyle and Virgil K. Whitaker, both of whom gave generously of valuable time to safeguard my passage through the mazes of Renaissance Latin quotation. David Dushkin, Susan Scarff Webster, and especially Estelle Fine represent, for me, the tactful guidance of Alfred A. Knopf, Inc. Barbara Damrosch Kerrigan showed intelligence and stamina at crucial points in the preparation of the manuscript. Irene gave of herself, both as scholar and helpmeet fit.

Contents

Michael Drayton

John Milton

Sir Kenelm Digby

William Drummond of Hawthornden

Thomas Carew

Henry Reynolds

George Herbert

Sir John Suckling

Sir William Davenant or D'Avenant

Thomas Hobbes

Andrew Marvell

Abraham Cowley

Thomas Sprat

John Wilmot, Earl of Rochester

John Dryden

Joseph Glanvill

Samuel Butler

Sir William Soames

Wentworth Dillon, Earl of Roscommon

Francis Atterbury

Charles Gildon

George Granville, Baron Lansdowne

Literary Criticism
of Seventeenth-Century
England

Introduction

Not long after the death of John Donne in 1931, Carew epitomized the achievement of his great predecessor in a famous elegiac couplet:

> Here lies a King, that rul'd as hee thought fit
> The universall Monarchy of wit—

thus anticipating the language, but not the meaning, of Dryden's complimentary lines to William Congreve in the closing decade of the century:

> Yet this I Prophecy: Thou shalt be seen
> (Tho' with some short Parenthesis between)
> High on the Throne of Wit. . . .

For Carew the one word "wit" evoked Donne's most kingly accomplishments: the "fresh invention" and "masculine expression," contrasting with the "servile imitation" and "soft melting Phrases" of the Petrarchan poetasters; the "giant Phansy," discovering in Nature such an array of bold correspondences that

> to the awe of thy imperious wit
> Our stubborn language bends. . . .

But in eulogizing Congreve's royal "wit" Dryden proposed to reveal his appreciation of an entirely different order of literary merit, for as he pointed out in the Epilogue to the Second Part of *The Conquest of Granada:*

> Wit's now arriv'd to a more high degree;
> Our native language more refin'd and free:
> Our ladies and our men now speak more wit
> In conversation, than those poets writ.

In this context "wit" denotes Congreve's gift for aristocratic repartee, his extraordinary ability to counterfeit in comic art the manners of a courtly society and to fix impeccably the minute variations from the ideal norm that constituted "wit," or the lack of it, among the gentlemen and ladies of the second half of the century. Although Dryden must be considered as accurate a critical prophet as Carew an elegiac critic, it is obviously in only the most superficial way that the two may be said to rely on the same literary vocabulary.

During the period from Donne to Dryden there occurred a radical shift in literary sensibility that betrays its presence not through dramatic changes in critical vocabulary but rather through the new meanings ascribed to old words. Although the existence of this kind of semantic prestidigitation correctly implies that the most significant changes occur in an indirect and, as it were, subterranean manner, the more obvious historical developments are of course important and provide the broad context needed for an understanding of the perplexing shift that takes place at a deeper level.

The literary criticism of the first half of the seventeenth century modifies and extends theories formulated during the preceding century, theories that owed much of their vitality and range to the recovery of classical sources, mainly through the editions and commentaries of the Renaissance Italians. Sixteenth-century literary criticism, insofar as it may be distinguished from the rhetorical criticism that flourished everywhere during the period, had established itself as a separate literary genre largely in response to those who attacked poetry. In the course of defending the Muse from moral zealots and from the poetasters who contributed to her unsavory reputation, the apologists, the most famous of whom is Sidney, sought to draw poetry into a systematic art after the examples provided by Greece and Rome so that, in the words of Puttenham's *Arte of English Poesie* (1589), the craft of feigning might be "corrected and reformed by discreet judgements." The eventual result is the critic and his criticism.

Ben Jonson's *Timber,* a compilation of critical and other dicta belonging to the first third of the seventeenth century, includes the essentials of the earlier body of doctrine and transmits them with renewed prestige to later writers.

> A *Poet* is . . . a Maker, or a fainer: His Art, an Art of imitation, or faining; expressing the life of man in fit measure, numbers, and harmony, according to *Aristotle*. . . . Now, the *Poesy* is the habit, or the Art: nay, rather the Queene of Arts: which had her Originall from heaven. . . . And, wheras they entitle *Philosophy* to bee a rigid, and austere *Poesie:* they have (on the contrary) stiled *Poesy,* a dulcet and gentle *Philosophy,* which leades on, and guides us by the hand to Action with a ravishing delight, and incredible Sweetnes. . . . And not thinke, hee can leape forth suddainely a *Poet,* by dreaming hee hath been in *Parnassus.* . . . For to Nature, Exercise, Imitation, and Studie, *Art* must bee added, to make all these perfect. . . . For . . . without Art, Nature can ne're bee perfect; &, without Nature, Art can clayme no being.

Poetry had her "Originall" from heaven, as the Renaissance neo-Platonists supposed; the end of poetry, as the Renaissance Horatians held, is to teach and delight; and, as the Renaissance Aristotelians assumed, the method of Art is to imitate Nature. Of these assumptions, usually conflated, that of imitation is central, the point from which theories radiate. It is a principle that shapes the course of criticism in the seventeenth century and that retains the glamour of certitude well into the eighteenth century. In matters such as these Jonson resists efforts to differentiate him from the critics of the sixteenth century in Italy, France, Holland, and England.

And yet the process of modification and extension has already begun. It is not that Jonson proclaims anything very different on the level of abstract theory, nor even that he forsakes the predominantly rhetorical cast of sixteenth-century criticism. Rather, there occurs a shift in emphasis as he comes gradually to show less interest in his earlier (neo-Platonic) view of the poet as divinely inspired and begins to dwell instead on problems of craft or technique. The shift from poet as *vates sacer* to poet as "maker" or craftsman may be associated with the effort, general among the Jacobeans, to avoid what was called, rather inaccurately, "Ciceronian" eloquence. Thus Jonson reverts in his search for rhetorical models to Martial, Horace, Pliny, Tacitus, and Petronius—those who "speke best Latine," it seems, are anti-Ciceronians all. The movement is away from the *genus grande*, the high style used (pre-eminently by Cicero) in affairs of state, and toward the *genus medium* and *genus humile*, the middle and low styles traditionally used for comedy, satire, and epigram. Jonson's poetry, as well as his criticism, reveals such preferences and also betrays the related effort, shared by Donne, to extend the range of the middle and low styles so as to include in them those matters, like divinity and statesmanship, that were traditionally reserved to the high style.

Whereas Sidney and Puttenham, the greatest critics of the sixteenth century, had directed their remarks to a courtly audience that had permitted its stylistic ideals to be formed chiefly by Cicero in prose and Petrarch in verse, Jonson's criticism represents a reaction against this "Asiatic" eloquence and the heightened diction of the Petrarchan poetasters: "You may sound these wits, and find the depth of them with your middle finger. They are *Creame-bowle,* or but puddle deepe." The sixteenth-century concern with the rhetoric of poetry is in the end qualified and extended, not only by the search for new models to imitate but also by the appeal to new authorities, many of them Renaissance writers who offered theoretical justifications for the "Attic" style: Hoskyns, Bacon, Vives, Lipsius, and, of course, the Erasmus of the *Ciceronianus*.

Although there assuredly exists no direct and easy relationship between these rhetorical theories and the actual process of versifying, it would be cavalier to suppose that this kind of criticism has nothing to do with the poetry Erasmus admired in one of his letters to Ammonius: "What particularly delights me is a rhetorical poem and a poetical oration, in which one can see the poetry in the prose and the rhetoric in the poetry." Knowing that the chameleon acquires his color only indirectly, from the leaf on which he perches, does not make him any the less green, though it should doubtless make us more attentive to the mysteries of metamorphosis. Even the negative influence of rhetorical training assumes some importance when we remember that the metaphysical style owes many of its most felicitous moments to the daring manipulation of such standard procedures as paradox, oxymoron, and "far-fet" analogy. The rhetorical ferment, particularly in the way it served to obliterate traditional classifications and standards of decorum, mirrors darkly the poetic moil out of which came the different, yet affiliated, "strong [or, as we now say, "metaphysical"] lines" of Chapman, Greville, Donne, and Jonson.

Yet it remains true that Jonson's modifications of sixteenth-century rhetorical criticism do not "explain" metaphysical verse. There is, in fact, no sizable body of doctrine in England that directly treats the subject at all. The most remarkable single fact about the literary criticism of the seventeenth century is that a great poetic style arose, reached its height in Donne, and then spent its force, without ever having its achievement defined or its principles expounded by contemporary critics. What we possess is in the nature of isolated comments, occurring more often than not in such improbable places as handbooks for preachers (the "metaphysical" manner of sermonizing attracted a few theorists), or in the entirely negative though useful responses of men like Drummond and North.

On the Continent, however, a number of critics argued theories of wit that have been considered more or less applicable to metaphysical poetry. These theorists, of whom the most interesting are probably the Spaniard Baltasar Gracián and the Italian Emanuele Tesauro, took Aristotle as their point of departure and used the provocative comments on metaphor in the *Poetics* and the third part of the *Rhetoric* to establish definitions of the "conceit" or conceptual metaphor. For Gracián the conceited poem declares a "subtle concord" among "extreme knowables," and the conceit itself represents an "intellectual act" that "expresses" the "correspondences" existing among "objects" in Nature. Thus, Gracián refuses to allow just "any simile" the name of "conceit," for the "conceptual" or "conceited" metaphor properly requires some "additional" kind of "mystery, contrariety, correspondence, disproportion." In Tesauro's treatise, *The Aristotelian Telescope*

(1654), the poet becomes through metaphor a Galileo, offering in the glass of language a strange view of Nature. Whereas the intellect operates directly upon reality, poetic "wit" (*ingegno*) effects delightful tricks in perspective, pleasurable examples of *trompe l'oeil*, by binding together the "remote and separate" and displaying "similarity in dissimilar things." Figures of speech generally "clothe concepts with words," but metaphor uniquely "clothes words with concepts" to produce urbanely fallacious arguments (*argomenti urbanamente fallaci*). Since in the view of this Aristotelian Jesuit the poet's *ingegno* is in some ways analogous to the "wit" of deity, the conceit acquires metaphysical dignity as the elegantly "fallacious" imitation of those "remote" signs that are in Nature the "work of the divine mind." But in England these theorizers had few if any followers, partly because the Italian influence was being progressively displaced by that of the Dutch, epitomized in the *De Tragoediæ Constitutione* (1611) of Daniel Heinsius, who helped make the rational classicism of Scaliger and Minturno available to the neoclassical Corneille and Dryden.

In England there were, of course, more than a few anachronistic attempts, like that of Reynolds in *Mythomystes,* to associate poetry with mystical or intuitive modes of apprehension and thus to liberate the poet from the literalists of the rhetorical imagination. But these theories of a "dark" or "closed" style provide little that illuminates the technique of metaphysical verse; and in any case they were soon to succumb to the prevailing rationalism, to the distaste for "enthusiasm"—thereafter to reappear only sporadically, as when Baudelaire or Yeats comes to cultivate an interest in occult doctrines of universal correspondence. The generality of English literary critics found themselves preoccupied with far other considerations: with polemics, the uses and abuses of poetry; with prefatorial self-justification; with the enunciation of general principles, largely rhetorical; with defining the "place" of poetry in relation to history and philosophy; and with, of course, controversies over classical versification and the propriety of rhyme. Although the poets themselves were constantly intrigued by the practical question of form in literature, their interest does not as a rule appear in literary criticism but has to be inferred from their forays into such alternative disciplines as rhetoric (Sidney's *Apologie for Poetrie* or Milton's *Areopagitica* as shaped by the form of the classical oration), dialectic (Marvell's "Coy Mistress," a subjunctive syllogism), or even numerology (Spenser's *Epithalamion*). But while the poets were exploring a variety of means to imitate the ordered Nature that is the "Art of God," the critics were perfecting in the heat of controversy those antithetical categories that still exert their negative influence on twentieth-century thought: science against poetry, logic against imagination, prose against verse, ideas against words, the general against the particular, and so on.

Analogous limitations appear in literary biography, literary editing, and literary history. Finding anything that resembles sustained analysis of the kind practiced widely today is rare, rare also to gain a sense of the man and the canon as produced in time and modified by circumstance. Criticism generally takes place, as it were, outside of history. Although there can be little doubt that the seventeenth-century version of the perennial debate between Ancients and Moderns stimulated an awareness of historical development, what was needed and yet only imperfectly achieved was the application of something like the idea of progress to literature. For in order to write sophisticated literary history, it was first necessary to recognize in a series like the old roll call of poets some kind of process or change, some kind of development or relation that could be appreciated independently of the widespread theories of degeneration or—as in William Temple—cyclical change: "Science and the arts have run their circles and had their periods in the several parts of the world." Critics like Atterbury, innocently discovering that all poetic history progresses to its culmination in Waller, succeed in avoiding the pessimistic view only by embracing simplicities of another order.

Sustained literary criticism of a particular work of art properly begins with Dryden, whose custom of writing critical prefaces stems ultimately from the old convention of printing, in the hope of patronage, fulsome letters of dedication that often disclosed something of literary method and purpose. Dryden had closer precedent in writers like Chapman and Jonson, both of whom had accustomed themselves to addressing "The Reader" at quite some length; and of course there is finally the immediate and compelling example of Corneille. The *Examens* that Corneille prefixed to each play in the collected edition of 1660 anticipate Dryden's habit of combining self-justification with specific attention to individual texts, a habit that, in works like Dryden's *A Discourse Concerning the Original and Progress of Satire* (1693) or *Preface to Fables Ancient and Modern* (1700), transforms the preface into literary criticism of a high order of excellence. (The famous *An Essay of Dramatic Poesy*, published in 1668, contains an extended *examen* of Ben Jonson's *Epicoene; or the Silent Woman*.) It is Dryden in whom almost alone there appear the beginnings of the historical imagination combined with an awareness that biography, editing, and criticism are not necessarily mutually exclusive modes of endeavor. And yet even in Dryden there are only vital intimations of what Samuel Johnson will achieve in the *Lives of the Poets*.

Given limitations such as these, it might be argued, with no more than a modest affection for paradox, that in seventeenth-century England the best criticism of poetry, including metaphysical poetry, is poetry. The earliest criticism of verse, as of almost everything else, was probably written in verse, and the tradition of imparting virtually all kinds of information in rhyme proved nearly as seductive to the writers of the Renaissance as it had to the encyclopedic versifiers of the Middle Ages. There was in addition the classical precedent set by Horace's *Ars Poetica*, imitations of which range from Drayton's verse-epistle to Reynolds, in which the influence resides mainly in tone and manner, through the Soames-Dryden version of Boileau's *Art Poétique* (itself the chief effort of the *législateur du Parnasse* to realize in seventeenth-century France the Horatian ideals of "reason" and "good sense"), to the more or less literal translations of the *Ars Poetica* produced by Jonson and Roscommon.

There are, of course, numerous varieties of poetry that owe little or nothing to Horace yet nevertheless embody direct and explicit literary criticism. There is, for instance, the spate of dedicatory or complimentary verse that generally accompanied a book of poems to the press, where in the midst of all the hyperbolic hackwork and extravagant eulogy there occasionally appear poems, like Marvell's on *Paradise Lost*, that are remarkable for critical insight and candid precision. There is as well the vast bulk of elegiac criticism in verse, which when practiced with the discriminating tact of Jonson on Shakespeare or Carew on Donne takes its place beside the best prose criticism of the period. The most popular variety of elegiac criticism made use of the ancient convention of the roll call of poets, a list subsuming brief biographical and critical comments that had its prose counterpart in the catalogues of writers like Francis Meres, Henry Peacham, and Edmund Bolton. The persistence of the form throughout the seventeenth century may be attributed to its flexible simplicity, the principle of enumeration being obviously susceptible to variation from without; and in retrospect it seems inevitable that the *Ragguagli di Parnaso* of Boccalini, the first "century" of which appeared in 1612 and initiated a European vogue, should have provided the necessary infusion. Boccalini's Lucianic fantasies, especially the intoxicating fiction of carrying out the "judicial" procedures of literature before the bar of Apollo, seized the English poetic imagination almost immediately and transformed the roll call into the "Sessions [judgments] of the Poets," thus affording wits like Suckling and Rochester the opportunity to deliver, with mock-Apollonian gravity, censures both personal and literary.

Less amusing but often more informative are the poems that avoid partisan compliment, either dedicatory or elegiac, and are in general also free of the element of personal invective that animates the "Sessions." Some of these works are prefatorial, as Chapman's crotchety "To the Reader"; some, like Cowley's "Of Wit" and "The Muse," pretend to definition and deal with special aspects of the craft; and some, like Milton's invocations or Herbert's "Jordan" poems, betray to a greater or lesser degree the poet's personal concern with the poetic act *sub specie divinitatis,* his concern with the implications of Donne's prayer in "A Litanie":

> When wee are mov'd to seeme religious
> Only to vent wit, Lord deliver us.

Toward the end of the period, criticism in verse comes increasingly to resemble Roscommon's "An Essay on Translated Verse" or Granville's "Upon unnatural Flights in Poetry"—urbanely the-

oretical, largely deductive in method, and nearly always legislative in purpose. It is not always easy to determine, in the course
of reading such productions, why the medium of verse should
have recommended itself to the writer, though the residuum of
truth in Matthew Arnold's witticism that Dryden and Pope are
classics of our prose implies that the problem of differentiating
the two mediums had become increasingly complicated.

But because of the peculiar resources available to the poet
there can be no question of the propriety of using poetry in what
may be called "oblique" or "indirect" literary criticism in verse.
Poets, whatever else they may be presumed to be up to, are forever glancing at the nature of their craft in the very process of
writing; even meter and rhyme constitute implicit comment on
the powers and limitations of language. I am not now referring
to the comparatively direct poetic pronouncements about art and
life occurring, say, in Dylan Thomas' "In my craft or sullen art,"
but rather to the obliquities of Wallace Stevens' "Anecdote of the
Jar," where the object of the title is "placed" in Nature to tell us
something of the whereabouts of that other object of well-
wrought Art, poetry. More traditional obliquities appear in "The
Man with the Blue Guitar," which resembles Wiat's "Blame not
my lute, for he must sound" in using a musical instrument to
glance, through synechdoche and analogy, at the sister artist. In
the most famous example of this type, Shelley's "To a Skylark,"
we are disposed to see, in the "profuse strains of unpremedi-
tated art," a parallel to the rapture of the Romantic poet. Many
Renaissance examples, when they do not depend on the established equations of poet with bird or lute, require a special effort
to appreciate because their techniques of allusion and double
reference become richly suggestive only in the appropriate historical and religious context. An easy illustration of potential difficulties may be found in Carew's fine poem to Sandys, which begins:

> I Presse not to the Quire, nor dare I greet
> The holy Place with my unhallowed feet—

then audaciously proceeds to exploit the pun on poetic "foot"
until finally the system of double reference prepares us fully to

experience the hope that the "Lyrick feet" of the "Muse" may "dance" in Davidic exaltation "before the Arke" of God. Carew's poem—to borrow a phrase from Jonson's Cary-Morison ode—delineates the "lines of life." Jonson, like Carew, manipulates throughout a punning parallel between Art and Nature, between the "measures" of poetry and the "proportions" of "life";

> for Life doth her great actions spell,
> By what was done and wrought
> In season, and so brought
> To light: her measures are, how well
> Each syllab'e answer'd, and was form'd, how faire;
> These make the lines of life, and that's her ayre.

This poetic double talk is, in effect, a dramatic embodiment of the critical dictum that Jonson shared with Milton, that the good poet must first of all be the good man, who "ought him selfe to bee a true Poem."

The practice of sacred parody requires similar responses, for parody is literary criticism of the work it "parallels." A quatrain (originally in couplets) of Dyer's love complaint—

> Mine Exercise naught ells
> But raginge agonies,
> My bookes of spightfull fortunes foiles
> And dreye tragedies—

may suddenly begin to jingle piously in Southwell:

> My exercise remorse,
> And dolefull sinners layes,
> My booke remembrance of my crimes
> And faults of former dayes.

Here again a parallel—this time between Art and Art—is sought, constituting by indirection an act of critical judgment that is quite consciously moral and literary. Such poems criticize adversely the poems by which they subsist, parasitic on the literary host they endeavor to transform *almost* beyond recognition.

In the work of great poets these techniques of parallel and allusion may exhibit even that ultimate parasitism in which the poem criticizes itself. In the ready example, Herbert's "The Collar," the "free" or uneven lines of the poem, as well as the "free" or unruly "life" of the speaker, submit to discipline in order that Art and Nature may undergo a parallel conversion to piety. Marvell's "The Coronet," a kind of heightened pastoral, provides an even more resonant illustration of the possibilities in oblique criticism. The "curious frame" of line twenty-two refers, of course, to the artful ("curious") "Coronet" or "Chaplet" of flowers that the shepherd in his spiritual ignorance ("so I myself deceive") plans to substitute for Christ's crown of "Thorns." But to understand only this much is to ignore the poet's gift for literary criticism and spiritual punditry. For the phrase "my curious frame" may refer as well to the intricate form of the natural man, likewise entangled through the divagations of his "curious" mind in the "winding Snare" of Satan: the Renaissance had not forgotten the medieval vice of *curiositas*, "that God hath made man upright; but they have sought out many inventions." And finally, the squinting context provided by words like "Coronet" (meaning also a circlet of poems, as in Chapman's "A Coronet for his Mistresse Philosophie" or Donne's "La Corona") and "Chaplet" (meaning wreath and prayer and poem) establishes yet another signification for "my curious frame": Marvell's poem itself, an object of "curious" Art that must, like the human "frame" and the "frame" of flowers, be "disentangled" from "Fame and Interest" so as to become a pure chaplet or psalm of praise. In this case, the poem is parasitic upon itself. As in "The Collar" (or Donne's "If poysonous mineralls . . .") a blasphemous or spiritually ignorant speaker is created expressly to be destroyed—the new Adam must replace the old—and "free" or "curious" lines are written expressly to be disciplined, recapitulating within the poem, both spiritually and esthetically, the Augustinian drama of conversion. Such poems record more than a little of the ways men might respond to the most insistent literary question of the day—What has Christ to do with Apollo? And as this is perhaps the ultimate esthetic question in an age of belief, so are these poems perhaps the ultimate in literary criticism: verse that obliquely criticizes itself, as it were, in process, and thereby invites Art so to imitate Nature that both may hope for Grace.

Although deficient in the subtlety that characterizes some of the criticism in verse, the prose criticism of the first half of the century has its peculiar and compelling interest in the way it consolidates and then modifies the mimetic theories developed in the previous century. After this first period, dominated by the "weight and fashion" of Jonson, historians find it useful to distinguish a transitional phase extending from about 1650 to 1674. Less arbitrary than many historical categories, this quarter century clearly reveals the intensification of the French influence that became steadily more fashionable during the last twenty-five years of the century. Charles I's choice of a French wife, Henrietta Maria, had proven to be a significant omen, for during the Interregnum the English court, already Frenchified, removed to France, where the exiles subjected to exotic theory included Cowley, Evelyn, Waller, Denham, and Hobbes. Political and cultural developments thus conspired, on their return, to intensify existing critical imbroglios.

After the death of the rationalistic and "anti-metaphysical" Malherbe in 1628, French literary theorists had carried out the program of codification and adaptation that crystallized the Italian interpretations of Horace and Aristotle into the famous "Rules." Poetry was to be considered a craft rather than a "fury" or divine madness; its "reform" was to be undertaken through systematic "imitation" of the classics, which were close to Nature; and imitation was to be conducted according to the Rules, which Reason had derived from the scrutiny of Nature. During the reign of Louis XIV (1661-1715), the authoritarianism evident in society had a parallel in literary criticism, where the Rules received disciplined form pre-eminently in the urbane poetic exposition of Boileau (1636–1711) but also in Le Bossu, Rapin, and others. The Rules consisted both of general principles—didacticism, imitation, decorum, "probability," and so on —and more specific determinations respecting matters like the "unities" or the doctrines of *kind*. Each *kind*, for example, was governed by its own proprieties that were derived from Nature and consequently not to be violated. Le Bossu, for instance, defined the epic as a species of narrative that through allegory propagates moral truth, going on to observe that the epic poet therefore first settles on the moral and then proceeds to lend

the pill its sugared coating. Among the Rules for the epic deduced by Reason and Good Sense from Nature were the necessity for perfection in the hero, for the intervention of the gods,
for action beginning *in medias res*, and so on. It is just such an
elaborate system that in the third quarter of the seventeenth
century—a convenient date is the publication of Boileau's *Art
Poétique* in 1674—increasingly exercised a hold on English theory; and it is, at least on the surface, chiefly in respect to the
influence of French neoclassicism that the quality of English letters appears to undergo so distinctive a metamorphosis during
the Restoration.

The French system was never so hopelessly pedestrian as a
superficial account implies; Boileau had, after all, introduced his
countrymen to the treatise *On the Sublime,* attributed to "Longinus," as well as popularized the Rules; and the more flexible
neoclassicists willingly acknowledged "a Grace beyond the
Reach of Art." But in any case there is a sense in which the
Rules had always been a part of the English mind so that metaphysical poetry—the one major phenomenon that appears to
controvert the generalization—ought to be viewed, in the perspective of the history of criticism, as poetic practice opposed to
theory, engulfed from both sides by waves of emergent neoclassicism. Lord North, around 1610, clearly anticipates the neoclassical aversion to "strong lines," and Drummond, whose critical
standards are essentially Elizabethan, early condemned those
who had lately "endeavored to abstract" poetry to "*Metaphysical*
Idea's, and *Scholastical* quiddities" on the Horatian principle
that such verse is as monstrous "as if Nature should bring forth
some new Animal." Dryden, who in his life of Lucian shows
himself keenly aware that "the union of two contraries may as
well produce a monster as a miracle," grounded his famous censure of Donne in 1693 on markedly similar principles: "He
affects the metaphysicks, not only in his satires, but in his amorous verses, where Nature only should reign; and perplexes the
minds of the fair sex with nice speculations of philosophy. . . ."

The mimetic theory, based on an appeal to Nature, provides a
link between earlier and later theorists, connects the Renaissance with the Restoration, and establishes affinities between
the pronouncements of Jonson ("Done for not keeping of accent

deserved hanging," "for not being understood would perish") and Dryden (Donne did not take "care of his words, and of his numbers"). From the sixteenth century to the eighteenth century the vast majority of educated Englishmen entertained ideas of Nature, Reason, and Art that could only, when pushed to their logical conclusion, produce something rather like the Rules. The logical extension, overtly the work of the French but latent among the English, developed mainly through subterranean shifts in the meanings of critical terms.

Aristotle and other classical thinkers had provoked interest in the idea that Nature is always and everywhere the same, which is the assumption behind the principle of the *consensus gentium* as reiterated by Hooker in the closing decade of the sixteenth century: "The general and perpetual voice of men is as the sentence of God himself. For that which all men have at all times learned, Nature herself must have needs taught; and God being the author of Nature, her voice is but his instrument." Compare Drummond's literary criticism:

> *Poesy* is not a Thing that is yet in the finding and search, or which may be otherwise found out, being already condescended on by all Nations, and as it were established *jure Gentium,* amongst *Greeks, Romans, Italians, French, Spaniards.*

Or compare Dr. Johnson on Shakespeare, "above all modern writers . . . the poet of nature": "His characters are not modified by the customs of particular places, unpractised by the rest of the world; by the peculiarities of studies or professions, which can operate but upon small numbers; or by the accidents of transient fashions or temporary opinions." In each instance it is assumed that Art is to imitate Nature, Nature as embodied in the *consensus gentium;* which is not to say that critics—think of Rymer and Johnson on Shakespeare—could not reach diametrically opposed conclusions from their diverse understanding of the same premises. But it is nevertheless easy to see that the renewed emphasis on the "norms," as distinct from the "varied plenitude," of Nature may be associated with the growing impatience excited by the individual fancies of metaphysical wit; with the intensified distrust of high-flown abstraction, of any sort of abstruse speculation simply because it *was* abstruse and therefore not sanctioned by the *consensus gentium;* with the accelerated attacks on any kind of sectarianism or "enthusiasm," including the "divine enthusiasm" of the poet who like Milton thereby constituted himself a sect of one.

Corollary to the principle of the *consensus gentium* is the tendency to regard history as the means of multiplying error, for if what is really valuable and true manifests itself to all men in virtue of the fact that they are men, the beautiful and good must have been supremely evident to the Ancients "ere Wit oblique had broke that steddy light" of Nature and Reason. Even Dryden, who managed to avoid the pessimistic view, assumes, in the *Parallel of Poetry and Painting* and elsewhere, that the "way to please" is to "imitate nature. . . . For nature is still the same in all ages, and can never be contrary to herself." And from this premise he is led in several passages to anticipate —with Rymer, Rapin, and others—Pope's final formulation:

> Those RULES of old *discover'd,* not *devis'd,*
> Are *Nature* still, but *Nature Methodiz'd.*

Thus when Waller is credited with having "reformed our numbers," we do well to attend to the original sense of "re-form"; otherwise the appeal may seem to imply the idea of progress, whereas the reformation is more likely to signify what Waller's "easy numbers" or meters in fact suggest—a cultivated reversion to first principles, an effort to realize in poetic form the primal regularities that may be presumed to underlie Nature. Similarly, the literary *kinds,* the "natural" genres, were often felt to have reached their peak without prior development, almost at the moment of inception. For most neoclassical thinkers, to progress usually involves a return, sloughing off the novel aberrations of the "Gothick" to recover the natural glory of Greece and the reasonable grandeur of Rome.

There is, of course, no warrant here to imitate the Nature of Sir Thomas Browne, whose metaphysical wit denied that there were any "Grotesques in Nature," thus providing a cosmic gloss on the fashionable genre of poems to a deformed mistress: "There is no deformity but in Monstrosity; wherein, notwithstanding, there is a kind of Beauty; Nature so ingeniously con-

triving the irregular parts, as they become sometimes more remarkable than the principle Fabrick." The neoclassic critic, on
the other hand, would be distressed by Donne's delight in unusual
complexions, or by Collop's lines to "A Crooked Lady, M. V."—
"Sure *Cupid* of thy shoulders makes a bow"—not merely because
such bizarre fancies violated decorum but also because the
anomalous was in itself repugnant. Insofar as his sense of value
relied on the norms of Nature, on "What oft was *Thought*, but
ne'er so well *Exprest*," he was that much less likely to appreciate
fully the variegated fabric or "disorderly order" that attracted the
rhetorician "E. K." to Spenser: "for oftimes we fynde our selves, I
knowe not how, singularly delighted with the shewe of such naturall rudenesse, and take great pleasure in that disorderly order."
It is this "disorderly order" that Dr. Johnson knew philosophically
but could not fully appreciate when he came to consider the
metaphysical wit of the preceding age:

> Wit, abstracted from its effects upon the hearer, may be more
> rigorously and philosophically considered as a kind of *discordia
> concors;* a combination of dissimilar images, or discovery of occult
> resemblances in things apparently unlike. Of wit, thus defined,
> they have more than enough. The most heterogeneous ideas are
> yoked by violence together; nature and art are ransacked for illus-
> trations, comparisons, and allusions.

Consequently, the "thoughts" of such poets "are often new, but
seldom natural."

The earlier view of Nature, though compounded of much the
same ingredients that appealed to the neoclassicists, seems less
coherent but more richly capacious, for principles like that of the
consensus gentium compete with a plurality of other, even conflicting, assumptions. To the English neo-Platonists the imitation
of Nature meant about what it had to Marsilio Ficino and the
Florentine Platonists: the expression of the forms of things, the
"exemplars" or "Ideas" realized fully in the divine mind alone. In
Sidney "there is no Arte delivered to mankinde that hath not the
workes of Nature for his principall object," but the poet is finally
bound "onely within the Zodiack of his owne wit," for "any understanding knoweth the skil of the Artificer standeth in that
Idea or fore-conceite of the work, and not in the work it selfe."

And even in writers more or less removed from direct Platonic influence there appears the related tendency to see Nature as *natura naturans,* as the cosmic power that testifies to God's sustaining grace and that somehow embodies the antithetical qualities of Plato's "god": insatiable variety and inexhaustible plenitude paradoxically combined with economy and "geometrical" regularity. In Milton's Eden, "Nature . . . plaid at will, . . . Wilde above Rule or Art," and yet Milton's God, like Browne's "Skilful Geometrician," takes up (in the person of His Son) "the gold'n Compasses" to "circumscribe" the "Universe, and all created things." Nature is regular, even geometrically ordered, but also, to borrow a word Milton applies again and again to Art as well as Nature, it is "various"; and the poem that properly imitates it must finally have more to do with "genius" and "Grace" than with the Rules.

But if we remove the paradoxical element from Nature and submit what remains to the shows of deductive logic, the result will in some measure resemble the Rules. De-emphasize the "Miltonic" principle of "variety" and emphasize the "order" of "disorderly order"—it then becomes easier to understand the revulsion from the anomalous that characterizes the criticism of the second half of the century. "The business of a poet," Johnson's Imlac was later to say, "is to examine, not the individual, but the species; . . . he does not number the streaks of the tulip, or describe the different shades in the verdure of the forest." Although the view of Nature as essence or "Idea," traditionally affiliated with the notions of "variety" and *discordia concors,* was of course available to Dryden and is utilized, among other places, in the *Parallel of Poetry and Painting,* his emphasis usually lies elsewhere. Similarly, the principle of *discordia concors,* which remains in modified form an important esthetic presupposition for Denham and even later writers, comes more and more to emphasize "concord" almost to the exclusion of "discord." In Dryden, as in Granville, Nature more usually refers to the order of empirical reality; and since empirical reality was increasingly conceived—early in Hobbes, later in Newton—to be distinguished by mechanical regularities, Nature tended to mean "species" in the sense of generic type or even, among prosaic thinkers, average type.

This tendency might in turn sanction the belief—once more the appeal is to a dehydrated version of the *consensus gentium* —that the beautiful and true could be ascertained by counting noses; "common sense suffices," declares Rymer, bracing us to accept the democratic verdict of "Women-judges." It is, basically, just such a concept of value that lies somewhere behind the "pure" sense of satisfaction Dryden derived from "pleasing," from being *read,* and that helps explain the neoclassic trust in breadth of appeal. In the light of such assumptions, the Horatian emphasis on the audience *qua* audience gains new significance and dignifies Dryden's so-called vulgar pragmatism. Whereas Milton could profess himself satisfied with the *"knowing* reader" and "fit audience . . . though few," such an admission on the part of the neoclassic poet might very well be taken to imply the lack of true poetic feeling. In this broad and "commonsensical" view of the poet's function, Art tends to become the codification of procedures, the body of Rules by which the poet achieves the Horatian end of keeping the audience seated, for in this way he might produce a poem, as did Gray for Dr. Johnson, that "abounds with images which find a mirrour in every mind, and with sentiments to which every bosom returns an echo."

And thus the neoclassical dilemma. However intense the patriot's distaste for Frenchified fashions and whatever the critic's tolerance for diversity, the Rules impressed most educated Englishmen as ineluctably reasonable; "to copy *Nature* is to copy *Them."* Dryden remains convinced that the Rules are somehow right and natural, and yet he could never lend himself to a rigorous application of the French system. Unlike the French, he confronted directly the example of Shakespeare, who illustrated the internal contradictions of the system by breaking the Rules while nevertheless appealing to all men; this prepossessing example, together with the sentiment of nationalism, made it impossible for Dryden and many other English men of letters to accept in entirety, and apply stringently, the doctrines of the French:

> But *Critic Learning* flourish'd most in *France.*
> The *Rules,* a Nation born to serve, obeys,
> And *Boileau* still in Right of *Horace* sways.
> But *we,* brave *Britons, Foreign Laws* despis'd. . . .

And then Pope's inevitable qualification: though Englishmen were "fierce for the *Liberties of Wit*," the "*sounder Few*" have "*restor'd* Wit's *Fundamental Laws*." The neoclassical dilemma appears perhaps most clearly in Dryden's ambiguous attitude toward the rigid procedures of Rymer. "He who undertakes to Answer this Excellent Critick . . . ," begins Dryden, thus testifying simultaneously to his desire to controvert and to his half conscious realization that there is, in the last analysis, no "Answer" —no answer if one begins, like Dryden, by sharing the premises of the adversary in regard to Nature and Art.

The genesis and growth of the dilemma may be glimpsed in the changing concept of decorum, one of the many important critical terms that retained its prestige but shifted its meaning in the course of the century. Milton had assumed in *Of Education* that men were to be trained to write "according to the fitted stile of lofty, mean, or lowly" and on this basis had proceeded to assert that "Decorum [is the] grand master peece to observe"—not knowing what use Rymer was to put the principle in observing the indecorums of Shakespeare:

> But what is most intolerable is *Iago*. He is no Black-amoor Souldier, so we may be sure he should be like other Souldiers of our acquaintance; yet never in Tragedy, nor in Comedy, nor in Nature was a Souldier with his Character. . . . *Horace* Describes a Souldier otherwise: *Impiger, iracundus, inexorabilis, acer.*
>
> *Shakespear* knew his Character of *Iago* was inconsistent. . . . This he knew, but to entertain the Audience with something new and surprising, against common sense, and Nature, he would pass upon us a close, dissembling, false, insinuating rascal, instead of a open-hearted, frank, plain-dealing Souldier, a character constantly worn by them for some thousands of years in the World.

Rymer was of course no stranger to the ways of the world or the habits of soldiers; he was wise, rather, in the decorum of character. For him, Nature refers to generic norms and thus has nothing to do with the unnatural "improbabilities" and "indecorums" of *Othello*.

The more limited understanding of decorum permitted neoclassic critics to denominate certain words, actions, and objects as intrinsically unpoetic. Such prejudices had of course occurred, though rather more rarely, to the earlier advocates of "aureate" diction and the like, for English literary criticism had begun by sharing the Renaissance concern with hierarchy, which is to say that the concept of decorum functioned as a social and meta-physical, as well as a stylistic, principle, receiving sustenance not only from the authority of classical rhetoricians but also from the structure of society and the universe. In such a context there is nothing irresponsible or precious in Donne's assertion that "wicked is not much worse then indiscreet." Decorum, thus comprehensively felt, could accommodate ranges of experience that were later designated unpoetic. Simplify the concept appropriate to this earlier view, codify its manner of application, and the result is a critical instrument of great precision, though the gain in utility has been achieved partly through the loss of meta-physical force and scope. The ultimate *reductio* of the old didac-ticism occurs in Rymer, where the concept of "poetical justice," a restricted version of Aristotle's distributive justice, points to-ward Nahum Tate's notorious adaptation of *Lear:* Cordelia is married off to Edgar.

But these underground movements in critical terminology have their best illustration in the tactical equivocations on the word "wit," which because of its inherent ambiguity fully justi-fied Pope's retrospective comment in 1711:

> Thus *Wit,* like *Faith,* by each Man is apply'd
> To *one small Sect,* and All are *damn'd beside.*

Wit had, however, *begun* the century by functioning as a middle term between "fancy" and "judgment," thus helping to mediate the sectarian and dualistic extremes that increasingly frag-mented seventeenth-century thought.

In literary criticism the word "wit" becomes, for a historical moment at mid-century, the battleground of the ancient combat between rhetorician and dialectician, between men of the word and men of the idea. Cicero's assertion that Socrates had sepa-rated the tongue and the mind anticipates Ascham's complaint in the sixteenth century. "Ye know not, what hurt ye do to learning that care not for Words, but for Matter; and so make a Di-vorce betwixt the Tongue and the Heart." Bacon's later condemnation of those who hunt more after "words" than "matter" continues the debate between *oratio et ratio, verba et res,* and lends a new prestige to the "thing" that, after the qualified approval of Greville, was fully acknowledged by Sprat in commending the efforts of the Royal Society "to return back to the primitive purity, and shortness, when men deliver'd so many *things,* almost in an equal number of *words.*" (Adequate protest had to await Swift's travesty of the Royal Society in Book III of *Gulliver:* "The other, was a Scheme for entirely abolishing all Words whatsoever. . . . An Expedient was therefore offered, that since Words are only Names for *Things,* it would be more convenient for all Men to carry about them, such *Things* as were necessary to express the particular Business they are to discourse on. . . .") The growing seventeenth-century distrust of the "word" in general gradually concentrated itself in the word "wit" in particular.

The process may be said to have begun with the *Novum Organum* (I, 55), for it was here that Bacon had directed attention to the provocative idea that the mind might be considered under the aspect of two primary powers: the power of perceiving resemblances and the power of discerning differences. This as yet unnamed distinction between synthetic and analytic commended itself immediately to many thinkers, for it appeared to offer a simple way of dealing more accurately with (among other things) the mystery of the creative process. And accordingly the terms "fancy" and "judgment" came to acquire new precision and utility as labels for the twin powers of the mind.

It has been argued that this development ought to be seen as a disguised resurgence of classical rhetoric. The separation of logic and rhetoric—largely the work of Peter Ramus (1515–72) —had allocated *inventio,* the finding of topics, and *dispositio,* the organization of topics, to the discipline of dialectic and thus had left rhetoric to shift as well as it could with the three remaining elements of the classical pentad—*memoria, elocutio, pronuntiatio.* But the emphasis placed upon the reform of language by Bacon and the members of the Royal Society helped create a situation in which it became once again feasible to regard the arts of style as directly the instrument of rational thought. In an age of scientific "things," *elocutio,* the art of tropes and schemes, could not retain its glamour; and in a period dominated by the written word, the oral art of *pronuntiatio* or *actio* had lost most of its relevance to literature; but invention, disposition, and memory remained to help lend shape to critical discourse. Gradually, through advancing interest in the poet himself and in the psychology of creation, the rhetorical term "invention," which as early as Gascoigne appears in the vernacular criticism of poetry, began to acquire much of its present meaning. Instead of signifying the *finding* of arguments *"discover'd, not devis'd"* (a corollary of the older understanding of the principle of *mimesis*), the word comes more and more to refer to the *original creation* of arguments, thus permitting rhetoricians like Obadiah Walker (in 1659) to speak of "fancy, or invention" as if they were synonyms. In this way "fancy," or "imagination," inherited much of the meaning and function formerly assigned to the classical *inventio*. And by mid-century, in *Leviathan*, Hobbes had found it possible to assimilate one of the two remaining terms, *memoria*, to the *inventio* that now masqueraded as "imagination": "This *decaying sense*, when we would express the thing it self, (I mean *fancy* it self,) we call *Imagination* . . . : But when we would express the *decay*, and signifie that the Sense is fading, old and past, it is called *Memory*. So that *Imagination* and *Memory*, are but one thing, which for divers considerations hath divers names." There remained now from the classical pentad only *dispositio* or organization, the meaning and function of which Hobbes refers to "judgment." The classical and early Renaissance pentad has thus been collapsed, neatly enough, into the dyad to be known as "fancy" and "judgment."

The result, of course, is the dualism that marks the literary criticism of the second half of the century. Typically, poetic composition will be explained and evaluated through recourse to the two contrasting elements that accord with Bacon's distinction between synthetic and analytic powers: "fancy" (or the "imaginative" power of the mind, the gift of Nature that "invents" by perceiving resemblances) and "judgment" (or the analytic power of the mind, the product of Art that "disposes" by noting differences). And soon the polarities will become attached to poets, always with some degree of oversimplification— Jonson as the exponent of Judgment and Art, and Shakespeare as the child of Fancy and Nature.

The direction of modern criticism does not invariably suggest
that we have found a way to free ourselves from such dichoto-
mies, but the thinkers of the earlier seventeenth century managed often enough to avoid, or transcend, the problem of oversimplification by using the word "wit." In its oldest signification
"wit" (from Anglo-Saxon *witan* and *gewitt*) had meant mind,
the rational faculty in general; and, especially in the plural, it
could be used to distinguish one kind of mentality from another,
as with Ascham's separation of "wits" into "quik" and "hard."
Thus "wit" is the usual translation of the Latin *ingenium* (from
whence the Italian *ingegno*), which to the Romans meant,
among other things, a man's intellectual quality, generally with
the favorable connotations that we attach to words like "talent"
and "genius." In literary discourse, therefore, "wit" (or *ingenium*) was a comprehensive designation for the poetic faculty,
for that sort of mind distinguished by poetic "talent" or "genius."
And so long as it could be employed thus comprehensively, the
word amply embraced a series of otherwise contrasting elements:
Nature and Art, Fancy and Judgment, Invention and Disposition.
For if "wit" is taken to mean mind in general, it is only by the
process of further analysis that potential antitheses will be allowed to emerge.

Yet "wit" seems almost always to have possessed the capacity
for internal opposition. It was this capacity that allowed John
Redford to reveal, in *Wyt and Science* (c. 1530), "what Wyt is
without Reson" and that forced all men forever to hold their
peace at *The Marriage of Wit and Wisdom* (c. 1579). Such writings assume an even earlier period in which it was possible to
see in the word a quality distinguishable from the mind in general. This fractional or more limited sense of the word corre-
sponds to one way of using *ingenium*, which in Quintilian and
other writers may on occasion be placed in opposition to *iudi-
cium* ("judgment"); and it is this restricted acceptation of "wit"
that moves toward the modern meaning of verbal agility, often
carrying with it the connotation of *mere* verbal agility. "Wit's an
unruly engine, wildly striking," says Herbert, aware of the proverbial truth that had been obvious, much earlier, to Lyly: "To
true it is that as the Sea Crab swimmeth alwayes agaynst the
streame, so wit alwayes striveth agaynst wisdome: And as the

Bee is oftentimes hurte with hir owne honny, so is wit not seldome plagued with his owne conceipte." There was thus no need
to wait for the writers of the middle of the seventeenth century
to provide the basis for Pope's conviction that "*Wit* and *Judgment* often are at strife."

It is nevertheless clear that the two main—and potentially antithetical—uses of the word Wit entered into full and open combat only toward the middle of the century. When Carew con-
ferred upon Donne the title to the "universall Monarchy of wit,"
the word at the time and in the context of the poem readily admitted its comprehensive interpretation: the *ingenium* or genius
of the poet-preacher whose Fancy combined with Judgment to
express, with great verbal dexterity, correspondences hidden to
men of lesser mind. But in 1660 Robert South would doubtless
have argued that Carew had really been using Wit in its limited
sense, not in its "true" or inclusive meaning at all. "Such are
wholly mistaken in the nature of wit: for true wit is a severe and
manly thing. Wit in divinity is nothing else, but sacred truth
suitably expressed. It is not shreds of Latin or Greek nor a *Deus
dixit,* and a *Deus benedixit,* nor those little quirks, or divisions.
. . . For that is not wit which consists not with wisdom." An
accurate enough, if unsympathetic, description of Donne's sermonizing—yet South denies this kind of thing "wisdom," hence
denies it "true wit," and therefore his "severe and manly" is only
superficially similar to Carew's "masculine expression." South's
definition is, like those of Dryden it resembles, mainly tactical;
in effect, a declaration of literary war.

It is the interplay of these two main interpretations of Wit,
particularly with respect to "fancy" and "judgment," that maps
the course of seventeenth-century literary criticism. During the
Jacobean period Wit had become firmly associated with the
"strong lines" of metaphysical and other coterie verse ("wee are
thought wits," says Jasper Mayne of a Donne poem, "when 'tis
understood"); to mention Wit was to suggest "strong lines." But
then the loss of belief in Nature as an ideal pattern of "various"
correspondences destroyed the rationale of metaphysical verse
so that what could previously have been considered analogical
truth was now more often dismissed as extravagant metaphorical ornament. The practitioners of the later style had rejected, in

Dryden's phrasing, the earlier "points of wit" in favor of Waller's "turns of words and thoughts," for these latter were held to be *really* based on Nature and therefore conformable to Baconian assumptions of the kind Cowley introduced into the preface to *A Proposition for the Advancement of Experimental Philosophy* (1661): "Our Reasoning Faculty as well as Fancy, does but Dream, when it is not guided by sensible Objects." Later critics could not, under such circumstances, permit Carew's "wit" to signify the rational faculty in general—that would be unreasonable and unnatural, prejudicial to the cause of poetry. Instead, the vulgar must be made to understand that such Wit carries no more than its delimited sense: for then it could be equated with Fancy, which in the older faculty psychology already possessed a reputation for irresponsibility and could therefore easily be held accountable for extravagant "conceits." So Davenant at mid-century: "That which is not, yet is accounted, *Wit*" consists in "what are commonly called *Conceits*, things that sound like the knacks or toyes of ordinary *Epigrammatists*," which "grow up to some force of Fancy" but "even then like young Hawks they stray and fly farre off."

Hobbes provides the clearest illustration of these involute developments, though even the philosopher's utterances are at times so inexact, not to say self-contradictory, as to point unmistakably to the widespread confusion in critical terminology. In *Human Nature* (published 1650 but dating from the earlier decade) Hobbes begins by relating the twin Baconian powers of the mind to Wit, Fancy, and Judgment:

> that *quick ranging* of mind . . . which is joined with *curiosity* of comparing the things that come into the mind, one with another: in which comparison, a man delighteth himself either with finding unexpected *similitude* of things, otherwise much unlike, in which men place the excellence of *fancy*, and from whence proceed those grateful similes, metaphors, and other tropes, by which both *poets* and *orators* have it in their power to make things please or displease, and shew well or ill to others, as they like themselves; or else in discerning suddenly *dissimilitude* in things that otherwise appear the same. And this virtue of the mind is that by which men attain to exact and perfect *knowledge;* and the pleasure thereof consisteth in continual instruction, and in distinction of places,

persons, and seasons, and is commonly termed by the name of *judgment:* for, to judge is nothing else, but to distinguish or discern: and both *fancy* and *judgment* are commonly comprehended under the name of *wit.*

The expository precision of this passage, in which Hobbes lends exact form to most of the major issues, is partly the result of his willingness, around 1640, to accept without question the inclusive view that "both *fancy* and *judgment* are commonly comprehended under the name of *wit.*"

By 1651, however, Hobbes had been exposed not only to the linguistic tangles of the English but also to the French quarrels over *esprit* and *jugement,* and perhaps as a consequence the definitions in the *Leviathan* finally betray a loss in expository control. We may begin by admiring the exactness with which Hobbes adjudicates the conflicting claims of Fancy and Judgment—even the clutter of adversatives communicates the proper sense of delicate equilibration: "In a good Poem, whether it be *Epique,* or *Dramatique;* as also in *Sonnets, Epigrams,* and other Pieces, both Judgment and Fancy are required: but the Fancy must be more eminent; because they please for the Extravagancy; but ought not to displease by Indiscretion." Elsewhere in the *Leviathan* this fine sense of contrast dissolves, for the presence of the word Wit—now insensibly allied to Fancy—threatens to disturb the precarious balance: "Where Wit is wanting, it is not Fancy that is wanting, but Discretion. Judgement therefore without Fancy is Wit, but Fancy without Judgement is not." Or, in recurring once more to the Baconian aphorism about the analytic and synthetic powers of the mind: "Those that observe their similitudes, in case they be such as are but rarely observed by others, are sayd to have a *Good Wit;* by which, in this occasion, is meant a *Good Fancy.* But they that observe their differences, and dissimilitudes; which is called *Distinguishing,* and *Discerning,* and *Judging* between thing and thing; in case, such discerning be not easie, are said to have a *good Judgement. . . .*" In the *Leviathan,* then, Wit no longer consistently comprehends "both *fancy* and *judgment.*"

First remark the tendency in the *Leviathan* to restrict the exercise of Wit by equating it with Fancy, then place Wit in the context of Hobbes' *Answer* to Davenant, which assigns the "strength and structure" of a poem to "Judgment" while relegating only the "ornaments" to "Fancy," and the two-fold result is likely to be, in a rationalistic age, the devaluation of both Wit and its product, the fanciful "ornaments" of poems written by "those that observe" unusual "similitudes." In the preface to *Homer's Odysses* (1675) Hobbes complained of the very situation he himself had helped to create: "For men more generally affect and admire Fancie than they do either Judgment, or Reason, or Memory, or any other intellectual vertue; and for the pleasantness of it, give to it alone the name of Wit. . . ."

So long as both "*fancy* and *judgment*" were "comprehended under the name of *wit*," the word remained equivalent to *ingenium* or *esprit* in the widest sense and could serve as an honorable name for the poetic faculty. But when Wit becomes a synonym for Fancy or Imagination (the tendency in the *Leviathan*) and is thus opposed to Judgment, the term once more emerges in its restricted sense and loses that much of its immediacy to reality. In the Baconians, in the Hobbes of the mid-century, and finally in popular usage the restricted sense becomes increasingly dominant, so that when Wit is used precisely it usually refers to the power of seeing resemblances in things apparently (or really) unlike and is therefore subordinated to the more admirable power of discerning differences. Equating Wit with Fancy permitted critics to continue the practice of associating the term with the poetic faculty, but the process of limitation thus merely hastened the decline of poetry as well as Wit. Since Wit and the (mainly metaphysical) poetry embodying it are by definition lacking in Judgment, there is evident need for the Rules of neoclassical Art or "*Nature Methodiz'd.*"

In *An Essay Concerning Humane Understanding* (1690) Locke, who fancied the opinion that "all the artificial and figurative applications of words . . . are for nothing else but to insinuate wrong ideas," adopts the "Baconian" division of the mind and precisely summarizes the major issues in the perspective of the new rationalism:

And hence, perhaps, may be given some Reason of that common Observation, That Men who have a great deal of Wit, and prompt

Memories, have not always the clearest Judgment, or deepest Reason. For *Wit* lying most in the assemblage of *Ideas,* and putting those together with quickness and variety, wherein can be found any resemblance or congruity, thereby to make up pleasant Pictures, and agreeable Visions in the Fancy: Judgment, on the contrary, lies quite on the other side, in separating carefully, one from another, *Ideas,* wherein can be found the least difference, therefore to avoid being misled by Similitude, and by affinity to take one thing for another. This is a way of proceeding quite contrary to metaphor and Allusion, wherein, for the most part, lies that entertainment and pleasantry of Wit, which strikes so lively on the Fancy; and therefore is so acceptable to all People, because its Beauty appears at first sight, and there is required no labor of thought, to examine what Truth and Reason there is in it. The Mind, without looking any further, rests satisfied with the agreeableness of the Picture, and the gayety of the Fancy. . . .

The sharp distinction between Wit (as Fancy), the aggregative power, and Judgment, the discriminative power, is scarcely new, and yet the patronizing tone and purport of the passage is decidedly more hostile to the literary imagination than anything in Hobbes.

To reinstate the prestige of verse in circumstances such as these it was necessary to re-establish "both *fancy* and *judgment*" under the "name of *wit."* And accordingly the typical effort of neoclassical literary criticism is to "re-form" the meaning of the term, to recover the comprehensive sense as a designation for their own style, and in this way to relegate the "extravagances" of the metaphysical conceit to the delimited usage:

> Some to *Conceit* alone their Taste confine,
> And glitt'ring Thoughts struck out at evry Line;
> Pleas'd with a Work where nothing's just or fit;
> One *glaring Chaos* and *wild Heap* of Wit.

"True wit," adds Pope tendentiously, "is *Nature* to Advantage drest." As early as 1704 he had written Wycherley to say that "True Wit I believe, may be defin'd a Justness of Thought, and a Facility of Expression," a tactical definition that accords well enough with Dryden's opinion in 1667: "a propriety of Thoughts and Words." Dryden, who knew intimately all the uses of the

term, was sufficiently fond of his neoclassical strategy on this occasion to repeat the definition in 1685 as a means of developing an invidious comparison with "conceits of epigrammatic wit and gross hyperbole." The attempt, everywhere evident, to rehabilitate Wit by restoring its "true" meaning is perhaps expressed most succinctly by La Rochefoucauld in Maxim XCVIII: "The making a Difference between *Wit* and *Judgment,* is a *Vulgar Error. Judgment* is nothing else but the *exceeding Brightness of Wit.*" It was a *"Vulgar Error"* that marks the center of seventeenth-century thought, making it possible for both Carew and Dryden to exalt diverse talents to witty eminence and for the modern reader with all his wits about him to find much on the Art of imitating Nature in the following pages.

George Chapman

1559?–1634

Anthony à Wood's claim that Chapman attended Oxford remains unsubstantiated, but the poet-translator-dramatist was deeply learned and fiercely proud of his "dark" erudition; he was associated with the circle, often suspected of occultism and atheism, that included Marlowe, Ralegh, and Harriot. Chapman's career as a playwright—mentioned by Meres as early as 1598—has obscured his talent as a poet, though Keats left famous testimony to his delight in the translation of Homer, and there have always been those who took pleasure in the "strong lines" of the original poetry.

Chapman's critical pronouncements represent one kind of passionate opposition to the neoclassical principles that were to dominate the Restoration: "that Poesy should be as perviall as Oratorie, and plainnes her speciall ornament, were the plaine way to barbarisme." Thus Scaliger is "soule-blind" and Chapman's Homer is a long way from Pope's. For Chapman the poet is vates, possessed by the divine "fury." This notion, stemming from Plato and elaborated by the neo-Platonism of the Florentine Academy under Marsilio Ficino, everywhere colors Chapman's view of the creative process—

> *where Gloweworme like doth shine*
> *In nights of sorrow, this hid soule of mine:*
> *And how her genuine formes struggle for birth,*
> *Under the clawes of this foule Panther earth.*

"To the Trulie Learned, and my worthy Friende, Ma. Mathew Roy-
den" is reproduced from Ovids Banquet of Sence (*1595*). *"To the*
Reader," which first appeared in Twelve Bookes of the Iliads (*1609*),
and "The Epistle Dedicatorie" ("To the Most Worthily Honored, My
Singular Good Lord, Robert, Earle of Somerset, Lord Chamberlaine"),
which was first appended to the Twelve Books of the Odysseys (*1614*)
and of which only the prose portion is given here, are both reprinted
from The Whole Works of Homer: Prince of Poetts (*1616*).

FROM

Ovids Banquet of Sence

TO THE TRULIE

LEARNED, AND MY WORTHY FRIENDE,

MA. *Mathew Royden*[1]

[*1595*]

Such is the wilfull povertie of judgements (sweet *Ma:*) wandring like pasportles men, in contempt of the divine discipline of
Poesie, that a man may well feare to frequent their walks: The
prophane multitude I hate, & onelie consecrate my strange
Poems to these serching spirits, whom learning hath made
noble, and nobilitie sacred; endevouring that materiall Oration,
which you call *Schema;* varying in some rare fiction, from popular custome, even for the pure sakes of ornament and utilitie;

---

[1] [Matthew Roydon, involved with Ralegh in the charges of atheism brought
against Marlowe, was a minor poet who flourished around the turn of the
century.]

This of *Euripides* exceeding sweetly relishing with mee; *Lentem coquens ne quicquam olentis addito.*[2]

But that Poesie should be as perviall as Oratorie, and plainnes her speciall ornament, were the plaine way to barbarisme: and to make the Asse runne proude of his eares; to take away strength from Lyons, and give Cammels hornes.

That, *Enargia*, or cleerenes of representation, requird in absolute Poems is not the perspicuous delivery of a lowe invention; but high, and harty invention exprest in most significant, and unaffected phrase; it serves not a skilfull Painters turne, to draw the figure of a face onely to make knowne who it represents; but hee must lymn, give luster, shaddow, and heightning; which though ignorants will esteeme spic'd, and too curious, yet such as have the judiciall perspective, will see it hath, motion, spirit and life.

There is no confection made to last, but it is admitted more cost and skill then presently to be used simples; and in my opinion, that which being with a little endevour serched, ads a kinde of majestie to Poesie; is better then that which every Cobler may sing to his patch.

Obscuritie in affection of words, & indigested conce[i]ts, is pedanticall and childish; but where it shroudeth it selfe in the hart of his subject, utterd with fitnes of figure, and expressive Epethites; with that darknes wil I still labour to be shaddowed; rich Minerals are digd out of the bowels of the earth, not found in the superficies and dust of it; charms made of unlerned characters are not consecrate by the Muses which are divine artists, but by *Evippes* daughters, that challengd them with meere nature, whose brests I doubt not had beene well worthy commendation, if their comparison had not turnd them into Pyes.[3]

Thus (not affecting glory for mine owne sleight labors, but desirous other should be more worthely glorious, nor professing sacred Poesie in any degree,) I thought good to submit to your apt judgment: acquainted long since with the true habit of Poesie, and now since your labouring wits endevour heaven-high thoughts of Nature, you have actual meanes to sound the philo-

2 [Originally, Aristotle's condemnation of the overly ornate in the style of Euripides: "When you are cooking lentils, add nothing in the way of flavor."]
3 [The nine daughters of Evippe challenged the Muses and were transformed into magpies.]

sophical conceits, that my new pen so seriously courteth. I know,
that empty, and dark spirits, wil complaine of palpable night:
but those that before-hand, have a radiant, and light-bearing intellect, will say they can passe through *Corynnas* Garden[4] without the helpe of a Lanterne.

Your owne most worthily
and sincerely affected,
George Chapman

FROM

Iliads

TO THE READER
[*1609*]

Lest with foule hands you touch these holy Rites;
  And with prejudicacies too prophane,
Passe Homer, *in your other Poets sleights;*
  Wash here. In this Porch to his numerous Phane,
Heare ancient Oracles speake, and tell you whom
  You have to censure. First then Silius *heare,*
Who thrice was Consull in renowned Rome;
  Whose verse (saith Martiall) *nothing shall out-weare.*

Silius Italicus. Lib. 13.

He, in *Elysium*, having cast his eye
  Upon the figure of a Youth, whose haire
With purple Ribands braided curiously,
  Hung on his shoulders wondrous bright and faire;
Said, Virgine, What is he whose heavenly face
  Shines past all others, as the Morne the Night;

4 [The garden of Ovid's "mistress" and the locale of Chapman's poem.]

Whom many marvelling soules, from place to place,
　Pursue, and haunt, with sounds of such delight?
Whose countenance (wer't not in the Stygian shade)
　Would make me, questionlesse, beleeve he were
A verie God. The learned Virgine made
　This answer: If thou shouldst beleeve it here,
Thou shouldst not erre: he well deserv'd to be
　Esteem'd a God; nor held his so-much breast
A little presence of the Deitie:
　His verse comprisde earth, seas, starres, soules at rest:
In song, the Muses he did equalise;
　In honor, *Phœbus:* he was onely soule;
Saw all things spher'd in Nature, without eyes,
　And raisde your *Troy* up to the starrie Pole.
Glad *Scipio,* viewing well this Prince of Ghosts,
　Said, O if Fates would give this Poet leave,
To sing the acts done by the Romane Hoasts;
　How much beyond, would future times receive
The same facts, made by any other knowne?
　O blest *Æacides!* [1] to have the grace
That out of such a mouth, thou shouldst be showne
　To wondring Nations, as enricht the race
Of all times future, with what he did know:
　Thy vertue, with his verse, shall ever grow.

Now heare an Angell sing our Poets Fame;
Whom Fate, for his divine song, gave that name. [2]

More living, then in old *Demodocus,*
　Fame glories to waxe yong in *Homers* verse.
And as when bright *Hyperion* holds to us
　His golden Torch; we see the starres disperse,
And every way flie heaven; the pallid Moone
　Even almost vanishing before his sight:
So with the dazling beames of *Homers* Sunne,
　All other ancient Poets lose their light.
Whom when *Apollo* heard, out of his starre,
　Singing the godlike Acts of honor'd men;
And equalling the actuall rage of warre,

1 [Achilles.]
2 Angelus Politianus, in Nutricia. [Angelo Politian (1454–94), Florentine critic and poet, praises Homer in "Nutricia."]

With onely the divine straines of his pen;
He stood amaz'd, and freely did confesse
   Himselfe was equall'd in *Mæonides*.

Next, heare the grave and learned Plinie *use*
His censure of our sacred Poets Muse.[3]

Whom shall we choose the glorie of all wits,
   Held through so many sorts of discipline,
And such varietie of workes, and spirits;
   But Grecian *Homer?* like whom none did shine,
For forme of worke and matter. And because
   Our proud doome of him may stand justified
By noblest judgements; and receive applause
   In spite of envie, and illiterate pride;
Great *Macedon,* amongst his matchlesse spoiles,
   Tooke from rich *Persia* (on his Fortunes cast)
A Casket finding (full of precious oyles)
   Form'd all of gold, with wealthy stones enchac't:
He tooke the oyles out; and his nearest friends
   Askt, in what better guard it might be usde?
All giving their conceipts, to severall ends;
   He answerd; His affections rather chusde
An use quite opposite to all their kinds:
   And *Homers* bookes should with that guard be serv'd;
That the most precious worke of all mens minds,
   In the most precious place, might be preserv'd.
The Fount of wit was *Homer;*[4] Learnings Syre,
   And gave Antiquitie, her living fire.[5]

Volumes of like praise, I could heape on this,
   Of men more ancient, and more learn'd then these:
But since true Vertue, enough lovely is
   With her owne beauties; all the suffrages
Of others I omit; and would more faine
   That *Homer,* for himselfe, should be belov'd
Who everie sort of love-worth did containe.
   Which how I have in my conversion prov'd,

3 Plin Nat. hist. lib. 7 Cap 29. Turnd into verse; that no Prose may come
neare *Homer.*
4 Idem. lib. 17. cap. 5.
5 Idem. lib. 25. cap. 3.

I must confesse, I hardly dare referre
  To reading judgements; since, so generally,
Custome hath made even th'ablest Agents erre
  In these translations; all so much apply   *Of Translation,*
Their paines and cunnings, word for word to render   *and the naturall*
  Their patient Authors; when they may as well,   *difference of*
Make fish with fowle, Camels with Whales engender;   *Dialects,*
  Or their tongues speech, in other mouths compell.   *necessarily to*
For, even as different a production   *be observed in*
  Aske Greeke and English; since as they in sounds,   *it.*
And letters, shunne one forme, and unison;
  So have their sense, and elegancie bounds
In their distinguisht natures, and require
  Onely a judgement to make both consent,
In sense and elocution; and aspire
  As well to reach the spirit that was spent
In his example; as with arte to pierce
  His Grammar, and etymologie of words.
But, as great Clerkes, can write no English verse;   *Ironicæ.*
  Because (alas! great Clerks) English affords
(Say they) no height, nor copie;[6] a rude toung,
  (Since tis their Native): but in Greeke or Latine
Their writs are rare; for thence true Poesie sprong:
  Though them (Truth knowes) they have but skil to chat-in,
Compar'd with that they might say in their owne;
  Since thither th'others full soule cannot make
The ample transmigration to be showne
  In Nature-loving Poesie: So the brake
That those Translators sticke in, that affect
  Their word-for-word traductions (where they lose
The free grace of their naturall Dialect
  And shame their Authors, with a forced Glose)
I laugh to see; and yet as much abhorre   *The necessarie*
  More licence from the words, then may expresse   *nearenesse of*
Their full compression, and make cleare the Author.   *translation to*
  From whose truth, if you thinke my feet digresse,   *the example.*
Because I use needfull Periphrases;
  Reade *Valla, Hessus,* that in Latine Prose,[7]

6 [L. *copia,* amplitude.]
7 [Lorenzo Valla (1406–57), a version in Latin prose that was published in 1497; Eobanus Hessus (1488–1540?), a German humanist, brought out a version in Latin verse in 1540.]

And Verse convert him; reade the *Messines*,[8]
　That into Tuscan turns him; and the Glose
Grave *Salel* [9] makes in French, as he translates:
　Which (for th'aforesaide reasons) all must doo;
And see that my conversion much abates
　The licence they take, and more showes him too:
Whose right, not all those great learn'd men have done
　(In some maine parts) that were his Commentars:
But (as the illustration of the Sunne
　Should be attempted by the erring starres)
They fail'd to search his deepe, and treasurous hart.
　The cause was, since they wanted the fit key
Of Nature, in their down-right strength of Art; *The power of*
　With Poesie, to open Poesie. *nature, above*
Which in my Poeme of the mysteries *Art in Poesie.*
　Reveal'd in *Homer*, I will clearely prove.
Till whose neere birth, suspend your Calumnies,
　And farre-wide imputations of selfe love.
Tis further from me, then the worst that reades;
　Professing me the worst of all that wright:
Yet what, in following one, that bravely leades,
　The worst may show, let this proofe hold the light.
But grant it cleere: yet hath detraction got
　My blinde side, in the forme, my verse puts on;
Much like a dung-hill Mastife, that dares not
　Assault the man he barkes at; but the stone
He throwes at him, takes in his eager jawes,
　And spoyles his teeth because they cannot spoyle.
The long verse hath by proofe receiv'd applause
　Beyond each other number: and the foile,
That squint-ey'd Envie takes, is censur'd plaine.
　For, this long Poeme askes this length of verse,
Which I my selfe ingenuously maintaine
　Too long, our shorter Authors to reherse.
And, for our tongue, that still is so empayr'd *Our English*
　By travailing linguists; I can prove it cleare, *language, above*
That no tongue hath the Muses utterance heyr'd *all others, for*
　For verse, and that sweet Musique to the eare *Rhythmicall*
Strooke out of rime, so naturally as this; *Poesie.*

[8] [La Badessa Messines (1520–78) published in 1564 an Italian translation of
the first five books in *versi sciolti*.]
[9] [Hughes Salel (1504?–53) brought out a French version of the first ten
books in 1545, though fragments of his translation had appeared earlier.]

Our Monosyllables, so kindly fall
And meete, opposde in rime, as they did kisse:
　French and Italian, most immetricall;
Their many syllables, in harsh Collision,
　Fall as they brake their necks; their bastard Rimes
Saluting as they justl'd in transition,
　And set our teeth on edge; nor tunes, nor times
Kept in their falles. And me thinkes, their long words
　Shew in short verse, as in a narrow place,
Two opposites should meet, with two-hand swords
　Unweildily, without or use or grace.
Thus having rid the rubs, and strow'd these flowers
　In our thrice sacred *Homers* English way;
What rests to make him, yet more worthy yours?
　To cite more prayse of him, were meere delay
To your glad searches, for what those men found,
　That gave his praise, past all, so high a place:
Whose vertues were so many, and so cround,
　By all consents, Divine; that not to grace,
Or adde increase to them, the world doth need
　Another *Homer;* but even to rehearse
And number them: they did so much exceed;
　Men thought him not a man; but that his verse
Some meere celestiall nature did adorne.
　And all may well conclude, it could not be,
That for the place where any man was borne,
　So long, and mortally, could disagree
So many Nations, as for *Homer* striv'd,
　Unlesse his spurre in them, had bene divine.
Then end their strife, and love him (thus reviv'd)
　As borne in *England:* see him over-shine
All other-Countrie Poets; and trust this,
　That whose-soever Muse dares use her wing
When his Muse flies, she will be truss't by his;
　And show as if a Bernacle[1] should spring
Beneath an Eagle. In none since was seene
　A soule so full of heaven as earth's in him.
O! if our moderne Poesie had beene
　As lovely as the Ladie he did lymne,
What barbarous worldling, groveling after gaine,
　Could use her lovely parts, with such rude hate,

1 [The wild barnacle goose.]

As now she suffers under every swaine?
   Since then tis nought but her abuse and Fate,
That thus empaires her; what is this to her
   As she is reall? or in naturall right?
But since in true Religion men should erre
   As much as Poesie, should th'abuse excite
The like contempt of her Divinitie?
   And that her truth, and right saint sacred Merites,
In most lives, breed but reverence formally;
   What wonder is't if Poesie inherits
Much lesse observance; being but Agent for her,
   And singer of her lawes, that others say?
Forth then ye Mowles, sonnes of the earth abhorre her;
   Keepe still on in the durty vulgar way,
Till durt receive your soules, to which ye vow;
   And with your poison'd spirits bewitch our thrifts.
Ye cannot so despise us as we you.
   Not one of you, above his Mowlehill lifts
His earthy Minde; but, as a sort of beasts,
   Kept by their Guardians, never care to heare
Their manly voices; but when, in their fists,
   They breathe wild whistles; and the beasts rude eare
Heares their Curres barking; then by heapes they flie,
   Headlong together: So men, beastly given,
The manly soules voice (sacred Poesie,
   Whose Hymnes the Angels ever sing in heaven)
Contemne, and heare not: but when brutish noises
   (For Gaine, Lust, Honour, in litigious Prose)
Are bellow'd-out, and cracke the barbarous voices
   Of Turkish *Stentors;* O! ye leane to those,
Like itching Horse, to blockes, or high May-poles;
   And breake nought but the wind of wealth, wealth, All
In all your Documents; your Asinine soules
   (Proud of their burthens) feele not how they gall.
But as an Asse, that in a field of weeds
   Affects a thistle, and falles fiercely to it;
That pricks, and gals him; yet he feeds, and bleeds;
   Forbeares a while, and licks; but cannot woo it
To leave the sharpnes; when (to wreake his smart)
   He beates it with his foote; then backward kickes,
Because the Thistle gald his forward part;
   Nor leaves till all be eate, for all the prickes;

Then falles to others with as hote a strife;
　And in that honourable warre doth waste
The tall heate of his stomacke, and his life:
　So, in this world of weeds, you worldlings taste
Your most-lov'd dainties; with such warre, buy peace;
　Hunger for torment; vertue kicke for vice;
Cares, for your states, do with your states increase:
　And though ye dreame ye feast in Paradise,
Yet Reasons Day-light, shewes ye at your meate
　Asses at Thistles, bleeding as ye eate.

F R O M

Odysseys

from THE EPISTLE DEDICATORIE
[*1614*]

And that your Lordship may in his Face, take view of his Mind:
the first word of his Iliads, is μηνιν, *wrath*: the first word of his
Odysses, ανδρα, *Man*: contracting in either word, his each workes
Proposition. In one, *Predominant Perturbation;* in the other,
over-ruling Wisedome: in one, the Bodies fervour and fashion
of outward Fortitude, to all possible height of Heroicall Action;
in the other, the Minds inward, constant, and unconquerd Empire; unbroken, unalterd, with any most insolent, and tyrannous
infliction. To many most soveraigne praises is this Poeme entitled; but to that *Grace* in chiefe, which sets on the Crowne, both
of Poets and Orators; το τα μικρα, μεγαλως; και τα κοίνα καινως: [1]
that is, *Parva magnè dicere; pervulgata novè; jejuna plenè:* To

[1] [*Cf.* Plato's *Phaedrus* 267.]

speake things litle, greatly; things commune, rarely; things
barren and emptie, fruitfully and fully. The returne of a man
into his Countrie, is his whole scope and object; which, in it
selfe, your Lordship may well say, is jejune and fruitlesse
enough; affoording nothing feastfull, nothing magnificent. And
yet even this, doth the divine inspiration, render vast, illustrous,
and of miraculous composure. And for this (my Lord) is this
Poeme preferred to his *Iliads:* for therein much magnificence,
both of person and action, gives great aide to his industrie; but in
this, are these helpes, exceeding sparing, or nothing; and yet is
the Structure so elaborate, and pompous, that the poore plaine
Ground worke (considered together) may seeme the naturally
rich wombe to it, and produce it needfully. Much wonderd at
therefore, is the Censure of *Dionysius Longinus* (a man otherwise affirmed, grave, and of elegant judgement) comparing
Homer in his *Iliads,* to the Sunne rising; in his *Odysses,* to his
descent or setting. Or to the *Ocean* robd of his æsture;[2] many
tributorie flouds and rivers of excellent ornament, withheld from
their observance. When this his worke so farre exceeds the
Ocean, with all his Court and concourse; that all his Sea, is onely
a serviceable streame to it. Nor can it be compared to any One
power to be named in nature; being an entirely wel-sorted and
digested Confluence of all. Where the most solide and grave, is
made as nimble and fluent, as the most airie and firie; the
nimble and fluent, as firme and well bounded as the most grave
and solid. And (taking all together) of so tender impression, and
of such Command to the voice of the *Muse;* that they knocke
heaven with her breath, and discover their foundations as low
as hell. Nor is this all-comprising *Poesie,* phantastique, or meere
fictive; but the most material, and doctrinall illations of *Truth;*
both for all manly information of Manners in the yong; all
prescription of Justice, and even Christian pietie, in the most
grave and high-governd. To illustrate both which, in both kinds,
with all height of expression, the Poet creates both a Bodie and
a Soule in them. Wherein, if the Bodie (being the letter, or historie) seemes fictive, and beyond Possibilitie to bring into Act:
the sence then and Allegorie (which is the Soule) is to be

2 [Turbulence. See the Preface for words like "composure," "pompous," and
"produce."]

sought: which intends a more eminent expressure of *Vertue,* for her lovelinesse; and of *Vice* for her uglinesse, in their severall effects; going beyond the life, then any Art within life, can possibly delineate. Why then is *Fiction,* to this end, so hatefull to our true Ignorants? Or why should a poore Chronicler of a Lord Maiors naked *Truth,* (that peradventure will last his yeare) include more worth with our moderne wizerds, then *Homer* for his naked *Ulysses,* clad in eternall Fiction? But this Prozer *Dionysius,* and the rest of these grave, and reputatively learned, (that dare undertake for their gravities, the headstrong censure of all things; and challenge the understanding of these Toyes in their childhoods: when even these childish vanities, retaine deepe and most necessarie learning enough in them, to make them children in their ages, and teach them while they live) are not in these absolutely divine Infusions, allowd either voice or relish: for, *Qui Poeticas ad fores accedit, &c.* (sayes the Divine Philosopher) he that knocks at the Gates of the *Muses; sine Musarum furore,*[3] is neither to be admitted entrie, nor a touch at their Thresholds: his opinion of entrie, ridiculous, and his presumption impious. Nor must Poets themselves (might I a litle insist on these contempts; not tempting too farre your Lordships *Ulyssean* patience) presume to these doores, without the truly genuine, and peculiar induction. There being in *Poesie* a twofold rapture, (or alienation of soule, as the abovesaid Teacher termes it) one *Insania,* a disease of the mind, and a meere madnesse, by which the infected is thrust beneath all the degrees of humanitie: *& ex homine, Brutum quodammodo redditur:*[4] (for which, poore *Poesie,* in this diseasd and impostorous age, is so barbarously vilified) the other is, *Divinus furor;* by which the sound and divinely healthfull, *supra hominis naturam erigitur, & in Deum transit.*[5] One a perfection directly infused from God: the other an infection, obliquely and degenerately proceeding from

[3] ["Without the inspiration of the Muses." (Chapman himself translates the preceding phrase.) The quotation—and the explanation of two kinds of poetic "fury" that follows—derives from Plato's *Ion* by way of the commentary of Marsilio Ficino (1433–99), *In Platonis Ionem, vel de furore poetico.* These ideas were also easily available in Seneca, *De Tranquillitate Animi* xvii.]

[4] ["And a brute is somehow produced from a man." From Ficino (see note 3).]

[5] [From Ficino (see note 3): "is elevated above the nature of man and translated into deity."]

man. Of the divine *Furie* (my Lord) your *Homer* hath ever bene, both first and last *Instance;* being pronounced absolutely, τον σοφωτατον: και τον θειοτατον ποιητην; the most wise and most divine Poet.

Samuel Daniel

1563?–1619

Educated at Oxford, Samuel Daniel later became tutor to the third Earl of Pembroke and so gained access to the Countess of Pembroke's famous literary circle. He wrote plays, masques, and enough poetry that shared the style of his The Civil Wars *(1595) to provoke Drayton's hearsay censure: "some wisemen him rehearse, / To be too much* Historian *in verse."*

The Defence *is a gentlemanly refutation of Campion's* Observations in the Art of English Poesie *(1602). Campion had attacked "Rime and Meeter," which in the "lack-learning times" of the Middle Ages and "in barbarized Italy, began that vulgar and easie kind of Poesie . . . now in use throughout most parts of Christendome." Although Campion, a practicing musician-poet of extraordinary delicacy, ornaments his lost cause with subtleties of technique that at times make his adversary appear clumsy, there is no doubt that Daniel, in arguing for rhyme and accent against the quantitative measures of classical prosody, correctly anticipated the main tendencies of later practice: after Daniel the problem of quantity assumes only secondary importance in English versification; and, similarly, there was to be little doubt as to the propriety or usefulness of rhyme, though even so late as 1668 Milton permitted himself a lordly denunciation of the "jingling sound of like endings" and Dryden was intermittently agitated by the question throughout his career. The measured eloquence of Daniel's argument derives its force from a dignified manipulation*

of the talismanic words of the Renaissance: "We could well have al-
lowed of his numbers had he not disgraced our Ryme; Which both
Custome and Nature doth most powerfully defend. Custome that is
before all Law, Nature that is above all Arte."

A Defence of Ryme: Against a Pamphlet entituled: Observations
in the Art of English Poesie *is reprinted from* A Panegyrike . . .
With a Defence of Ryme, heeretofore written, and now published by
the Author (*n.d.*). *The* Defence *was entered in the* Stationers' Register *30 May 1603 but was probably written in late 1602.*

A Defence of Ryme
[*1602?*]

TO
WILLIAM HERBERT EARLE
OF PEMBROOKE

The Generall Custome, and use of Ryme in this kingdome, Noble
Lord, having beene so long (as if from a Graunt of Nature) held
unquestionable; made me to imagine that it lay altogither out of
the way of contradiction, and was become so natural, as we
should never have had a thought to cast it off into reproch, or be
made to thinke that it ill-became our language. But now I see,
when there is opposition made to all things in the world by
wordes, wee must nowe at length likewise fall to contend for
words themselves; and make a question, whether they be right or
not. For we are tolde how that our measures goe wrong, all
Ryming is grosse, vulgare, barbarous, which if it be so, we have

lost much labour to no purpose: and for mine owne particular, I cannot but blame the fortune of the times and mine owne Genius that cast me uppon so wrong a course, drawne with the current of custome, and an unexamined example. Having beene first incourag'd or fram'd thereunto by your most Worthy and Honourable Mother,[1] receiving the first notion for the formall ordering of those compositions at *Wilton*, which I must ever acknowledge to have beene my best Schoole, and thereof alwayes am to hold a feeling and gratefull Memory. Afterward, drawne farther on by the well-liking and approbation of my worthy Lord, the fosterer of mee and my *Muse*, I adventured to bestow all my whole powers therein, perceiving it agreed so well, both with the complexion of the times, and mine owne constitution, as I found not wherein I might better imploy me. But yet now, upon the great discovery of these new measures, threatning to overthrow the whole state of Ryme in this kingdom, I must either stand out to defend, or else be forced to forsake my selfe, and give over all. And though irresolution and a selfe distrust be the most apparent faults of my nature, and that the least checke of reprehension, if it savour of reason, will as easily shake my resolution as any mans living: yet in this case I know not how I am growne more resolved, and before I sinke, willing to examine what those powers of judgement are, that must beare me downe, and beat me off from the station of my profession, which by the law of nature I am set to defend.

And the rather for that this detractor (whose commendable Rymes albeit now himselfe an enemy to ryme, have given heretofore to the world the best notice of his worth) is a man of faire parts, and good reputation, and therefore the reproach forcibly cast from such a hand may throw downe more at once then the labors of many shall in long time build up againe, specially upon the slippery foundation of opinion, and the worlds inconstancy, which knowes not well what it would have, and:

> *Discit enim citius, meminitque libentius illud*
> *Quod quis deridet quam quod probat & veneratur.*[2]

1 [Mary, sister of Sir Philip Sidney and patroness of poets.]
2 [Horace, *Epistulae* ii.1.262–63: "For men learn faster, and remember with more pleasure, what they deride than what they approve and venerate."]

And he who is thus, become our unkinde adversarie, must pardon us if we be as jealous of our fame and reputation, as hee is desirous of credite by his new-old arte, and must consider that we cannot, in a thing that concernes us so neere, but have a feeling of the wrong done, wherein every Rymer in this universall Iland as well as my selfe, stands interressed. So that if his charitie had equally drawne with his learning hee would have forborne to procure the envie of so powerfull a number upon him, from whom he cannot but expect the returne of a like measure of blame, and onely have made way to his owne grace, by the proofe, of his abilitie, without the disparaging of us, who would have bin glad to have stood quietly by him, & perhaps commended his adventure, seeing that evermore of one science an other may be borne, & that these Salies made out of the quarter of our set knowledges, are the gallant proffers onely of attemptive spirits, and commendable though they worke no other effect than make a Bravado: and I know it were *Indecens, & morosum nimis, alienæ industriæ, modum ponere.*[3] We could well have allowed of his numbers had he not disgraced our Ryme; Which both Custome and Nature doth most powerfully defend. Custome that is before all Law, Nature that is above all Arte. Every language hath her proper number or measure fitted to use and delight, which, Custome intertaining by the allowance of the Eare, doth indenize, and make naturall. All verse is but a frame of wordes confinde within certaine measure; differing from the ordinarie speach, and introduced, the better to expresse mens conceipts, both for delight and memorie. Which frame of wordes consisting of *Rithmus* or *Metrum,* Number or Measure, are disposed into divers fashions, according to the humour of the Composer and the set of the time; And these *Rhythmi* as *Aristotle* saith are familiar amongst all Nations, and *è naturali & sponte fusa compositione:*[4] And they fall as naturally already in our language as ever Art can make them; being such as the Eare of it selfe doth marshall in their proper roomes, and they of themselves will not willingly be put out of their ranke; and that in such a verse as best comports with the Nature of our language. And for our Ryme (which is an excellencie added to this

3 ["Indecorous and ill-natured to set limits for the work of another."]
4 ["is natural and willy-nilly makes a shaped composition."]

worke of measure, and a Harmonie, farre happier than any proportion Antiquitie could ever shew us) dooth adde more grace,
and hath more of delight than ever bare numbers, howsoever
they can be forced to runne in our slow language, can possibly
yeeld. Which, whether it be deriv'd of *Rhythmus*, or of *Romance*
which were songs the *Bards* & *Druydes* about Rymes used, &
therof were caled *Remensi*, as some Italians hold; or howsoever,
it is likewise number and harmonie of words, consisting of an
agreeing sound in the last silables of severall verses, giving both
to the Eare an Eccho of a delightfull report & to the Memorie a
deeper impression of what is delivered therein. For as Greeke
and Latine verse consists of the number and quantitie of sillables, so doth the English verse of measure and accent. And
though it doth not strictly observe long and short sillables, yet it
most religiously respects the accent: and as the short and the
long make number, so the Acute and grave accent yeelde harmonie: And harmonie is likewise number, so that the English
verse then hath number, measure and harmonie in the best proportion of Musike. Which being more certain & more resound-
ing, works that effect of motion with as happy successe as either
the Greek or Latin. And so naturall a melody is it, & so universall as it seems to be generally borne with al the nations of the
world, as an hereditary eloquence proper to all mankind. The
universallitie argues the generall power of it: for if the Barbarian
use it, then it shews that it swais th'affection of the Barbarian, if
civil nations practise it, it proves that it works upon the harts of
civil nations: If all, then that it hath a power in nature on all.
Georgievez de Turcarum moribus,[5] hath an example of the
Turkish Rymes just of the measure of our verse of eleven sillables, in feminine Ryme: never begotten I am perswaded by any
example in *Europe*, but borne no doubt in *Scythia*, and brought
over *Caucasus* and *Mount Taurus*. The Sclavonian and Arabian
tongs acquaint a great part of *Asia* and *Affrique* with it, the Mos-
covite, Polack, Hungarian, German, Italian, French, and Spaniard use no other harmonie of words. The Irish, Briton, Scot,
Dane, Saxon, English, and all the Inhabiters of this Iland, either

---

[5] [Bartholomaeus Georgevicz published *De Turcarum Moribus Epitome* in
1553, an account of Turkish customs that includes an earlier treatise published
as *Epitomen de Turcarum Ritu, Moribus et Ceremoniis* in 1545.]

have hither brought, or here found the same in use. And such a force hath it in nature, or so made by nature, as the Latine numbers notwithstanding their excellencie, seemed not suffi-cient to satisfie the eare of the world thereunto accustomed, without this Harmonicall cadence: which made the most learned of all nations labour with exceeding travaile to bring those num-bers likewise unto it: which many did with that happinesse, as neither their puritie of tongue, nor their materiall contemplations are thereby any way disgraced, but rather deserve to be rever-enced of all gratefull posteritie, with the due regard of their worth. And for *Schola Salerna,* and those *Carmina Proverbialia,*[6] who finds not therein more precepts for use, concerning diet, health, and conversation, then *Cato, Theognes,* or all the Greekes and Latines can shew us in that kinde of teaching: and that in so few words, both for delight to the eare, and the hold of mem-orie, as they are to be imbraced of all modest readers that studie to know and not to deprave.

Me thinkes it is a strange imperfection, that men should thus over-runne the estimation of good things with so violent a cen-sure, as though it must please none else, because it likes not them. Whereas *Oportet arbitratores esse non contradictores eos qui verum judicaturi sunt,*[7] saith *Arist.* though he could not ob-serve it himselfe. And milde Charitie tells us:

> *non ego paucis*
> *Offendor maculis quas aut incuria fudit*
> *Aut humana parum cavet natura.*[8]

For all men have their errors, and we must take the best of their powers, and leave the rest as not appertaining unto us.

Ill customes are to be left, I graunt it: but I see not howe that can be taken for an ill custome, which nature hath thus ratified, all nations received, time so long confirmed, the effects such as it performes those offices of motion for which it is imployed;

6 [The "school of Salerno," says Puttenham, made "their verses goe all in ryme" to enforce their "medicinall rules." The *Carmina Proverbialia* is a sixteenth-century book of quotations.]
7 [*De Caelo* i.10: "Those who are going to point the way to the truth should be arbiters, not litigants."]
8 [Horace, *Ars Poetica* 351–53: "I am not offended by small blemishes that lack of care produced or that human weakness failed to avoid."]

delighting the eare, stirring the heart, and satisfying the judgement in such sort as I doubt whether ever single numbers will do in our Climate, if they shew no more worke of wonder then yet we see. And if ever they proove to become any thing, it must be by the approbation of many ages that must give them their strength for any operation, or before the world will feele where the pulse, life, and enargie lies, which now we are sure where to have in our Rymes, whose knowne frame hath those due staies for the minde, those incounters of touch as makes the motion certaine, though the varietie be infinite. Nor will the Generall sorte, for whom we write (the wise being above bookes) taste these laboured measures but as an orderly prose when wee have all done. For this kinde acquaintance and continuall familiaritie ever had betwixt our eare and this cadence, is growne to so intimate a friendship, as it will nowe hardly ever be brought to misse it. For be the verse never so good, never so full, it seemes not to satisfie nor breede that delight as when it is met and combined with a like sounding accent. Which seemes as the jointure without which it hangs loose, and cannot subsist, but runnes wildely on, like a tedious fancie without a close: suffer then the world to injoy that which it knowes, and what it likes. Seeing that whatsoever force of words doth moove, delight and sway the affections of men, in what Scythian sorte soever it be disposed or uttered: that is true number, measure, eloquence, and the perfection of speach: which I said, hath as many shapes as there be tongues or nations in the world, nor can with all the tyrannicall Rules of idle Rhetorique be governed otherwise then custome, and present observation will allow. And being now the trym, and fashion of the times, to sute a man otherwise cannot but give a touch of singularity, for when hee hath all done, hee hath but found other clothes to the same body, and peradventure not so fitting as the former. But could our Adversary hereby set up the musicke of our times to a higher note of judgement and discretion, or could these new lawes of words better our imperfections, it were a happy attempt; but when hereby we shall but as it were change prison, and put off these fetters to receive others, what have we gained, as good still to use ryme and a little reason, as neither ryme nor reason, for no doubt as idle wits will write, in that kinde, as do now in this, imitation wil after, though it breake her necke. *Scribimus indocti doctique poemata passim.*[9] And this multitude of idle writers can be no disgrace to the good, for the same fortune in one proportion or other is proper in a like season to all States in their turne: and the same unmeasurable confluence of Scriblers hapned, when measures were most in use among the Romanes, as we finde by this reprehension,

> *Mutavit mentem populus levis, & calet uno*
> *Scribendi studio, pueri, patrésque severi,*
> *Fronde comas vincti cœnant, & carmina dictant.*[1]

So that their plentie seems to have bred the same waste and contempt as ours doth now, though it had not power to disvalew what was worthy of posteritie, nor keep backe the reputation of excellencies, destined to continue for many ages. For seeing it is matter that satisfies the judiciall, appeare it in what habite it will, all these pretended proportions of words, howsoever placed, can be but words, and peradventure serve but to embroyle our understanding, whilst seeking to please our eare, we inthrall our judgement: to delight an exterior sense, wee smoothe up a weake confused sense, affecting sound to be unsound, and all to seeme *Servum pecus,*[2] onely to imitate the Greekes and Latines, whose felicitie, in this kind, might be something to themselves, to whome their owne *idioma* was naturall, but to us it can yeeld no other commoditie then a sound. We admire them not for their smooth-gliding words, nor their measures, but for their inventions: which treasure, if it were to be found in Welch, and Irish, we should hold those languages in the same estimation, and they may thanke their sword that made their tongues so famous and universall as they are. For to say truth, their Verse is many times but a confused deliverer of their excellent conceits, whose scattered limbs we are faine to looke out and joyne together, to discerne the image of what they represent unto us. And even the Latines, who professe not to be so licentious as the Greekes,

9 [Horace, *Epistulae* ii.1.117: "Learned and unlearned, we all at times write verse."]
1 [Horace, *Epistulae* ii.1.108–10: "The giddy populace has shifted its taste and burns with the rage to write: sons and stern fathers eat dinner while crowned with laurel, and dictate verses."]
2 [Horace, *Epistulae* i.19.19: "a servile herd."]

shew us many times examples but of strange crueltie, in tortur-
ing and dismembring of wordes in the middest, or disjoyning
such as naturally should be married and march together, by setting them as farre asunder, as they can possibly stand: that
sometimes, unlesse the kind reader, out of his owne good nature,
wil stay them up by their measure, they will fall downe into
flatte prose, and sometimes are no other indeede in their naturall
sound: and then againe, when you finde them disobedient to
their owne Lawes, you must hold it to be *licentia poetica,* and so
dispensable. The striving to shew their changable measures in
the varietie of their Odes, have beene very painefull no doubt
unto them, and forced them thus to disturbe the quiet streame of
their wordes, which by a naturall succession otherwise desire to
follow in their due course.

But such affliction doth laboursome curiositie still lay upon
our best delights (which ever must be made strange and variable) as if Art were ordained to afflict Nature, and that we could
not goe but in fetters. Every science, every profession, must be
so wrapt up in unnecessary intrications, as if it were not to fashion, but to confound the understanding, which makes me much
to distrust man, and feare that our presumption goes beyond our
abilitie, and our Curiositie is more than our Judgement: labor-
ing ever to seeme to be more than we are, or laying greater
burthens upon our mindes, then they are well able to beare, because we would not appeare like other men.

And indeed I have wished there were not that multiplicitie of
Rymes as is used by many in Sonets, which yet we see in some
so happily to succeed, and hath beene so farre from hindering
their inventions, as it hath begot conceit beyond expectation,
and comparable to the best inventions of the world: for sure in
an eminent spirit whome Nature hath fitted for that mysterie,[2a]
Ryme is no impediment to his conceit, but rather gives him
wings to mount and carries him, not out of his course, but as it
were beyond his power to a farre happier flight. Al excellencies
being sold us at the hard price of labour, it followes, where we
bestow most thereof, we buy the best successe: and Ryme being
farre more laborious then loose measures (whatsoever is objected) must needs, meeting with wit and industry, breed

[2a] [Craft or art.]

greater and worthier effects in our language. So that if our labours have wrought out a manumission from bondage, and that
wee goe at libertie, notwithstanding these ties, wee are no longer
the slaves of Ryme, but we make it a most excellent instrument
to serve us. Nor is this certaine limit observed in Sonnets, any
tyrannicall bounding of the conceit, but rather a reducing it in
girum,[3] and a just forme, neither too long for the shortest project, nor too short for the longest, being but onely imployed for a
present passion. For the body of our imagination, being as an
unformed *Chaos* without fashion, without day, if by the divine
power of the spirit it be wrought into an Orbe of order and
forme, is it not more pleasing to Nature, that desires a certaintie,
and comports not with that which is infinite, to have these
clozes, rather than, not to know where to end, or how farre to
goe, especially seeing our passions are often without measure:
and wee finde the best of the latines many times, either not concluding, or els otherwise in the end then they began. Besides, is
it not most delightfull to see much excellently ordred in a small
roome, or little, gallantly disposed and made to fill up a space of
like capacitie, in such sort, that the one would not appeare so
beautifull in a larger circuite, nor the other do well in a lesse:
which often we find to be so, according to the powers of nature,
in the workeman. And these limited proportions, and rests of
Stanzes: consisting of 6. 7. or 8. lines are of that happines, both
for the disposition of the matter, the apt planting the sentence
where it may best stand to hit, the certaine close of delight with
the full body of a just period well carried, is such, as neither the
Greekes or Latines ever attained unto. For their boundlesse running on, often so confounds the Reader, that having once lost
himselfe, must either give off unsatisfied, or uncertainely cast
backe to retrive the escaped sence, and to find way againe into
his matter.

Me thinkes we should not so soone yeeld our consents captive
to the authoritie of Antiquitie, unlesse we saw more reason: all
our understandings are not to be built by the square of *Greece*
and *Italie*. We are the children of nature as well as they, we are
not so placed out of the way of judgement, but that the same
Sunne of Discretion shineth uppon us, wee have our portion of

3 [I.e., reducing it into a circle, the "just forme."]

the same vertues as well as of the same vices, *Et Catilinam Quocunque in populo videas, quocunque sub axe.*[4] Time and the turne of things bring about these faculties according to the present estimation: and, *Res temporibus non tempora rebus servire opportet.*[5] So that we must never rebell against use: *Quem penes arbitrium est, & jus & norma loquendi.*[6] It is not the observing of *Trochaicques* nor their *Iambicques*, that wil make our writings ought the wiser: All their Poesie, all their Philosophie is nothing, unlesse we bring the discerning light of conceipt with us to apply it to use. It is not bookes, but onely that great booke of the world, and the all-overspreading grace of heaven that makes men truely judiciall. Nor can it be but a touch of arrogant ignorance, to hold this or that nation Barbarous, these or those times grosse, considering how this manifold creature man, wheresoever hee stand in the world, hath alwayes some disposition of worth, intertaines the order of societie, affects that which is most in use, and is eminent in some one thing or other, that fits his humour and the times. The Grecians held all other nations barbarous but themselves, yet *Pirrhus* when he saw the well ordered marching of the Romanes, which made them see their presumptuous errour, could say it was no barbarous maner of proceeding. The *Gothes, Vandales* and *Longobards,* whose comming downe like an inundation overwhelmed, as they say, al the glory of learning in *Europe,* have yet left us still their lawes and customes, as the originalls of most of the provinciall constitutions of Christendome; which well considered with their other courses of governement, may serve to cleere them from this imputation of ignorance. And though the vanquished never yet spake well of the Conquerour: yet even thorow the unsound coverings of malediction appeare those monuments of trueth, as argue wel their worth and proves them not without judgement, though without Greeke and Latine.

Will not experience confute us, if wee shoulde say the state of *China,* which never heard of Anapestiques, Trochies, and Tribracques, were grosse, barbarous, and uncivile? And is it not a most apparant ignorance, both of the succession of learning in

[4] ["And you may see a Cataline in a crowd, under any part of the heavens."]
[5] ["Business ought to fit the times, not times the business."]
[6] [Horace, *Ars Poetica* 72: "In whom lies the power of judgment, the law and norm of speaking."]

Europe, and the generall course of things, *to say, that all lay pittifully deformed in those lacke-learning times from the declining of the Romane Empire, till the light of the Latine tongue was revived by* Rewcline, Erasmus *and* Moore.[7] When for three hundred yeeres before them about the comming downe of *Tamburlaine* into *Europe, Franciscus Petrarcha* (who then no doubt likewise found whom to imitate) shewed all the best notions of learning, in that degree of excellencie, both in Latin, Prose and Verse, and in the vulgare Italian, as all the wittes of posteritie have not yet much over-matched him in all kindes to this day: his great Volumes written in Moral Philosophie, shew his infinite reading, and most happy power of disposition: his twelve Ǽglogues, his *Affrica* containing nine Bookes of the last Punicke warre, with his three Bookes of Epistles in Latine verse, shew all the transformations of wit and invention, that a Spirite naturally borne to the inheritance of Poetrie & judiciall knowledge could expresse: All which notwithstanding wrought him not that glory & fame with his owne Nation, as did his Poems in Italian, which they esteeme above al whatsoever wit could have invented in any other forme then wherein it is: which questionles they wil not change with the best measures, Greeks or Latins can shew them; howsoever our Adversary imagines. Nor could this very same innovation in Verse, begun amongst them by *C. Tolomæi,*[8] but die in the attempt, and was buried as soone as it came borne, neglected as a prodigious & unnaturall issue amongst them: nor could it never induce *Tasso* the wonder of *Italy,* to write that admirable Poem of *Jerusalem,* comparable to the best of the ancients, in any other forme then the accustomed verse. And with *Petrarch* lived his scholer *Boccacius,* and neere about the same time, *Johannis Ravenensis,* and from these *tanquam ex equo Troiano,*[9] seemes to have issued all those famous Italian Writers, *Leonardus Aretinus, Laurentius Valla, Pog-*

---

7 [Quoting Campion's *Observations.* "Rewcline" is Johann Reuchlin (1455–1522), German humanist.]

8 [Claudio Tolomei, attempting to "classicize" the vernacular, published *Versi et Regole della Nuova Poetica* in 1539.]

9 ["As if out of the Trojan Horse." "Boccacius" is Giovanni Boccaccio (1313–75), the author of the *Decameron* and *De Genealogia Deorum.* "Johannis Ravenensis" is probably Giovanni da Ravenna, Italian author who flourished around the turn of the fourteenth century.]

gius, B[i]ondus,[1] and many others. Then *Emanuel Chrysolaras* a Constantinopolitan gentleman, renowmed for his learning and vertue, being imployed by *John Paleologus* Emperour of the East, to implore the ayde of christian Princes, for the succouring of perishing *Greece:* and understanding in the meane time, how *Bajazeth* was taken prisoner by *Tamburlan,* and his country freed from danger, stayed still at *Venice,* and there taught the Greeke tongue, discontinued before, in these parts the space of seaven hundred yeeres. Him followed *Bessarion, George Trapezantius, Theodore Gaza,*[2] & others, transporting Philosophie beaten by the Turke out of *Greece* into christendome. Hereupon came that mightie confluence of Learning in these parts, which returning, as it were *per postliminium,*[3] and heere meeting then with the new invented stampe of Printing, spread it selfe indeed in a more universall sorte then the world ever heeretofore had it. When *Pomponius Lætus, Æneas Sylvius, Angelus Politianus, Hermolaus Barbarus, Johannes Picus de Mirandula*[4] the miracle & Phoenix of the world, adorned *Italie,* and wakened up other Nations likewise with this desire of glory, long before it brought foorth, *Rewclen, Erasmus,* and *Moore,* worthy men I confesse, and the last a great ornament to this land, and a Rymer. And yet long before all these, and likewise with these, was not our Nation behind in her portion of spirite and worthinesse, but concurrent with the best of all this lettered worlde: witnesse venerable *Bede,* that flourished above a thousand yeeres since: *Aldelmus Durotelmus* that lived in the yeere 739. of whom we finde this commendation registred. *Omnium Poetarum sui temporis facilè primus, tantæ eloquentiæ, majestatis & eruditionis homo fuit, ut nunquam satis admirari possim unde illi in tam barbara*

1 [Not Pietro but Leonardo Aretino (1369–1444), who wrote lives of Dante and Petrarch; Lorenzo Valla (1406–57); Poggio Bracciolini (1380–1459); Flavio Biondo (1388–1463).]
2 [Daniel offers a historical sketch of humanism, beginning with the Byzantine Chrysolorus (1355–1415); moving to Johannes Bessarion (1389–1472), patriarch of Constantinople; then to the philosopher George of Trebizond (1395–1484); ending with Theodorus Gaza (1400?–78), Byzantine scholar.]
3 [Term drawn from Roman law, meaning "through a restoration of former rights and privileges."]
4 [Pomponius Laetus (1428–98), leader of the Roman academy; Aeneas Sylvius Piccolomini (1406–64), later Pope Pius II; Angelo Politian (1454–94), author of the *Sylvae* containing the famous "Nutricia"; Ermolao Barbaro (1454–1493 or 1495), Italian philosopher and humanist; Pico della Mirandola (1463–94).]

ac rudi ætate facundia accreverit, usque adeo omnibus numeris tersa, elegans & rotunda, versus edidit cum antiquitate de palma contendentes.[5] Witnesse *Josephus Devonius,*[6] who wrote *de bello Troiano,* in so excellent manner, and so neere resembling Antiquitie, as Printing his Worke beyond the Seas, they have ascribed it to *Cornelius Nepos,* one of the Ancients.

What should I name *Walterus Mape, Gulielmus Nigellus, Gervasius Tilburiensis, Bracton, Bacon, Ockam,*[7] and an infinite Catalogue of excellent men, most of them living about foure hundred yeares since, and have left behinde them monuments of most profound judgement and learning in all sciences. So that it is but the clowds gathered about our owne judgement that makes us thinke all other ages wrapt up in mists, and the great distance betwixt us, that causes us to imagine men so farre off, to be so little in respect of our selves. We must not looke upon the immense course of times past, as men over-looke spacious and wide countries, from off high Mountaines and are never the neere to judge of the true Nature of the soyle, or the particular syte and face of those territories they see. Nor must we thinke, viewing the superficiall figure of a region in a Mappe that wee know strait the fashion and place as it is. Or reading an Historie (which is but a Mappe of men, and dooth no otherwise acquaint us with the true Substance of Circumstances, than a superficiall Card dooth the Sea-man with a Coast never seene, which alwayes prooves other to the eye than the imagination forecast it) that presently wee know all the world, and can distinctly judge of times, men and maners, just as they were. When the best measure of man is to be taken by his owne foote, bearing ever the neerest proportion to himselfe, and is never so farre different and unequall in his powers, that he hath all in perfection at one

5 ["Easily the foremost poet of his time, he was a man of so much eloquence, majesty, and erudition that I cannot wonder enough at how his command of language grew in so barbarous and rude an age, so that his discourse was polished in all meters—elegant and complete—and issued in verses contending for the palm with antiquity." (Aldelmus Durotelmus or Ealdhelm of Sherbourne who died in 709?).]
6 [Joseph of Exeter, whose history of the Trojan War had been attributed to Cornelius Nepos and Dares Phrygius.]
7 [Walter Map (*fl.* 1200) wrote *De Nugis Curialium;* Nigel "Wireker" (*fl.* 1190) wrote *Speculum Stultorum;* Tilburiensis (*fl.* 1210) wrote *Otia Imperialia;* Henry Bracton, thirteenth-century jurist, wrote a *De Legibus Angliae;* Roger Bacon, thirteenth-century philosopher; William of Ockham, nominalist of the fourteenth century.]

time, and nothing at an other. The distribution of giftes are universall, and all seasons hath them in some sort. We must not
thinke, but that there were *Scipioes, Cæsars, Catoes* and *Pom-
peies,* borne elsewhere then at *Rome,* the rest of the world hath
ever had them in the same degree of nature, though not of state.
And it is our weakenesse that makes us mistake, or misconceive
in these deliniations of men the true figure of their worth. And
our passion and beliefe is so apt to leade us beyond truth, that
unlesse we try them by the just compasse of humanitie, and as
they were men, we shall cast their figures in the ayre when we
should make their models upon Earth. It is not the contexture of
words, but the effects of Action that gives glory to the times: we
finde they had *mercurium in pectore* though not *in lingua,*[8] and
in all ages, though they were not Ciceronians, they knew the Art
of men, which onely is, *Ars Artium,*[9] the great gift of heaven,
and the chiefe grace and glory on earth, they had the learning of
Governement, and ordring their State, Eloquence inough to shew
their judgements. And it seemes the best times followed *Lycur-
gus* councell: *Literas ad usum saltem discebant, reliqua omnis
disciplina erat, ut pulchre parerent ut labores perferrent &c.*[1]
Had not unlearned *Rome* laide the better foundation, and built
the stronger frame of an admirable state, eloquent *Rome* had
confounded it utterly, which we saw, ranne the way of all confusion, the plaine course of dissolution in her greatest skill: and
though she had not power to undoe her selfe, yet wrought she so
that she cast her selfe quite away from the glory of a common-
wealth, and fell upon that forme of state she ever most feared
and abhorred of all other: and then scarse was there seene any
shadowe of pollicie under her first Emperours, but the most hor-
rible and grosse confusion that could bee conceved, notwithstanding it stil indured, preserving not only a Monarchie, locked
up in her own limits, but therewithall held under her obedience,
so many Nations so farre distant, so ill affected, so disorderly
commanded & unjustly conquerd, as it is not to be attributed to
any other fate but to the first frame of that commonwealth,
which was so strongly joynted and with such infinite combina-

8 ["the god of eloquence in their breasts" though not "on their tongues."]
9 ["The art of art."]
1 ["They used to learn letters for use anyway—it was the last discipline of all
—so that they might appear elegant as they carried out their labors."]

tions interlinckt, as one naile or other ever held up the Majestie thereof. There is but one learning, which *omnes gentes habent scriptum in cordibus suis*,[2] one and the selfe-same spirit that worketh in all. We have but one body of Justice, one body of Wisedome throughout the whole world, which is but apparaled according to the fashion of every nation.

Eloquence and gay wordes are not of the Substance of wit, it is but the garnish of a nice time, the Ornaments that doe but decke the house of a State, & *imitatur publicos mores:*[3] Hunger is as well satisfied with meat served in pewter as silver. Discretion is the best measure, the rightest foote in what habit soever it runne. *Erasmus, Rewcline* and *More*, brought no more wisdome into the world with all their new revived wordes then we finde was before, it bred not a profounder Divine than Saint *Thomas*, a greater Lawyer than *Bartolus*,[4] a more accute Logician than *Scotus:* nor are the effects of all this great amasse of eloquence so admirable or of that consequence, but that *impexa illa antiquitas*[5] can yet compare with them. Let us go no further, but looke upon the wonderfull Architecture of this state of *England*, and see whether they were deformed times, that could give it such a forme. Where there is no one the least piller of Majestie, but was set with most profound judgement and borne up with the just conveniencie of Prince and people. No Court of Justice, but laide by the Rule and Square of Nature, and the best of the best commonwealths that ever were in the world. So strong and substantial, as it hath stood against al the storms of factions, both of beliefe & ambition, which so powerfully beat upon it, and all the tempestuous alterations of humorous times whatsoever. Being continually in all ages furnisht with spirites fitte to maintaine the majestie of her owne greatnes, and to match in an equall concurrencie all other kingdomes round about her with whome it had to incounter. But this innovation, like a Viper, must ever make way into the worlds opinion, thorow the bowelles of her owne breeding, & is alwayes borne with reproch in her mouth; the disgracing others is the best grace it can put on, to winne reputation of wit, and yet is it never so wise as it

---

2 ["all men have inscribed in their hearts."]
3 ["and ape public fashions."]
4 [Italian jurist of the fourteenth century.]
5 ["that unpolished antiquity."]

would seeme, nor doth the world ever get so much by it, as it imagineth: which being so often deceived, and seeing it never performes so much as it promises, me thinkes men should never give more credite unto it. For, let us change never so often, wee can not change man, our imperfections must still runne on with us. And therefore the wiser Nations have taught menne alwayes to use, *Moribus legibusque presentibus etiamsi deteriores sint.*[6] The Lacedemonians, when a Musitian, thincking to winne him- selfe credite by his new invention, and be before his fellowes, had added one string more to his Crowde,[7] brake his fiddle, and banished him the Cittie, holding the Innovator, though in the least things, dangerous to a publike societie. It is but a fantastike giddinesse to forsake the way of other men, especially where it lies tollerable: *Ubi nunc est respublica, ibi simus potius quam dum illam veterem sequimur, simus in nulla.*[8] But shal we not tend to perfection? Yes, and that ever best by going on in the course we are in, where we have advantage, being so farre onward, of him that is but now setting forth. For we shall never proceede, if wee be ever beginning, nor arrive at any certayne Porte, sayling with all windes that blow: *Non convalescit planta quæ sæpius transfertur,*[9] and therefore let us hold on in the course wee have undertaken, and not still be wandring. Perfec- tion is not the portion of man, and if it were, why may wee not as well get to it this way as an other? and suspect these great undertakers, lest they have conspired with envy to betray our proceedings, and put us by the honor of our attempts, with cast- ing us backe upon an other course, of purpose to overthrow the whole action of glory when we lay the fairest for it, and were so neere our hopes? I thanke God that I am none of these great Schollers, if thus their hie knowledges doe but give them more eyes to looke out into uncertaintie and confusion, accounting my selfe, rather beholding to my ignorance, that hath set me in so lowe an under-roome of conceipt with other men, and hath given me as much distrust, as it hath done hope, daring not adventure to goe alone, but plodding on the plaine tract I finde beaten by

6 ["The present laws and customs, even if they may be worse."]
7 [Ancient Celtic stringed instrument, hence "fiddle."]
8 ["Where the state is at present, there we must be, rather than be in no state as we follow the old ways."]
9 ["A plant that is too often moved does not grow strong."]

Custome and the Time, contenting me with what I see in use. And surely mee thinkes these great wittes should rather seeke to adorne, than to disgrace the present, bring something to it, without taking from it what it hath. But it is ever the misfortune of Learning, to be wounded by her owne hand. *Stimulos dat emula virtus*,[1] and when there is not abilitie to match what is, malice wil finde out ingines, either to disgrace or ruine it, with a perverse incounter of some new impression: and which is the greatest misery, it must ever proceed from the powers of the best reputation, as if the greatest spirites were ordained to indanger the worlde, as the grosse are to dishonour it, and that we were to expect *ab optimis periculum, à pessimis dedecus publicum*.[2] Emulation the strongest pulse that beates in high mindes, is oftentimes a winde, but of the worst effect: For whilst the Soule comes disappoynted of the object it wrought on, it presently forges an other, and even cozins it selfe, and crosses all the world, rather than it wil stay to be under hir desires, falling out with all it hath, to flatter and make faire that which it would have. So that it is the ill successe of our longings that with *Xerxes* makes us to whippe the Sea, and send a cartel of defiance to mount *Athos:* and the fault laide upon others weakenesse, is but a presumptuous opinion of our owne strength, who must not seeme to be maistered. But had our Adversary taught us by his owne proceedings, this way of perfection, and therein fram'd us a Poeme of that excellencie as should have put downe all, and beene the maister-peece of these times, we should all have admired him. But to deprave the present forme of writing, and to bring us nothing but a few loose and uncharitable Epigrammes, and yet would make us believe those numbers were come to raise the glory of our language, giveth us cause to suspect the performance, and to examine whether this new Arte, *constat sibi*, or, *aliquid sit dictum quod non sit dictum prius*.[3]

First we must heere imitate the Greekes and Latines, and yet we are heere shewed to disobey them, even in their owne numbers and quantities: taught to produce what they make short, and make short what they produce: made beleeve to be shewd meas-

---

1 ["Exemplary virtue lends incentive."]
2 ["At the best, danger; at the worst, public disgrace."]
3 ["has fully established itself" or "permits something to be said that was not said before."]

ures in that forme we have not seene, and no such matter: tolde that heere is the perfect Art of versifying, which in conclusion is yet confessed to be unperfect, as if our Adversary to be opposite to us, were become unfaithfull to himselfe, and seeking to leade us out of the way of reputation, hath adventured to intricate and confound him in his owne courses, running upon most un-even groundes, with imperfect rules, weake proofes, and unlawfull lawes. Whereunto the world, I am perswaded, is not so unreasonable as to subscribe, considering the unjust authoritie of the Law-giver. For who hath constituted him to be the *Radamanthus* thus to torture sillables, and adjudge them their perpetuall doome, setting his *Theta*[4] or marke of condemnation uppon them, to indure the appoynted sentence of his crueltie, as hee shall dispose. As though there were that disobedience in our wordes, as they would not be ruled or stand in order without so many intricate Lawes, which would argue a great perversenesse amongst them, according to that, *in pessima republica plurimæ leges:*[5] or, that they were so farre gone from the quiet freedome of nature, that they must thus be brought backe againe by force. And now in what case were this poore state of words, if in like sorte another tyrant the next yeere should arise and abrogate these lawes and ordaine others cleane contrary according to his humor, and say that they were onely right, the others unjust, what disturbance were there here, to whome should we obey? Were it not farre better to holde us fast to our old custome, than to stand thus distracted with uncertaine Lawes, wherein Right shal have as many faces as it pleases Passion to make it, that wheresoever mens affections stand, it shall still looke that way. What trifles doth our unconstant curiositie cal up to contend for, what colours are there laid upon indifferent things to make them seeme other then they are, as if it were but only to intertaine contestation amongst men; who standing according to the prospective of their owne humour, seeme to see the selfe same things to appeare otherwise to them, than either they doe to other, or are indeede in themselves, being but all one in nature. For what a doe have we heere, what strange precepts of Arte about the framing of an Iambique verse in our language, which when all is

---

4 [Rhadamanthus judged the dead, the Greek "theta" meaning death.]
5 ["in the worst state there are the most laws."]

done, reaches not by a foote, but falleth out to be the plaine ancient verse consisting of tenne sillables or five feete, which hath ever beene used amongest us time out of minde. And for all this cunning and counterfeit name can or will be any other in nature then it hath beene ever heretofore: and this new *Dimeter* is but the halfe of this verse divided in two, and no other then the *Cæsura* or breathing place in the middest thereof, and therefore it had bene as good to have put two lines in one, but only to make them seeme diverse. Nay it had beene much better for the true English reading and pronouncing thereof, without violating the accent, which now our Adversarie hath heerein most unkindely doone: for, being, as wee are to sound it, according to our English March, we must make a rest, and raise the last sillable, which falles out very unnaturall in *Desolate, Funerall, Elizabeth, Prodigall,* and in all the rest saving the Monosillables. Then followes the English *Trochaicke,* which is saide to bee a simple verse, and so indeede it is, being without Ryme; having here no other grace then that in sound it runnes like the knowne measure of our former ancient Verse, ending (as we terme it according to the French) in a feminine foote, saving that it is shorter by one sillable at the beginning, which is not much missed, by reason it falles full at the last. Next comes the *Elegiacke,* being the fourth kinde, and that likewise is no other then our old accustomed measure of five feete, if there be any difference, it must be made in the reading, and therein wee must stand bound to stay where often we would not, and sometimes either breake the accent, or the due course of the word. And now for the other foure kinds of numbers, which are to be employed for *Odes,* they are either of the same measure, or such as have ever beene familiarly used amongst us. So that of all these eight severall kindes of new promised numbers you see what we have. Onely what was our owne before, and the same but apparelled in forraine Titles, which had they come in their kinde and naturall attire of Ryme, wee should never have suspected that they had affected to be other, or sought to degenerate into strange manners, which now we see was the cause why they were turnd out of their proper habite, and brought in as Aliens, onely to induce men to admire them as farre-commers. But see the power of Nature, it is not all the artificiall coverings of wit that can hide their native and originall condition which breakes out thorow the strongest bandes of affectation, and will be it selfe, doe Singularitie what it can. And as for those imagined quantities of sillables, which have bin ever held free and indifferent in our language, who can inforce us to take knowlege of them, being *in nullius verba jurati*,[6] & owing fealty to no forraine invention; especially in such a case where there is no necessitie in Nature, or that it imports either the matter or forme, whether it be so, or otherwise. But every Versifier that wel observes his worke, findes in our language, without all these unnecessary precepts, what numbers best fitte the Nature of her Idiome, and the proper places destined to such accents, as she will not let in, to any other roomes then into those for which they were borne. As for example, you cannot make this fall into the right sound of a Verse.

None thinkes reward rendred worthy his worth:

unlesse you thus misplace the accent uppon *Rendrèd* and *Worthìe*, contrary to the nature of these wordes: which sheweth that two feminine numbers (or Trochies, if so you wil call them) will not succeede in the third and fourth place of the Verse. And so likewise in this case,

Though Death doth consume, yet Virtue preserves,

it wil not be a Verse, though it hath the just sillables, without the same number in the second, and the altering of the fourth place, in this sorte:

Though Death doth ruine, Virtue yet preserves.

Againe, who knowes not that we cannot kindely answere a feminine number with a masculine Ryme, or (if you will so terme it) a *Trochei* with a *Sponde*, as *Weakenes* with *Confesse*, *Nature* and *Indure*, onely for that thereby wee shall wrong the accent, the chiefe Lord and grave Governour of Numbers. Also you cannot in a Verse of foure feete, place a *Trochei* in the first, without the like offence, as,

6 ["bound by no man's word."]

Yearely out of his watry Cell:

for so you shall sound it *Yeareliè* which is unnaturall. And other such like observations usually occurre, which Nature and a judiciall eare, of themselves teach us readily to avoyde.

But now for whom hath our Adversary taken all this paines? For the Learned, or for the Ignorant, or for himselfe, to shew his owne skill? If for the Learned, it was to no purpose, for everie Grammarian in this land hath learned his *Prosodia,* and alreadie knowes all this Arte of Numbers: if for the Ignorant, it was vaine: For if they become Versifiers, wee are like to have leane Numbers, instede of fat Ryme: and if *Tully*[7] would have his Orator skilld in all the knowledges appertaining to God and man, what should they have, who would be a degree above Orators? Why then it was to shew his owne skill, and what himselfe had observed: so he might well have done, without doing wrong to the fame of the living, and wrong to *England,* in seeking to lay reproach uppon her native ornaments, and to turne the faire streame and full course of her accents, into the shallow current of a lesse uncertaintie, cleane out of the way of her knowne delight. And I had thought it could never have proceeded from the pen of a Scholler (who sees no profession free from the impure mouth of the scorner) to say the reproach of others idle tongues is the curse of Nature upon us, when it is rather her curse upon him, that knowes not how to use his tongue. What, doth he think himselfe is now gotten so farre out of the way of contempt, that his numbers are gone beyond the reach of obloquie, and that how frivolous, or idle soever they shall runne, they shall be protected from disgrace, as though that light rymes and light numbers did not weigh all alike in the grave opinion of the wise. And that it is not Ryme, but our ydle Arguments that hath brought downe to so base a reckning, the price and estimation of writing in this kinde. When the few good things of this age, by comming together in one throng and presse with the many bad, are not discerned from them, but over-looked with them, and all taken to be alike. But when after-times shall make a quest of inquirie, to examine the best of this Age, peradventure there will be found in the now contemned recordes of Ryme, matter not unfitting the

[7] [Cicero.]

gravest Divine, and severest Lawyer in this kingdome. But these things must have the date of Antiquitie, to make them reverend and authentical: For ever in the collation of Writers, men rather weigh their age then their merite, & *legunt priscos cum reverentia, quando coetaneos non possunt sine invidia.*[8] And let no writer in Ryme be any way discouraged in his endevour by this brave allarum, but rather animated to bring up all the best of their powers, and charge withall the strength of nature and industrie upon contempt, that the shew of their reall forces may turne backe insolencie into her owne holde. For, be sure that innovation never workes any overthrow, but upon the advantage of a carelesse idlenesse. And let this make us looke the better to our feete, the better to our matter, better to our maners. Let the Adversary that thought to hurt us, bring more profit and honor, by being against us, then if he had stoode still on our side. For that (next to the awe of heaven) the best reine, the strongst hand to make men keepe their way, is that which their enemy beares upon them: and let this be the benefite wee make by being oppugned, and the meanes to redeeme backe the good opinion, vanitie and idlenesse have suffered to be wonne from us; which, nothing but substance and matter can effect. For,

Scribendi rectè sapere est & principium & fons.[9]

When we heare Musicke, we must be in our eare, in the utterroome of sense, but when we intertaine judgement, we retire into the cabinet and innermost withdrawing chamber of the soule: And it is but as Musicke for the eare,

Verba sequi fidibus modulanda Latinis,[1]

but it is a worke of power for the soule,

Numerósque modósque ediscere vitæ.[2]

---

8 ["And they read the Ancients with reverence when they cannot read their contemporaries without envy."]
9 [Horace, *Ars Poetica* 309: "Knowledge is the source and fount of good writing."]
1 [Horace, *Epistulae* ii.2.143: "To find out words faithful to Latin measures."]
2 [Horace, *Epistulae* ii.2.144: "To learn the rhythms and meters of life."]

The most judiciall and worthy spirites of this Land are not so delicate, or will owe so much to their eare, as to rest uppon the out-side of wordes, and be intertained with sound: seeing that both Number, Measure, and Ryme, is but as the ground or seate, whereupon is raised the work that commends it, and which may be easily at the first found out by any shallow conceipt: as wee see some fantasticke to beginne a fashion, which afterward gravity itselfe is faine to put on, because it will not be out of the weare of other men, and *Recti apud nos locum tenet error ubi publicus factus est.*[3] And power and strength that can plant itselfe any where, having built within this compasse, and reard it of so high a respect, wee now imbrace it as the fittest dwelling for our invention, and have thereon bestowed all the substance of our understanding to furnish it as it is: and therefore heere I stand foorth, onelie to make good the place we have thus taken up, and to defend the sacred monuments erected therein, which containe the honour of the dead, the fame of the living, the glory of peace, and the best power of our speach, and wherin so many honorable spirits have sacrificed to Memorie their dearest passions, shewing by what divine influence they have beene moved, and under what starres they lived.

But yet now notwithstanding all this which I have heere delivered in the defence of Ryme, I am not so farre in love with mine owne mysterie,[4] or will seeme so froward, as to bee against the reformation, and the better setling these measures of ours. Wherein there be many things, I could wish were more certaine and better ordered, though my selfe dare not take upon me to be a teacher therein, having so much neede to learne of others. And I must confesse, that to mine owne eare, those continuall cadences of couplets used in long and continued Poemes, are very tyresome, and unpleasing, by reason that still, me thinks, they runne on with a sound of one nature, and a kinde of certaintie which stuffs the delight rather then intertaines it. But yet notwithstanding, I must not out of mine owne daintinesse, condemne this kinde of writing, which peradventure to another may seeme most delightfull, and many worthy compositions we see to

[3] ["Among us, where a wrong is committed for the state it holds the place of right."]
[4] [Craft or art.]

have passed with commendation in that kinde. Besides, me thinkes sometimes, to beguile the eare, with a running out, and passing over the Ryme, as no bound to stay us in the line where the violence of the matter will breake thorow, is rather gracefull then otherwise. Wherein I finde my *Homer-Lucan,* as if he gloried to seeme to have no bounds, albeit hee were confined within his measures, to be in my conceipt most happy. For so thereby, they who care not for Verse or Ryme, may passe it over without taking notice thereof, and please themselves with a well-measured Prose. And I must confesse my Adversary hath wrought this much upon me, that I thinke a Tragedie would indeede best comporte with a blank Verse, and dispence with Ryme, saving in the *Chorus* or where a sentence shall require a couplet. And to avoyde this over-glutting the eare with that alwayes certaine, and ful incounter of Ryme, I have assaid in some of my Epistles to alter the usuall place of meeting, and to sette it further off by one Verse, to trie how I could disuse my owne eare and to ease it of this continuall burthen, which indeede seemes to surcharge it a little too much, but as yet I cannot come to please my selfe therein: this alternate or crosse Ryme holding still the best place in my affection.

Besides, to me this change of number in a Poem of one nature sits not so wel, as to mixe uncertainly, feminine Rymes with masculine, which, ever since I was warned of that deformitie by my kinde friend and countriman Maister *Hugh Samford,* I have alwayes so avoyded it, as there are not above two couplettes in that kinde in all my Poem of the Civill warres: and I would willingly if I coulde, have altered it in all the rest, holding feminine Rymes to be fittest for Ditties, and either to be set certaine, or else by themselves. But in these things, I say, I dare not take upon mee to teach that they ought to be so, in respect myselfe holdes them to be so, or that I thinke it right; for indeede there is no right in these things that are continually in a wandring motion, carried with the violence of our uncertaine likings, being but onely the time that gives them their power. For if this right, or truth, should be no other thing then that wee make it, we shall shape it into a thousand figures, seeing this excellent painter Man, can so well lay the colours which himselfe grindes in his owne affections, as that hee will make them serve for any shadow, and any counterfeit. But the greatest hinderer to our proceedings, and the reformation of our errours, is this Selfe-love, whereunto we Versifiers are ever noted to be especially subject; a disease of all other, the most dangerous, and incurable, being once seated in the spirits, for which there is no cure, but onely by a spirituall remedy. *Multos puto, ad sapientiam potuisse pervenire, nisi putassent se pervenisse:*[5] and this opinion of our sufficiencie makes so great a cracke in our judgement, as it wil hardly ever holde any thing of worth, *Cœcus amor sui,*[6] and though it would seeme to see all without it, yet certainely it discernes but little within. For there is not the simplest writer that will ever tell himselfe, he doth ill, but as if he were the parasite onely to sooth his owne doings, perswades him that his lines can not but please others, which so much delight himselfe:

> *Suffenus est quisque sibi. —neque idem unquam.*
> *Æque est beatus, ac poema cum scribit,*
> *Tam gaudet in se tamque se ipse miratur.*[7]

And the more to shew that he is so, we shall see him evermore in all places, and to all persons repeating his owne compositions: and,

> *Quem vero arripuit, tenet occidítque legendo.*[8]

Next to this deformitie stands our affectation, wherein we alwayes bewray our selves to be both unkinde, and unnaturall to our owne native language, in disguising or forging strange or unusuall wordes, as if it were to make our verse seeme an other kind of speach out of the course of our usuall practise, displacing our wordes, or investing new, onely upon a singularitie: when our owne accustomed phrase, set in the due place, would expresse us more familiarly and to better delight, than all this

[5] ["I am convinced that many might have achieved wisdom had they not assumed they had already attained it."]
[6] [Horace, *Odes* i.18.14: "blind self-love."]
[7] [Mainly from Catullus xxii: "Each one is a Suffenus unto himself—and one is never so happy as when one writes a poem, for then one takes pleasure in oneself and is overcome with self-admiration." Suffenus, a hack poet whom Catullus twitted in several poems.]
[8] [Horace, *Ars Poetica* 475: "Whomever he catches he holds and reads to death."]

idle affectation of antiquitie, or noveltie can ever doe. And I can not but wonder at the strange presumption of some men that dare so audaciously adventure to introduce any whatsoever forraine wordes, be they never so strange; and of themselves as it were, without a Parliament, without any consent, or allowance, establish them as Free-denizens in our language. But this is but a Character of that perpetuall revolution which wee see to be in all things that never remaine the same, and we must heerein be content to submit our selves to the law of time, which in few yeeres wil make al that, for which we now contend, *Nothing*.

FINIS

Ben Jonson

1572/3–1637

One of the great figures of English literature, Jonson was translator, dramatist, poet, literary critic—even the author of an English Gram- mar—and within various genres he was, variously, capable of ease, power, delicacy, and compression. But because his manipulation of tone is so exact, his metrical effects so subtle, he has always been difficult to appreciate; as T. S. Eliot points out, a writer like Shake- peare has much to offer even the man with the untrained ear, but the "polished veneer of Jonson reflects only the lazy reader's fatuity." After attending Westminster school, where he came to reverence his master Camden, and through Camden, to revere the writers of an- tiquity as "Guides, not Commanders," Jonson fully established his reputation as a dramatist with such enduring plays as Volpone *(1606),* The Alchemist *(1610), and* Bartholomew Fair *(1614). He also consumed a large portion of his literary life in writing a series of great masques for the court of King James, where he was first friend and later enemy to Inigo Jones. His acquaintance numbered Bacon, Selden, Donne, Shakespeare, and of course the group of younger poets who were honored to be the Sons of Ben.*

Jonson made a (rather awkward) translation of Horace's Ars Poet- ica, *which was published unrevised after his death, and apparently wrote an "art of poetry" of his own that may have been burned in the conflagration that destroyed the larger part of his library in 1623. The poet in person, his "mountaine belly" and "rockie face," must have been a formidable figure, and it may be supposed that his witty* obiter dicta, *delivered at the Mermaid Tavern and elsewhere, exerted considerable influence on the literary men of the time. Something of his "conversation" was preserved by Drummond, though in reading the excerpts offered here it ought to be remembered that the laird of Hawthornden was rather a solemn fellow and Jonson a hard-drinking master of what Puttenham calls "Ironia, or the Drie Mock." Jonson also shaped critical opinion by writing prefaces and prologues to his plays, thus anticipating the habit of self-justification that Corneille and Dryden were to elevate to an art of criticism.*

But Jonson's most important critical pronouncements occur in Timber: or, Discoveries; Made Upon Men and Matter: As They have flow'd out of his daily Readings; or had their refluxe to his peculiar Notion of the Times, *published posthumously by Sir Kenelm Digby, Jonson's literary executor. The title is quite literal, for about three-quarters of these "discoveries . . . flow'd out of his daily Readings" —of Quintilian, Vives, Heinsius, the two Senecas, Hoskyns, and others—and then are given, often with only minor rephrasing, by strategic juxtaposition, some "refluxe to his peculiar Notion of the Times." In this rare facility for recognizing the presentness of the past resides the force and relevance of* Timber; *not merely useful as a compendium, the work is a commonplace book of a practicing poet who has contrived to apply the words of a Seneca or a Quintilian to contemporary figures and events, bringing ancient Rome and seventeenth-century London into abrupt and meaningful alignment. It is a "refluxive" practice that affords insight into Jonson's poetry as well as his criticism, and probably it is not too much to say that the practice characterizes the period as a whole.*

"A Fit of Rime against Rime" is reprinted from Under-Woods: Consisting of Divers Poems *in* The Workes of Benjamin Jonson *(1641; dated 1640). Herford and Simpson speculate that the poem may date from the Campion-Daniel controversy, about which Jonson expressed his dissatisfaction to Drummond. "The Epistle" to* Volpone *is reprinted from the 1607 edition. Drummond's ms. of the "Conversations" is lost, so that editors have had to work from the transcript made by Sir Robert Sibbald (1641–1722). Although the transcript seems to have been done with care, its orthography and pointing are such as to make it unacceptable for a volume of this kind: I have, accordingly, taken considerable liberties with the text, basing the present version on David Laing's more readable edition of 1842 but taking care to amend in the light of later editions. The poem "To . . . Shakespeare" comes from the first folio (1623).* Timber *(separately dated*

*1641), checked against Herford and Simpson, is reprinted without
marginalia from The Workes. (Since one can hardly hope to appreciate Timber without some awareness of what Jonson was using from
the past for the present, I have indicated most of his main sources in
the notes. Anyone interested in more detailed information may begin
by consulting Volume XI of Ben Jonson, edited by Herford and Simpson.) Despite its miscellaneous character, I have used points of ellip-
sis to indicate omission in Timber but have not repeated the practice
with the wholly fragmentary "Conversations."*

FROM

Under-Woods

A FIT OF RIME AGAINST RIME

[1603?]

Rime the rack of finest wits,
That expresseth but by fits,
      True Conceipt,
Spoyling Senses of their Treasure,
Cosening Judgement with a measure,
      But false weight.
Wresting words, from their true calling;
Propping Verse, for feare of falling
      To the ground.
Joynting Syllabes, drowning Letters,
Fastning Vowells, as with fetters
      They were bound!
Soone as lazie thou wert knowne,

All good Poëtrie hence was flowne,
And [Art] banish'd.
For a thousand yeares together,
All *Pernassus* Greene did wither,
And wit vanish'd.
Pegasus did flie away,
At the Wells no Muse did stay,
But bewail'd.
So to see the Fountaine drie,
And Apollo's Musique die,
All light failed!
Starveling rimes did fill the Stage,
Not a Poët in an Age,
Worth crowning.
Not a worke deserving Baies,
Nor a lyne deserving praise,
Pallas frowning;
Greeke was free from Rimes infection,
Happy Greeke by this protection!
Was not spoyled.
Whilst the Latin, Queene of Tongues,
Is not yet free from Rimes wrongs,
But rests foiled.
Scarce the hill [1] againe doth flourish,
Scarce the world a Wit doth nourish,
To restore,
Phœbus to his Crowne againe;
And the Muses to their braine;
As before.
Vulgar Languages that want
Words, and sweetnesse, and be scant
Of true measure,
Tyran Rime hath so abused,
That they long since have refused,
Other ceasure;[2]
He that first invented thee,
May his joynts tormented bee,
Cramp'd forever;
Still may Syllabes jarre with time,

1 [Parnassus.]
2 [Caesura.]

Still may reason warre with rime,
                            Resting never.
May his Sense when it would meet,
The cold tumor in his feet,
                            Grow unsounder.
And his Title be long foole,
That in rearing such a Schoole,
                            Was the founder.

F R O M

Volpone

THE EPISTLE

[*1607*]

Never (*most æquall* Sisters[1]) had any man a wit so presently
excellent, as that it could raise it selfe; but there must come both
Matter, Occasion, Commenders, and Favourers to it. If this be
true, and that the Fortune of all *Writers* doth daily prove it, it
behoves the carefull to provide, well, toward these accidents;
and, having acquir'd them, to preserve that part of reputation
most tenderly, wherein the benefit of a Friend is also defended.
Hence is it, that I now render my selfe gratefull, and am studious to justifie the bounty of your act: To which, though your
mere authority were satisfying, yet, it being an age, wherein *Poëtry* and the Professors of it heare so ill, on all sides, there will a
reason bee look'd for in the subject. It is certaine, nor can it with
any forehead be oppos'd, that the too-much licence of *Poëtasters*,
in this time, hath much deform'd their *Mistresse;* that, every day
their manifold, and manifest ignorance doth stick unnaturall re-

[1] [Oxford and Cambridge.]

proches upon her: But for their petulancy, it were an act of the greatest injustice, either to let the learned suffer; or so divine a *skill* (which indeed should not be attempted with uncleane hands) to fall, under the least contempt. For if men will impartially, and not à-squint, looke toward the offices, and function of a *Poët*, they will easily conclude to themselves, the impossibility of any mans being the good *Poët*, without first being a good *Man*. He that is sayd to be able to informe *yong-men* to all good disciplines, inflame *growne-men* to all great vertues, keepe *old men* in their best and supreme state, or as they decline to child-hood, recover them to their first strength; that comes forth the Interpreter, and Arbiter of *Nature*, a Teacher of things divine, no lesse then humane, a Master in manners; and can alone (or with a few) effect the busines of Man-kind. This, I take him, is no subject for *Pride*, and *Ignorance* to exercise their railing *rhetorique* upon. But, it will here be hastily answer'd, that the *Writers* of these dayes are other things; that, not onely their manners, but their natures are inverted; and nothing remaining with them of the dignity of *Poët*, but the abused name, which every Scribe usurpes: that now, especially in *Dramatick*, or (as they terme it) Stage-*Poëtry*, nothing but Ribaldry, Profanation, Blasphemy, al Licence of offence to God, and Man, is practisd. I dare not deny a great part of this (and am sory, I dare not) because in some mens abortive *Features* (and would they had never boasted the light) it is over-true: But, that all are embarqu'd in this bold adventure for Hell, is a most uncharitable thought, and, utterd, a more malicious slander. For my particular, I can (and from a most cleare conscience) affirme that I have ever trembled to thinke toward the least Prophanenesse; have loathed the use of such foule, and un-washd Baudr'y, as is now made the foode of the *Scene:* And, howsoever I cannot escape, from some, the imputation of sharpnesse, but that they wil say, I have taken a pride, or lust to be bitter, and not my yongest Infant[2] but hath come into the world with all his teeth; I would aske of these supercilious *Politiques*, what Nation, Society, or generall Order, or State I have provokd? what publique Person? whether I have not (in all these) preserv'd their dignity, as mine owne person,

---

2 [*Sejanus*, the tragedy that because of its supposed political "applications" brought Jonson before the Privy Council.]

safe? My WORKES are read, allow'd, (I speake of those that are
intirely mine) looke into them, what broad reproofes have I usd:
Where have I bin particular? Where personall, except to a
Mimick, Cheater, Baud, or Buffon, creatures (for their inso-
lencies) worthy to be tax'd? or to which of these so pointingly, as
he might not, either ingeniously have confest, or wisely dissembled his disease? [3] But it is not Rumour can make men guilty,
much lesse entitle me, to other mens crimes. I know, that nothing can be so innocently writ, or carried, but may be made obnox-
ious to[4] construction; mary, whilst I beare mine innocence
about me, I feare it not. Application, is now, growne a Trade
with many; and there are, that professe to have a *Key* for the
deciphering of every thing, but let wise and noble Persons take
heed how they bee too credulous, or give leave to these invading
Interpreters to be over-familiar with their fames, who cunningly,
& often, utter their owne virulent malice, under other mens simplest meanings. As for those, that wil (by faults which charity
hath rak'd up, or common honesty conceald) make themselves a
name with the Multitude, or (to drawe their rude, and beastly
clappes) care not whose living faces they intrench with their
petulant stiles; may they doe it, without a rivall, for mee: I
chuse rather to live grav'd in obscuritie, then share with them, in
so preposterous a fame. Nor can I blame the wishes of those
grave, and wiser *Patriotes*, who providing[5] the hurts these licentious spirits may do in a State, desire rather to see Fooles, and
Divells, and those antique reliques of Barbarisme retriv'd, with
all other ridiculous, and exploded follies: then behold the
wounds of Private men, of Princes, and Nations. For as HORACE,
makes *Trebatius* speake, in these

Sibi quisque timet, quanquam est intactus, & odit.[6]

And men may justly impute such rages, if continu'd, to the
Writer, as his sports. The encrease of which lust in liberty, together with the present trade of the Stage, in all their misc'line

3 ["Mimick" means "actor," and "ingeniously" means "ingenuously."]
4 [Open to (construction).]
5 [Foreseeing.]
6 [*Satires* ii.1.23: "Each one fears, and hates, for himself, though he remains
untouched."]

Enterludes,[7] what learned or liberall soule doth not already abhor? where nothing but the garbage of the time is utter'd, & that
with such impropriety of *phrase,* such plenty of *solœcismes,*
such dearth of *sense,* so bold *prolepse's,*[8] so rackt *metaphor's,*
with brothelry able to violate the eare of a *Pagan,* and blasphemy, to turne the bloud of a *Christian* to water. I cannot but
be serious in a cause of this nature, wherein my fame, & the
reputations of diverse honest, & learned are the question; when
a NAME, so full of authority, antiquity, and all great marke, is
(through their insolence) become the lowest scorne of the *Age:*
and those MEN subject to the petulancie of every vernaculous
Orator, that were wont to be the care of *Kings,* and happiest
Monarchs. This it is that hath not onely rap't mee to present
indignation, but made mee studious, heretofore, and, by all my
actions, to stand of, from them; which may most appeare in this
my latest WORKE: (which you, *most learned* ARBITRESSES, have
seene, judg'd, & to my crowne, approv'd) wherein I have la-
bourd, for their instruction, and amendment, to reduce,[9] not
onely the antient formes, but manners of the *Scene,* the easinesse, the propriety, the innocence, and last the doctrine, which
is the principall end of POESY to informe men, in the best reason
of living. And though my *Catastrophe* may, in the strict rigour of
Comick Law, meete with censure, as turning back to my promise; I desire the learned, and charitable *Critick* to have so much
faith in me, to thinke it was done off industrye:[1] For with what
ease I could have varied it, nearer his *scale* (but that I feare to
boast my owne faculty) I could here insert. But my special aime
being to put the snafle in their mouths, that crie out, we never
punish vice in our *Enterludes* &c. I tooke the more liberty;
though not with out some lines of example drawne even in the
Antients themselves, the goings out of whose *Comœdies* are not
alwayes joyfull, but oftimes, the Baudes, the Servants, the Rivals, yea and the maisters are mulcted: and fitly, it beeing the
office of a Co*mick*-POET to imitate justice, and instruct to life, as
well as puritie of language, or stirre up gentle affections. To
which, upon my next opportunity toward the examining & di-

[7] From the Latin *ludi miscelli,* a variety show.]
[8] [Prolepsis in the sense of anachronism.]
[9] [Restore.]
[1] [On purpose.]

gesting of my *notes,* I shall speake more wealthily, and pay the World a debt.

In the meane time (*most reverenced* SISTERS) as I have car'd to be thankefull for your affections past, and here made the understanding acquainted with some ground of your favors; let me not dispayre their continuance, to the maturing of some worthier fruits: wherein, if my MUSES bee true to me, I shall raise the dispis'd head of POETRY againe, & stripping her out of those rotten and base ragges, wherewith the *Times* have adulterated her forme, restore her to her primitive habite, feature, and majesty, and render her worthy to be imbraced, and kist, of all the great and Maister *Spirits* of our World. As for the vile, and slothfull, who never affected an act, worthy of celebration, or are so inward with their owne vicious natures, as they worthely feare her; and thinke it a high point of policie, to keepe her in contempt with their declamatory, and windy invectives: shee shall out of just rage incite her Servants (who are *Genus iritabile*) to spout inke in their faces, that shall eate, farder then their marrow, into their fames; and not CINNAMUS the Barber,[2] with his
art, shall be able to take out the brands, but they shall
live, and be read, till the Wretches die, as Things
worst deserving of themselves in chiefe,
and then of all mankind.

From my house in the Black-Friars
this 11. of February. 1607

2 [Martial vi.64.24–26. Martial threatens a writer of bad verses: If my anger brands you, the mark will cling and be read all over town, and not even Cinnamus, the barber-surgeon, will be able to efface the stigma.]

BEN JONSON'S CONVERSATIONS
WITH
WILLIAM DRUMMOND OF HAWTHORNDEN

CERTAIN INFORMATIONS AND MANERS OF BEN JOHNSONS
TO W. DRUMOND
[*1619*]

1

That he had ane intention to perfect ane Epick Poeme intitled
Heroologia, of the Worthies of his Country, rowsed by fame,
and was to dedicate it to his Country, it is all in Couplets, for
he detesteth all other Rimes, said he had written a Discourse
of Poesie both against Campion and Daniel [1] especially this
last, wher he proves couplets to be the bravest sort of verses,
especially when they are broken, like Hexameters and that
crosse Rimes and Stanzaes (becaus the purpose would lead
him beyond 8 lines to conclude) were all forced.

He recommended to my reading Quintilian, (who (he said)
would tell me the faults of my Verses as if he had lived with
me) and Horace, Plinius 2dus Epistles, Tacitus, Juvenall,
Martiall, whose Epigrame *Vitam quæ faciunt beatiorem* &c. he
heth translated.[2]

HIS CENSURE OF THE ENGLISH POETS WAS THIS,

That Sidney did not keep a Decorum in making every one speak
as well as himself.

Spencers stanzaes pleased him not, nor his matter, the meaning
of which Allegorie he had delivered in papers to Sir Walter
Raughlie.

1 [Thomas Campion's *Observations in the Art of English Poesie* (1602), the
most subtle of Renaissance attempts to apply principles of classical prosody
to English verse, was tolerantly demolished by Samuel Daniel, *A Defence of
Ryme: Against a Pamphlet entituled: Observations in the Art of English Poesie*
(1602?). *Cf.* above, Jonson's "A Fit of Rime against Rime."]
2 [Martial x.47. See Jonson's translation (*Under-Woods* xc), "The Things that
make the happier life, are these."]

Samuel Daniel was a good honest man, had no children, bot no poet.

That Michael Draytons Polyabion,[3] if [he] had performed what he promised to writte (the deeds of all the Worthies) had been excellent: His long verses pleased him not.

That Silvesters translation of Du Bartas was not well done, and that he wrote his Verses befor it err he understood to conferr.[4] Nor that of Fairfax his.[5]

That the translations of Homer and Virgill in long Alexandrines were but Prose.

That John Haringtones Ariosto, under all translations was the worst. That when Sir John Harrington desyred him to tell the truth of his Epigrames, he answered him that he loved not the Truth, for they were Narrations, and not Epigrames.

That Warner since the King's comming to England had marrd all his Albions England.

That Dones Anniversarie was profane and full of Blasphemies: that he told Mr Donne, if it had been written of the Virgin Marie it had been something to which he answered that he described the Idea of a Woman and not as she was. That Done for not keeping of accent deserved hanging.

That Shaksperr wanted Arte.

That Abram Francis in his English Hexameters was a Foole.[6]

That next himself only Fletcher and Chapman could make a Mask.

HIS JUDGEMENT OF STRANGER POETS WAS

That he thought not Bartas a Poet but a Verser, because he wrote not Fiction.

He cursed Petrarch for redacting Verses to Sonnets, which he said were like that Tirrants bed, wher some who were too short were racked, others too long cut short.

---

3 [*Poly-Olbion, or a Chorographicall description of* . . . *Great Britain* (1612).]
4 [Jonson means that he wrote his commendatory verses before he knew enough to compare *Bartas: His Devine Weekes and Workes* (collected edition 1605) with the French original; see Jonson's *Epigrammes* cxxxii.]
5 [*Godfrey of Bulloigne or the Recoverie of Jerusalem* (1600), translated from Tasso.]
6 [Abraham France, *The Lamentations of Amintas for the death of Phillis, paraphrastically translated out of Latine into English Hexameteres* (1587) and *The Countesse of Pembrokes Yvychurch* (1591).]

That Guarini, in his Pastor Fido keept not decorum in making Shepherds speek as well as himself could.

That Lucan taken in parts was good divided, read altogidder, merited not the name of a Poet.

He esteemeth John Done the first poet in the World in some things: his verses of the Lost Chaine, he heth by heart and that passage of the Calme, *That dust and feathers doe not stirr, all was so quiet.* Affirmeth Done to have written all his best pieces err he was 25 years old.

Sir Edward [7] Wottons verses of a happie lyfe he hath by heart, and a peice of Chapman's translation of the 13 of the Iliads, which he thinketh well done.

That Done said to him he wrott that Epitaph on Prince Henry, *Look to me, Fa[i]th,* to match Sir Ed: Herbert in obscurenesse.

He hath by heart some verses of Spensers Calender about wyne between Coline and Percye.

The conceit of Dones Transformation, or μετεμψύχωσις,[8] was that he sought the soule of that Aple which Eva pulled, and therafter made it the soule of a Bitch, then of a shee wolf, and so of a woman: his generall purpose was to have brought in all the bodies of the Hereticks from the soule of Cain and at last left it in the bodie of Calvin: of this he never wrotte but one sheet, and now since he was made Doctor repenteth highlie, and seeketh to destroy all his poems.

Of their Nation, Hookers Ecclesiasticall historie (whose children are now beggars) for church matters. Seldens Titles of Honour for Antiquities here and ane book of the Gods of the Gentiles whose names are in the Scripture of Seldens.

For a Heroik poeme he said ther was no such ground as King Arthurs fiction and that S. P. Sidney had ane intention to have transformd all his Arcadia to the stories of King Arthure.

HIS ACQUAINTANCE AND BEHAVIOUR WITH POETS LIVING WITH HIM.

Daniel was at jealousies with him.

Drayton feared him, and he esteemed not of him.

[7] [Sir *Henry* Wotton.]
[8] ["Metempsycosis: Poema Satyricon" or "The Progresse of the Soule."]

That Francis Beaumont loved too much himself and his own verses.

That Sᵣ John Roe loved him; and when they two were ushered by my Lord Suffolk from a Mask, Roe wrott a moral Epistle to him, which began, *That next to playes, the Court and the State were the best. God threateneth Kings, Kings Lords, and Lords do us.*

Sir W. Alexander was not half kinde unto him and neglected him because a friend to Drayton.

Nid Field [9] was his Schollar and he had read to him the Satyres of Horace and some Epigrames of Martiall.

That Markam [1] (who added his English Arcadia) was not of the number of the Faithfull, *i.* [*e.*] *Poets*, and but a base fellow.

And such were Day and Midleton.

That Chapman and Fletcher were loved of him.

Overbury was first his friend, then turn'd his mortall enimie.

PARTICULARS OF THE ACTIONS OF OTHER POETS AND APOTHEGMES.

That the Irish having robd Spensers goods, and burnt his house and a litle child new born he and his wyfe escaped, and after he died for lake of bread in King Street and refused 20 pieces sent to him by my Lord of Essex and said he was sorrie he had no time to spend them. That in that paper S. W. Raughly had of the Allegories of his Fayrie Queen by the Blating Beast the Puritans were understood by the false Duessa the Q. of Scots.

That Southwell was hanged yett so he had written that piece of his, the Burning Babe, he would have been content to destroy many of his.

That S. J. Davies played in ane Epigrame on Draton, who in a sonnet concluded his Mistriss might been the [Tenth Worthy] and said he used a phrase like Dametas in Arcadia, who said for wit his Mistresse might be a Gyant.

9 [Nathaniel Field (1587–1633), actor and dramatist, acted in Jonson's *Cynthias Revels* (1600) and other plays.]
1 [Gervase Markham, a prolific hack: *The English Arcadia, alluding his beginning from Sir Philip Sydnes ending* (1607) and *The Seconde and Laste Parte of the First Book of the English Arcadia, making a complete end* (1613).]

Dones Grandfather on the mother side was Heywood the Epigrammatist. That Done himself for not being understood would perish.

That Sir W. Raughlye esteemed more of fame than conscience. The best wits of England were employed for making of his historie. Ben himself had written a piece to him of the punick warre, which he altered and set in his booke.

S. W. heth written the lyfe of Queen Elizabeth, of which ther is copies extant.

Sir P. Sidney had translated some of the Psalmes, which went abroad under the name of the Countesse of Pembrock.

Marston wrott his Father-in-lawes preachings, and his Father-in-law his Commedies.

Sheakspear in a play brought in a number of men saying they had suffered Shipwrack in Bohemia, wher ther is no sea neer by some 100 miles.

Daniel wrott Civill Warres and yett hath not one batle in all his Book.

The Countess of Rutland was nothing inferior to her Father Sir P. Sidney in poesie. Sir Th: Overburie was in love with her, and caused Ben to read his Wyffe to her, which he with ane excellent grace did and praised the Author. That the morne therafter he discorded with Overburie, who would have him to intend a sute that was unlawfull. The lines my Lady keepd in remembrance, *He comes to near who comes to be denied.* Beaumont wrot that Elegie on the death of the Countess of Rutland, and in effect her husband wanted the half of his in his travells.

Owen[2] is a pure Pedantique Schoolmaster sweeping his living from the Posteriors of litle children, and hath no thinge good in him, his Epigrames being bare narrations.

Chapman hath translated Musæus in his verses like his Homer.

Flesher and Beaumont ten yeers since hath written the Faithfull Shipheardesse a Tragicomedie well done.

Dyer died unmaried.

Sir P. Sidney was no pleasant man in countenance, his face

[2] [John Owen was headmaster of King Henry VIII's School in Warwick and published several collections of epigrams.]

being spoilled with Pimples and of high blood and long: that my Lord Lisle now Earle of [Leicester] his eldest son resembleth him.

OF HIS OWNE LYFE.

When the King came in England, at that tyme the Pest was in London, he being in the country at Sr Robert Cottons house with old Cambden, he saw in a vision his eldest sone (then a child and at London) appear unto him with the Marke of a bloodie crosse on his forehead as if it had been cutted with a suord, at which amazed he prayed unto God, and in the morning he came to Mr. Cambden's chamber to tell him, who persuaded him it was but ane appreehension of his fantasie at which he sould not be disjected; in the mean tyme comes there letters from his wife of the death of that Boy in the plague. He appeared to him he said of a manlie shape and of that grouth that he thinks he shall be at the resurrection.

He had many quarrels with Marston beat him and took his pistol from him, wrote his Poetaster on him; the beginning of them were that Marston represented him in the stage.

S. W. Raulighe sent him Governour with his Son anno 1613 to France. This youth being knavishly inclyned, among other pastimes (as the setting of the favour of Damosells on a Codpiece) caused him to be Drunken and dead drunk, so that he knew not wher he was, therafter laid him on a Carr, which he made to be drawen by Pioners through the streets, at every corner showing his Governour streetched out and telling them that was a more lively image of the Crucifix then any they had, at which sporte young Raughlies mother delyghted much (saying, his father young was so inclyned) though the Father abhorred it.

Every first day of the new year he had 20lb. sent him from the Earl of Pembrok to buy bookes.

After he was reconciled with the Church and left of to be a recusant, at his first communion in token of true reconciliation, he drank out all the full cup of wyne.

Being at the end of my Lord Salisburies table with Inigo Jones and demanded by my Lord, why he was not glad? My Lord said he yow promised I should dine with yow, bot I doe not, for he had none of his meate; he esteamed only that his meate which was of his owne dish.

He heth consumed a whole night in lying looking to his great toe, about which he hath seen tartars and turks, Romans and Carthaginions feight in his imagination.

Northampton was his mortall enimie for brauling, on a St. Georges day, one of his attenders, he was called before the Councell for his Sejanus, and accused both of popperie and treason by him.

Sundry tymes he hath devoured his bookes, *i.* [*e.*] *sold them all for Necessity.*

He heth a minde to be a churchman, and so he might have favour to make one Sermon to the King, he careth not what therafter sould befall him, for he would not flatter though he saw Death.

At his hither comming Sʳ Francis Bacon said to him, he loved not to sie poesy goe on other feet than poeticall dactilus and spondaius.

Pembrok and his Lady discoursing the Earl said the Woemen were mens shadowes, and she maintained them, both appealing to Johnson, he affirmed it true, for which my Lady gave a pennance to prove it in Verse, hence his Epigrame.

His OPINIONE OF VERSES.

That he wrott all his first in prose, for so his master Cambden had learned him.

That Verses stood by sense without either Colours or accent, which yett other tymes he denied.

A great many Epigrams were ill, because they expressed in the end, what sould have been understood, by what was said.

Some loved running verses, *plus mihi complacet.*[3]

He scorned such verses as could be transponed.

> Wher is the man that never yett did hear
> Of faire Penelope Ulisses Queene?

[3] [The quotation from an anonymous epitaph on Lucan, famed for his end-stopped lines, should read: *plus mihi comma placet*, by which Jonson means to register his preference for the end-stopped line as against the excessively loose enjambment of "running verses"; he is not condemning the more "sinewy" use of run-over lines, of which there are plenty in his own verse.]

Of faire Penelope Ulisses Queene
Wher is the man that never yett did hear? [4]

OF HIS WORKES.

That the half of his Comedies were not in print.

He hath intention to writt a fisher or Pastorall play and sett the stage of it in the Lowmond Lake.

That Epithalamium that wants a name in his printed Workes was made at the Earl of Essex mariage.

He is to writt his foot Pilgrimage hither, and to call it a Discoverie in a poem he calleth Edinborough. . . .

He heth commented and translated Horace Art of Poesie, it is in dialogue wayes; by Criticus he understandeth Dr. Done. The old book that goes about (The Art of English Poesie) was done 20 yeers since and keept long in wrytt as a secret.

OF HIS JEASTS AND APOTHEGMS.

The greatest sport he saw in France, was the picture of our Saviour with the Apostles eating the Pascall lamb that was all Larded.

At a supper wher a Gentlewoman had given him unsavoury wild-foul and therfter, to wash, sweet water, he commendet her that shee gave him sweet water, because her flesh stinked.

He said to Prince Charles of Inigo Jones, that when he wanted words to express the greatest Villaine in the world he would call him ane Inigo.

Jones having accused him for naming him behind his back a foole: he denied it; but, says he, I said he was ane arrant knave and I avouch it.

A Gentleman reading a Poem that began with

Wher is that man that never yet did hear
Of fair Penelope, Ulisses Queene?

calling his Cook, asked if he had ever hard of her? Who answering no, demonstrate to him

Lo, ther the man that never yet did hear
Of fair Penelope Ulisses Queene!

[4] [The opening lines of Sir John Davies' *Orchestra* (1596). Jonson found the couplet variously amusing; see below, under "Jeasts."]

Of all his Playes he never gained 2 hundreth pounds.

He had oft this Verse, though he scorned it:

> So long as we may, let us enjoy this breath,
> For nought doth kill a man so soone, as Death.

His Impressa was a Compass with one foot in Center, the other broken, the word, *Deest quod duceret orbem*.[5]

He was better Versed and knew more in Greek and Latin, than all the Poets in England and quintessence[th] their braines.

Of all stiles he loved most to be named honest, and hath of that ane hundreth letters so naming him.

In his merry humor he was wont to name himself the Poet.

He went from Lieth homeward the 25 of January 1619 in a pair of shoes, which he told lasted him since he came from Darnton,[6] which he minded to take back that farr againe: they were appearing like Coriats,[7] the first two dayes he was all excoriate.

If he died by the way, he promised to send me his papers of this Country, hewen as they were.

I have to send him descriptions of Edinbrough Borrow lawes, of the Lowmond.

That piece of the Pucelle of the Court,[8] was stollen out of his pocket by a Gentleman who drank him drousie and given Mistriss Boulstraid, which brought him great displeasur.

January 19, 1619

He [Jonson] is a great lover and praiser of himself, a contemner and scorner of others, given rather to losse a friend, than a jest, jealous of every word and action of those about him (especiallie after drink, which is one of the elements in which he liveth), a dissembler of ill parts which raigne in him, a bragger of some good that he wanteth, thinketh nothing well bot what either he himself, or some of his friends and Countrymen

---

5 ["What might fashion the world is absent."]
6 [Darlington (in Durham).]
7 [Thomas Coryate (1577–1617), whose *Crudities* (1611) has for its engraved title page a picture of the author's traveling clothes, including the boots in which he walked from Venice.]
8 [See *Under-Woods* xlix.]

*hath said or done, he is passionately kynde and angry, careless
either to gaine or keep, vindicative, but if he be well answered,
at himself.*

*For any religion, as being versed in both. Interpreteth best say-
ings and deeds often to the worst: oppressed with fantasie,
which hath ever mastered his reason, a generall disease in
many poets. His inventions are smooth and easie, but above
all he excelleth in a translation.*

*When his play of a Silent Woman was first acted, ther was found
Verses after on the stage against him, concluding that, that
play was well named the Silent Woman, ther was never one
man to say plaudite to it.*

FINIS

To THE MEMORY OF MY BELOVED,

THE AUTHOR

MR. WILLIAM SHAKESPEARE:

AND

WHAT HE HATH LEFT US

[1623]

To draw no envy (*Shakespeare*) on thy name,
    Am I thus ample to thy Booke, and Fame:
While I confesse thy writings to be such,
    As neither *Man*, nor *Muse*, can praise too much.
'Tis true, and all mens suffrage. But these wayes
    Were not the paths I meant unto thy praise:
For seeliest Ignorance on these may light,
    Which, when it sounds at best, but eccho's right;
Or blinde Affection, which doth ne're advance
    The truth, but gropes, and urgeth all by chance;
Or crafty Malice, might pretend this praise,
    And thinke to ruine, where it seem'd to raise.
These are, as some infamous Baud, or whore,

Should praise a Matron. What could hurt her more?
But thou art proofe against them, and indeed
  Above th'ill fortune of them, or the need.
I, therefore will begin. Soule of the Age!
  The applause! delight! the wonder of our Stage!
My *Shakespeare*, rise; I will not lodge thee by
  Chaucer, or *Spenser*, or bid *Beaumont* lye
A little further, to make thee a roome:
  Thou art a Moniment, without a tombe,
And art alive still, while thy Booke doth live,
  And we have wits to read, and praise to give.
That I not mixe thee so, my braine excuses;
  I meane with great, but disproportion'd Muses:
For, if I thought my judgement were of yeeres,
  I should commit thee surely with thy peeres,
And tell, how farre thou didstst our *Lily* out-shine,
  Or sporting *Kid*, or *Marlowes* mighty line.
And though thou hadst small *Latine*, and lesse *Greeke*,
  From thence to honour thee, I would not seeke
For names; but call forth thund'ring *Æschilus*,
  Euripides, and *Sophocles* to us,
Paccuvius, *Accius*, him of *Cordova* dead,[1]
  To life againe, to heare thy Buskin tread,
And shake a Stage: Or, when thy Sockes were on,
  Leave thee alone, for the comparison
Of all, that insolent *Greece*, or haughtie *Rome*
  Sent forth, or since did from their ashes come.
Triúmph my *Britaine*, thou hast one to showe,
  To whom all Scenes of *Europe* homage owe.
He was not of an age, but for all time!
  And all the *Muses* still were in their prime,
When like *Apollo* he came forth to warme
  Our eares, or like a *Mercury* to charme!
Nature her selfe was proud of his designes,
  And joy'd to weare the dressing of his lines!
Which were so richly spun, and woven so fit,
  As, since, she will vouchsafe no other Wit.
The merry *Greeke*, tart *Aristophanes*,
  Neat *Terence*, witty *Plautus*, now not please;
But antiquated, and deserted lye

---

[1] [For Pacuvius and Accius, tragic dramatists, see Horace, *Epistulae* ii.1.50.
The "him of Cordova" is Seneca.]

As they were not of Natures family.
Yet must I not give Nature all : Thy Art,
  My gentle *Shakespeare*, must enjoy a part.
For though the *Poets* matter, Nature be,
  His Art doth give the fashion. And, that he,
Who casts to write a living line, must sweat,
  (Such as thine are) and strike the second heat
Upon the *Muses* anvile : turne the same,
  (And himselfe with it) that he thinkes to frame;
Or for the lawrell, he may gaine a scorne,
  For a good *Poet's* made, as well as borne.
And such wert thou. Looke how the fathers face
  Lives in his issue, even so, the race
Of *Shakespeares* minde, and manners brightly shines
  In his well torned, and true-filed lines :
In each of which, he seemes to shake a Lance,
  As brandish'd at the eyes of Ignorance.
Sweet Swan of Avon ! what a sight it were
  To see thee in our waters yet appeare,
And make those flights upon the bankes of *Thames*,
  That so did take *Eliza*, and our *James*!
But stay, I see thee in the *Hemisphere*
  Advanc'd, and made a Constellation there !
Shine forth, thou Starre of *Poets*, and with rage,
  Or influence, chide, or cheere the drooping Stage;
Which, since thy flight from hence, hath mourn'd like **night**,
  And despaires day, but for thy Volumes light.

F R O M
Timber: or, Discoveries

[*1610?–35?*]

. . . .

What a deale of cold busines doth a man mis-spend the better part of life in! in scattering *complements*, tendring *visits*, gathering and venting *newes*, following *Feasts* and *Playes*, making a little winter-love in a darke corner.

. . .

A man should so deliver himselfe to the nature of the subject, whereof hee speakes, that his hearer may take knowledge of his discipline with some delight: and so apparell faire, and good matter, that the studious of elegancy be not defrauded; redeeme Arts from their rough, and braky seates, where they lay hid, and overgrowne with thornes, to a pure, open, and flowry light: where they may take the eye, and be taken by the hand.

I cannot thinke *Nature* is so spent, and decay'd, that she can bring forth nothing worth her former yeares. She is always the same, like her selfe: And when she collects her strength, is abler still. Men are decay'd, and *studies*: Shee is not.

I know *Nothing* can conduce more to letters, then to examine the writings of the *Ancients*, and not to rest in their sole Authority, or take all upon trust from them; provided the plagues of *Judging*, and *Pronouncing* against them, be away; such as are *envy, bitternesse, precipitation, impudence,* and *scurrile scoffing.* For to all the observations of the *Ancients*, wee have our owne experience: which, if wee will use, and apply, wee have better meanes to pronounce. It is true they open'd the gates, and made the way that went before us; but as Guides, not Commandders: *Non Domini nostri, sed Duces fuêre.*[1] Truth lyes open to all; it is

1 [Seneca, *Epistulae* xxxiii.11.]

no mans *severall. Patet omnibus veritas; nondum est occupata. Multum ex illâ, etiam futuris relictum est.*[2]

If in some things I dissent from others, whose *Wit, Industry, Diligence,* and *Judgement* I looke up at, and admire: let me not therefore heare presently of Ingratitude, and Rashnesse. For I thanke those, that have taught me, and will ever: but yet dare not thinke the *scope* of their labour, and enquiry, was to envy their posterity, what they also could adde, and find out.

If I erre, pardon me: *Nulla ars simul & inventa est, & absoluta.*[3] I doe not desire to be equall to those that went before; but to have my reason examin'd with theirs, and so much faith to be given them, or me, as those shall evict.[4] I am neither *Author,* or *Fautor*[5] of any sect. I will have no man addict himselfe to mee; but if I have any thing right, defend it as Truth's, not mine (save as it conduceth to a common good.) It profits not me to have any man fence, or fight for me, to flourish, or take a side. Stand for *Truth,* and 'tis enough.

Arts that respect the mind were ever reputed nobler, then those that serve the body: though wee lesse can bee without them. As *Tillage, Spinning, Weaving, Building, &c.* without which, wee could scarce sustaine life a day. But these were the workes of every hand; the other of the braine only, and those the most generous, and exalted wits, and spirits that cannot rest, or *acquiesce.* The mind of man is still fed with labour: *Opere pascitur.*[6]

There is a more secret *Cause:* and the power of liberall studies lyes more hid, then that it can bee wrought out by profane wits. It is not every mans way to hit. They are men (I con-

---

2 ["Truth lies open to all; it has not yet been taken possession of. Much has come forth from it, and even more remains for the future." ("Severall" means "private property.")]

3 [Juan Luis Vives (1492–1540), *In Libros Disciplinis Praefatio* (*Opera* [1555], I, 325): "No art is simultaneously discovered and perfected." This and the following paragraph, together with the larger part of the preceding paragraphs, have been extracted and condensed from the various works—Jonson owned a copy of the *Opera, in duos distincta tomos*—of this Spanish humanist, friend to Erasmus and More and great educator, who lectured for a time at Oxford.]

4 ["Evict" means to prove through disputation.]

5 [A partisan.]

6 [Condensed from Vives, *De Causis Corruptarum Artium* (*Opera,* I, 326): "He feasts upon work."]

fesse) that set the *Caract,* and *Value* upon things, as they love them; but *Science* is not every mans *Mistresse.* It is as great a spite to be praised in the wrong place, and by a wrong person, as can be done to a noble nature.

.   .   .

Envy is no new thing, nor was it borne onely in our times. The Ages past have brought it forth, and the comming Ages will. So long as there are men fit for it, *quorum odium virtute relictâ placet,*[7] it will never be wanting. It is a barbarous envy, to take from those mens vertues, which because thou canst not arrive at, thou impotently despaires to imitate. Is it a crime in me that I know that, which others had not yet knowne, but from me? or that I am the Author of many things, which never would have come in thy thought, but that I taught them? It is a new, but a foolish way you have found out, that whom you cannot equall, or come neere in doing, you would destroy, or ruine with evill speaking: As if you had bound both your wits, and natures prentises to slander, and then came forth the best Artificers, when you could forme the foulest calumnies.

Indeed, nothing is of more credit, or request now, then a petulant paper, or scoffing verses; and it is but convenient to the times and manners wee live with; to have then the worst writings, and studies flourish, when the best begin to be despis'd. *Ill Arts* begin, where good end.

The time was, when men would learne, and study good things; not envie those that had them. Then men were had in price for learning: now, letters onely make men vile. Hee is upbraydingly call'd a *Poet,* as if it were a most contemptible *Nickname.* But the *Professors* (indeed) have made the learning cheape. Rayling, and tinckling *Rimers,* whose Writings the vulgar more greedily reade; as being taken with the scurrility, and petulancie of such wits. Hee shall not have a Reader now, unlesse hee jeere and lye. It is the food of mens natures: the diet of the

7 [Joseph Justus Scaliger (1540–1609), *Confutatio fabulae Burdonum* (*Opuscula* [1612], p. 419), saying that great men will be hated unless they are willing to forsake virtue; Jonson misquotes so as to say, "to whom hatred becomes pleasure by forsaking virtue." This and the following two paragraphs come from this, the younger, Scaliger, great literary dictator and teacher of Daniel Heinsius.]

times! *Gallants* cannot sleepe else. The Writer must lye, and the gentle Reader rests happy, to heare the worthiest workes misinterpreted; the clearest actions obscured; the innocent'st life traduc'd; And in such a licence of lying, a field so fruitfull of slanders, how can there be matter wanting to his laughter? Hence comes the *Epidemicall* Infection. For how can they escape the contagion of the Writings, whom the virulency of the calumnies hath not stav'd off from reading?

Nothing doth more invite a greedy Reader, then an unlook'd for *subject*. And what more unlook'd for, then to see a person of an unblam'd life, made ridiculous, or odious, by the Artifice of lying? But it is the disease of the Age: and no wonder if the world, growing old, begin to be infirme: Old age it selfe is a disease. It is long since the sick world began to doate, and talke idly: Would she had but doated still; but her dotage is now broke forth into a madnesse, and become a meere phrency.

It is an Art to have so much judgement, as to apparell a Lye well, to give it a good dressing; that though the nakednesse would shew deform'd and odious, the suiting of it might draw their Readers. Some love any Strumpet (be shee never so shoplike, or meritorious[8]) in good clothes. But these, nature could not have form'd them better, to destroy their owne testimony; and over-throw their calumny.

Memory of all the *powers* of the mind, is the most *delicate,* and *fraile*: it is the first of our *faculties,* that Age invades. *Seneca,* the father, the *Rhetorician,* confesseth of himselfe, hee had a miraculous one; not only to receive, but to hold. I my selfe could in my youth, have repeated all, that ever I had made; and so continued, till I was past fortie: Since, it is much decay'd in me. Yet I can repeate whole books that I have read, and *Poems,* of some selected friends, which I have lik'd to charge my memory with. It was wont to be faithfull to me, but shaken with *age* now, and *sloath* (which weakens the strongest abilities) it may performe somewhat, but cannot promise much. By exercise it is to be made better, and serviceable. Whatsoever I pawn'd

8 [Retaining the Latin sense of to make money by prostitution.]

with it, while I was young, and a boy, it offers me readily, and without stops: but what I trust to it now, or have done of later yeares, it layes up more negligently, and often times loses; so that I receive mine owne (though frequently call'd for) as if it were new, and borrow'd. Nor doe I alwayes find presently from it, what I doe seek; but while I am doing another thing, that I labour'd for, will come: And what I sought with trouble, will offer it selfe, when I am quiet. Now in some men I have found it as happy as nature, who, whatsoever they reade, or pen, they can say without booke presently; as if they did then write in their mind. And it is more a wonder in such, as have a swift stile; for their *memories* are commonly slowest; such as torture their writings, and go into councell for every word, must needs fixe somewhat, and make it their owne at last, though but through their owne vexation.[9]

·　　·　　·

I doe heare them say often: Some men are not witty, because they are not every where witty; then which nothing is more foolish. If an eye or a nose bee an excellent part in the face, therefore be all eye or nose? I thinke the eye-brow, the fore-head, the cheeke, chyn, lip, or any part else, are as necessary, and naturall in the place. But now nothing is good that is naturall: Right and naturall language seeme[s] to have least of the wit in it; that which is writh'd and tortur'd, is counted the more exquisite. Cloath of Bodkin, or Tissue, must be imbrodered; as if no face were faire, that were not pouldred, or painted? No beauty to be had, but in wresting, and writhing our owne tongue? Nothing is fashionable, till it bee deform'd; and this is to write like a *Gentleman*. All must bee as affected, and preposterous as our Gallants cloathes, sweet bags, and night-dressings: in which you would thinke our men lay in, like *Ladies*: it is so curious.

Nothing in our Age, I have observ'd, is more preposterous, then the *running Judgements* upon *Poetry*, and *Poets*; when wee shall heare those things commended, and cry'd up for the best writings, which a man would scarce vouchsafe, to wrap any wholsome drug in; hee would never light his *Tobacco* with them.

9 [This paragraph is lifted from M. Seneca's *Controversiae* and about half of the following paragraph from Quintilian's *Institutio Oratoria*.]

And those men almost nam'd for *Miracles,* who yet are so vile, that if a man should goe about, to examine, and correct them, hee must make all they have done, but one blot. Their good is so intangled with their bad, as forcibly one must draw on the others death with it. A Sponge dipt in Inke will doe all:

> *Comitetur punica librum*
> *Spongia.*

Et paulò post,

> *Non possunt . . . multæ, una litura potest.*[1]

Yet their vices have not hurt them: Nay, a great many they have profited; for they have beene lov'd for nothing else. And this false opinion growes strong against the best men: if once it take root with the *Ignorant. Cestius* in his time, was preferr'd to *Cicero;* so farre, as the Ignorant durst: They learn'd him without booke, and had him often in their mouthes: But a man cannot imagine that thing so foolish, or rude, but will find, and enjoy an Admirer; at least, a Reader, or *Spectator.* The Puppets are seene now in despight of the Players: *Heath's Epigrams,*[2] and the *Skullers Poems*[3] have their applause. There are never wanting, that dare preferre the worst *Preachers,* the worst *Pleaders,* the worst *Poets:* not that the better have left to write, or speake better, but that they that heare them judge worse; *Non illi pejus dicunt, sed hi corruptiùs judicant.*[4] Nay, if it were put to the question of the Water-rimers workes, against *Spencers;* I doubt not, but they would find more *Suffrages;* because the most favour common vices, out of a Prerogative the vulgar have, to lose their judgements; and like that which is naught.

Poetry in this latter Age, hath prov'd but a meane *Mistresse,* to such as have wholly addicted themselves to her; or given their

---

1 [Martial, *Epigrams* iv.10, sending a friend a copy of his poems on which the ink is barely dry: "Let a punic sponge go with the book." Then Jonson adds, "And, a little later," before returning to Martial: "Many (corrections) cannot (emend my witticisms)—one erasure can."]
2 [John Heath brought out his *Two Centuries of Epigrammes* in 1610.]
3 [John Taylor (1580–1653), prolific writer of doggerel and self-styled "Water Poet" (having been a waterman on the Thames).]
4 ["Those do not speak worse, but these judge more corruptly."]

names up to her family. They who have but saluted her on the by; and now and then tendred their visits, shee hath done much for, and advanced in the way of their owne professions (both the *Law,* and the *Gospel*) beyond all they could have hoped, or done for themselves, without her favour. Wherein she doth emulate the judicious, but preposterous bounty of the times *Grandes*: who accumulate all they can upon the *Parasite,* or *Fresh-man* in their friendship; but thinke an old Client, or honest servant, bound by his place to write, and starve.

Indeed, the multitude commend Writers, as they doe Fencers, or Wrastlers; who if they come in robustiously, and put for it, with a deale of violence, are received for the *braver-fellowes:* when many times their owne rudenesse is a cause of their disgrace; and a slight touch of their Adversary, gives all that boisterous force the foyle. But in these things, the unskilfull are naturally deceiv'd, and judging wholly by the bulke, thinke rude things greater then polish'd; and scatter'd more numerous, then compos'd: Nor thinke this only to be true in the sordid multitude but the neater sort of our *Gallants:* for all are the multitude; only they differ in cloaths, not in judgement or understanding.[5]

I remember, the Players have often mentioned it as an honour to *Shakespeare,* that in his writing, (whatsoever he penn'd) hee never blotted out line. My answer hath beene, would he had blotted a thousand. Which they thought a malevolent speech. I had not told posterity this, but for their ignorance, who choose that circumstance to commend their friend by, wherein he most faulted. And to justifie mine owne candor, (for I lov'd the man, and doe honour his memory (on this side of Idolatry) as much as any.) Hee was (indeed) honest, and of an open, and free nature: had an excellent *Phantsie;* brave notions, and gentle expressions: wherein hee flow'd with that facility, that sometime it was necessary he should be stop'd: *Sufflaminandus erat;*[6] as *Augustus* said of *Haterius.* His wit was in his owne power; would the rule of it had beene so too. Many times hee fell into those things, could not escape laughter: As when hee said in the per-

[5] [Much of this paragraph derives from Quintilian, *Institutio Oratoria*, and reappears in Jonson's preface to the 1612 quarto of *The Alchemist.*]
[6] [M. Seneca, *Controversiae* iv: "He needed a drag-chain," for, as Seneca explains, the eloquence of Quintus Haterius not only flowed, it flowed downhill.]

son of *Cæsar*, one speaking to him; *Cæsar, thou dost me wrong.*
Hee replyed: *Cæsar did never wrong, but with just cause:* and
such like; which were ridiculous.[7] But hee redeemed his vices,
with his vertues. There was ever more in him to be praysed, then
to be pardoned.

In the difference of wits, I have observ'd; there are many
notes: And it is a little *Maistry* to know them: to discerne, what
every nature, every disposition will beare: For, before wee sow
our land, we should plough it. There are no fewer formes of
minds, then of bodies amongst us. The variety is incredible; and
therefore wee must search. Some are fit to make *Divines*, some
Poets, some *Lawyers*, some *Physicians;* some to be sent to the
plough, and trades.

There is no doctrine will doe good, where nature is wanting.
Some wits are swelling, and high; others low and still: Some hot
and fiery; others cold and dull: One must have a bridle, the
other a spurre.

There be some that are forward, and bold; and these will doe
every little thing easily: I meane that is hard by, and next them;
which they will utter, unretarded, without any shamefastnesse.
These never performe much, but quickly. They are, what they
are on the sudden; they shew presently like *Graine*, that, scatter'd on the top of the ground, shoots up, but takes no root; has a
yellow blade, but the eare empty. They are wits of good promise
at first, but there is an *Ingeni-stitium:*[8] They stand still at six-
teene, they get no higher.

You have others, that labour onely to ostentation; and are ever
more busie about the colours, and surface of a worke, then in the
matter, and foundation: For that is hid, the other is seene.

Others, that in composition are nothing, but what is rough,
and broken: *Quæ per salebras, altaque saxa cadunt.*[9] And if it
would come gently, they trouble it of purpose. They would not
have it run without rubs, as if that stile were more strong and

---

7 [A misquotation of *Julius Caesar*, III, i.]
8 [The marginal gloss says "A wit-stand," i.e., a case of arrested intellectual
development. These paragraphs on the "difference of wits" seem to rely on
remarks made by Seneca and Quintilian.]
9 [Martial, *Epigrams* xc.2: "Those who tumble over rough places and high
cliffs." (The conclusion of the paragraph comes mainly from Seneca.)]

manly, that stroke the eare with a kind of unevenesse. These men erre not by chance, but knowingly, and willingly; they are like men that affect a fashion by themselves, have some singularity in a Ruffe, Cloake, or Hat-band; or their beards, specially cut to provoke beholders, and set a marke upon themselves. They would be reprehended, while they are look'd on. And this vice, one that is in authority with the rest, loving, delivers over to them to bee imitated: so that oft-times the faults which he fell into, the others seeke for: This is the danger, when vice becomes a *Precedent*.

Others there are, that have no composition at all; but a kind of tuneing, and riming fall, in what they write. It runs and slides, and onely makes a sound. Womens-*Poets* they are call'd: as you have womens-*Taylors*.

> *They write a verse, as smooth, as soft, as creame;*
> *In which there is no torrent, nor scarce streame.*

You may sound these wits, and find the depth of them, with your middle finger. They are *Creame-bowle,* or but puddle deepe.

Some that turne over all bookes, and are equally searching in all papers, that write out of what they presently find or meet, without choice; by which meanes it happens, that what they have discredited, and impugned in one worke, they have before, or after, extolled the same in another. Such are all the *Essayists,* even their Master *Mountaigne*. These, in all they write, confesse still what bookes they have read last; and therein their owne folly, so much, that they bring it to the *Stake* raw, and undigested: not that the place did need it neither; but that they thought themselves furnished, and would vent it.

Some againe, who (after they have got authority, or, which is lesse, opinion, by their writings, to have read much) dare presently to faine whole bookes, and Authors, and lye safely. For what never was, will not easily be found; not by the most *curious*.

And some, by a cunning protestation against all reading, and false venditation of their owne *naturals,* thinke to divert the *sagacity* of their Readers from themselves, and coole the sent of their owne *fox-like* thefts; when yet they are so ranke, as a man may find whole pages together usurp'd from one Author, their necessities compelling them to read for present use, which could

not be in many books; and so come forth more ridiculously, and
palpably guilty, then those, who, because they cannot trace, they
yet would slander their industry.

But the Wretcheder are the obstinate contemners of all helpes,
and Arts: such as presuming on their owne *Naturals* (which
perhaps are excellent) dare deride all diligence, and seeme to
mock at the termes, when they understand not the things; thinking that way to get off wittily, with their Ignorance. These are
imitated often by such, as are their Peeres in negligence, though
they cannot be in nature: And they utter all they can thinke,
with a kind of violence, and *indisposition;* unexamin'd, without
relation, either to person, place, or any fitnesse else; and the
more wilfull, and stubborne, they are in it, the more learned they
are esteem'd of the *multitude,* through their excellent vice of
Judgement: Who thinke those things the stronger, that have no
Art: as if to breake, were better then to open; or to rent asunder,
gentler then to loose.

It *cannot* but come to passe, that these men, who commonly
seeke to doe more then enough, may sometimes happen on some
thing that is good, and great; but very seldome: And when it
comes, it doth not recompence the rest of their ill. For their jests,
and their sentences[9a] (which they onely, and ambitiously seeke
for) sticke out, and are more eminent; because all is sordid, and
vile about them; as lights are more discern'd in a thick darkenesse, then a faint shadow. Now because they speake all they
can (how ever unfitly) they are thought to have the greater
copy;[1] Where the learned use ever election, and a meane; they
looke back to what they intended at first, and make all an even,
and proportion'd body. The true Artificer will not run away from
nature, as hee were afraid of her; or depart from life, and the
likenesse of Truth; but speake to the capacity of his hearers. And
though his language differ from the vulgar somewhat; it shall
not fly from all humanity, with the *Tamerlanes,* and *Tamer-
Chams* of the late Age, which had nothing in them but the *sceni-
call* strutting, and furious vociferation, to warrant them to the
ignorant gapers. Hee knowes it is his onely Art, so to carry it, as

9a [From L. *sententia,* a (high) thought or apothegm.]
1 [From L. *copia,* suggesting in the Renaissance the ability to "vary" and to
write with inventive amplitude. (This and the preceding paragraph draw on
Quintilian.)]

none but Artificers perceive it. In the meane time perhaps hee is call'd barren, dull, leane, a poore Writer (or by what contumelious word can come in their cheeks) by these men, who without labour, judgement, knowledge, or almost sense, are received, or preferr'd before him. He gratulates them, and their fortune. An other Age, or juster men, will acknowledge the vertues of his studies: his wisdome, in dividing: his subtilty, in arguing: with what strength hee doth inspire his Readers; with what sweetnesse hee strokes them: in inveighing, what sharpenesse; in Jest, what urbanity hee uses. How he doth raigne in mens affections; how invade, and breake in upon them; and makes their minds like the thing he writes. Then in his Elocution to behold, what word is proper: which hath ornament: which height: what is beautifully translated:[2] where figures are fit: which gentle, which strong to shew the composition *Manly.* And how hee hath avoyded faint, obscure, obscene, sordid, humble, improper, or effeminate *Phrase;* which is not only prais'd of the most, but commended, (which is worse) especially for that it is naught.

I know no disease of the *Soule,* but *Ignorance;* not of the Arts, and Sciences, but of it selfe: Yet relating to those, it is a pernicious *evill*: the darkner of mans life: the disturber of his *Reason,* and common Confounder of *Truth*: with which a man goes groping in the darke, no otherwise, then if hee were blind. Great understandings are most wrack'd and troubled with it: Nay, sometimes they will rather choose to dye, then not to know the things they study for. Thinke then what an evill it is; and what good the contrary.

Knowledge is the action of the *Soule;* and is perfect without the *senses,* as having the seeds of all *Science,* and *Vertue* in its selfe; but not without the service of the *senses*: by those Organs, the *Soule workes*: She is a perpetuall Agent, prompt and subtile; but often flexible, and erring; intangling her selfe like a Silke-worme: But her *Reason* is a weapon with two edges, and cuts through. In her Indagations[3] oft-times new Sents put her by; and shee takes in errors into her, by the same conduits she doth Truths.

[2] [From Latin *translatio*, meaning "made figurative or metaphorical."]
[3] [Investigations.]

Ease, and relaxation, are profitable to all studies. The mind is
like a Bow, the stronger by being unbent. But the temper in
Spirits is all, when to command a mans wit; when to favour it. I
have knowne a man vehement on both sides; that knew no
meane, either to intermit his studies, or call upon them againe.
When hee hath set himselfe to wri[t]ing, hee would joyne night
to day; presse upon himselfe without release, not minding it, till
hee fainted: and when hee left off, resolve himselfe into all
sports, and loosenesse againe; that it was almost a despaire to
draw him to his booke: But once got to it, hee grew stronger, and
more earnest by the ease. His whole Powers were renew'd: he
would worke out of himselfe, what hee desired; but with such
excesse, as his study could not bee rul'd: hee knew not how to
dispose his owne Abilities, or husband them, hee was of that
immoderate power against himselfe. Nor was hee only a strong,
but an absolute *Speaker,* and *Writer*: but his subtilty did not
shew it selfe; his judgement thought that a vice. For the ambush
hurts more that is hid. Hee never forc'd his language, nor went
out of the high way of *speaking;* but for some great necessity, or
apparent profit. For hee denied *Figures* to be invented for ornament, but for ayde; and still thought it an extreme madnesse to
bend, or wrest that which ought to be right.[4]

It is no *Wonder,* mens eminence appeares but in their owne
way. *Virgils* felicity left him in prose, as *Tullies*[5] forsooke him
in verse. *Salusts* Orations are read in the honour of Story: yet
the most eloquent *Plato*'s speech, which he made for *Socrates,* is
neither worthy of the *Patron,* or the *Person* defended. Nay, in the
same kind of *Oratory,* and where the matter is one, you shall
have him that reasons strongly, open negligently: another that
prepares well, not fit so well: and this happens, not onely to
braines, but to bodies. One can wrastle well; another runne well;
a third leape, or throw the barre; a fourth lift, or stop a Cart
going: Each hath his way of strength. So in other creatures;
some dogs are for the Deere: some for the wild Boare: some are

4 [This paragraph utilizes M. Seneca's characterization of Porcius Latro in
Controversiae i, and the next paragraph leans on *Controversiae* iii where the
rhetorician Cassius Severus is quoted.]
5 [I.e., Cicero.]

Fox-hounds: some Otter-hounds. Nor are all horses for the Coach, or Saddle; some are for the Cart, and Panniers.

I have knowne many excellent men, that would speake suddenly, to the admiration of their hearers; who upon study, and premeditation have beene forsaken by their owne wits; and no way answered their fame: Their eloquence was greater, then their reading: and the things they uttered, better then those they knew. Their fortune deserved better of them, then their care. For men of present spirits, and of greater wits, then study, doe please more in the things they invent, then in those they bring. And I have heard some of them compell'd to speake, out of necessity, that have so infinitly exceeded themselves, as it was better, both for them, and their Auditory, that they were so surpriz'd, not prepar'd. Nor was it safe then to crosse them, for their adversary, their anger made them more eloquent. Yet these men I could not but love, and admire, that they return'd to their studies. They left not diligence (as many doe) when their rashnesse prosper'd. For diligence is a great ayde, even to an indifferent wit; when wee are not contented with the examples of our owne Age, but would know the face of the former. Indeed, the more wee conferre with, the more wee profit by, if the persons be chosen.[6]

One, though hee be excellent, and the chiefe, is not to bee imitated alone. For never no Imitator, ever grew up to his *Author;* likenesse is alwayes on this side Truth: Yet there hapn'd, in my time, one noble *Speaker*, who was full of gravity in his speaking. His language, (where hee could spare, or passe by a jest) was nobly *censorious*. No man ever spake more neatly, more presly,[6a] more weightily, or suffer'd lesse emptinesse, lesse idlenesse, in what hee utter'd. No member of his speech, but consisted of the owne graces: His hearers could not cough, or looke aside from him, without losse. Hee commanded where hee spoke; and had his Judges angry, and pleased at his devotion. No man had their affections more in his power. The feare of every man that heard him, was, lest hee should make an end.

6 [This and the following paragraph rely on M. Seneca, *Controversiae* iii.]
6a [I.e., "pressly," concisely.]

Cicero is said to bee the only wit, that the people of *Rome* had equall'd to their *Empire. Ingenium par imperio.* We have had many, and in their severall Ages, (to take in but the former *Seculum.*) *Sir Thomas Moore,* the elder *Wiat; Henry,* Earle of *Surrey; Chaloner, Smith, Eliot,* B. *Gardiner*[7] were for their times admirable: and the more, because they began Eloquence with us. Sir *Nico: Bacon,*[8] was singular, and almost alone, in the beginning of Queene *Elizabeths* times. Sir *Philip Sidney,* and Mr. *Hooker*[9] (in different matter) grew great Masters of wit, and language; and in whom all vigour of Invention, and strength of judgement met. The Earle of *Essex,* noble and high; and Sir *Walter Rawleigh,* not to be contemn'd, either for judgement, or stile. Sir *Henry Savile*[1] grave, and truly letter'd; Sir *Edwin Sandes,*[2] excellent in both: Lo: *Egerton,*[3] the Chancellor, a grave, and great Orator; and best, when hee was provok'd. But his learned, and able (though unfortunate) *Successor*[4] is he, who hath fill'd up all numbers; and perform'd that in our tongue, which may be compar'd, or preferr'd, either to insolent *Greece,* or haughty *Rome.* In short, within his view, and about his times, were all the wits borne, that could honour a language, or helpe study. Now things daily fall: wits grow downe-ward, and *Eloquence* growes back-ward: So that hee may be nam'd, and stand as the *marke,* and ἀκμὴ of our language.

I have ever observ'd it, to have beene the office of a wise Patriot, among the greatest affaires of the *State,* to take care of the

7 [Sir Thomas Chaloner (1521–65), diplomatist and translator, in 1549, of Erasmus' *Praise of Folly;* Sir Thomas Smith (1513–77), professor of Greek and Secretary of State; Sir Thomas Elyot (1490?–1546), author of *The Governor* (1531) and other works; Bishop Stephen Gardiner (1483?–1555), religious controversialist.]
8 [Sir Nicholas Bacon (1509–79), Keeper of the Seal and father of Francis Bacon.]
9 [Richard Hooker (1533–1600), the "judicious" Anglican apologist who produced the great *Lawes of Ecclesiasticall Politie.*]
1 [Sir Henry Savile (1549–1622), learned scholar and editor, who tutored Elizabeth in Greek and was one of the translators of the authorized version of the Bible.]
2 [Sir Edwin Sandys (1561–1629), statesman and author; father of George Sandys, the poet.]
3 [Sir Thomas Egerton, Baron Ellesmere and Viscount Brackley (1540?–1617), Lord Chancellor; father of John Egerton, for whom Milton wrote *Comus.*]
4 [The allusion is to Sir Francis Bacon, who is here commended in words borrowed from M. Seneca, *Controversiae* i.]

Common-wealth of Learning. For Schooles, they are the *Seminaries* of State: and nothing is worthier the study of a Statesman, then that part of the *Republicke*, which wee call the *advancement* of Letters. Witnesse the care of *Julius Cæsar*; who, in the heat of the civill warre, writ his bookes of *Analogie*, and dedicated them to *Tully*.[5] This made the late Lord S. *Albane*, entitle his worke, *novum Organum*.[6] Which though by the most of superficiall men, who cannot get beyond the Title of *Nominals*,[7] it is not penetrated, nor understood: it really openeth all defects of Learning, whatsoever; and is a Booke,

Qui longum noto scriptori porriget œvum.[8]

My conceit of his Person was never increased toward him, by his place, or honours. But I have, and doe reverence him for the greatnesse, that was onely proper to himselfe, in that hee seem'd to mee ever, by his worke, one of the greatest men, and most worthy of admiration, that had beene in many Ages. In his adversity I ever prayed, that *God* would give him strength: for *Greatnesse* hee could not want. Neither could I condole in a word, or syllable for him; as knowing no Accident could doe harme to vertue; but rather helpe to make it manifest.[9]

There cannot be one colour of the mind; an other of the wit. If the mind be staid, grave, and compos'd, the wit is so; that vitiated, the other is blowne, and deflowr'd. Doe wee not see, if the mind languish, the members are dull? Looke upon an effeminate person: his very gate confesseth him. If a man be fiery, his motion is so: if angry, 'tis troubled, and violent. So that wee may conclude: Wheresoever, manners, and fashions are corrupted, Language is. It imitates the publicke riot. The excesse of Feasts,

5 [I.e., Cicero. (Caesar's *De Analogia* is lost.)]
6 [Bacon's *Novum Organum* (1620) was the "second" part of the "Great Instauration," the "first" part being the *De Augmentis* (1623), which was the enlarged Latin version of the *Advancement of Learning* (1605).]
7 [That which subsists by name alone, distinct from "reals."]
8 [Adapted from Horace, *Ars Poetica* 346: "which will prolong the fame of its author into a far-off age."]
9 [This appreciation of Bacon is lifted, perhaps by way of Thomas Hobbes' translation, from a letter written by the Venetian Fr. Fulgenzio Micanza in 1621 to the Earl of Devonshire.]

and apparell, are the notes of a sick State; and the wantonnesse of language, of a sick mind.[1]

There be some men are borne only to sucke out the poyson of bookes: *Habent venenum pro victu: imò, pro deliciis.*[2] And such are they that only rellish the obscene, and foule things in *Poets:* Which makes the profession taxed. But by whom? men, that watch for it, and (had they not had this hint) are so unjust valuers of Letters; as they thinke no Learning good, but what brings in gaine. It shewes they themselves would never have beene of the professions they are; but for the profits and fees. But, if an other Learning, well used, can instruct to good life, informe manners; no lesse perswade, and leade men, then they threaten, and compell, and have no reward: is it therefore the worse study? I could never thinke the study of *Wisdome* confin'd only to the Philosopher: or of *Piety* to the *Divine:* or of *State* to the *Politicke.*[3] But that he which can faine a *Common-wealth* (which is the *Poet*) can governe it with *Counsels,* strengthen it with *Lawes,* correct it with *Judgements,* informe it with *Religion,* and *Morals;* is all these. Wee doe not require in him meere *Elocution;* or an excellent faculty in verse; but the exact knowledge of all vertues; and their Contraries; with ability to render the one lov'd, the other hated, by his proper embattaling them. The Philosophers did insolently, to challenge only to themselves that which the greatest *Generals,* and gravest *Counsellors* never durst. For such had rather doe, then promise the best things.

Some *Controverters* in Divinity are like Swaggerers in a Taverne, that catch that which stands next them; the candlesticke, or pots; turne every thing into a weapon: ofttimes they fight blind-fold; and both beate the Ayre. The one milkes a Hee-goat, the other holds under a Sive. Their Arguments are as fluxive as liquour spilt upon a Table; which with your finger you may draine as you will. Such Controversies, or Disputations, (carried with more labour, then profit) are odious: where most times the Truth is lost in the midst; or left untouch'd. And the fruit of their

1 [This paragraph draws on Seneca, *Epistulae* cxiv.]
2 ["They have poison for food; rather, for pleasure." (The last part of this paragraph comes from Quintilian.)]
3 [I.e., politician.]

fight is; that they spit one upon another, and are both defil'd.
These Fencers in Religion, I like not.

. . .

I *have* considered, our whole life is like a *Play:* wherein every
man, forgetfull of himselfe, is in travaile with expression of another. Nay, wee so insist in imitating others, as wee cannot
(when it is necessary) returne to our selves: like Children, that
imitate the vices of *Stammerers* so long, till at last they become
such; and make the habit to another nature, as it is never forgotten.

Good men are the Stars, the Planets of the Ages wherein they
live, and illustrate the times. *God* did never let them be wanting
to the world: As *Abel,* for an example, of Innocency; *Enoch* of
Purity, *Noah* of Trust in Gods mercies, *Abraham* of Faith, and so
of the rest. These, sensuall men thought mad, because they
would not be partakers, or practisers of their madnesse. But
they, plac'd high on the top of all vertue, look'd downe on the
Stage of the world, and contemned the Play of *Fortune.* For
though the most be Players, some must be *Spectators.*

. . .

Poetry, and *Picture,* are Arts of a like nature; and both are
busie about imitation. It was excellently said of *Plutarch, Poetry*
was a speaking Picture, and *Picture* a mute Poesie.[4] For they
both invent, faine, and devise many things, and accommodate
all they invent to the use, and service of nature. Yet of the two,
the Pen is more noble, then the Pencill. For that can speake to
the Understanding; the other, but to the Sense. They both behold
pleasure, and profit, as their common Object; but should ab-
staine from all base pleasures, lest they should erre from their
end: and while they seeke to better mens minds, destroy their
manners. They both are borne *Artificers,* not made. Nature is
more powerfull in them then study.

Whosoever loves not *Picture,* is injurious to Truth: and all the
wisdome of *Poetry.* Picture is the invention of Heaven: the most
ancient, and most a kinne to Nature. It is it selfe a silent worke:
and alwayes of one and the same habit: Yet it doth so enter, and

4 [A saying of Simonides. Jonson apparently encountered it, among many other
places, in Plutarch, *Quomodo adolescens poetas audire debeat, Moralia* i.17F–
18.]

penetrate the inmost affection (being done by an excellent Artificer) as sometimes it orecomes the power of speech, and oratory. There are diverse graces in it; so are there in the Artificers.
One excels in care, another in reason, a third in easinesse, a
fourth in nature and grace. Some have diligence, and comeli-
nesse: but they want Majesty. They can expresse a humane
forme in all the graces, sweetnesse, and elegancy; but they
misse the Authority. They can hit nothing but smooth cheeks;
they cannot expresse roughnesse, or gravity. Others aspire to
Truth so much, as they are rather Lovers of likenesse, then
beauty. *Zeuxis,* and *Parrhasius,* are said to be contemporaries:
The first, found out the reason of lights, and shadowes in Picture: the other, more subtily examined the lines.[5]

In Picture, light is requir'd no lesse then shadow: so in stile,
height, as well as humblenesse. But beware they be not too humble; as *Pliny* pronounc'd of *Regulus* writings:[6] You would thinke
them written, not on a child, but by a child. Many, out of their
owne obscene Apprehensions, refuse proper and fit words; as
occupie, nature, and the like: So the curious industry in some of
having all alike good, hath come neerer a vice, then a vertue.

Picture tooke her faining from *Poetry:* from *Geometry* her
rule, compasse, lines, proportion, and the whole *Symmetry. Parrhasius* was the first wan reputation, by adding *Symmetry* to Picture: hee added subtility to the countenance, elegancy to the
haire, love-lines[s] to the face; and, by the publike voice of all Artificers, deserved honour in the outer lines. *Eupompus* gave it
splendor by numbers, and other elegancies. From the *Opticks* it
drew reasons; by which it considered, how things plac'd at distance, and a farre off, should appeare lesse: how above, or beneath the head, should deceive the eye, &c. So from thence it
tooke shadowes, recessor,[7] light, and heightnings. From morall
Philosophy it tooke the soule, the expression of Senses, Perturbations, Manners, when they would paint an angry person, a
proud, an inconstant, an ambitious, a brave, a magnanimous,
a just, a mercifull, a compassionate, an humble, a dejected, a

[5] [This paragraph draws on Quintilian, *Institutio Oratoria* xii.10.]
[6] [Pliny, *Epistulae* iii.13. But Jonson is working indirectly, relying in this paragraph on the Jesuit Antonio Possevino (1534–1611), *Bibliotheca Selecta* (1593), XVII, xxiii.]
[7] [Probably from L. *recessus*, "background."]

base, and the like. They made all heightnings bright, all shad-owes darke, all swellings from a plane; all solids from breaking. See where he[8] complaines of their painting *Chimæra's*, by the vul-gar unaptly called *Grottesque:* Saying, that men who were borne truly to study, and emulate nature, did nothing but make mon-sters against nature; which *Horace* so laught at. The Art *Plas-ticke* was moulding in clay, or potters earth anciently. This is the Parent of *Statuary: Sculpture, Graving* and *Picture;* cutting in brasse, and marble, all serve under her. *Socrates* taught *Parrhas-ius,* and *Clito* (two noble Statuaries) first to expresse manners by their looks in Imagery, *Polygnotus,* and *Aglaophon* were an-cienter. After them *Zeuxis,* who was the Law-giver to all Paint-ers, after *Parrhasius.* They were contemporaries, and liv'd both about *Philips* time, the Father of *Alexander* the Great. There liv'd in this latter Age six famous Painters in *Italy*: who were excellent, and emulous of the Ancients: *Raphael de Urbino, Michel Angelo Buonarota, Titian, Antonie of Correggio, Sebas-tian of Venice, Julio Romano,* and *Andrea Sartorio.*

. . .

It *pleas'd* your Lordship[9] of late, to aske my opinion, touching the education of your sonnes, and especially to the advancement of their studies. To which, though I return'd somewhat for the present; which rather manifested a will in me, then gave any just resolution to the thing propounded: I have upon better cogi-tation call'd those ayds about mee, both of mind, and memory; which shall venter my thoughts clearer, if not fuller, to your Lordships demand. I confesse, my Lord, they will seeme but petty, and minute things I shall offer to you, being writ for chil-dren, and of them. But studies have their Infancie, as well as creatures. Wee see in men, even the strongest compositions had their beginnings from milke, and the Cradle; and the wisest tar-ried sometimes about apting their mouthes to Letters, and sylla-bles. In their education therefore, the care must be the greater had of their beginnings, to know, examine, and weigh their na-

---

[8] [I.e., Vitruvius, *De Architectura* vii.173. (Again Jonson is relying on sum-maries in Possevino, who is also the source of the list of painters at the end of the paragraph.)]

[9] [Probably William Cavendish, Duke of Newcastle (1592–1676). (This para-graph draws heavily on the first book of Quintilian's *Institutio Oratoria;* in-deed, the next four paragraphs owe much to various books of the *Institutio.*)]

tures; which though they bee proner in some children to some disciplines; yet are they naturally prompt to taste all by degrees, and with change. For change is a kind of refreshing in studies, and infuseth knowledge by way of recreation. Thence the Schoole it selfe is call'd a Play, or Game: and all Letters are so best taught to Schollers. They should not be afrighted, or deterr'd in their Entry, but drawne on with exercise, and emulation. A youth should not be made to hate study, before hee know the causes to love it: or taste the bitternesse before the sweet; but call'd on, and allur'd, intreated, and praised: Yea, when hee deserves it not. For which cause I wish them sent to the best schoole, and a publike; which I thinke the best. Your Lordship I feare, hardly heares of that, as willing to breed them in your eye, and at home; and doubting their manners may bee corrupted abroad. They are in more danger in your owne Family, among ill servants, (allowing, they be safe in their Schoole-Master) then amongst a thousand boyes, however immodest: would wee did not spoyle our owne children, and overthrow their manners our selves by too much Indulgence. To breed them at home, is to breed them in a shade; where in a schoole they have the light, and heate of the Sunne. They are us'd, and accustom'd to things, and men. When they come forth into the Commonwealth, they find nothing new, or to seeke. They have made their friendships and ayds; some to last till their Age. They heare what is commanded to others, as well as themselves, much approv'd, much corrected; all which they bring to their owne store, and use; and learne as much, as they heare. *Eloquence* would be but a poore thing, if wee should onely converse with singulars; speake, but man and man together. Therefore I like no private breeding. I would send them where their industry should be daily increas'd by praise; and that kindled by emulation. It is a good thing to inflame the mind: And though Ambition it selfe be a vice, it is often the cause of great vertue. Give me that wit, whom praise excites, glory puts on, or disgrace grieves: hee is to bee nourish'd with Ambition, prick'd forward with honour; check'd with Reprehension; and never to bee suspected of sloath. Though hee be given to play, it is a signe of spirit, and livelinesse; so there be a meane had of their sports, and relaxations. And from the rodde, or ferule, I would have them free, as from the menace of them: for it is both deformed, and servile.

For a man to write well, there are required three Necessaries. To reade the best Authors, observe the best Speakers: and much exercise of his owne style. In style to consider, what ought to be written; and after what manner; Hee must first thinke, and excogitate his matter; then choose his words, and examine the weight of either. Then take care in placing, and ranking both matter, and words, that the composition be comely; and to doe this with diligence, and often. No matter how slow the style be at first, so it be labour'd, and accurate: seeke the best, and be not glad of the forward conceipts, or first words, that offer themselves to us, but judge of what wee invent; and order what wee approve. Repeat often, what wee have formerly written; which beside, that it helpes the consequence, and makes the juncture better, it quickens the heate of imagination, that often cooles in the time of setting downe, and gives it new strength, as if it grew lustier, by the going back. As wee see in the contention of leaping, they jumpe farthest, that fetch their race largest: or, as in throwing a Dart, or Javelin, wee force back our armes, to make our loose the stronger. Yet, if we have a faire gale of wind, I forbid not the steering out of our sayle, so the favour of the gale deceive us not. For all that wee invent doth please us in the conception, or birth; else we would never set it downe. But the safest is to returne to our Judgement, and handle over againe those things, the easinesse of which might make them justly suspected. So did the best Writers in their beginnings; they impos'd upon themselves care, and industry. They did nothing rashly. They obtain'd first to write well, and then custome made it easie, and a habit. By little and little, their matter shew'd it selfe to 'hem more plentifully; their words answer'd, their composition followed; and all, as in a well-order'd family, presented it selfe in the place. So that the summe of all is: Ready writing makes not good writing; but good writing brings on ready writing: Yet when wee thinke wee have got the faculty, it is even then good to resist it: as to give a Horse a check sometimes with [the] bit, which doth not so much stop his course, as stirre his mettle. Againe, wh[i]ther a mans *Genius* is best able to reach, thither it should more and more contend, lift and dilate it selfe, as men of low stature, raise themselves on their toes; and so oft times get even, if not eminent. Besides, as it is fit for grown and able Writers to stand of themselves, and worke with their owne strength, to trust and endeavour by their owne faculties: so it is fit for the beginner, and learner, to study others, and the best. For the mind, and memory are more sharpely exercis'd in comprehending an other mans things, then our owne; and such as accustome themselves, and are familiar with the best Authors, shall ever and anon find somewhat of them in themselves, and in the expression of their minds, even when they feele it not, be able to utter something like theirs, which hath an Authority above their owne. Nay, sometimes it is the reward of a mans study, the praise of quoting an other man fitly: And though a man be more prone, and able for one kind of writing, then another, yet hee must exercise all. For as in an Instrument, so in style, there must be a Harmonie, and concent of parts.

I take this labour in teaching others, that they should not be alwayes to bee taught; and I would bring my Precepts into practise. For rules are ever of lesse force, and valew, then experiments. Yet with this purpose, rather to shew the right way to those that come after, then to detect any that have slipt before by errour, and I hope it will bee more profitable. For men doe more willingly listen, and with more favour, to precept, then reprehension. Among diverse opinions of an Art, and most of them contrary in themselves, it is hard to make election; and therefore, though a man cannot invent new things after so many, he may doe a welcome worke yet to helpe posterity to judge rightly of the old. But Arts and Precepts availe nothing, except nature be beneficiall, and ayding. And therefore these things are no more written to a dull disposition, then rules of husbandry to a barren Soyle. No precepts will profit a Foole; no more then beauty will the blind, or musicke the deafe. As wee should take care, that our style in writing, be neither dry, nor empty: wee should looke againe it be not winding, or wanton with far-fetcht descriptions; Either is a vice. But that is worse which proceeds out of want,

then that which riots out of plenty. The remedy of fruitful-
nesse is easie, but no labour will helpe the contrary; I will like,
and praise some things in a young Writer; which yet if hee continue in, I cannot but justly hate him for the same. There is a
time to bee given all things for maturity; and that even your
Countrey-husband-man can teach; who to a young plant will not
put the proyning knife, because it seemes to feare the iron, as
not able to admit the scarre. No more would I tell a greene
Writer all his faults, lest I should make him grieve and faint,
and at last despaire. For nothing doth more hurt, then to make
him so afraid of all things, as hee can endeavour nothing. Therefore youth ought to be instructed betimes, and in the best
things: for we hold those longest, wee take soonest. As the first
sent of a Vessell lasts: and that tinct the wooll first receives.
Therefore a Master should temper his owne powers, and descend
to the others infirmity. If you powre a glut of water upon a Bot-
tle, it receives little of it; but with a Funnell, and by degrees, you
shall fill many of them, and spill little of your owne; to their
capacity they will all receive, and be full. And as it is fit to reade
the best Authors to youth first, so let them be of the openest, and
clearest. As *Livy* before *Salust*, *Sydney* before *Donne*: and beware of letting them taste *Gower*, or *Chaucer* at first, lest falling
too much in love with Antiquity, and not apprehending the
weight, they grow rough and barren in language onely. When
their judgements are firme, and out of danger, let them reade
both, the old and the new: but no lesse take heed, that their new
flowers, and sweetnesse doe not as much corrupt, as the others
drinesse, and squallor, if they choose not carefully. *Spencer*, in
affecting the Ancients writ no Language: Yet I would have him
read for his matter; but as *Virgil* read *Ennius*. The reading of
Homer and *Virgil* is counsell'd by *Quintilian*, as the best way of
informing youth, and confirming man. For besides that the
mind is rais'd with the height, and sublimity of such a verse, it
takes spirit from the greatnesse of the matter, and is tincted
with the best things. *Tragicke*, and *Liricke* Poetry is good too:
and *Comicke* with the best, if the manners of the Reader be once
in safety. In the *Greeke* Poets, as also in *Plautus*, wee shall see
the Oeconomy, and disposition of *Poems*, better observed then in

Terence, and the later: who thought the sole grace, and vertue of their Fable, the sticking in of sentences,[9a] as ours doe the forcing in of jests.

Wee should not protect our sloath with the patronage of difficulty. It is a false quarrell against nature, that shee helpes understanding, but in a few; when the most part of mankind are inclin'd by her thither, if they would take the paines; no lesse then birds to fly, horses to run, &c. Which if they lose, it is through their owne sluggishnesse, and by that meanes become her prodigies, not her children. I confesse, nature in children is more patient of labour in study, then in Age; for the sense of the paine, the judgement of the labour is absent, they doe not measure what they have done. And it is the thought, and consideration, that affects us more, then the wearinesse it selfe. *Plato* was not content with the Learning, that *Athens* could give him, but sail'd into *Italy* for *Pythagoras* knowledge: And yet not thinking himselfe sufficiently inform'd, went into *Egypt* to the Priests, and learned their mysteries. Hee labour'd, so must wee. Many things may be learn'd together, and perform'd in one point of time; as Musicians exercise their memory, their voice, their fingers, and sometime their head, and feet at once. And so a Preacher in the invention of matter, election of words, composition of gesture, looke, pronunciation, motion, useth all these faculties at once. And if wee can expresse this variety together, why should not diverse studies, at diverse houres, delight, when the variety is able alone to refresh, and repaire us? As when a man is weary of writing, to reade; and then againe of reading, to write. Wherein, howsoever wee doe many things, yet are wee (in a sort) still fresh to what wee begin: wee are recreated with change, as the stomacke is with meats. But some will say, this variety breeds confusion, and makes, that either wee loose all, or hold no more then the last. Why doe wee not then perswade husbandmen, that they should not till Land, helpe it with Marle, Lyme, and Compost? plant Hop-gardens, prune trees, looke to Bee-hives, reare sheepe, and all other Cattell at once? It is easier to doe many things, and continue, then to doe one thing long.

9a [Apothegms or maxims.]

It is not the passing through these Learnings that hurts us, but the dwelling and sticking about them. To descend to those extreame anxieties, and foolish cavils of *Grammarians*, is able to breake a wit in pieces; being a worke of manifold misery, and vainenesse, to bee *Elementarii senes*.[1] Yet even Letters are as it were the Banke of words, and restore themselves to an Author, as the pawnes of Language. But talking and Eloquence are not the same: to speake, and to speake well, are two things. A foole may talke, but a wise man speakes, and out of the observation, knowledge, and use of things. Many Writers perplexe their Readers, and Hearers with meere *Non-sense*. Their writings need sunshine. Pure and neat Language I love, yet plaine and customary. A barbarous Phrase hath often made mee out of love with a good sense; and doubtfull writing hath wrackt mee beyond my patience. The reason why a *Poet* is said, that hee ought to have all knowledges, is that hee should not be ignorant of the most, especially of those hee will handle. And indeed when the attaining of them is possible, it were a sluggish, and base thing to despaire. For frequent imitation of any thing, becomes a habit quickly. If a man should prosecute as much, as could be said of every thing; his worke would find no end.

Speech is the only benefit man hath to expresse his excellencie of mind above other creatures. It is the Instrument of *Society*. Therefore *Mercury,* who is the President of Language, is called *Deorum hominumque interpres*.[2] In all speech, words and sense, are as the body, and the soule. The sense is as the life and soule of Language, without which all words are dead. Sense is wrought out of experience, the knowledge of humane life, and actions, or of the liberall Arts, which the *Greeks* call'd *Ε'γκυκλοπαιδείαν*.[3] Words are the Peoples; yet there is a choise of them to be made. For *Verborum delectus, origo est eloquentiæ*.[4] They are to be chose according to the persons wee make speake, or the things wee speake of. Some are of the Campe, some of the Councell-

1 ["Old men, dealing still with elementary matters."]
2 ["The interpreter of gods and men."]
3 ["A liberal education."]
4 [So Cicero (*Brutus* lxxii) quotes Caesar's *De Analogia:* "Choice of words was the basis of eloquence," adapted by Jonson to read: "Delight in words is the origin of eloquence."]

board, some of the Shop, some of the Sheepe-coat, some of the Pulpit, some of the Barre, &c. And herein is seene their Elegance, and Propriety, when wee use them fitly, and draw them forth to their just strength and nature, by way of Translation, or *Metaphore*. But in this Translation wee must only serve necessity (*Nam temerè nihil transfertur à prudenti*[5]) or commodity, which is a kind of necessity; that is, when wee either absolutely want a word to expresse by, and that is necessity; or when wee have not so fit a word, and that is commodity. As when wee avoid losse by it, and escape [obscenenesse], and gaine in the grace and property, which helpes significance. *Metaphors* farfet hinder to be understood, and affected, lose their grace. Or when the person fetcheth his translations from a wrong place. As if a Privie-Counsellor should at the Table take his *Metaphore* from a Dicing-house, or Ordinary, or a Vintners Vault; or a Justice of Peace draw his similitudes from the *Mathematicks;* or a *Divine* from a Bawdyhouse, or Tavernes; or a Gentleman of *Northampton-shire, Warwick-shire,* or the *Mid-land,* should fetch all his Illustrations to his country neighbours from shipping, and tell them of the maine *sheat,* and the Boulin.[6] *Metaphors* are thus many times deform'd, as in him that said, *Castratam morte Aphricani Rempublicam.*[7] And an other, *stercus curiæ Glauciam.* And *Canâ nive conspuit Alpes.*[8] All attempts that are new in this kind, are dangerous, and somewhat hard, before they be softned with use. A man coynes not a new word without some perill, and lesse fruit; for if it happen to be received, the praise is but moderate; if refus'd, the scorne is assur'd. Yet wee must adventure, for things, at first hard and rough, are by use made tender and gentle. It is an honest errour that is committed, following great *Chiefes*.

Custome is the most certaine Mistresse of Language, as the publicke stampe makes the current money. But wee must not be too frequent with the mint, every day coyning. Nor fetch words from the extreme and utmost ages; since the chiefe vertue of a style is perspicuitie, and nothing so vitious in it, as to need an

5 ["For nothing is rashly transferred (into metaphor) by the prudent."]
6 [Bowline.]
7 [Quintilian, *Institutio Oratoria* viii.6.15: "The Republic is gelded by the death of Africanus."]
8 [*Institutio Oratoria* viii.6.17: "Glaucia, the turd of the senate" and "The Alps bespewed with white snow." This paragraph comes mainly from Vives, *De Ratione Dicendi* i.]

Interpreter. Words borrow'd of Antiquity, doe lend a kind of Majesty to style, and are not without their delight sometimes. For they have the Authority of yeares, and out of their intermission doe win to themselves a kind of grace like newnesse. But the eldest of the present, and [newest] of the past Language is the best. For what was the ancient Language, which some men so doate upon, but the ancient Custome? Yet when I name Custome, I understand not the vulgar Custome: For that were a precept no lesse dangerous to Language, then life, if wee should speake or live after the manners of the vulgar: But that I call Custome of speech, which is the consent of the Learned; as Custome of life, which is the consent of the good. *Virgill* was most loving of Antiquity; yet how rarely doth hee insert *aquai,* and *pictai!*[9] *Lucretius* is scabrous and rough in these; hee seekes 'hem: As some doe *Chaucerismes* with us, which were better expung'd and banish'd. Some words are to be cull'd out for ornament and colour, as wee gather flowers to straw houses, or make Garlands; but they are better when they grow to our style; as in a Meadow, where though the meere grasse and greennesse delights; yet the variety of flowers doth heighten and beautifie. Marry, we must not play, or riot too much with them, as in *Paranomasies:*[1] Nor use too swelling, or ill-sounding words; *Quæ per salebras, altaque saxa cadunt.*[2] It is true, there is no sound but shall find some Lovers, as the bitter'st confections are gratefull to some palats. Our composition must bee more accurate in the beginning and end, then in the midst; and in the end more, then in the beginning; for through the midst the streame beares us. And this is attain'd by Custome more then care, or diligence. Wee must expresse readily, and fully, not profusely. There is difference betweene a liberall, and a prodigall hand. As it is a great point of Art, when our matter requires it, to enlarge, and veere out all sayle; so to take it in, and contract it, is of no lesse praise when the Argument doth aske it. Either of them hath their fitnesse in the place. A good man alwayes profits by his endeavour, by his helpe; yea, when he is absent; nay, when he is dead, by his example and memory. So good Authors in their style: A

9 [Examples of the old genitives; see *Aeneid* vii.464 and ix.26.]
1 [Plays on words, usually puns.]
2 [Martial, *Epigrams* xc.2: "Those that tumble over rough places and high cliffs."]

strict and succinct style is that, where you can take away nothing without losse, and that losse to be manifest. The briefe style
is that which expresseth much in little. The concise style, which
expresseth not enough, but leaves somewhat to bee understood.
The abrupt style, which hath many breaches, and doth not
seeme to end, but fall. The congruent, and harmonious fitting of
parts in a sentence, hath almost the fastning, and force of knitting, and connexion: As in stones well squar'd, which will rise
strong a great way without mortar.

Periods are beautifull, when they are not too long: for so they
have their strength too, as in a Pike or Javelin. As wee must take
the care that our words and sense bee cleare; so if the obscurity
happen through the Hearers, or Readers want of understanding,
I am not to answer for them; no more then for their not listning
or marking; I must neither find them eares, nor mind. But a man
cannot put a word so in sense, but some thing about it will illustrate it, if the Writer understand himselfe. For Order helpes
much to Perspicuity, as Confusion hurts. *Rectitudo lucem ad-
fert; obliquitas et circumductio offuscat.*[3] We should therefore
speake what wee can, the neerest way, so as wee keepe our gate,
not leape; for too short may as well be not let into the memory,
as too long not kept in. Whatsoever looseth the grace, and
clearenesse, converts into a Riddle; the obscurity is mark'd, but
not the valew. That perisheth, and is past by, like the Pearle in
the Fable. Our style should be like a skeine of silke to be carried,
and [w]ound by the right thred, not ravel'd, and perplex'd; then
all is a knot, a heape. There are words, that doe as much raise a
style, as others can depresse it. Superlation, and overmuchnesse
amplifies. It may be above faith, but never above a meane. It was
ridiculous in *Cestius,* when hee said of *Alexander: Fremit Oce-
anus, quasi indignetur, quòd terras relinquas;* But propitiously
from *Virgil:—*

*Credas innare revulsas
Cycladas.*[4]

3 [Vives, *De Ratione Dicendi* i: "Straight-forwardness produces light, obliquity
and round-aboutness obfuscates." This whole section on composition and style
derives mainly from Vives, *Opera*, I, 93–101.]
4 [*Aeneid* viii.691–92: "you would believe the Cyclades uprooted and floating."
This example, like the preceding one ("The Ocean roars, as if indignant, because you may leave the land"), is taken from M. Seneca, *Suasoriae* i.2.12.]

Hee doth not say it was so, but seem'd to be so. Although it be somewhat incredible, that is excus'd before it be spoken. But there are *Hyperboles,* which will become one Language, that will by no means admit another. As *Eos esse* P. R. *exercitus, qui cœlum possint perrumpere:*[5] who would say this with us, but a mad man? Therefore wee must consider in every tongue what is us'd, what receiv'd. *Quintilian* warnes us, that in no kind of Translation, or *Metaphore,* or *Allegory,* wee make a turne from what wee began; As if wee fetch the originall of our *Metaphore* from sea, and billowes; wee end not in flames and ashes; It is a most fowle inconsequence. Neither must wee draw out our *Allegory* too long, lest either wee make our selves obscure, or fall into affectation, which is childish. But why doe men depart at all from the right, and naturall wayes of speaking? Sometimes for necessity, when wee are driven, or thinke it fitter to speake that in obscure words, or by circumstance, which utter'd plainely would offend the hearers. Or to avoid obscenenesse, or sometimes for pleasure, and variety; as Travailers turne out of the high way, drawne, either by the commodity of a foot-path, or the delicacy, or freshnesse of the fields. And all this is call'd ἐσχηματισμένη, or figur'd Language.

Language most shewes a man: speake that I may see thee. It springs out of the most retired, and inmost parts of us, and is the Image of the Parent of it, the mind. No glasse renders a mans forme, or likenesse, so true as his speech. Nay, it is likened to a man; and as we consider feature, and composition in a man; so words in Language: in the greatnesse, aptnesse, sound, structure, and harmony of it. Some men are tall, and bigge, so some Language is high and great. Then the words are chosen, their sound ample, the composition full, the absolution plenteous, and powr'd out, all grave, sinnewye and strong. Some are little, and Dwarfes: so of speech it is humble, and low, the words poore and flat; the members and *Periods,* thinne and weake, without knitting, or number. The middle are of a just stature. There the Language is plaine, and pleasing: even without stopping, round

---

[5] [Misquotation, by way of Vives, of the boast attributed to Caesar in *De Bello Hispaniensi* xlii: "These are the armies of the Roman people, who could storm the heavens."]

without swelling; all well-torn'd, compos'd, elegant, and accurate. The vitious Language is vast, and gaping, swelling, and irregular; when it contends to be high, full of Rocke, Mountaine, and pointednesse: As it affects to be low, it is abject, and creeps, full of bogs, and holes. And according to their Subject, these stiles vary, and lose their names: For that which is high and lofty, declaring excellent matter, becomes vast and tumorous, speaking of petty and inferiour things: so that which was even, and apt in a meane and plaine subject, will appeare most poore and humble in a high Argument. Would you not laugh, to meet a great Counsellor of state in a flat cap, with his trunck hose, and a hobby-horse Cloake, his Gloves under his girdle, and yond Haberdasher in a velvet Gowne, furr'd with sables? There is a certaine latitude in these things, by which wee find the degrees. The next thing to the stature, is the figure and feature in Language: that is, whether it be round, and streight, which consists of short and succinct *Periods,* numerous, and polish'd; or square and firme, which is to have equall and strong parts, every where answerable, and weighed. The third is the skinne, and coat, which rests in the well-joyning, cementing, and coagmentation of words; when as it is smooth, gentle, and sweet; like a Table, upon which you may runne your finger without rubs, and your nayle cannot find a joynt; not horrid, rough, wrinckled, gaping, or chapt: After these the flesh, blood, and bones come in question. Wee say it is a fleshy style, when there is much *Periphrases,* and circuit of words; and when with more then enough, it growes fat and corpulent; *Arvina orationis,* full of suet and tallow. It hath blood, and juyce, when the words are proper and apt, their sound sweet, and the *Phrase* neat and pick'd. *Oratio uncta, & benè pasta.* But where there is Redundancy, both the blood and juyce are faulty, and vitious. *Redundat sanguine, quæ multò plus dicit, quàm necesse est.* Juyce in Language is somewhat lesse then blood; for if the words be but becomming, and signifying, and the sense gentle, there is Juyce: but where that wanteth, the Language is thinne, flagging, poore, starv'd; scarce covering the bone; and shewes like stones in a sack. Some men to avoid Redundancy, runne into that; and while they strive to have no ill blood, or Juyce, they loose their good. There be some

styles againe, that have not lesse blood, but lesse flesh, and corpulence. These are bony, and sinnewy: *Ossa habent, et nervos.*[6]
It was well noted by the late L. St. *Alban,* that the study of words is the first distemper of Learning.[7] Vaine matter the second: And a third distemper is deceit, or the likenesse of truth. Imposture held up by credulity. All these are the Cobwebs of Learning, and to let them grow in us, is either sluttish or foolish. Nothing is more ridiculous, then to make an Author a *Dictator,* as the schooles have done *Aristotle.* The dammage is infinite, knowledge receives by it. For to many things a man should owe but a temporary beliefe, and a suspension of his owne Judgement, not an absolute resignation of himselfe, or a perpetuall captivity. Let *Aristotle,* and others have their dues; but if wee can make farther Discoveries of truth and fitnesse then they, why are we envied? Let us beware, while wee strive to adde, wee doe not diminish, or deface; wee may improve, but not augment. By discrediting falshood, Truth growes in request. Wee must not goe about like men anguish'd, and perplex'd, for vitious affectation of praise: but calmely study the separation of opinions, find the errours have intervened, awake Antiquity, call former times into question; but make no parties with the present, nor follow any fierce undertakers, mingle no matter of doubtfull credit, with the simplicity of truth, but gently stirre the mould about the root of the Question, and avoid all digladiations,[8] facility of credit, or superstitious simplicity; seeke the consonancy, and concatenation of Truth; stoope only to point of necessity; and what leads to convenience. Then make exact animadversion where style hath degenerated, where flourish'd, and thriv'd in choisenesse of Phrase, round and cleane composition of sentence, sweet falling of the clause, varying an illustration by tropes and figures, weight of Matter, worth of Subject, soundnesse of Argument, life of Invention, and depth of Judgement. This is *Monte potiri,* to get the hill. For no perfect Discovery can bee made upon a flat or a levell.

6 [This paragraph is quarried from Vives, *De Ratione Dicendi* ii.]
7 [Jonson here begins to summarize the famous analysis of the "distempers" of learning, using substantially the same words as did Bacon in the first book of the *Advancement of Learning* (1605).]
8 [Fencing with words.]

Now, that I have informed you in the knowing these things; let mee leade you by the hand a little farther, in the direction of the use; and make you an able Writer by practice. The conceits of the mind are Pictures of things, and the tongue is the Interpreter of those Pictures. The order of Gods creatures in themselves, is not only admirable, and glorious, but eloquent; Then he who could apprehend the consequence of things in their truth, and utter his apprehensions as truly, were the best Writer, or Speaker. Therefore *Cicero* said much, when hee said, *Dicere rectè nemo potest, nisi qui prudenter intelligit.*[9] The shame of speaking unskilfully were small, if the tongue onely thereby were disgrac'd: But as the Image of a *King,* in his Seale ill-represented, is not so much a blemish to the waxe, or the Signet that seal'd it, as to the Prince it representeth; so disordered speech is not so much injury to the lips that give it forth, as to the disproportion, and incoherence of things in themselves, so negligently expressed. Neither can his mind be thought to be in tune, whose words doe jarre; nor his reason in frame, whose sentence is preposterous;[1] nor his Elocution cleare and perfect, whose utterance breakes it selfe into fragments and uncertainties: Were it not a dishonour to a mighty Prince, to have the Majesty of his embassage spoyled by a carelesse Ambassadour? and is it not as great an Indignity, that an excellent conceit and capacity, by the indiligence of an idle tongue should be disgrac'd? Negligent speech doth not onely discredit the person of the Speaker, but it discrediteth the opinion of his reason and judgement; it discrediteth the force and uniformity of the matter, and substance. If it be so then in words, which fly and escape censure, and where one good *Phrase* begs pardon for many incongruities, and faults; how shall he then be thought wise, whose penning is thin and shallow? How shall you looke for wit from him, whose leasure and head, assisted with the examination of his eyes, yeeld you no life, or sharpenesse in his writing?

---

9 [*Brutus* vi.23: "No one can be a proper speaker who is not a sound thinker." In this paragraph and the following one on epistolary style, Jonson follows John Hoskyns, "Directions for Speech and Style" (which circulated in ms. around 1600 and after), even to a minor misquotation in the sentence from Cicero's *Brutus;* Hoskyns himself drew on Quintilian and, especially, Lipsius' *Epistolica Institutio.*]

1 [Retaining the sense of the L. *praeposterus,* making first what should be last. Similarly, "sentence," from L. *sententia,* a sententious or pointed saying.]

In writing [of letters] there is to be regarded the Invention, and the Fashion. For the *Invention*, that ariseth upon your busines; whereof there can bee no rules of more certainty, or precepts of better direction given, then conjecture can lay downe, from the severall occasions of mens particular lives, and vocations: But sometimes men make businesse of kindnesse: As (*I could not satisfie my selfe, till I had discharged my remembrance, and charged my Letter with commendations to you.*) Or, (*My busines is no other, then to testifie my love to you, and to put you in mind of my willingnesse to doe you all kind offices.*) Or, (*Sir, have you leasure to descend to the remembring of that assurance you have long possest in your servant; and upon your next opportunity, make him happy with some commands from you?*) Or, the like; that goe a begging for some meaning, and labour to be deliver'd of the great burthen of nothing. When you have invented, and that your busines bee matter, and not bare forme, or meere Ceremony, but some earnest: then are you to proceed to the ordering of it, and digesting the parts, which is had out of two circumstances. One is the understanding of the Persons, to whom you are to write; the other is the coherence of your Sentence.[2] For mens capacity to weigh, what will be apprehended with greatest attention, or leisure; what next regarded, and long'd for especially; and what last will leave [most] satisfaction, and (as it were) the sweetest memoriall, and beliefe of all that is past in his understanding, whom you write to. For the consequence of Sentences, you must bee sure, that every clause doe give the Q. one to the other, and be bespoken ere it come. So much for *Invention* and *order*.

Now for fashion, it consists in foure things, which are Qualities of your style. The first is *Brevity*. For they must not be Treatises, or Discourses (your Letters) except it be to learned men. And even among them, there is a kind of thrift, and saving of words. Therefore you are to examine the clearest passages of your understanding, and through them to convey the sweetest, and most significant words you can devise; that you may the easier teach them the readiest way to an other mans apprehension, and open their meaning fully, roundly, and distinctly. So as the Reader may not thinke a second view cast away upon your

[2] [I.e., thought (from L. *sententia*).]

letter. And though respect bee a part following this; yet now
here, and still I must remember it. If you write to a man, whose
estate and senses[3] you are familiar with, you may the bolder (to
set a taske to his braine) venter on a knot. But if to your Superior, you are bound to measure him in three farther points: First,
your interest in him: Secondly, his capacity in your Letters:
Thirdly, his leasure to peruse them. For your interest, or favour
with him, you are to bee the shorter, or longer, more familiar, or
submisse, as hee will afford you time. For his capacity you are
to be quicker, and fuller of those reaches, and glances of wit, or
learning, as hee is able to entertaine them. For his leasure, you
are commanded to the greater briefnesse, as his place is of
greater discharges, and cares. But with your betters, you are not
to put Riddles of wit, by being too scarse of words: not to cause
the trouble of making *Breviates*,[4] by writing too riotous, and
wastingly. *Brevity* is attained in matter, by avoiding idle Complements, Prefaces, Protestations, Parentheses, superfluous circuit of figures, and digressions: In the composition, by omitting
Conjunctions, (*Not onely; But Also*) (*Both the one, and the
other*) (*Whereby it commeth to passe*) and such like idle Particles, that have no great busines in a serious Letter, but breaking
of sentences; as often times a short journey is made long, by
unnecessary baits.[4a]

But as *Quintilian* saith, there is a briefnesse of the parts
sometimes, that makes the whole long, as *I came to the staires, I
tooke a paire of oares, they launch'd out, rowed a pace, I landed
at the Court-gate, I paid my fayre, went up to the Presence, ask'd
for my Lord, I was admitted.* All this is but, *I went to the Court,
and spake with my Lord.* This is the fault of some Latine Writers, within these last hundred years, of my reading, and perhaps
Seneca may be appeacht of it; I accuse him not.

The next property of *Epistolarie* style is *Perspicuity*, and is
oftentimes [indangered by the former qualitie (brevity), often-
times] by affectation of some wit ill angled for, or ostentation of
some hidden termes of Art. Few words they darken speech, and
so doe too many: as well too much light hurteth the eyes, as too

---

[3] [Meaning "rank," from L. *census.*]
[4] [Précis.]
[4a] [A halt, for food and rest.]

little; and a long Bill of *Chancery* confounds the understanding, as much as the shortest note. Therefore, let not your Letters be penn'd like English Statutes, and this is obtain'd. These vices are eschewed by pondering your busines well, and distinctly [conceiving] your selfe, which is much furthered by uttering your thoughts, and letting them as well come forth to the light, and Judgement of your owne outward senses, as to the censure of other mens eares: For that is the reason, why many good Schollers speake but fumblingly; like a rich man, that for want of particular note and difference, can bring you no certaine ware readily out of his shop. Hence it is, that talkative shallow men doe often content the Hearers, more then the wise. But this may find a speedier redresse in writing; where all comes under the last examination of the eyes. First mind it well, then pen it, then examine it, then amend it; and you may bee in the better hope of doing reasonably well. Under this vertue may come Plainenesse, which is not to be curious in the order, as to answer a letter, as if you were to answer to Intergatories. As to the first, first; and to the second, secondly, &c. But both in method [and wordes] to use (as Ladies doe in their attyre) a diligent kind of negligence, and their sportive freedome; though with some men you are not to jest, or practise tricks: yet the delivery of the most important things, may be carried with such a grace, as that it may yeeld a pleasure to the conceit of the Reader. There must bee store, though no excesse of termes; as if you are to name *Store*, sometimes you may call it choyse, sometimes plenty; sometimes copiousnesse, or variety: but ever so, that the word which comes in lieu, have not such difference of meaning, as that it may put the sense of the first in hazard to be mistaken. You are not to cast a Ring for the perfumed termes of the time, as *Accommodation, Complement, Spirit, &c.* But use them properly in their place, as others.

There followeth *Life,* and *Quicknesse,* which is the strength and sinnewes (as it were) of your penning by [pithy] Sayings, Similitudes, and Conceits, Allusions [to] some knowne History, or other common place, such as are in the *Courtier,*[5] and the second booke of *Cicero de oratore.*

The last is; Respect to discerne, what fits your selfe; him to

5 [Castiglione's *Cortegiano* (1528) was translated by Thomas Hoby in 1561.]

whom you write; and that which you handle, which is a quality
fit to conclude the rest, because it doth include all. And that
must proceed from ripenesse of judgement, which as one truly
saith, is gotten by foure meanes, *God, Nature, Diligence, and
Conversation.* Serve the first well, and the rest will serve you.

We have spoken sufficiently of Oratory; let us now make a
diversion to *Poetry. Poetry* in the Primogeniture, had many peccant humours, and is made to have more now, through the Levity, and inconstancie of mens Judgements. Whereas indeed, it
is the most prevailing Eloquence, and of the most exalted *Char-
act.* Now the discredits and disgraces are many it hath receiv'd,
through mens study of Depravation or Calumny: their practise
being to give it diminution of Credit, by lessening the Professors
estimation, and making the Age afraid of their Liberty: And the
Age is growne so tender of her fame, as she cals all writings
Aspersions. That is the State-word, the Phrase of Court, (*Placen-
tia Colledge*[6]) which some call *Parasites Place,* the Inne of *Ignorance.*

Whilst I name no persons, but deride follies; why should any
man confesse, or betray himselfe? why doth not that of S. *Hierome* come into their minde; *Ubi generalis est de vitiis disputa-
tio, ibi nullius esse personæ injuriam?*[7] Is it such an inexpiable
crime in *Poets,* to taxe vices generally; and no offence in them
who, by their exception, confesse they have committed them
particularly? Are wee fal'ne into those times that wee must not

Auriculas teneras mordaci rodere vero?

Remedii votum semper verius erat, quàm spes.[8] If men may by
no meanes write freely, or speake truth, but when it offends not;
why doe *Physicians* cure with sharpe medicines, or corrosives?
Is not the same equally lawfull in the cure of the minde, that is

6 [Courteousness College (a place rather overly genteel).]
7 [From "S. Hierome" or St. Jerome, *Epistulae* cxxv, by way of Erasmus' misquotation: "Where the discussion concerns vice in general, no individual is in-
jured." (The paragraph draws throughout on Erasmus' "Letter to Martin
Dorp," an apology for *The Praise of Folly.*)]
8 [Misquoted from Persius, *Satires* i.107–08: "Gnaw tender little ears with a
biting truth," and, "The promise of reform was always more solid than the
hope." (Persius has *radere,* "grate," for Jonson's *rodere,* "gnaw.")]

in the cure of the body? Some vices, (you will say) are soe foule,
that it is better they should bee done, then spoken. But they that
take offence where no Name, Character, or Signature doth
blazon them, seeme to mee like affected as woemen; who, if they
heare any thing ill spoken of the ill of their Sexe, are presently
mov'd, as if the contumely respected their particular: and, on
the contrary, when they heare good of good woemen, conclude,
that it belongs to them all. If I see any thing that toucheth mee,
shall I come forth a betraier of my selfe, presently? No; if I be
wise, I'le dissemble it; if honest, I'le avoid it: lest I publish that
on my owne forehead, which I saw there noted without a title. A
man, that is on the mending hand, will either ingeniously[9] confesse, or wisely dissemble his disease. And, the wise, and vertuous, will never thinke any thing belongs to themselves that is
written, but rejoyce that the good are warn'd not to bee such;
and the ill to leave to bee such. The Person offended hath no
reason to bee offended with the writer, but with himselfe; and so
to declare that properly to belong to him, which was so spoken of
all men, as it could bee no mans severall, but his that would
willfully and desperately clayme it. It sufficeth I know, what
kinde of persons I displease, men bred in the declining, and
decay of vertue, betroth'd to their owne vices; that have aban-
doned, or prostituted their good names; hungry and ambitious of
infamy, invested in all deformity, enthrall'd to ignorance and
malice, of a hidden and conceal'd malignitie, and that hold a
concomitancy with all evill.

What is a Poet?

A *Poet* is that, which by the *Greeks* is call'd κατ᾽ ἐξοχὴν, ὁ
ποιητής,[1] a Maker, or a fainer: His Art, an Art of imitation, or
faining; expressing the life of man in fit measure, numbers, and
harmony, according to *Aristotle*: From the word ποιεῖν, which signifies to make or fayne. Hence, hee is call'd a *Poet*, not hee
which writeth in measure only; but that fayneth and formeth a
fable, and writes things like the Truth. For, the Fable and Fiction
is (as it were) the forme and Soule of any Poeticall worke, or
Poeme.

9 [Ingenuously.]
1 [The maker par excellence.]

What meane you by a Poeme?

A *Poeme* is not alone any worke, or composition of the Poets in many, or few verses; but even one alone verse sometimes makes a perfect *Poeme*. As, when *Aeneas* hangs up, and consecrates the Armes of *Abas*, with this Inscription;

> *Aeneas hæc de Danais victoribus arma.*[2]

And calls it a *Poeme*, or *Carmen*. Such are those in *Martiall.*

> *Omnia, Castor, emis: sic fiet, ut omnia vendas.*

And,

> *Pauper videri Cinna vult, & est pauper.*[3]

So were *Horace* his *Odes* call'd, *Carmina;* his *Lirik* Songs. And *Lucretius* designes a whole booke, in his sixt:

> *Quod in primo quoque carmine claret.*[4]

And anciently, all the Oracles were call'd, *Carmina;* or, what ever Sentence was express'd, were it much, or little, it was call'd, an *Epick, Dramatick, Lirike, Elegiake,* or *Epigrammatike Poeme.*

But, how differs a Poeme from what wee call Poesy?

A *Poeme*, as I have told you, is the worke of the Poet; the end, and fruit of his labour, and studye. *Poesy* is his skill, or Crafte of making: the very Fiction it selfe, the reason, or forme of the worke. And these three voices differ, as the thing done, the doing, and the doer; the thing fain'd, the faining, and the fainer: so the *Poeme*, the *Poesy*, and the *Poet.* Now, the *Poesy* is the habit, or the Art: nay, rather the Queene of Arts: which had her

---

[2] [*Aeneid* iii.288: "These arms, Aeneas, from the victorious Grecians."]
[3] [*Epigrams* vii.98: "Since you buy everything, Castor, it may be that you will sell everything." And viii.19: "Cinna wants to seem poor—and is poor."]
[4] [*De Rerum Natura* vi.937: "Which is also made clear in my first poem (book)." I.e., Lucretius "designes" or designates a "whole booke" a "carmen."]

Originall from heaven, received thence from the *'Ebrewes,* and
had in prime estimation with the *Greeks,* transmitted to the *Latines,* and all Nations, that profess'd Civility. The Study of it (if
wee will trust *Aristotle*) offers to mankinde a certaine rule, and
Patterne of living well, and happily; disposing us to all Civill
offices of Society. If wee will beleive *Tully,*[5] it nourisheth, and
instructeth our Youth; delights our Age; adornes our prosperity;
comforts our Adversity; entertaines us at home; keepes us company abroad, travailes with us; watches; devides the times of our
earnest, and sports; shares in our Country recesses, and recrea-
tions; insomuch as the wisest and best learned have thought her
the absolute Mistresse of manners, and neerest of kin to Vertue.
And, wheras they entitled *Philosophy* to bee a rigid, and austere
Poesie: they have (on the contrary) stiled *Poesy,* a dulcet, and
gentle *Philosophy,* which leades on, and guides us by the hand to
Action, with a ravishing delight, and incredible Sweetnes. But,
before wee handle the kindes of *Poems,* with their speciall
differences; or make court to the Art it selfe, as a Mistresse, I
would leade you to the knowledge of our *Poet,* by a perfect Information, what he is, or should bee by nature, by exercise, by imitation, by Studie; and so bring him downe through the disciplines of *Grammar, Logicke, Rhetoricke,* and the *Ethicks,* adding
somewhat, out of all, peculiar to himselfe, and worthy of your
Admittance, or reception.

First, wee require in our *Poet,* or maker, (for that Title our
Language affordes him, elegantly, with the *Greeke*) a goodnes of
naturall wit. For, wheras all other Arts consist of Doctrine, and
Precepts: the *Poet* must bee able by nature, and instinct, to
powre out the Treasure of his minde; and, as *Seneca* saith, *Ali-
quando secundum Anacreontem insanire, jucundum esse:*[6] by
which hee understands, the *Poeticall Rapture.* And according to
that of *Plato; Frustrà Poeticas fores sui compos pulsavit:*[7] And
of *Aristotle; Nullum magnum ingenium sine mixturâ dementiæ
fuit. Nec potest grande aliquid, & supra cæteros loqui, nisi mota*

5 [Cicero, *Pro Archia* vii. The opening of this paragraph comes from Pontanus,
Poeticae Institutiones (1594), as appended to Joannes Buchler's *Poeticarum
Thesaurus* (1633).]
6 [*De Tranquillitate Animi* xvii (misquoted): "According to Anacreon, it is
sometimes joyful to be mad."]
7 [Misquoted from *ibid.* (Seneca is alluding to Plato's *Ion*): "The one in control of himself knocked in vain at the portals of poetry."]

mens.[8] Then it riseth higher, as by a devine Instinct, when it contemnes common, and knowne conceptions. It utters somewhat above a mortall mouth. Then it gets a loft, and flies away with his Ryder, wh[i]ther, before, it was doubtfull to ascend. This the *Poets* understood by their *Helicon, Pegasus,* or *Parnassus;* and this made *Ovid* to boast:

> *Est, Deus in nobis; agitante calescimus illo:*
> *Sedibus æthereis spiritus ille venit.*[9]

And *Lipsius,* to affirme; *Scio, Poetam neminem præstantem fuisse, sine parte quâdam uberiore divinæ auræ.*[1] And, hence it is, that the comming up of good Poets, (for I minde not *mediocres,* or *imos*) is so thinne and rare among us; Every beggerly Corporation affoords the State a *Maior,* or two *Bailiffs,* yearly: but, *solus Rex, aut Poeta, non quotannis nascitur.*[2] To this perfection of Nature in our *Poet,* wee require Exercise of those parts, and frequent. If his wit will not arrive soddainly at the dignitie of the Ancients, let him not yet fall out with it, quarrell, or be over hastily Angry: offer, to turne it away from Study, in a humor; but come to it againe upon better cogitation; try an other time, with labour. If then it succeed not, cast not away the Quills, yet: nor scratch the Wainescott, beate not the poore Deske; but bring all to the forge, and file, againe; tourne it a newe. There is no Statute *Law* of the Kingdome bids you bee a Poet, against your will; or the first Quarter. If it come, in a yeare, or two, it is well. The common Rymers powre forth Verses, such as they are, (*ex tempore*) but there never come from them one Sense, worth the life of a Day. A Rymer, and a *Poet,* are two things. It is said of the incomparable *Virgil,* that he brought forth his verses like a

---

8 [Also from the passage in *De Tranquillitate* (Seneca appears to have used Aristotle, *Problemata* xxx.i.): "There was never great genius without admixture of madness." The next sentence is not from Aristotle but from Seneca: "Nor can one rise to what is great and above the ordinary unless the mind is excited."]

9 [A combination of Ovid's *Fasti* vi.5 and his *Ars Amatoria* iii.550: "There is a god in us, and when he excites us we wax inspired; that spirit comes from the heavens."]

1 [*Electorum Liber* ii.17: "I know there has never been a great poet without a very large share of the divine spirit."]

2 [Florus, *Fragmenta:* "Only a King, or a Poet, is not born yearly."]

Beare, and after form'd them with licking. *Scaliger*, the Father,[3] writes it of him, that he made a quantitie of verses in the morning, which a fore night hee reduced to a lesse number. But, that which *Valerius Maximus* hath left recorded of *Euripides*, the *tragicke Poet*, his answer to *Alcestis*, an other *Poet*, is as memorable, as modest: who, when it was told to *Alcestis*, that *Euripides* had in three daies brought forth, but three verses, and those with some difficultie, and throwes; *Alcestis*, glorying hee could with ease have sent forth a hundred in the space; *Euripides* roundly repl[y]'d, like enough. But, here is the difference; Thy verses will not last those three daies; mine will to all time. Which was, as to tell him, he could not write a verse. I have met many of these Rattles, that made a noyse, and buz'de. They had their humme; and, no more. Indeed, things, wrote with labour, deserve to be so read, and will last their Age. The third requisite in our *Poet*, or Maker, is *Imitation*, to bee able to convert the substance, or Riches of an other *Poet*, to his owne use. To make choise of one excellent man above the rest, and so to follow him, till he grow very *Hee*: or, so like him, as the Copie may be mistaken for the Principall. Not, as a Creature, that swallowes, what it takes in, crude, raw, or indigested; but, that feedes with an Appetite, and hath a Stomacke to concoct, devide, and turne all into nourishment. Not, to imitate servilely, as *Horace* saith, and catch at vices, for vertue: but, to draw forth out of the best, and choisest flowers, with the Bee, and turne all into Honey, worke it into one relish, and savour: make our *Imitation* sweet: observe, how the best writers have imitated, and follow them. How *Virgil*, and *Statius* have imitated *Homer*; how *Horace, Archilochus;* how *Alcæus*, and the other *Liricks*: and so of the rest. But, that, which wee especially require in him is an exactnesse of Studie, and multiplicity of reading, which maketh a full man, not alone enabling him to know the *History*, or Argument of a *Poeme*, and to report it: but so to master the matter, and Stile, as to shew, hee knowes, how to handle, place, or dispose of either, with *elegancie*, when need shall bee. And not thinke, hee can leape forth

---

[3] [I.e., Julius Caesar Scaliger (1484–1558), author of the influential, "neoclassical" *Poetice* (published 1561), defender of Vergil over Homer, and father of Joseph Justus Scaliger (see note 7 on p. 97).]

suddainely a *Poet,* by dreaming hee hath been in *Parnassus,* or, having washt his lipps (as they say) in *Helicon.* There goes more to his making, then so. For to Nature, Exercise, Imitation, and Studie, *Art* must bee added, to make all these perfect. And, though these challenge to themselves much, in the making up of our Maker, it is Art only can lead him to perfection, and leave him there in possession, as planted by her hand. It is the assertion of *Tully,*[4] If to an excellent nature, there happen an accession, or conformation of Learning, and Discipline, there will then remaine somewhat noble, and singular. For, as *Simylus* saith in *Stobæus;*

Οὔτε φύσις ἱκανὴ γίνεται τέχνης ἄτερ,

οὔτε πᾶν τέχνη μὴ φύσιν κεκτημένη.[5]

without Art, Nature can ne're bee perfect; &, without Nature, Art can clayme no being. But, our Poet must beware, that his Studie bee not only to learne of himself; for, hee that shall affect to doe that, confesseth his ever having a Foole to his master. Hee must read many; but, ever the best, and choisest: those, that can teach him any thing, hee must ever account his masters, and reverence: among whom *Horace,* and (hee that taught him) *Aristotle,* deserve to bee the first in estimation. *Aristotle* was the first accurate *Criticke,* and truest Judge; nay, the greatest *Philosopher,* the world ever had: for, hee noted the vices of all knowledges, in all creatures, and out of many mens perfections in a Science, hee formed still one Art. So hee taught us two Offices together, how we ought to judge rightly of others, and what wee ought to imitate specially in our selves. But all this in vaine, without a naturall wit, and a Poeticall nature in chiefe. For, no man, so soone as hee knowes this, or reades it, shall be able to write the better; but as he is adapted to it by Nature, he shall grow the perfecter Writer. Hee must have *Civil prudence,* and *Eloquence,* & that whole; not taken up by snatches, or peeces, in Sentences, or remnants, when he will handle businesse, or carry Counsells, as if he came then out of the Declam-

4 [Cicero, *Pro Archia* vii.]
5 [*Florilegium* ii. (Simylus [*fl.* 350 B.C.] wrote comedies. Stobaeus compiled his anthology about A.D. 500.) Jonson apparently derived the quotation from Pontanus, *Poeticae Institutiones.*]

ors Gallerie, or Shadowe, furnish'd but out of the body of the State, which commonly is the Schoole of men. The *Poet* is the neerest Borderer upon the Orator, and expresseth all his vertues, though he be tyed more to numbers; is his equall in ornament, and above him in his strengths. And, (of the kind) the *Comicke* comes neerest: Because, in moving the minds of men, and stirring of affections (in which Oratory shewes, and especially approves her eminence) hee chiefly excells. What figure of a Body was *Lysippus* ever able to forme with his Graver; or *Apelles* to paint with his Pencill, as the Comedy to life expresseth so many, and various affections of the minde? There shall the Spectator see some, insulting with Joy; others, fretting with Melancholy; raging with Anger; mad with Love; boiling with Avarice; undone with Riot; tortur'd with expectation; consum'd with feare: no perturbation in common life, but the Orator findes an example of it in the Scene. And then, for the Elegancy of Language, read but this Inscription on the *Grave* of a *Comicke Poet:*

Immortales mortales, si fas esset, flere,
Flerent divæ Camœnæ Nævium Poetam;
Itaque postquam est Orcino traditus thesauro,
Obliti sunt Romæ, linguâ loqui Latinâ.[6]

Or, that modester Testimonie given by *Lucius Aelius Stilo* upon *Plautus;* who affirmed, *Musas, si latinè loqui voluissent, Plautino sermone fuisse loquuturas.*[7] And that illustrious judgement by the most learned *M. Varro* of him; who pronounced him the *Prince* of *Letters,* and *Elegancie,* in the *Roman* Language.[8]

I am not of that opinion to conclude a *Poets* liberty within the narrowe limits of lawes, which either the *Grammarians,* or *Philosophers* prescribe. For, before they found out those Lawes, there were many excellent Poets, that fulfill'd them. Amongst

[6] [Aulus Gellius, *Noctes Atticae* i.24, quoting the epitaph the poet Naevius wrote for himself: "If the immortals may grieve for mortals, the divine Muses would weep for the poet Naevius. After he was carried away as treasure to the abode of Orcus (in Hades), the Romans forgot how to speak Latin."]
[7] ["If the Muses had wanted to speak in Latin, they would have used the language of Plautus." *Cf.* Quintilian, *Institutio Oratoria* x.1.99.]
[8] [This paragraph and all those that follow owe a great deal, more or less directly, to the great Dutch "neoclassical" critic and humanist, Daniel Heinsius, particularly to his *De Tragoediae Constitutione* (1611) and the *Dissertatio* prefixed to his 1618 edition of Terence.]

whome none more perfect then *Sophocles,* who liv'd a little before *Aristotle.* Which of the *Greekelings* durst ever give precepts
to *Demosthenes?* or to *Pericles,* (whom the Age surnam'd *heavenly*) because he seem'd to thunder, and lighten, with his Language? or to *Alcibiades,* who had rather Nature for his guide,
then Art for his master?

But, whatsoever Nature at any time dictated to the most happie; or long exercise to the most laborious; that the wisdome, and
Learning of *Aristotle,* hath brought into an Art: because, he understood the Causes of things: and what other men did by
chance or custome, he doth by reason; and not only found out
the way not to erre, but the short way we should take, not to
erre.

Many things in *Euripides* hath *Aristophanes* wittily reprehended; not out of Art, but out of Truth. For, *Euripides* is sometimes peccant, as he is most times perfect. But, Judgement when
it is greatest, if reason doth not accompany it, is not ever absolute.

To judge of Poets is only the facultie of Poets; and not of all
Poets, but the best. *Nemo infælicius de Poetis judicavit, quàm
qui de Poetis scripsit.*[9] But, some will say, *Criticks* are a kind of
Tinkers; that make more faults, then they mend ordinarily. See
their diseases, and those of *Grammarians.* It is true, many
bodies are the worse for the medling with: And the multitude of
Physicians hath destroyed many sound patients, with their
wrong practise. But the office of a true *Critick,* or *Censor,* is, not
to throw by a letter any where, or damne an innocent Syllabe, but
lay the words together, and amend them; judge sincerely of the
Author, and his matter, which is the signe of solid, and perfect
learning in a man. Such was *Horace,* an Author of much Civili-
tie; and (if any one among the heathen can be) the best master,
both of vertue, and wisdome; an excellent, and true judge upon
cause, and reason; not because he thought so; but because he
knew so, out of use and experience.

Cato, the *Grammarian,* a defender of *Lucilius.*

---

9 [J. J. Scaliger, *Confutatio fabulae Burdonum:* "No one judged the poets
more infelicitously than he who wrote *Of Poets.*" Scaliger means the Italian
critic Giraldi (1479–1552). That only the poet may properly judge the poet
appears in the *Rhetorica ad Herrenium* iv.2, a work the Renaissance attributed to Cicero; the idea is a Renaissance commonplace.]

Cato Grammaticus, Latina Syren,
Qui solus legit, & facit Poetas.[1]

Quintilian of the same heresie, but rejected.

Horace his judgement of *Chœrillus*, defended against *Joseph Scaliger*. And, of *Laberius*, against *Julius*.

But chiefly his opinion of *Plautus*, vindicated against many, that are offended, and say, it is a hard Censure upon the parent of all conceipt, and sharpnesse. And, they wish it had not fallen from so great a master, and Censor in the Art: whose bondmen knew better how to judge of *Plautus*, then any that dare patronize the family of learning in this Age; who could not bee ignorant of the judgement of the times, in which hee liv'd, when *Poetrie*, and the *Latin* Language were at the height: especially, being a man so conversant, and inwardly familiar with the censures of great men, that did discourse of these things daily amongst themselves. Againe, a man so gratious, and in high favour with the Emperour, as *Augustus* often called him his wittie *Manling*, (for the littlenes of his stature;) and (if wee may trust Antiquity) had design'd him for a Secretary of Estate; and invited him to the P[a]lace, which he modestly praid off, and refus'd.

Horace did so highly esteeme *Terence* his Comedies, as he ascribes the Art in Comedie to him alone, among the *Latines*, and joynes him with *Menander*.

Now, let us see what may be said for either, to defend *Horace* his judgement to posterity; and not wholly to condemne *Plautus*.

The parts of a Comedie are the same with a *Tragedie*, and the end is partly the same. For, they both delight, and teach; the *Comicks* are call'd διδάσκαλοι,[2] of the *Greekes;* no lesse then the *Tragicks.*

Nor, is the moving of laughter alwaies the end of *Comedy*, that is rather a fowling for the peoples delight, or their fooling. For, as *Aristotle* saies rightly,[3] the moving of laughter is a fault in Comedie, a kind of turpitude, that depraves some part of a

---

[1] [Quoted by Suetonius, *De Grammaticis* xi: "The grammarian Cato, the Latin Siren, who alone reads and makes poets." (Jonson is again following Heinsius.)]
[2] [Teachers.]
[3] [*Poetics* v.1, but Jonson, through his source, Heinsius, misunderstands Aristotle on this point.]

mans nature without a disease. As a wry face without paine
moves laughter, or a deformed vizard, or a rude Clowne, drest in
a Ladies habit, and using her actions, wee dislike, and scorne
such representations; which made the ancient Philosophers ever
thinke laughter unfitting in a wise man. And this induc'd *Plato*
to esteeme of *Homer,* as a sacrilegious Person; because he presented the *Gods* sometimes laughing. As, also it is divinely said
of *Aristotle,* that to seeme ridiculous is a part of dishonesty, and
foolish.

So that, what either in the words, or Sense of an Author, or in
the language, or Actions of men, is a wry, or depraved, doth
strangely stirre meane affections, and provoke for the most part
to laughter. And therfore it was cleare that all insolent, and obscene speaches, jest[s] upon the best men; injuries to particular
persons; perverse, and sinister[4] Sayings (and the rather unexpected) in the old Comedy did move laughter; especially, where
it did imitate any dishonesty; and scurrility came forth in the
place of wit: which who understands the nature and *Genius* of
laughter, cannot but perfectly know.

Of which *Aristophanes* affords an ample harvest, having not
only out gone *Plautus,* or any other in that kinde; but express'd
all the moods, and figures, of what is ridiculous, oddly. In short,
as Vinegar is not accounted good, untill the wine be corrupted:
so jests that are true and naturall, seldome raise laughter, with
the beast, the multitude. They love nothing, that is right, and
proper. The farther it runs from reason, or possibility with them,
the better it is. What could have made them laugh, like to see
Socrates presented, that Example of all good life, honesty, and
vertue, to have him hoisted up with a Pullie, and there play the
Philosopher, in a basquet? Measure, how many foote a Flea
could skip *Geometrically,* by a just Scale, and edifie the people
from the ingine? This was *Theatricall* wit, right Stage-jesting,
and relishing a Play-house, invented for scorne, and laughter;
whereas, if it had savour'd of equity, truth, perspicuity, and Candor, to have tasten a wise, or a learned Palate, spit it out pres-
antly; this is bitter and profitable, this instructs, and would informe us: what neede wee know any thing, that are nobly borne,

4 [Misleading, oblique, prejudicial.]

more then a Horse-race, or a hunting-match, our day to breake
with Citizens, and such innate mysteries?

This is truly leaping from the Stage, to the Tumbrell [5] againe,
reducing all witt to the Originall Dungcart.

Of the magnitude, and compasse of any Fable, Epicke, or Dramatick.

To the resolving of this *Question*, wee must first agree in the
definition of the Fable. The Fable is call'd the *Imitation* of one
intire, and perfect Action; whose parts are so joyned, and knitt
together, as nothing in the structure can be chang'd, or taken
away, without impairing, or troubling the whole; of which there
is a proportionable magnitude in the members. As for example;
if a man would build a house, he would first appoint a place to
build it in, which he would define within certaine bounds: So in
the Constitution of a *Poeme*, the Action is aym'd at by the *Poet*,
which answers Place in a building; and that Action hath his
largenesse, compasse, and proportion. But, as a Court or Kings
Palace, requires other dimensions then a private house: So the
Epick askes a magnitude, from other Poëms. Since, what is
Place in the one, is Action in the other, the difference is in space.
So that by this definition wee conclude the fable, to be the *imitation* of one perfect, and intire Action; as one perfect, and intire
place is requir'd to a building. By perfect, wee understand that,
to which nothing is wanting; as Place to the building, that is
rais'd, and Action to the fable, that is form'd. It is perfect, perhaps, not for a Court, or Kings Palace, which requires a greater
ground; but for the structure wee would raise. So the space of
the Action, may not prove large enough for the *Epick Fable*, yet
bee perfect for the *Dramatick*, and whole.

Whole, wee call that, and perfect, which hath a *beginning*, a
mid'st, and an *end*. So the place of any building may be whole,
and intire, for that worke; though too little for a palace. As, to a
Tragedy or a *Comedy*, the Action may be convenient, and perfect, that would not fit an *Epicke Poeme* in Magnitude. So a Lion
is a perfect creature in himselfe, though it bee lesse, then that of

[5] [The "cart" of Thespis.]

a *Buffalo,* or a *Rhinocerote.* They differ; but *in specie:* either in
the kinde is absolute. Both have their parts, and either the
whole. Therefore, as in every body; so in every Action, which is
the subject of a just worke, there is requir'd a certaine proportionable greatnesse, neither too vast, nor too minute. For that
which happens to the Eyes, when wee behold a body, the same
happens to the Memorie, when wee contemplate an action. I
looke upon a monstrous Giant, as *Tityus,* whose body cover'd
nine Acres of Land, and mine eye stickes upon every part; the
whole that consists of those parts, will never be taken in at one
intire view. So in a *Fable,* if the Action be too great wee can
never comprehend the whole together in our Imagination.
Againe, if it be too little, there ariseth no pleasure out of the
object, it affords the view no stay: It is beheld and vanisheth at
once. As if wee should looke upon an Ant or Pismyre, the parts
fly the sight, and the whole considered is almost nothing. The
same happens in Action, which is the object of Memory, as the
body is of sight. Too vast oppresseth the Eyes, and exceeds the
Memory: too little scarce admits either.

Now, in every Action it behooves the *Poet* to know which is his
utmost bound, how farre with fitnesse, and a necessary proportion, he may produce, and determine it. That is, till either good
fortune change into the worse, or the worse into the better. For
as a body without proportion cannot be goodly, no more can the
Action, either in *Comedy,* or *Tragedy,* without his fit bounds.
And every bound, for the nature of the Subject, is esteem'd the
best that is largest, till it can increase no more: so it behooves
the Action in *Tragedy,* or *Comedy,* to be let grow, till the necessity aske a Conclusion: wherin two things are to be considered;
First, that it exceed not the compasse of one Day: Next, that
there be place left for digression, and Art. For the *Episodes,* and
digressions in a Fable, are the same that houshold stuffe, and
other furniture are in a house. And so farre for the measure,
and extent of a *Fable Dramaticke.*

Now, that it should be one, and intire. One is considerable two
waies: either, as it is only separate, and by it self: or as being
compos'd of many parts, it beginnes to be one, as those parts
grow, or are wrought together. That it should be one the first way
alone, and by it self, no man that hath tasted letters ever would

say, especially having required before a just Magnitude, and equall Proportion of the parts in themselves. Neither of which can possibly bee, if the Action be single and separate, not compos'd of parts, which laid together in themselves, with an equall and fitting proportion, tend to the same end; which thing out of Antiquitie it selfe, hath deceiv'd many; and more this Day it doth deceive.

So many there be of old, that have thought the Action of one man to be one: As of *Hercules, Theseus, Achilles, Ulysses,* and other *Heroes;* which is both foolish and false; since by one and the same person many things may be severally done, which cannot fitly be referred, or joyned to the same end: which not only the excellent *Tragick-Poets,* but the best Masters of the *Epick, Homer,* and *Virgil* saw. For though the Argument of an *Epick-Poeme* be farre more diffus'd, & powr'd out, then that of *Tragedy;* yet *Virgil* writing of *Aeneas* hath pretermitted many things. He neither tells how he was borne, how brought up; how he fought with *Achilles;* how he was snatch'd out of the battaile by *Venus;* but that one thing, how *he came into Italie,* he prosecutes in twelve bookes. The rest of his journey, his error by Sea, the Sacke of *Troy,* are put not as the Argument of the worke, but *Episodes* of the Argument. So *Homer* lai'd by many things of *Ulysses* and handled no more, then he saw tended to one and the same end.

Contrarie to which and foolishly those *Poets* did, whom the *Philosopher* taxeth; Of whom one gather'd all the Actions of *Theseus;* another put all the Labours of *Hercules* in one worke. So did he, whom *Juvenal* mentions[6] in the beginning, *hoarse Codrus,* that recited a volume compil'd, which he call'd his *Theseide,* not yet finish'd, to the great trouble both of his hearers and himself: Amongst which there were many parts had no coherence, nor kindred one with other, so farre they were from being one Action, one *Fable.* For as a house, consisting of diverse materialls, becomes one structure, and one dwelling; so an Action, compos'd of diverse parts, may become one *Fable Epicke,* or *Dramaticke.* For *example,* in a *Tragedy* looke upon *Sophocles* his *Ajax: Ajax* depriv'd of *Achilles's* Armour, which he hop'd from the suffrage of the *Greekes,* disdaines; and, grow-

6 [*Satires* i.2; but there Cordus, not Codrus.]

ing impatient of the Injurie, rageth, and turnes mad. In that humour he doth many senselesse things; and at last falls upon the *Grecian* flocke, and kills a great Ramme for *Ulysses:* Returning to his Sense, he growes asham'd of the scorne, and kills himself; and is by the *Chiefes* of the *Greekes* forbidden buriall. These things agree, and hang together, not as they were done; but as seeming to be done, which made the Action whole, intire, and absolute.

For the *whole,* as it consisteth of parts; so without all the parts it is not the whole; and to make it absolute, is requir'd, not only the parts, but such parts as are true. For a part of the whole was true; which if you take away, you either change the whole, or it is not the whole. For if it be such a part, as being present or absent, nothing concernes the whole, it cannot be call'd a part of the whole: and such are the *Episodes,* of which hereafter. For the present, here is one example; The single Combat of *Ajax* with *Hector,* as it is at large describ'd in *Homer,* nothing belongs to this *Ajax* of *Sophocles.*

.   .   .

FINIS

Sir Francis Bacon

1561–1626

Bacon, educated at Cambridge, entered Parliament in 1584, but his advancement was delayed until the time of King James: Solicitor-General in 1607, Attorney-General in 1613, Lord Keeper in 1617, Lord Chancellor in 1618—and then convicted of having accepted bribes by the just judgment of a corrupt judicial system.

Bacon's influence—as essayist, legal philosopher, politician, scientist, and "advancer" of learning—is so important and pervasive as to evade summary; his prestige, range, and persuasiveness were such that he was made use of, like the Bible, as authority for various (sometimes conflicting) purposes, and he has consequently been made accountable for large items like The Birth of Science and The Death of Poetry. He affected all departments of learning during the century, not least that of imaginative writing; poetry he referred, after the manner of the Spaniard Huarte and other theorizers, solely to the "imagination," thus allowing his authority to be used by the movement that tended ultimately to the trivializing of verse by divorcing it from the "reason." Probably Bacon's own intentions lay elsewhere: he was really not so much interested in depreciating poetry (or Christianity, or whatever) as in dignifying and preserving utilitarian learning. Although his longest "literary" work is De Sapientia Veterum (1609; translated as The Wisdom of the Ancients in 1619), this popular venture into the "scientific" allegoresis of the ancient myths was finally less influential than the concise pronouncements

of The Advancement of Learning (*1605*), *together with their fuller
exposition in* De Augmentis Scientiarum (*1623*).

The first excerpt is taken from Book II of The Twoo Bookes of
Francis Bacon, Of the Proficience and advancement of Learning,
divine and humane (*1605*); *the inserts in brackets represent additions made by Bacon when he came to include the* Twoo Bookes *in
the* De Augmentis Scientiarum, *given here from the edition of 1674
in the translation made by Gilbert Wats in 1640. The second selection
comes from Book VII, Chapter 1, of the* De Augmentis *where Bacon
addresses himself to the problem of discourse in general and the place
of poetry in this larger picture; also from the edition of 1674 in the
translation of Wats.*

FROM

The Twoo Bookes of Francis Bacon,

Of the Proficience

and ADVANCEMENT of LEARNING,

DIVINE AND HUMANE

[1605]

THE PARTS of humane learning have reference to the three
partes of Mans understanding, which is the seate of Learning:
HISTORY to his MEMORY, POESIE to his IMAGINATION, and PHI-
LOSOPHIE to his REASON: Divine learning receiveth the same distribution, for the Spirit of Man is the same: though the Revelation of Oracle and Sense be diverse: So as the Theologie consisteth also of HISTORIE of the Church; of PARABLES, which is
Divine *Poesie*: and of holie DOCTRINE or *Precept*. For as for that

part, which seemeth supernumerarie, which is *Prophecie:* it is but Divine Historie: which hath that prerogative over humane, as the Narration may bee before the fact, aswell as after.

POESIE is a part of Learning in measure of words for the most part restrained: but in all other points extreamely licensed: and doth truly referre to the Imagination: which beeing not tyed to the Lawes of Matter; may at pleasure joyne that which Nature hath severed: & sever that which Nature hath joyned, and so make unlawfull Matches & divorses of things: *Pictoribus atque Poetis &c.*[1] It is taken in two senses in respect of Wordes or Matter; In the first sense it is but a *Character* of stile, and belongeth to Arts of speeche, and is not pertinent for the present. In the later, it is (as hath beene saide) one of the principall Portions of learning: and is nothing else but FAINED HISTORY, which may be stiled as well in Prose as in Verse.

The use of this FAINED HISTORIE, hath beene to give some shadowe of satisfaction to the minde of Man in those points, wherein the Nature of things doth denie it, the world being in proportion inferiour to the soule: by reason whereof there is agreeable to the spirit of Man, a more ample Greatnesse, a more exact Goodnesse; and a more absolute varietie then can bee found in the Nature of things. Therefore, because the Acts or Events of *true Historie*, have not that Magnitude, which satisfieth the minde of Man, *Poesie* faineth Acts and Events Greater and more Heroicall; because *true Historie* propoundeth the successes and issues of actions, not so agreable to the merits of Vertue and Vice, therefore *Poesie* faines them more just in Retribution, and more according to Revealed Providence, because *true Historie* representeth Actions and Events, more ordinarie and lesse interchanged, therefore *Poesie* endueth them with more Rarenesse, and more unexpected, and alternative Variations. So as it appeareth that *Poesie* serveth and conferreth to Magnanimitie, Moralitie, and to Delectation. And therefore it was ever thought to have some participation of divinesse, because it doth raise and erect the Minde, by submitting the shewes of things to the

[1] [Horace, *Ars Poetica* 9. A critical catch-phrase during the Renaissance, introducing the notion that poets and painters may hazard anything so long as they do not violate Nature by having birds couple with serpents and the like impossibilities.]

desires of the Mind; whereas reason doth buckle and bowe the Mind unto the Nature of things. And we see that by these insinuations and congruities with mans Nature and pleasure, joyned also with the agreement and consort it hath with Musicke, it hath had accesse and estimation in rude times, and barbarous Regions, where other learning stoode excluded.

The division of Poesie which is aptest in the propertie therof (besides those divisions which are common unto it with history: as fained Chronicles, fained lives, & the Appendices of History, as fained Epistles, fained Orations, and the rest) is into POESIE NARRATIVE; REPRESENTATIVE, and ALLUSIVE. The NARRATIVE is a meere imitation of History with the excesses before remembred; Choosing for subject commonly Warrs, and Love; rarely State, and sometimes Pleasure or Mirth. REPRESENTATIVE is as a visible History, and is an Image of Actions as if they were present, as History is of actions in nature as they are, (that is) past; ALLUSIVE or PARABOLICALL, is a NARRATION applied onely to expresse some speciall purpose or conceit.

[*Dramatical, or Representative Poesie, which brings the World upon the stage,* is of excellent use, if it were not abused. For the Instructions, and Corruptions of the *Stage,* may be great; but the corruptions in this kind abound; the Discipline is altogether neglected in our times. For although in Modern Commonwealths, *Stage-playes* be but esteemed a sport or pastime, unless it draw from the Satyr, and be mordent; yet the care of the Ancients was, that it should instruct the minds of men unto virtue. Nay, wise men and great Philosophers have accounted it, as the Archer, or musical Bow of the Mind. And certainly it is most true, and as it were, a secret of nature, *that the minds of men are more patent to affections, and impressions, Congregate, than solitary.*]

[But *Poesie Allusive, or Parabolical, excels the rest, and seemeth to be a sacred and venerable thing; especially seeing Religion it self hath allowed it in a work of that nature, and by it, traficks divine commodities with men.* But even *this* also hath been contaminate by the levity and indulgence of mens wits about *Allegories.* And it is of ambiguous use, and applied to contrary ends. For it serves for *Obscuration;* and it serveth also for *Illustration:* in this it seems, there was sought a way how to

teach; in that an Art how to conceal.] Which later kind of Parabolical wisedome was much more in use in the ancient times, as
by the Fables of *Aesope,* and the briefe sentences of the seven,[2]
and the *use* of *Hieroglyphikes* may appeare. And the cause was
for that it was then of necessitie to expresse any point of reason,
which was more sharpe or subtile then the vulgar in that maner,
because men in those times wanted both varietie of examples,
and subtiltie of conceit: And as *Hierogliphikes* were before Letters, so parables were before arguments: And neverthelesse now
and at all times they doe retaine much life and vigor, because
reason cannot bee so sensible, nor examples so fit.

But there remaineth yet another use of POESY PARABOLICAL,
opposite to that which we last mentioned: for that tendeth to
demonstrate, and illustrate that which is taught or delivered,
and this other to retire and obscure it: That is when the Secrets
and Misteries of Religion, Pollicy, or Philosophy, are involved in
Fables or Parables. Of this in divine Poesie, wee see the use is
authorised. In Heathen Poesie, wee see the exposition of Fables
doth fall out sometimes with great felicitie, as in the Fable that
the Gyants beeing overthrowne in their warre against the Gods,
the Earth their mother in revenge thereof brought forth Fame.

Illam terra Parens ira irritata Deorum,
Extremam, ut perhibent, Cœo Enceladoque Sororem Progenuit.[3]

Expounded that when Princes & Monarches have suppressed actuall and open Rebels, then the malignitie of people, (which is
the mother of Rebellion,) doth bring forth Libels & slanders,
and taxations of the states, which is of the same kind with Rebellion, but more Feminine: So in the Fable that the rest of the
Gods having conspired to binde *Jupiter, Pallas* called *Briareus*
with his hundreth hands to his aide, expounded, that Monarchies neede not feare any courbing of their absolutenesse by
Mightie Subjects, as long as by wisedome they keepe the hearts
of the people, who will be sure to come in on their side: So in the

2 [Gnomic utterances of The Seven Wise Men of Greece; lists differ but
include such persons as Solon and Thales.]
3 [Vergil, *Aeneid* iv.178–80: "Provoked to anger against the gods, Mother
Earth, as they say, gave birth to that one last, as sister to Coeus and
Enceladus."]

fable, that *Achilles* was brought up under *Chyron* the *Centaure*, who was part a man, & part a beast, Expounded Ingeniously, but corruptly by Machiavell, that it belongeth to the education and discipline of Princes, to knowe as well how to play the part of the Lyon, in violence, and the Foxe in guile, as of the Man in vertue & Justice. Neverthelesse in many the like incounters, I doe rather think that the fable was first, and the exposition devised, then that the Morall was first, & thereupon the fable framed. For I finde it was an auncient vanitie, in *Chrisippus,* that troubled himselfe with great contention to fasten the assertions of the *Stoicks* upon the fictions of the ancient Poets: But yet that all the Fables and fictions of the Poets, were but pleasure and not figure, I interpose no opinion. Surely of those Poets which are now extant, even *Homer* himselfe, (notwithstanding he was made a kinde of Scripture, by the later Schooles of the Grecians) yet I should without any difficultie pronounce, that his Fables had no such inwardnesse in his owne meaning: But what they might have, upon a more originall tradition, is not easie to affirme: for he was not the inventor of many of them. In this third part of Learning which is Poesie, I can report no deficience. For being as a plant that commeth of the lust of the earth, without a formall seede, it hath sprung up, and spread abroad, more then any other kinde: But to ascribe unto it that which is due for the expressing of affections, passions, corruptions and customes, we are beholding to Poets, more then to the Philosophers workes, and for wit and eloquence not much lesse then to Orators harangues. But it is not good to stay too long in the Theater: let us now passe on to the judicial Place or Pallace of the Mind, which we are to approach and view, with more reverence and attention.

TRANSLATED FROM

De Augmentis Scientiarum

[*1623*]

The Knowledge *concerning the Organ of Speech* generally re-ceiv'd, which is also called *Grammar,* hath two Parts; the one of *Speech;* the other of *Writing.* For *Aristotle* saith well, *Words are the Images of Cogitations; Letters are the Images of Words;*[1] we will assign both to *Grammar.* But to derive the Matter somewhat higher before we come to *Grammar,* and the Parts thereof now set down; we must speak of the *Organ of Tradition* in general. For there seems to be other *Traditive Emanations* besides *Words* and *Letters.* For this is certain whatsoever may be distinguisht into differences, sufficient for number, to express the variety of Notions (so those differences be perceptible to sense) may be the Convoy of the Cogitations from man to man. For we see Na-tions of different Language to trade one with the other, well enough to serve their turn by *Gestures.* Nay, in the practice of many, that have been dumb and deaf from their birth, and otherwise were ingenious, we have seen strange Dialogues held between them, and their friends, who have learn'd their Ges-tures. *Moreover it is now* generally known that in *China,* and the Provinces of the high *Levant,* there are at this day in use, certain *Real,* and not *Nominal Characters;* that is, such as express nei-ther *Letters* nor *Words;* but *Things* and *Notions:* in so much, that many Countries that understand not one anothers Lan-guage, but consenting in such kind of *Characters* (which are more generally receiv'd amongst them) can communicate one with another by such *Figures* written; so as every Country can read and deliver in his own native Tongue, the meaning of any Book written with these *Characters.*

[1] *De Interpret.* [In *De Interpretatione* and elsewhere. (But at the end of the paragraph, in speaking of Chinese characters, Bacon is probably drawing on Juan Gonzalez Mendoza's *History of the Great and Mighty Kingdom of China,* Englished in 1588 by R. Parke.)]

Notes therefore of things, which without the help and mediation of *Words* signfie *Things,* are of two sorts; whereof the first sort is significant of *Congruity;* the other *ad placitum.* Of the former sort are *Hieroglyphicks* and *Gestures;* of the later are those which we call *Characters Real.* The use of *Hieroglyphicks* is very ancient, and had in a kind of Veneration; especially amongst the Egyptians, one of the most Ancient Nations: So that *Hieroglyphicks* seem to have been a *first-born writing,* and elder than the *Elements* of *Letters;* unless, it may be, the *Letters* of the Hebrews. *As for Gestures,* they are, as it were, Transitory *Hieroglyphicks.* For as words pronounced vanish, *writings* remain; so *Hieroglyphicks* expressed by *Gestures,* are transient, but *painted,* permanent. As when *Periander* being consulted with, how to preserve a Tyranny, bid the Messenger stand still, *and he walking in a Garden, topt all the highest Flowers;*[2] signifying the cutting off, and the keeping low of the Nobility; did as well make use of a *Hieroglyphick,* as if he had drawn the same upon Paper. This in the mean is plain, that *Hieroglyphicks* and *Gestures* ever have some similitude with the thing signified, and are kind of *Emblems;* wherefore we have named them the *Notes of things from Congruity.* But *Characters Real* have nothing of Emblem in them; but are plainly dumb and dead Figures, as the *Elements* of *Letters* are; and only devised *ad Placitum,* and confirmed by Custom, as by a tacit agreement. And it is manifest also that there must needs be a vast number of them for writing; at least so many as there are Radical words. Wherefore this portion of Knowledge *concerning the Organ of Speech, which is of the Notes of Things, we report as Deficient.* And though it may seem of no great use, considering that *Words* and *writings by Letters* are the most apt *Organs* of *Tradition;* yet we thought good to make mention of it here, as of a knowledge not to be despised. For we here handle, as it were, the *Coyns of things Intellectual;* and it will not be amiss to know, that as Money may be made of other matter besides Gold and Silver; so there may be stamped other *Notes* of things besides *Words* and *Letters.*

Let us proceed to *Grammar; this doth bear the office as it were, of an Usher to other Sciences; a place not very honourable, yet*

[2] *Herodot. Laert.* [Herodotus v.92.]

*very necessary, especially seeing that in our age Sciences are
chiefly drawn from Learned Languages, and not from Mother-
tongues.* Nor is the dignity thereof to be esteemed mean, seeing
it supplies the place of an Antidote, against that *Malediction* of
the *Confusion* of *Tongues.* Surely the Industry of man striveth to
restore, and redintegrate himself in those Benedictions, which
by his guilt he forfeited; and by all other Arts, arms and
strengthens himself against that first general Curse of the *steril-
ity of the earth, and the eating of his bread in the sweat of his
brows.*[3] But against that second Curse, which was the *Confusion*
of *Tongues, he calls in the assistance of Grammar.* The use
hereof in some Mother-tongues is indeed very small; in forreign
tongues more large; but most ample in such tongues, as have
ceased to be vulgar, and are perpetuated only in Books.

*We will divide Grammar into two sorts, whereof the one is
Literary, the other Philosophical.* The one is merely applied to
Languages, that they may be more speedily learned; or more correctly and purely spoken. *The other* in a sort doth minister,
and is subservient to *Philosophy.* In this later part which is *Philosophical,* we find *that Cæsar writ Books De Analogia;*[4] and it is
a question whether those Books handled this Philosophical
Grammar whereof we speak? Our opinion is, that not any high
and subtil matter in them, but only that they deliver'd Precepts
of a pure and perfect speech, not depraved by popular Custom;
nor corrupted and polluted by over-curious affectation; in which
kind *Cæsar* excell'd. *Notwithstanding,* admonish'd by such a
work, we have conceiv'd and comprehended in our mind, a kind
of Grammar, that may diligently enquire, not the *Analogy of
words one* with another, but the *Analogy* between Words and
Things, or Reason; besides that *Interpretation of Nature,* which
is subordinate to *Logick.* Surely *Words* are the *foot-steps of Reason;* and foot-steps do give some indications of the Body; wherefore we will give some general description of this. And first we do
not allow that curious enquiry which *Plato* an excellent man pursued, touching the *imposition* and *original Etymology of names,*
conceiving it, *as if words had not been imposed at first, ad Placi-*

3 *Gen. 3:*
4 *Suet. in Jul.* [Suetonius, "Life" of Julius Caesar; *De Analogia* is lost.]

tum; but were significantly derived and deduced from a certain reason and intendment.[5] Certainly an elegant and pliant speculation, which might be aptly fain'd and made square to the purpose: and by reason it seemeth to search the secrets of Antiquity, in some kind reverend. But yet sparingly mixt with truth, and without fruit. *But without* question that would be a most excellent kind of *Grammar:* as we suppose if some man throughly instructed in many *Languages,* as well *Learned,* as *Mother-tongues,* should write a Treatise of the divers Proprieties of *Languages;* shewing in what points every particular Language did excel; and in what points it was *Deficient.* For so *Tongues* might be enricht and perfected by mutual intertraffick one with another; and a most fair Image of speech (like the *Venus* of *Apelles*[6]); and a goodly pattern for the true expression of the inward sence of the mind, might be drawn from every part which is excellent in every Language. *And withal* no slight Conjectures, but such as were well worth the observation, might be taken (which a man perchance would little think) touching the natural dispositions and customs of People, and Nations, even from their Languages. *For I willingly* give ear to *Cicero* noting that the Grecians have not a word which may express this Latine word, *Ineptum;*[7] *because* (saith he) *this vice was so familiar to the Grecians, that they did not so much as acknowledge themselves guilty thereof.* Certainly a Censure worthy a Roman gravity. And what may that infer, that the Grecians used such a Liberty in composition of words; contrarywise the Romans were in this point severe? Surely a man may plainly collect that the Grecians were more fit to study Arts; the Romans to manage affairs of state. For distinctions of Arts, for most part, require composition of words; but matters and business, simple words. *But the Hebrews so shun Composition, that they make choice rather to strain a Metaphor too far, than to bring in a Composition.* Nay they use so few words, and so unmingled, that a man may plainly perceive by their Tongue, that they were a Nazarite People, and separate from other Nations. *And is not that* worthy

5 *In Cratyl.* [In the *Cratylus* Socrates and Hermogenes explore the relation of words to things.]
6 [Probably the Helen of Zeuxis.]
7 *De Orat. lib.*2. [*De Oratore* ii.4: "tasteless," "indecorous," "ungrammatical" in "composition."]

observation? (though it may serve to abate our high conceit of our own times) *that ancient Languages were more full of Declensions; Cases; Conjugations; Tenses, and the like; the modern commonly destitute of these, do loosely deliver themselves in many expressions by Prepositions, and auxiliary verbs.* Certainly a man may easily conjecture (however we may please our selves) that the wits of former times were far more acute and subtil than ours are. There are an infinite number of observations of this kind which might make up a just Volume. Wherefore it will not be amiss to distinguish *Grammar Philosophical,* from *mere and literary Grammar,* and to set it down as *Deficient.* Unto *Grammar* also belongs the consideration of all *Accidents* of words; such as are *Measure; Sound; Accent;* but those first infancies of simple Letters (as, with what Percussion of the Tongue, with what opening of the mouth; with what drawing of the lips, with what straining of the throat; the sound of every Particular *Letter* is to be made) belongs not unto *Grammar;* but is a Portion of the *knowledge of sounds,* to be handled *under sense* and *sensibility. Grammatical sound,* whereof we speak, belongs only to sweetness and harshness of sounds; of which some are common; for there is no Tongue but in some sort shuns the too much overture of concurrent Vowels, and the asperities of concurrent Consonants. There are other respective sounds which are pleasing, or unpleasing to the ear, according to the temper of divers Nations. *The Greek Tongue* is full of Diphthongs; the Latin is far more sparing; the Spanish Tongue hates small-sounding Letters, and presently changeth them into Letters of a middle tone; the Tongues derived from the *Goths* delight in Aspirates; there are innumerable of this nature, but perchance these are more than enough.

But the measure of words hath brought us forth an immense Body of Art, namely *Poesie;* not in respect of the Matter (of which we have spoken before) but in respect of stile, and the form of words, as *Metre* or *Verse;* touching which the Art is very small and brief, but the access of Examples large and infinite. Neither ought that Art (which the Grammarians call *Prosodia*) to be only restrain'd to the kinds and measures of *Verse;* for their are Precepts to be annext, what kind of *Verse* best fitteth every Matter or Subject. The Ancients applied *Heroical Verse* to

Histories and *Laudatories; Elegies* to *Lamentations; Iambicks* to *Invectives; Lyricks* to *Songs* and *Hymns.* And this Wisdom of the Ancients is not wanting in the *Poets* of later Ages, in Mother-tongues; only this is to be reprehended, that some of them too studious of Antiquity have endeavoured to draw Modern Languages to Ancient Measures (as *Heroick, Elegiack, Saphick,* and the rest) which the Fabrick and composition of those Languages, will not bear; and withal is no less harsh unto the ear. In the Matters of this Nature the Judgement of Sense is to be preferr'd before Precepts of Art, as he saith,

Cœnæ Fercula nostræ
Mallem Convivis quam placuisse Coquis.[8]

Nor is *this Art,* but the abuse of Art, seeing it doth not perfect, but perverts Nature. *As for Poesie (whether we speak of Fables, or Metre) it is, as we have said before, as a Luxuriant Herb brought forth without seed, and springs up from the strength and rankness of the soyl. Wherefore it runs along every where, and is so amply spread, as it were a superfluous labour to be curious of any Deficients therein;* the care therefore for this is taken already.

[8] *Mart. Ep. 9.* [Martial ix.81: "I would prefer the courses of my dinner to please the guests rather than the cooks."]

Dudley North,
3rd Baron North

1581–1666

Educated at Cambridge, Lord North was, according to his grandchild Roger, a "person full of spirit and flame"; "after he had consumed the greatest part of his estate in the gallantrys of King James (or rather his son Prince Henry's) Court, retired and lived more honourably in the country upon what was left than ever he had done before"; "being a courtier, and withall a person of much witt, and more fancy, affected a state answerable to his education and former course of life." North wrote love poems, religious verse, and essays; his rambling style is doubtless a matter of temperament, but it also derives from his idols Montaigne and Burton. ("Burtons Book of Melancholy" defined the nature of North's fashionable malady and also makes use of the indestructible simile of the spaniel that reappears in the preface to Dryden's Annus Mirabilis.) North's essay is extremely valuable for the indirect (and unflattering) light it sheds on the "strong lines" of "metaphysical verse." According to L. A. Beaurline ("Dudley North's Criticism of Metaphysical Poetry," Huntington Library Quarterly, XXV [1962], 299–313), North helps controvert Rosemond Tuve's theory, as stated in Elizabethan and Metaphysical Imagery, that the Jacobeans emphasized different aspects of the rhetorical tradition but remained generally faithful to the theory and practice of the Eliza-

bethans. In any case, there is no doubt that North, like Drummond, regarded the "strong lines" of metaphysical verse with disaffection. Condemning fashionable Jacobean verse, he looked both toward the past—the example of Sidney—and toward the future—the "easy" Suckling, who as late as 1638 flattered North with a "request" for "the preface concerning poetry."

The preface "Concerning petty Poetry" is reprinted from A Forest of Varieties (1645); Beaurline dates its composition as early as 1610–12. Words bracketed in the text represent additions made by North as they appear in the copy held by The Huntington Library.

FROM

A Forest of Varieties:

OR RATHER A WYLDERNESSE

CONCERNING PETTY POETRY, MADE

MORE GENERALL IN ADDRESSE THEN AT FIRST

[1610–12?]

Preludium to the first Verses

Madam,[1]
In ancient offerings to Deity, Turtles, Incense, and Flowers have beene acceptable for the zeale of obedience, though of little worth, or advantage; let my respect to your command make the more excusable the worthlesse following lines, which otherwise in my knowledge of the sleightnesse of their stuffe and making

[1] [Lady Mary Wroth, literary patroness and niece to Sir Philip Sidney.]

should never have presumed to undergoe the weight of your censure: True Turtles you shall find them, full of simple love, and
unfurnisht of all Serpentine climbing art of subtilty and knowledge: Incense and Smoake, they are but of the gentlest nature,
not far fetcht Aromatiques, troublesome and intoxicating to the
brain, but mild as flowers unmedicinall for morality, meere Po-
seys or Nosegays, gay to the first sense; which if happily you
prove them, favour them so far as to give them their passe without further examination, I promise not my self that they shal
please, for they please not my selfe; (especially in a serious humour) I know them full of faults, but thinke them not worth the
mending. And if to bee an Author of such toyes bee a fault, it is
surely doubled to make them too great a businesse. Idlenesse
was their mother, which though I pleased my selfe to avoyd by
their destroying her in their birth, yet to good judgements they
may well bee as ill pleasing, as ill natur'd: If time were mis-
spent in them, yet there was not much cast away; for the idle
howers of three moneths brought them forth, except some few,
the children of little more then my childhood. As they are farre
from deserving good opinion, so am I farre from the humour
of some so well conceited of such their workes (like Peacocks
proud of their feathers) that they are never at an end of their
labour, but still with child to utter them: my travell [2] ended with
their first birth, and so I hope or wish the readers may at the first
reading; for if they bee not plaine and easie, it is against my
will, which as it wants strength to imitate, so cannot approve the
ridling humour lately affected by many, who thinke nothing
good that is easie, nor any thing becomming passion that is not
exprest with an hyperbole above reason. These tormentors of
their owne and their Readers braines I leave to bee admired in
their high obscure flight, (while my selfe will bee happy, if I can
procure but a familiar delight to a superficiall reading) they
affect to shew more wit then love, and in truth so much, that
whilst they commend beyond reason, they shew that either they
want reason to commend, or their subject to bee commended;
like ill ranging Spaniells they spring figures, and ravished with
their extravagant fancies, pursue them in long excursions, neglecting their true game and pretended affection: Bee the matter,

2 [Travail or the labor of childbirth.]

or the discoursers capacitie never so poore and meane, I ever affect a man that maketh right conclusions. And for my selfe, I would rather bee thought to want invention and knowledge, then judgement and good consequence in what I utter. The Poetry of these times abounds in wit, high conceit, figure, and proportions; thinne, light, and emptie in matter and substance; like fine colored ayery bubbles or Quelque-choses, much ostentation and little food; conceits, similes, and allegories are good, so the matter bee carried along in them, and not interrupted by them. *Venus* is here drawne by her Doves, not Serpents; and as I professe my selfe to want art in all things, so in matters of love I thinke it may bee best spared, as being an affection meerely[3] naturall, and where Art is seldome comely, but authorised with a native disposition; besides, Verses of love are commonly made for women, whose chiefest beautie consists in being unsophisticated by Art, and are the more pleasing in conversation by possessing a free puritie of unadulterated wit. And as wee often see that those women that have bestowed on themselves the most Art and costly dressing, nay many times that have the best proportion, are not yet the most winning: So in Verses there is to bee exprest a naturall spirit and moving ayre (or accent) more alluring and charming the affection, then others of a farre more rich, faire and curious composition. The world in all things is full of Critiques, that are sharpe sighted to reprehend, and will approve nothing but according to their owne rule; (many times out of square). But for my part I hold the same opinion of Verses as of Ayres in Musick, or Houses, that let them bee delightfull and pleasant to the first appearance with conveniency to the designe, and for the fantasticated rules of Art, Architecture, and proportion, let them observe them that list: and commonly who most affects them, most failes in the generall delightfulnesse and use. Poetry is in truth a kind of Musick, the fable of *Orpheus* expressed as much; Musick hath its Anthems, Pavens, Fantesies, Galliards, Courantoes, Ayres, Sarabands, Toyes, Cromatiques, &c. And Verses have their Hymmes, Tragedies, Satyres, Heroiques, Sonets, Odes, Songs, Epigrams, Distiques, and Strong lines, which are their Cromatiques, and of themselves may bee excellent in their Art; but long dwelt upon grow harsh and dis-

3 [Purely.]

tastefull. The commandements and preceptives are none of the poeticall parts of Scripture. Though I am no part of a Scholar, yet thus much by casuall opening of books I know, that *Horace* in matter of love hates difficulty: and though I beleeve it an imitation of his abrupt and harsh veine in his more serious peeces, that upon the worthinesse of his name and matter, hath debaucht many from the formerly used, more open, familiar and pleasing manner of versifying; yet I finde that even himselfe (howsoever either naturally or affectedly rugged, except his Lyrick veine) when hee uttereth his judgement, or prescribeth to others concerning measured compositions, no man is more frequent in recommendation of a round, current, cleare and gracefull delivery: but what his morall, solid and satyrick matter dispenst with, is in slighter stuffe intolerable: there shall you find the rough hands, but not the voyce and substance; let them rather imitate his best, then his worst. It cannot bee good in limited lines, which are a purposed pause to the voyce, to carry with a counter-time the period of the sense to the body of the next line, much lesse to dismember an innocent word, that every child according to nature, and use, in spelling would put together; and words have a naturall ayre, accent, and quantitie, whence to strayne them is to rack both them and the reader: Who will set himselfe to daunce, or his horse to manage, let him seeke to observe good time, ayre, and fashion: no man is fit for all things; whose Genius was borne for prose, let him write prose, rather then affecting Verse to make such unnaturall stuffe, as shall bee good neither. I pity both in my selfe and others to see the best of our matter in one place so extreamly prest, that it is a labour to discover it, and yet in another part of the same peece slight and superfluous stuffe dilated at large. A Poet should raise light from smoak, not blow that which is light with him to carry but smoak to another. I am of his Majesties[4] mind, that the best eloquence is to make our selves clearely understood, and that to him who hath leasure, there need no abbreviations: I had rather pay for a little more paper then to bee put to the cost of my braine. The admirable inventions and matter of your unimitable Uncles[5] extant works flourish in applause of all,

---

4 *King James.*
5 *Sir Philip Sidney.*

by a happy and familiar display of their beauties to the meanest, including withall such generositie of truely and profoundly extracted conceit to the most inward life of whatsoever hee expresseth, that the strongest and clearest seeing judgements may rest satisfied, yea transported in contemplation of the most lively and pleasing touches that a soule can apprehend, or a pen distill. Yet somewhat more to authorise my selfe, *Lipsius* upon perspicuity holds it the greatest misery in writing, not onely not to be understood, but to be understood with difficulty: and the sharp-witted *Martial* [6] in contempt of the more formall and severe censurers and Writers, professeth that hee would have his verses need neither an *Apollo,* nor *Grammarian;* and howsoever some may deny him to be exact, himself in his entertainments affects rather to please his Guests then Cooks. Verses of love should be verses of pleasure, & to please in love, the smoother fac'd the better.

I may be crabbed and rugged, but will never affect to bee so, especially in verses, whose true nature and use is to worke a kind of a Charme upon the mind, even with slightnesse of matter, by the well wrought and exquisite harmony of their Cadence, and sound: There being to be transfused into verse sometimes such a naturall spirit of magnanimity, sometimes such a soft, wanton, and melting aire of passion, that the one shall never faile to affect a generous and heroick mind, nor the other to work a kind of tender and relenting disposition in a sensible[7] and well-natur'd constitution; neither of which shall easily be seene effected from a harsh and rude (though never so witty) an expression: for as in persons, so in Verses; some, let them meane never so lovingly, shall yet by their naturall verjuyce[8] be ever out of the way of *Bacchus* and *Venus.* But in point of obscurity, in some sort to excuse my selfe with others, I feare wee all often unwillingly incurre the errour of it by thinking our meaning as open to others, as to our selves, when indeed the Characters of our expression are fully supplyed by our owne understanding to our selves, whilst to others they are lamely contracted and imperfect. Thus much I have been bold to write, not onely to ex-

[6] *Hunc volo qui fiat non sine pane satur.* [Martial x.59.6: "I want one who would not be satisfied without bread."]
[7] [I.e., susceptible to feeling.]
[8] ["Green juice" of crab apple or unripe fruit.]

cuse a poore Mother wit, but somewhat to give a passe upon
their strange and uneasie habit, who I doubt not but they will
have many a gird at my easie and naturall nakednesse; I meane
those lofty dimme shooting Archers, whom I wish to remember,
that hee who shootes highest, shootes not ever nearest the
marke; and hee that may walke in the light, is to bee suspected
for choosing the darke. Now (Madam) I grant that all I can
write (especially what these lines containe) is but vanity and a
most idle vanity; yet thus farre I will excuse both the writing
and the reading, that all the world is little better: wee often condemn vaine pleasures, and remember not that the most things
the best of us most seriously doe, have indeed no other end. For
God being served and nature sustained, what fruit proceeds
from our authority, learning, wealth, policy, and earnest intent
to profit, but to satisfie our impulsive affections, which either
propound to themselves a felicity whereof they faile in the possession, or seeke to divert by such imployments the dulnesse
and otherwise obtruding miseries of their condition? which if
you please to consider, you will the more excuse many pursuers
of lawful and naturall delights, and value those pleasures at the
better rate which are most perdurable and communicable. May
the following wanton (but as modest Babes as their Mother *Venus* could produce) though they cannot profit, yet afford some
delight to that your Worthy well furnish't mind, to which I wish
all happinesse that ever Noble nature possest, or can possesse. I
must yet bee so much longer, as to crave pardon for my unin-
tended and I feare unpleasant length, it is the vice of writing to
bee endlesse; thus hath my enmity to obscurity brought forth
tediousnesse, yet not so much, but that all this may bee sooner
read, then some one passage of our Night pieces understood:
they had need afford profitable stuffe, who utter it at so hard a
rate. I wish your Ladiships authority would so abate the price
that our poorer abilities might hold trade without straining. And
seeing I am upon the Theame of verses, whither I meane not
shortly to returne, I humbly crave your favour after my fashion,
disorderly to say thus much more, that howsoever some of the
stricter sort approve onely of verses so close, usefull, and substantially woven, that there must bee neither list, loosenesse, nor the
least superfluity of words: for my part, I am not of that strict

order, nor ever yet saw it observed in any Author. Nature hath mingled stalkes with flowers, and Huskes with Corne, and hath raised ornament from our excrementiciall [9] haires: conceits and matter over-crusht, afford commonly as little grace as pleasure; and to write all in abbreviations, would take indeed lesse room, but much more time and trouble. A *Geneva* print weakens the sight, nor is it good to hold your bow ever bent, or your horse streight rained. Sometimes amongst pithy and tough lines I thinke it not amisse to interpose one of an easie straine, like resting places in lofty staires, to ease the Reader. Some fluency of weak water helpes the better in nourishment to convey what is more solid. Lamp-oile yeelds no good savour nor in sallet nor verse. *Difficilia quæ pulchra*,[1] is to bee understood of the attaining, and not the exercising of faculties. You know how it is said of *Poems*, that they should bee such, *ut sibi quivis speret, idem sudet frustraque laboret ausus idem.*[2] Strong lines may bee drawne on with Cartropes, but the fairest have generally an easie birth. It is rare for any thing to be well and hardly performed. The French expression, *A Delivre*,[3] implyes as well perfectnesse, as facility and dexterity. There may bee imployed such an extraordinary (yet gentle) finenesse of conceit, and Conclusions so designed, wrought, limned and coloured, touches so bold, covert allegories and subtilties so neat [transitions so easy], Epithets so materiall, Metaphors and ambiguities so doubly fine, as shall bee more masterlike then more sententious, sublime, abstruse, and strong appearing lines. Worth of matter and conception supposed, nothing more commends a piece then termes well chosen, proper, lively, and significant, with a free comming on, and as free a close and conclusion. Also a faire, cleare and even thorough carriage with well wrought joints and connexions gives credit to the workman. I love as much a great deale of force and depth couched in one word, as I hate little in many. We ordinarily write and speake the same things and notions, and to the same purpose, but infinitely differ in the de-

9 [Retaining the L. sense of a "growing out" or "excresence."]
1 ["The beautiful is difficult," a Renaissance commonplace stemming from Plato (usually by way of Plutarch and Erasmus).]
2 [Horace, *Ars Poetica* 240–42 is slightly abbreviated by North. "So that anyone may hope for the same success, may sweat but work in vain in attempting it."]
3 ["*A Delivre*," meaning with ease and without encumbrance. "Deliver," from the French, could be used as an adjective in Renaissance English.]

livery and expression; some proceed in a stuttering confused
obliquity, groping as in a mist or darknesse; some goe more directly, and exhibit their Idea's and conceptions with so cleare
and distinct a light, illustrations, instances, demonstrations, en-
forcements, and arguments so pertinent, perspicuous and concluding, that the understanding and assent are captivate beyond
evasion or subterfuge. Sophistry and figures may appeare fine
and witty, but prevaile little upon the best judgements: Reason
must convince the intellectuall soule. May I write clearly and
strongly, rather then finely and artificially; hence is the difference of elocution, hence of perswasion, the one is light and aery,
the other weighty and solid; most lovely and commanding is the
beauty of a faire ingenuous and rich soule fairely mounted, and
armed upon well shaped and unanimously received vertue,
goodnesse and reason. Verses are then good, when turned to
prose they hold a faire and currant sense, and when translated
into another language, there is such mastery found in their conception by the advantage of what is genuine unto them, that
there will bee either more words or lesse conceit[4] and matter. The
priviledge they have over common phrase, consists in the war-
ranted becomming ornament of a lofty well ordered spirit, and
wantonnesse, such as shall make toyes passe for Jewels, and
give to what of it selfe is precious, an acquisite[5] lustre of workmanship beyond what prose can beare, and that in little room;
Their voice is more constrained, and consequently more shrill
and piercing. Nor is it in writing the least perfection (howsoever
it hath found little observation) so to order and contract our expressions, that one well adapted word may run into, and govern
many of diverse and strong sense) for nothing gives more pleasure and satisfaction to a diligent inquisitive and judicious
Reader, then much matter and conceit compendiously digested
with sufficiency of perspicuity. To conclude, lines of a farre
fetcht and labour'd fancy with allusions and curiosity, and in
similes of little more fruit or consequence, then to ravish the
Reader into the writers fine *Chamæleon* colours, and feed him
with aire, I approve not so much, as heighth and force of spirit
sententiously and weightily exhibited; wit needs not rack it self

4 [I.e., thought, as also later in this paragraph.]
5 [Acquired.]

where matter flowes; embroideries become not a rich stuffe; and art is best exprest where it least appeares.

A strong wing is to be preferred before a painted, and good sense and matter elegantly delivered before extravagancy of fancy and conceit; such unnaturall impertinency serves rather to shadow then illustrate, to overwhelme then set forth the subject: as well apposite as accurate writing is the Authors glory.

Edmund Bolton

1575–post 1634

Bolton, a Catholic, was educated at Cambridge and the Inner Temple.
Always full of schemes and projects—his idea for an "Academ Roial"
expired with King James—he was in one way or another acquainted
with a great many antiquarians and literary men of the day. He contributed to Englands Helicon (1600), wrote Latin and English verse
and a variety of works in prose, of which the most important is
Hypercritica, a treatise on historiography that argues the patriotic
significance of the "matter of Brute" and defends the moral and
practical utility of literature. It is the first original "art of history"
in English, though there are a number of Continental examples,
particularly in Italy after the middle of the sixteenth century. The
literary criticism included in Hypercritica, a variation on the old
roll call of poets, is distinguished by Bolton's professional effort
to find models in literature for the proper writing of history; the
historiographical emphasis lends the roll call a more than usual
interest and goes far toward explaining Bolton's willingness to recognize the virtues of "plain" as against "sugared" eloquence.

The first complete Hypercritica appeared at the end of Antony
Hall's Nicolai Triveti Annalium Continuatio in 1722 (Thomas Hearne
had published a fragment in 1719), but Bolton apparently began work
on the essay as early as 1603. His public references to Hypercritica, as
well as the appearance of the "1st Addresse" in William Camden's
notebooks, imply that the work enjoyed a fairly wide circulation in

manuscript. *Reprinted here are the first two sections of "Addresse the first.," Sections 4 and 5 of "Addresse. III.," and Sections 1–4 and 7–8 of "Addresse. IV." The text, from which I have removed the marginalia, was prepared by Thomas H. Blackburn of Swarthmore College, who has made a fresh collation of the mss. (Bodleian mss. Wood F. 9, Rawlinson D. 1, and the recently discovered autograph North B. 24); for a description of the mss. and an account of the evolution of the treatise, see Blackburn, "The Date and Evolution of Edmund Bolton's Hypercritica," Studies in Philology, LXIII (1966).*

FROM

Hypercritica,

OR A RULE OF JUDGMENT,
FOR WRITING, OR READING OUR HISTORIES
[*1621*]

ADDRESSE the first

To write the Historie of England is a worke superfluous, if it ever had an Historie: but having had all other honors it only wanteth that. Polydor Vergil [1] in England, and Paulus Æmilius[2] in France; both of them Italians, were entertaind of purpose. As if their narrations ought to have most beeleif, which were written by their penns, who had least interest in the argument, or relation to the parties. This counsel, whatsoever it seemed to the

1 [Italian humanist brought to England by Henry VIII to write *Anglica Historia* (first edition in 1534).]
2 [Italian humanist brought to the French court to write *De Rebus Gestis Francorum* (1516).]

givers, or receavers, found lesse in successe among us then it
had in probabilitie. Many great volumnes carrie among us the
titles of Histories. But learned men, and Syr Henrie Savile one of
them, absolutely denye, that any of ours discharge that office
which the titles promise. For my part I thincke that the most of
them have their praises, and all of them their uses towards the
composition of an universal Historie for England.

2. Among the greatest wants in our auncient authors are
the wants of Art, & Style: which as they add to the luster of the
workes & delights of the reader; yet add they nothing to the
trueth: which they soe esteemed, as they seeme to have regarded
nothing else. For without truthe, Art & Style come into the nature of crimes by imposture. It is an act of high wisdome, and
not of eloquence only, to write the Historie of soe great, & noble
a people as the English. For the causes of things are not only
wonderfully wrapt one within the other, but placed oftentymes
farr above the ordinarie reaches of humane witt: and hee who
relates events without their pr*ae*mises, and circumstances deserves not the name of an Historian; as being like to him who
numbers the bones of a man anatomised, or presenteth unto us
the bare Skeleton, without declaring the nature of the fabrick, or
teaching the use of the parts.

.   .   .   .

ADDRESSE. III

4. Historie in general hath as many prayses as any Muse
among the nine. One[3] tells us, as from out of auncient authors,
that Historie is nothing els but a kinde of Philosophie using examples; another, that Historie is the Metropolis of Philosophie,
the mother-cittie of Philosophie. Plainlier, & more to our purpose,
Tullie,[4] among other tytles calls her The light of truthe, & Mistresse of life, S. Gregorie Nazianzen, (that excellent Greek father) styleth her A world of wisdom, for soe his *quaedam con-
globata sapientia* (as his translatour calls it) may be Englished.
Our Malmesburie saith well, & worthely that it is *jucunda quaedam gestorum notitia mores condiens, qua ad BONA SE-*

3 [Bolton's note ("Isa Casaubo") indicates that the reference is to Isaac
Casaubon (1559–1614), the great classical scholar.]
4 [Cicero, whose definition of history (*De Oratore* ii.ix.36) was a Renaissance
commonplace.]

QUENDA, vel MALA CAVENDA, legentes exemplis irritat.[5] To
like purpose writes Venerable Beda to king Ceolulph. Excellent
is that of S[r.] Thomas North, in his praeface to his Plutarchs
lives: Histories (saith hee there) are fitt for every place, serve
for all tymes, reach to all persons, teach the living, revive the
dead, so excelling all other bookes, as it is better to see learning
in noble mens lives, then to read it in Philosophers writings.

5. What Grammatical Criticks (from whose penns let no man
greatlie hope for any thing in historie noble) do teach unto us,
it is not mainlie by any free Maister to bee regarded. For who
did ever write well, simplie as a disciple of theirs? Because to
make an Historian, there are also requisite certain guiftes of God,
and nature, ripened, and perfected by experience, peculiar to
that dutie, which Lucian himself placeth not within purchase,
as natural Wisdome, & Eloquence. And Lucians praecepts, or
observations are the best for Historiographers among all the
heathen, unless perhaps' you will praefer Dionysius Halicarnas-
saeus, where hee, in a special tract, compares Thucydides, and
Salust. A principal dutie of an Historian, everywhere agreed
upon, is to handle the counsels, & causes of affaires. Causes
againe are two fowld, considered (according to Savile) as they
are in composition (wherein he saith that Tacitus did not looke
soe well about him) and as they are in division, or as S[r.] Francis
Bacon ([new] Vicount S. Alban) doth far better for my capacitie distinguish them into causes, Secund or Scattred, and into
causes confaederate, and knit togeather. In this poinct consisteth the principal difficulty and mysterie of Historical office, and
not only difficultie, & mysterie, but faelicitie also, according to
that of the poet; *Faelix qui potuit rerum cognoscere causas.*[6]

. . .

ADDRESSE. IV

As for language and style (the coat, and appareil of matter) hee
who would penn our affairs in English, and compose unto us an
entire bodie of them, ought to have a singular care thereof. For

5 [From the historian William of Malmesbury, whose *De Gestis Regum
Anglorum* was finished in 1125: it is "a certain felicitous knowledge of human
actions seasoning the forms of conduct, so that it excites readers to pursue
the good and avoid the evil."]
6 [Vergil, *Georgics* ii.490. "Happy is he who has been able to discover the
causes of things."]

our tongue (though it have no noted dialects, nor accentual notes, as the Greeks, nor any receaved, or enacted certaintie of Grammar, or Orthographie) is very copious, and few there bee, who have the best, and most proper graces therof. In which the rule cannot bee but variable, because the peoples judgments are uncertain. The bookes also out of which wee gather the most warrantable English are not many to my remembrance. The principal which I have seene, and can in pr*ae*sent cal to minde either for prose, or verse, are those whose names doe followe.

2. The Histories written by S^r. Thomas More (some few antiquated words excepted) contain a clear, and proper phrase. The Arcadia of S^r. Phillip Sidney is most famous for ritch conceipt, and splendor of courtly expressions, warely to bee used by an Historian; whose style should have glosse and luster, but otherwise rather soliditie, and fluencie, then singularitie of Oratorical, or Poetical notions.

Such things as I have read of Q. Elizabeths own doing carry in them a most princely, & vital character, not without a singular Energie, and force of sought elegancie, wch. makes mee consent in a sort to the praise even of those things, which I have not seen of hers, set forth by S^r. Henrie Savile, in these words of his dedicatorie Epistle before translated Tacitus: The cause that I published it under yor. Majesties name and protection (besides the testification of my bounden dutie) was &ct. principallie to incite your Majestie by this, as by a foil, to communicate to the world, if not those admirable compositions of your owne, yet at the least those most rare, and excellent Translations of Histories (if I may call them translations which have so infinitelie exceeded the originalls) makeing evident demonstration to all who have seen them, that as the great actions of princes are the subject of stories, so Stories composed, or amended by princes are not only the best pattern, and rule of great actions, but also the most natural Registers therof, the writers beeing persons of like degree, and proportionable conceipts with the doers. Somewhat it may detract from the credit of this seeming Hyperbolical praise, both because it was written in her life-tyme, and also to herselfe. But I can beleive that they were excellent. For perhapps' the world never saw a ladie in whose person more greatnesses of parts mett then in hers; unlesse it were in that most noble prin-

cesse, & Heroine, Marie. Q. of Scots, inferior to her only in her
outward fortunes, in all other respects, and abilities at least her
equal.

A princelie, grave, and florishing peice of natural, and exquisite
English is Cardinal Alans Apologie said to bee;[7] and many have
commended the style, and phrase of Father Robert Persons
highly.[8] The end of Nero, and beginning of Galba, praefixed to
the translated Histories of Tacitus, and thought to bee S^r· Henrie
Saviles own (as whose else should so rare a piece bee?) is the
work of a very great M^r· indeed, both in our tongue, and in that
Storie. That tractate which goeth under the name of the Earl of
Essex his Apologie, was thought by some to bee M^r· Anthonie
Bacons; but as it bears that Earls name, so doe I also thinck that
it was the Earls own, as also his advises for travail to Roger Earl
of Rutland;[9] then which nothing almost can bee more honorablie
uttred, nor more to the writers praise, so farr as beelongs to a
noble English Orator. M^r· Hookers Praeface to his books of Ec-
clesiastical Policie is a singular, and choyse parcel of our vulgar
language.

Doctor Haywards phrase, and words are very good: onlie some
have wisht that in his Henrie, 4. hee had not called S^r· Hugh
Linn by so light a word, as Mad-cap, though hee were such; and
that hee had not changed his Historical state into a drammati-
call, where hee induceth a mother uttering a womans passion, in
the case of her sonn.[1] S^r· Walter Raleighs Guiana, and his praef-
atorie Epistle before his mightie undertaking in the Historie of
the World, are full of proper, clear, and courtly graces of speech.
Most of all, Sr. Francis Bacons writings, w^{ch}· have the freshest,
and most savorie formes, and aptest utterances, that (as I suppose) our tongue can bear.

These, next to his Majesties own most roial style, are the principal prose-writers, whom out of my present memorie I dare com-

---

7 [Cardinal William Allen (1532–94), *A True Sincere and Modest Defence
of English Catholics* (1584).]
8 [Robert Parsons, like Allen an English Catholic, wrote controversial works,
including the influential *A Christian directorie*, which went through many editions in the late sixteenth and early seventeenth centuries.]
9 [Actually Francis Bacon wrote both the *Apologie* (1604) and the letter.]
1 [Sir John Hayward (1564?–1627), *The First Part of the Life and Rayne of
King Henrie the IIII* (1599).]

mend for the best garden-plotts, out of which to gather English language.

3. In verse there are Edmund Spencers Hymns. I cannot advise the allowance of other his poems, as for practick English, no more then I can do Geffrey Chaucer, Lydgate, Peirce Ploughman, or Laureat Skelton. It was laid as a fault to the charge of Salust, that hee used some old outworn words, stoln out of Cato his book de Originibus. And for an Historian in our tongue to affect the like out of those our poets would bee accounted a fowl oversight. That therefore must not bee, unlesse perhaps' wee cite the words of some old moniment, as Livie cites carmen Martium, or as other Latins might allege Pacuvius, Andronicus, or lawes of the Twelve Tables, or what els soever of the antient. My judgment is nothing at all in poems, or poesie, and therefore I dare not goe far, but will simply deliver my minde concerning those authors among us, whose English hath in my conceipt most proprietie, and is nearest to the phrase of Court, and to the speech used among the noble, and among the better sort in London; the two sovereign seats, & as it were Parlament-tribunals to trye the question in. Brave language are Chapmans Iliads, those I meane which are translated into Tessera-decasyllabons, or lines of fowrteen syllables. The works of Samuel Daniel contain somewhat a flatt, but yet withal a very pure, & copious English, and words as warrantable as any mans, and fitter perhapps' for prose, then measure. Michael Draitons heroical Epistles are well worth the reading also, for the purpose of our subject; which is; to furnish an English Historian with choyse, and copie of tongue.[2]

Q. Elizabeths verses, those which I have seen and read (some extant in the elegant, wittie, and artificial book of the Art of English Poesie, the work (as the fame is) of one of her Gentlemen, Pensionars, Puttenham,) are princely, as her prose.

Never must bee forgotten S. Peters Complainct, and those other serious poems said to bee Father Southwells, the English wherof as it is most proper, so the sharpnesse, and light of witt is verie rare in them.

Noble Henrie Constable was a great Maister in English tongue,

2 ["Copie" from L. *copia*, referring to the rhetorical ability to "vary" and amplify.]

nor had any gentleman of our nation a more pure, quick, or higher deliverie of conceipt, witnesse among all other, that Sonnet of his beefore his Maties Lepanto. I have not seen much of Sr. Edward Dyers poetrie. Among the lesser late poets, Georg Gascoigns works may bee endured. But the best of those times (if Albions England bee not praeferred) for our businesse, is the Mirrour of Magistrates, and in that Mirrour, Sackvilles Induction, the work of Thomas, afterward Earl of Dorset, and Lord Treasurer of England, whose also the famous tragedie of Gorboduc was, the best of that tyme, even in Sr. Phillip Sydneys judgment, and all skillfull Englishmen cannot but ascribe asmuch therto, for his phrase, and eloquence therin. But before in age, if not also in noble, courtlie, and lustrous English, is that of the songs, and Sonnets of Henrie Howard, E. of Surrey (sonn of that victorious prince, the Duke of Norfolk, and father of that learned Howard his most livelie image, Henrie Earl of Northampton) written chiefly by him, and by Sr. Thomas Wyat, not the daungerous Commotioner, but his worthie father. Nevertheless they who most commend those poems, and exercises of honorable witt, if they have seen that incomparable Earl of Surrey his English translation of Vergils Æneids, which for a book, or two, hee admirably rendreth, almost line for line, will bear mee witnesse that those others were but foils, and sportives. The English poems of Sr. Walter Raleigh, of John Donn, of Hugh Holland, but speciallie of Sr. Foulk Grevile, in his matchlesse Mustapha, are not easelie to bee mended.

I dare not presume to speak of his Maties exercises in this heroick kind. Because I see them all lefte out in that edition, wch. Montague, lord Bishop of Winchester hath given us of his roial writings.

But if I should declare mine owne rudenesse rudely, I should then confesse, that I never tasted English more to my liking, nor more smart, and put to the heighth of use in poetrie, then in that vital, judicious, and most practicable language of Benjamin Jonsons poems.[3]

---

3 [In ms. Rawlinson D. 1—a late (1625) copy of an early outline for *Hypercritica*—this list of authors includes an item not in other texts: "Shakespeare, Mr. Francis Beaumont, and innumerable other writers for the stage, and presse tenderly to be used in this argument." Bolton means that the historian should use such writers warily, if at all.]

4. I hope nowe that no man will bee so captious, or ungentle, as to make it a matter of quarel to mee, if I have left out many other for want of memorie, or knowledg of them: or if in those of whom herein I have made mention, I have spoken either other, or otherwise then as they themselves would. Because it is enough that I dissemble not; and for that the subject, to the purpose wherof I bring this tumultuarie Catalogue, and private free opinion upon it, is rather Parergon,[4] then the thing it selfe I write of. For though it bee honor, and necessitie that the body of man bee cloathed, yet that it should bee cloathed in this, or that stuff, or in stuff of this, or that fashion, is a poinct indifferent, & arbitrarie at the writers pleasure, so as truthe bee under. And this is the present case of cloathing the bodie of Historie in the garment of English idiom.

· · ·

7. God almightie, I hope, hath now gratiously brought me to the conclusion of this high, and Hypercritical argument, which to his glorie I cloze up with this final admonition to my self, or to whosoever else doth meditate the Herculean, and trulie noble labour of composing an entire, and complete body of English affairs, a corpus rerum Anglicarum, a general Historie of England, to which not only the exquisite knowledge of our own matters is altogether necessarie, but of all other our neighbours whosoever, yea of all the world, for where our armes, and armies have not beene, our arts, and Navies have. Knowe therefore whosoever art in love with glorie for good, & heroick desarts, that in writing an Historie thou bearest a fowr fowld person; and in regard of that empersonation, thou standest charged w[th.] a fowr fowld dutie.

1. As a Christian Cosmopolite to discover Gods assistences, disappoinctments, and overrulings in human affairs, as hee is sensiblie conversant in the actions of men; to establish the just feare of his celestial Ma.[tie], against Atheists, and Voluptuaries, for the general good of mankinde, and the world.

2. As a Christian Patriot to disclose the causes, and authors of

---

4 [Something accessory or subordinate; also a "Herculean . . . labour" (see below, Section 7) not usually numbered among the standard twelve labors of Hercules.]

all thy countreys good, or evill to establish therby the lawful
libertie of nations.

3. As a Christian Subject to observe to thy reader, the benefit
of obedience, and damage of rebellions; to establish therby the
regular authoritie of Monarcks, and peoples safetie.

4. As a Christian Paterfamilias so to order thy studies, that
thou neglect not thy private, because the publick hath few real
friends; and labours of this noble nature are fitter to get renown
then riches, which they will need not amplifie.

8. Of such writings thou needest not fain with Dio, the consul
of Rome, any promise in vision, that thy name, & praise shall
bee immortal by meanes of them. For they will outlast the nations themselves, whose acts in competent style they memorize.
And of such works the late Earl of Essex under the letters A.B.
(for fame gives it him) in an Epistle before the translated [T]aci-
tus of his friend, S^r· Henrie Savile, it is as probablie pronounced
for true, as if an Oracle had uttered it: That there is no treasure
so much enriches the minde of man as learning; there is no
learning so proper for the direction of the life of man as Historie; there is no Historie so well worth reading (I say not with
him) as Tacitus, but as that of thine whosoever.

DEO GRATIAS

Michael Drayton

1563–1631

Drayton—there is no evidence of his having attended a university—
apparently began writing verse while in the service of Sir Henry
Goodere, whose daughter Anne was the "Idea" of the sonnets; later
patrons included Sir Walter Aston and the Countess of Bedford.
"Among schollers, souldiers, poets, and all sorts of people," says
Francis Meres, Drayton "is helde for a man of vertuous disposition,
honest conversation, and well-governed carriage." Popular as well as
prolific, he was quoted at least a hundred and fifty times in Englands
Parnassus alone; he was pre-eminently a craftsman, continually engaged in revising and enlarging, as with the gigantic loco-descriptive
Poly-Olbion, which had been begun by 1598, came out some fifteen
years later, and then was largely revised in 1622. His literary acquaintance included the younger Spenserians—Drummond, Wither,
William Browne—and his criticism, like his verse, stands in the
tradition of Spenser and Sidney; the verse-epistle to Reynolds, "Of
Poets and Poesie," is constructed on the venerable principle of the
roll call of poets and is chiefly remarkable for its personal reminis-
cences and Horatian tone.

The text comes from the 1627 edition of the poems.

To my most dearely-loved friend
HENERY REYNOLDS Esquire, of
Poets and Poesie
[*1627*]

My dearely loved friend how oft have we,
In winter evenings (meaning to be free,)
To some well chosen place us'd to retire;
And there with moderate meate, and wine, and fire,
Have past the howres contentedly with chat,
Now talk'd of this, and then discours'd of that,
Spoke our owne verses 'twixt our selves if not
Other mens lines, which we by chance had got,
Or some Stage pieces famous long before,
Of which your happy memory had store;
And I remember you much pleased were,
Of those who lived long agoe to heare,
As well as of those, of these latter times,
Who have inricht our language with their rimes,
And in succession, how still up they grew,
Which is the subject, that I now pursue;
For from my cradle (you must know that) I,
Was still inclin'd to noble Poesie,
And when that once *Pueriles*[1] I had read,
And newly had my *Cato*[2] construed,
In my small selfe I greatly marveil'd then,
Amonst all other, what strange kinde of men
These Poets were; And pleased with the name,

1 [*Sententiae Pueriles*, a manual of Latin "sentences" used by Renaissance
schoolboys.]
2 [The *Disticha de Moribus*, in the Renaissance thought to be by Cato the
Elder, is, like the *Pueriles*, an elementary manual.]

To my milde Tutor merrily I came,
(For I was then a proper goodly page,
Much like a Pigmy, scarse ten yeares of age)
Clasping my slender armes about his thigh.
O my deare master! cannot you (quoth I)
Make me a Poet, doe it; if you can,
And you shall see, Ile quickly be a man,
Who me thus answered smiling, boy quoth he,
If you'le not play the wag, but I may see
You ply your learning, I will shortly read
Some Poets to you; *Phœbus* be my speed,
Too't hard went I, when shortly he began,
And first read to me honest *Mantuan*.[3]
Then *Virgils Eglogues*, being entred thus,
Me thought I straight had mounted *Pegasus*,
And in his full Careere could make him stop,
And bound upon *Parnassus* by-clift top.
I scornd your ballet then though it were done
And had for Finis, *William Elderton*.[4]
But soft, in sporting with this childish jest,
I from my subject have too long digrest,
Then to the matter that we tooke in hand,
Jove and *Apollo* for the *Muses* stand.

    That noble *Chaucer*, in those former times,
The first inrich'd our *English* with his rimes,
And was the first of ours, that ever brake,
Into the *Muses* treasure, and first spake
In weighty numbers, delving in the Mine
Of perfect knowledge, which he could refine,
And coyne for currant, and as much as then
The *English* language could expresse to men,
He made it doe; and by his wondrous skill,
Gave us much light from his abundant quill.

    And honest *Gower*, who in respect of him,
Had only sipt at *Aganippas* brimme,
And though in yeares this last was him before,
Yet fell he far short of the others store.

    When after those, foure ages very neare,

3 [Baptista Spagnuoli (1448–1516), born at Mantua, whose Latin pastorals
served as a textbook.]
4 [A ballad-writer, attorney in Sheriff's Court, leader of a group of comedians;
he wrote "scurile balates" on the execution of Campion the Jesuit martyr in
1581.]

They with the Muses which conversed, were
That Princely *Surrey*, early in the time
Of the Eight *Henry*, who was then the prime
Of *Englands* noble youth; with him there came
Wyat; with reverence whom we still doe name
Amongst our Poets, *Brian*[5] had a share
With the two former, which accompted are
That times best makers, and the authors were
Of those small poems, which the title beare,
Of songs and sonnets, wherein oft they hit
On many dainty passages of wit.

   Gascoine and *Churchyard* [6] after them againe
In the beginning of *Eliza's* raine,
Accoumpted were great Meterers many a day,
But not inspired with brave fier, had they
Liv'd but a little longer, they had seene,
Their workes before them to have buried beene.

   Grave morrall *Spencer* after these came on
Then whom I am perswaded there was none
Since the blind *Bard* his *Iliads* up did make,
Fitter a taske like that to undertake,
To set downe boldly, bravely to invent,
In all high knowledge, surely excellent.

   The noble *Sidney*, with this last arose,
That *Heroe* for numbers, and for Prose.
That throughly pac'd our language as to show,
The plenteous *English* hand in hand might goe
With *Greeke* and *Latine*, and did first reduce
Our tongue from *Lillies* writing then in use;
Talking of Stones, Stars, Plants, of fishes, Flyes,
Playing with words, and idle Similies,
As th' *English*, Apes and very Zanies be
Of every thing, that they doe heare and see,
So imitating his ridiculous tricks,
They spake and writ, all like meere lunatiques.

   Then *Warner*[7] though his lines were not so trim'd,
Nor yet his Poem so exactly lim'd
And neatly joynted, but the Criticke may
Easily reproove him, yet thus let me say;

5 [Sir Francis Bryan (d. 1550), courtier, diplomat, and poet.]
6 [George Gascoigne (1539?–77), critic, translator, and poet. Thomas Church-
yard (1520?–1604), a good literary hack, best known for *Shore's Wife* (1563).]
7 [William Warner (1558?–1609), author of *Albion's England*.]

For my old friend, some passages there be
In him, which I protest have taken me,
With almost wonder, so fine, cleere, and new
As yet they have bin equalled by few.

    Neat *Marlow* bathed in the *Thespian* springs
Had in him those brave translunary things,
That the first Poets had, his raptures were,
All ayre, and fire, which made his verses cleere,
For that fine madnes still he did retaine,
Which rightly should possesse a Poets braine.

    And surely *Nashe*, though he a Proser were
A branch of Lawrell yet deserves to beare,
Sharply *Satirick* was he, and that way
He went, since that his being, to this day
Few have attempted, and I surely thinke
Those words shall hardly be set downe with inke;
Shall scorch and blast, so as his could, where he,
Would inflict vengeance, and be it said of thee,
Shakespeare thou hadst as smooth a Comicke vaine,
Fitting the socke, and in thy naturall braine,
As strong conception, and as Cleere a rage,[8]
As any one that trafiqu'd with the stage.

    Amongst these *Samuel Daniel*, whom if I
May spake of, but to sensure doe denie,
Onely have heard some wisemen him rehearse,
To be too much *Historian* in verse;
His rimes were smooth, his meeters well did close
But yet his maner better fitted prose:
Next these, learn'd *Johnson*, in this List I bring,
Who had drunke deepe of the *Pierian* spring,
Whose knowledge did him worthily prefer,
And long was Lord here of the Theater,
Who in opinion made our learn'st to sticke,
Whether in Poems rightly dramatique,
Strong *Seneca* or *Plautus*, he or they,
Should beare the Buskin, or the Socke away.
Others againe here lived in my dayes,
That have of us deserved no lesse praise
For their translations, then the daintiest wit
That on *Parnassus* thinks, he highst doth sit,
And for a chaire may mongst the Muses call,

8 [Poetic inspiration.]

As the most curious maker of them all;
As reverent *Chapman*, who hath brought to us,
Musæus, Homer, and *Hesiodus*
Out of the Greeke; and by his skill hath reard
Them to that height, and to our tongue endear'd,
That were those Poets at this day alive,
To see their bookes thus with us to survive,
They would think, having neglected them so long,
They had bin written in the *English* tongue.

    And *Silvester* who from the *French* more weake,
Made *Bartas*[9] of his sixe dayes labour speake
In naturall *English*, who, had he there stayd,
He had done well, and never had bewraid,
His owne invention, to have bin so poore
Who still wrote lesse, in striving to write more.

    Then dainty *Sands*[1] that hath to *English* done,
Smooth sliding *Ovid,* and hath made him run
With so much sweetnesse and unusuall grace,
As though the neatnesse of the *English* pace,
Should tell the jetting *Lattine* that it came
But slowly after, as though stiffe and lame.

    So *Scotland* sent us hither, for our owne
That man, whose name I ever would have knowne,
To stand by mine, that most ingenious knight,
My *Alexander,*[2] to whom in his right,
I want extreamely, yet in speaking thus
I doe but shew the love, that was twixt us,
And not his numbers which were brave and hie,
So like his mind, was his cleare Poesie,
And my deare *Drummond* to whom much I owe
For his much love, and proud I was to know,
His poesie, for which two worthy men,
I *Menstry* still shall love, and *Hauthorne-den,*
Then the two *Beamounts* and my *Browne*[3] arose,
My deare companions whom I freely chose

---

9 [Guillaume de Salluste, sieur du Bartas (1544–90), began publishing the hexameral *Semaines* in 1578, and Joshua Sylvester (1563–1618) first collected his translations as *Bartas: His Divine Weekes and Workes* in 1605.]
1 [George Sandys (1578–1644) began publishing his translation of the *Metamorphoses* in 1621.]
2 [Sir William Alexander (1567?–1640), Scottish statesman and poet.]
3 [William Browne (1591–1643?), pastoral poet. Of the three literary Beaumonts—Joseph (1616–99), Francis (1584?–1616), and Sir John (1583?–1627) —it seems clear that the latter two are meant.]

My bosome friends; and in their severall wayes,
Rightly borne Poets, and in these last dayes,
Men of much note, and no lesse nobler parts,
Such as have freely tould to me their hearts,
As I have mine to them; but if you shall
Say in your knowledge, that these be not all
Have writ in numbers, be inform'd that I
Only my selfe, to these few men doe tye,
Whose workes oft printed, set on every post,
To publique censure subject have bin most;
For such whose poems, be they ne're so rare,
In private chambers, that incloistered are,
And by transcription daintyly must goe;
As though the world unworthy were to know,
Their rich composures,[4] let those men that keepe
These wonderous reliques in their judgement deepe,
And cry them up so, let such Peeces bee
Spoke of by those that shall come after me,
I passe not for them: nor doe meane to run,
In quest of these, that them applause have wonne,
Upon our Stages in these latter dayes,
That are so many, let them have ther bayes
That doe deserve it; let those wits that haunt
Those publique circuits, let them freely chaunt
Their fine Composures, and their praise pursue
And so my deare friend, for this time adue.

[4] [I.e., compositions.]

John Milton

1608–74

There is no need in this instance for a rehearsal of biographical fact, but the peculiar nature of Milton's contribution to literary criticism deserves brief notice. At St. Paul's, and to a lesser degree at Cambridge, Milton received the Christian-classical training of the day, which he then supplemented with a rigorous program of self-education in order to learn, as he advised others in 1644, "that sublime art which in Aristotle's Poetics, in Horace, and the Italian commentaries of Castelvetro, Tasso, Mazzoni, and others teaches what the laws are of a true epic poem, what of a dramatic, what of a lyric." Given such a background, together with the classical and Renaissance rhetoricians Milton read as a matter of course, it may seem strange that a man of his temperament and interests did not in any way aspire to the kind of literary dictatorship exercised by Ben Jonson. Although Milton wrote treatises on education and the art of logic, he left no formal criticism as such, not even a practical ars poetica of the kind Gascoigne provided in his Certayne Notes of Instruction: mainly what we possess is instead by way of lordly apologetic, as in the prefaces to Paradise Lost and Samson Agonistes, or consists of quasi-biographical utterances that appear with fervid abruptness in the course of arguments against episcopacy. In the last analysis, Milton is a literary critic who explains, if he "explains" anything at all, only himself, for it is in the nature of the poetic theory to which he gave his allegiance that the relationship of the vates with the "Heavenly Muse" must in the

end remain as undefinable as the source of the relationship itself.
The texts are based on The Works of John Milton, *ed. F. A. Patterson et al.,* Columbia University Press, 1931–38.

ANNO ÆTATIS 19. *At a Vacation Exercise*
in the Colledge, *part* LATIN, *part* ENGLISH.
The LATIN *speeches ended, the* ENGLISH
thus began
[1628]

Hail native Language, that by sinews weak
Didst move my first endeavouring tongue to speak,
And mad'st imperfect words with childish tripps,
Half unpronounc't, slide through my infant-lipps,
Driving dum silence from the portal dore,
Where he had mutely sate two years before:
Here I salute thee and thy pardon ask,
That now I use thee in my latter task:
Small loss it is that thence can come unto thee,
I know my tongue but little Grace can do thee:
Thou needst not be ambitious to be first,
Believe me I have thither packt the worst:
And, if it happen as I did forecast,
The daintiest dishes shall be serv'd up last.
I pray thee then deny me not thy aide
For this same small neglect that I have made:
But haste thee strait to do me once a Pleasure,
And from thy wardrope bring thy chiefest treasure;
Not those new fangled toys, and triming sight
Which takes our late fantasticks with delight,
But cull those richest Robes, and gay'st attire

Which deepest Spirits, and choicest Wits desire:
I have some naked thoughts that rove about
And loudly knock to have their passage out;
And wearie of their place do only stay
Till thou hast deck't them in thy best aray;
That so they may without suspect or fears
Fly swiftly to this fair Assembly's ears;
Yet I had rather, if I were to chuse,
Thy service in some graver subject use,
Such as may make thee search thy coffers round,
Before thou cloath my fancy in fit sound:
Such where the deep transported mind may soare
Above the wheeling poles, and at Heav'ns dore
Look in, and see each blissful Deitie
How he before the thunderous throne doth lie,
Listening to what unshorn *Apollo* sings
To th' touch of golden wires, while *Hebe* brings
Immortal Nectar to her Kingly Sire:
Then passing through the Spherse of watchful fire,
And mistie Regions of wide air next under,
And hills of Snow and lofts of piled Thunder,
May tell at length how green-ey'd *Neptune* raves,
In Heav'ns defiance mustering all his waves;
Then sing of secret things that came to pass
When Beldam Nature in her cradle was;
And last of Kings and Queens and *Hero's* old,
Such as the wise *Demodocus* once told
In solemn Songs at King *Alcinous* feast,
While sad *Ulisses* soul and all the rest
Are held with his melodious harmonie
In willing chains and sweet captivitie.
But fie my wandring Muse how thou dost stray!
Expectance calls thee now another way,
Thou know'st it must be now thy only bent
To keep in compass of thy Predicament:[1]
Then quick about thy purpos'd business come,
That to the next I may resign my Roome.

1 [Referring to the Aristotelian "categories" that Milton played with in the
"Vacation Exercise."]

TRANSLATED FROM

A LETTER TO CHARLES DIODATI
[*September or November 1637*]

What besides God has resolved concerning me I know not, but this at least: He has instilled into me, if into any one, a vehement love of the beautiful. Not with so much labour, as the fables have it, is Ceres said to have sought her daughter Proserpina as it is my habit day and night to seek for this idea of the beautiful, as for a certain image of supreme beauty, through all the forms and faces of things (for many are the shapes of things divine)[1] and to follow it as it leads me on by some sure traces which I seem to recognize. Hence it is that, when any one scorns what the vulgar opine in their depraved estimation of things, and dares to feel and speak and be that which the highest wisdom throughout all ages has taught to be best, to that man I attach myself forthwith by a kind of real necessity, wherever I find him. If, whether by nature or by my fate, I am so circumstanced that by no effort and labour of mine can I myself rise to such an honour and elevation, yet that I should always worship and look up to those who have attained that glory, or happily aspire to it, neither gods nor men, I reckon, have bidden nay.

But now I know you wish to have your curiosity satisfied. You make many anxious inquiries, even as to what I am at present thinking of. Hearken, Theodotus, but let it be in your private ear, lest I blush; and allow me for a little to use big language with you. You ask what I am thinking of? So may the good Deity help me, of immortality! And what am I doing? Growing my wings and meditating flight; but as yet our Pegasus raises himself on very tender pinions. Let us be lowly wise!

1 [A tag line from Euripides.]

FROM

The Reason of Church-Government

URG'D AGAINST PRELATY

[*January or February* 1642]

. . . I would be heard only, if it might be, by the elegant &
learned reader, to whom principally for a while I shal beg leav I
may addresse my selfe. To him it will be no new thing though I
tell him that if I hunted after praise by the ostentation of wit and
learning, I should not write thus out of mine own season, when I
have neither yet compleated to my minde the full circle of my
private studies, although I complain not of any insufficiency to
the matter in hand, or were I ready to my wishes, it were a folly
to commit any thing elaborately compos'd to the carelesse and
interrupted listening of these tumultuous times. Next if I were
wise only to mine own ends, I would certainly take such a subject as of it self might catch applause, whereas this hath all the
disadvantages on the contrary, and such a subject as the publishing whereof might be delayd at pleasure, and time enough to
pencill it over with all the curious touches of art, even to the
perfection of a faultlesse picture, whenas in this argument the
not deferring is of great moment to the good speeding, that if
solidity have leisure to doe her office, art cannot have much.
Lastly, I should not chuse this manner of writing wherin knowing my self inferior to my self, led by the genial power of nature
to another task, I have the use, as I may account it, but of my
left hand. And though I shall be foolish in saying more to this
purpose, yet since it will be such a folly, as wisest men going
about to commit, have only confest and so committed, I may
trust with more reason, because with more folly to have courte-
ous pardon. For although a Poet soaring in the high region of his
fancies with his garland and singing robes about him might
without apology speak more of himself then I mean to do, yet for
me sitting here below in the cool element of prose, a mortall

thing among many readers of no Empyreall conceit,[1] to venture and divulge unusual things of my selfe, I shall petition to the gentler sort, it may not be envy to me. I must say therefore that after I had from my first yeeres by the ceaselesse diligence and care of my father, whom God recompence, bin exercis'd to the tongues, and some sciences, as my age would suffer, by sundry masters and teachers both at home and at the schools, it was found that whether ought was impos'd me by them that had the overlooking, or betak'n to of mine own choise in English, or other tongue, prosing or versing, but chiefly this latter, the stile by certain vital signes it had, was likely to live. But much latelier in the privat Academies of *Italy*, whither I was favor'd to resort, perceiving that some trifles which I had in memory, compos'd at under twenty or thereabout (for the manner is that every one must give some proof of his wit and reading there) met with acceptance above what was lookt for, and other things which I had shifted in scarsity of books and conveniences to patch up amongst them, were receiv'd with written Encomiums, which the Italian is not forward to bestow on men of this side the *Alps*, I began thus farre to assent both to them and divers of my friends here at home, and not lesse to an inward prompting which now grew daily upon me, that by labour and intent study (which I take to be my portion in this life) joyn'd with the strong propensity of nature, I might perhaps leave something so written to aftertimes, as they should not willingly let it die. These thoughts at once possess me, and these other. That if I were certain to write as men buy Leases, for three lives and downward, there ought no regard be sooner had, then to Gods glory by the honour and instruction of my country. For which cause, and not only for that I knew it would be hard to arrive at the second rank among the Latines, I apply'd my selfe to that resolution which *Ariosto* follow'd against the perswasions of *Bembo*, to fix all the industry and art I could unite to the adorning of my native tongue; not to make verbal curiosities the end, that were a toylsom vanity, but to be an interpreter & relater of the best and sagest things among mine own Citizens throughout this Iland in the mother dialect. That what the greatest and choycest wits of *Athens, Rome,* or modern *Italy,* and those He-

1 [I.e., thought.]

brews of old did for their country, I in my proportion with this
over and above of being a Christian, might doe for mine: not
caring to be once nam'd abroad, though perhaps I could attaine to
that, but content with these British Ilands as my world, whose
fortune hath hitherto bin, that if the Athenians, as some say,
made their small deeds great and renowned by their eloquent
writers, *England* hath had her noble atchievments made small by
the unskilfull handling of monks and mechanicks.

Time servs not now, and perhaps I might seem too profuse to
give any certain account of what the mind at home in the spacious circuits of her musing hath liberty to propose to her self,
though of highest hope, and hardest attempting, whether that
Epick form whereof the two poems of *Homer,* and those other
two of *Virgil* and *Tasso* are a diffuse, and the book of *Job* a brief
model: or whether the rules of *Aristotle* herein are strictly to be
kept, or nature to be follow'd, which in them that know art, and
use judgement is no transgression, but an inriching of art. And
lastly what K.[ing] or Knight before the conquest might be
chosen in whom to lay the pattern of a Christian *Heroe.* And as
Tasso gave to a Prince of *Italy* his chois whether he would command him to write of *Godfreys* expedition against the infidels, or
Belisarius against the Gothes, or *Charlemain* against the Lom-
bards; if to the instinct of nature and the imboldning of art
ought may be trusted, and that there be nothing advers in our
climat, or the fate of this age, it haply would be no rashnesse
from an equal diligence and inclination to present the like offer
in our own ancient stories. Or whether those Dramatick constitutions, wherein *Sophocles* and *Euripides* raigne shall be found
more doctrinal and exemplary to a Nation, the Scripture also
affords us a divine pastoral Drama in the Song of *Salomon* consisting of two persons and a double *Chorus,* as *Origen* rightly
judges. And the Apocalyps of Saint *John* is the majestick image
of a high and stately Tragedy, shutting up and intermingling her
solemn Scenes and Acts with a sevenfold *Chorus* of Halleluja's
and harping symphonies: and this my opinion the grave authority of *Pareus*[2] commenting that booke is sufficient to confirm. Or

2 [David Pareus (1548–1622), German theologian whose exegetical work (1628)
on the Book of Revelations Milton read with care; he could also have found
in Pareus the reference to Origen and the Song of Solomon.]

if occasion shall lead to imitat those magnifick Odes and Hymns wherein *Pindarus* and *Callimachus* are in most things worthy, some others in their frame judicious, in their matter most an end faulty: But those frequent songs throughout the law and prophets beyond all these, not in their divine argument alone, but in the very critical art of composition may be easily made appear over all the kinds of Lyrick poesy, to be incomparable. These abilities, wheresoever they be found, are the inspired guift of God rarely bestow'd, but yet to some (though most abuse) in every Nation: and are of power beside the office of a pulpit, to inbreed and cherish in a great people the seeds of vertu, and publick civility, to allay the perturbations of the mind, and set the affections in right tune, to celebrate in glorious and lofty Hymns the throne and equipage of Gods Almightinesse, and what he works, and what he suffers to be wrought with high providence in his Church, to sing the victorious agonies of Martyrs and Saints, the deeds and triumphs of just and pious Nations doing valiantly through faith against the enemies of Christ, to deplore the general relapses of Kingdoms and States from justice and Gods true worship. Lastly, whatsoever in religion is holy and sublime, in vertu amiable, or grave, whatsoever hath passion or admiration in all the changes of that which is call'd fortune from without, or the wily suttleties and refluxes of mans thoughts from within, all these things with a solid and treatable smoothnesse to paint out and describe. Teaching over the whole book of sanctity and vertu through all the instances of example with such delight to those especially of soft and delicious temper who will not so much as look upon Truth herselfe, unlesse they see her elegantly drest, that whereas the paths of honesty and good life appear now rugged and difficult, though they be indeed easy and pleasant, they would then appeare to all men both easy and pleasant though they were rugged and difficult indeed. And what a benefit this would be to our youth and gentry, may be soon guest by what we know of the corruption and bane which they suck in dayly from the writings and interludes of libidinous and ignorant Poetasters, who having scars ever heard of that which is the main consistence of a true poem, the choys of such persons as they ought to introduce, and what is morall and decent to each one, doe for the most part lap up vitious principles

in sweet pils to be swallow'd down, and make the tast of vertuous documents harsh and sowr. But because the spirit of man
cannot demean it selfe lively in this body without some recreat-
ing intermission of labour, and serious things, it were happy for
the Common wealth, if our Magistrates, as in those famous governments of old, would take into their care, not only the decid-
ing of our contentious Law cases and brauls, but the managing
of our publick sports, and festival pastimes, that they might be,
not such as were autoriz'd a while since, the provocations of
drunkennesse and lust, but such as may inure and harden our
bodies by martial exercises to all warlike skil and performance,
and may civilize, adorn and make discreet our minds by the
learned and affable meeting of frequent Academies, and the pro-
curement of wise and artfull recitations sweetned with eloquent
and gracefull inticements to the love and practice of justice,
temperance and fortitude, instructing and bettering the Nation at
all oportunities, that the call of wisdom and vertu may be heard
every where, as *Salomon* saith, *She crieth without, she uttereth*
her voice in the streets, in the top of high places, in the chief
concours, and in the openings of the Gates.[3] Whether this may
not be not only in Pulpits, but after another persuasive method,
at set and solemn Paneguries,[4] in Theaters, porches, or what
other place, or way may win most upon the people to receiv at
once both recreation, & instruction, let them in autority consult. The thing which I had to say, and those intentions which
have liv'd within me ever since I could conceiv my self any
thing worth to my Countrie, I return to crave excuse that urgent
reason hath pluckt from me by an abortive and foredated discovery. And the accomplishment of them lies not but in a power
above mans to promise; but that none hath by more studious
ways endeavour'd, and with more unwearied spirit that none
shall, that I dare almost averre of my self, as farre as life and
free leasure will extend, and that the Land had once infranchis'd
her self from this impertinent yoke of prelaty, under whose in-
quisitorius and tyrannical duncery no free and splendid wit can
flourish. Neither doe I think it shame to covnant with any knowing reader, that for some few yeers yet I may go on trust with

3 [Proverbs 1:20–21 and 8:2.]
4 [Public assemblies.]

him toward the payment of what I am now indebted, as being a work not to be rays'd from the heat of youth, or the vapours of wine, like that which flows at wast from the pen of some vulgar Amorist, or the trencher fury of a riming parasite, nor to be obtain'd by the invocation of Dame Memory and her Siren daughters, but by devout prayer to that eternall Spirit who can enrich with all utterance and knowledge, and sends out his Seraphim with the hallow'd fire of his Altar to touch and purify the lips of whom he pleases:[5] to this must be added industrious and select reading, steddy observation, insight into all seemly and generous arts and affaires, till which in some measure be compast, at mine own peril and cost I refuse not to sustain this expectation from as many as are not loath to hazard so much credulity upon the best pledges that I can give them. Although it nothing content me to have disclos'd thus much before hand, but that I trust hereby to make it manifest with what small willingnesse I endure to interrupt the pursuit of no lesse hopes then these, and leave a calme and pleasing solitarynes fed with cherful and confident thoughts, to imbark in a troubl'd sea of noises and hoars disputes, put from beholding the bright countenance of truth in the quiet and still air of delightfull studies to come into the dim reflexion of hollow antiquities sold by the seeming bulk, and there be fain to club quotations with men whose learning and beleif lies in marginal stuffings, who when they have like good sumpters laid ye down their hors load of citations and fathers at your dore, with a rapsody of who and who were Bishops here or there, ye may take off their packsaddles, their days work is don, and episcopacy, as they think, stoutly vindicated.

5 [See Isaiah 6:1–7.]

FROM

An Apology Against a Pamphlet

CALL'D A MODEST CONFUTATION
OF THE ANIMADVERSIONS UPON THE REMONSTRANT
AGAINST SMECTYMNUUS [1]
[*April 1642*]

. . . I had my time Readers, as others have, who have good learning bestow'd upon them, to be sent to those places, where the opinion was it might be soonest attain'd: and as the manner is, was not unstudied in those authors which are most commended; whereof some were grave Orators & Historians; whose matter me thought I lov'd indeed, but as my age then was, so I understood them; others were the smooth Elegiack Poets,[2] whereof the Schooles are not scarce. Whom both for the pleasing sound of their numerous writing, which in imitation I found most easie; and most agreeable to natures part in me, and for their matter which what it is, there be few who know not, I was so allur'd to read, that no recreation came to me better welcome. For that it was then those years with me which are excus'd though they be least severe, I may be sav'd the labour to remember ye. Whence having observ'd them to account it the chiefe glory of their wit, in that they were ablest to judge, to praise, and by that could esteeme themselves worthiest to love those high perfections which under one or other name they took to celebrate, I thought with my selfe by every instinct and presage of nature which is not wont to be false, that what imboldn'd them to this task might with such diligence as they us'd imbolden me, and that what judgement, wit, or elegance was my share, would herein best appeare, and best value it selfe, by how much more

1 [The initials of the five Presbyterian ministers who wrote *An Answer to . . .* "*An Humble Remonstrance*" (1641), which occasioned Robert or Edward Hall's *A Modest Confutation*, which in turn occasioned Milton's *Apology* for "Smectymnuus."]
2 [Poets like Ovid, who wrote in "smooth Elegiack" meter.]

wisely, and with more love of vertue I should choose (let rude eares be absent) the object of not unlike praises. For albeit these thoughts to some will seeme vertuous and commendable, to others only pardonable, to a third sort perhaps idle, yet the mentioning of them now will end in serious. Nor blame it Readers, in those yeares to propose to themselves such a reward, as the noblest dispositions above other things in this life have sometimes preferr'd. Whereof not to be sensible, when good and faire in one person meet, argues both a grosse and shallow judgement, and withall an ungentle, and swainish brest. For by the firme setling of these perswasions I became, to my best memory, so much a proficient, that if I found those authors any where speaking unworthy things of themselves; or unchaste of those names which before they had extoll'd, this effect it wrought with me, from that time forward their art I still applauded, but the men I deplor'd; and above them all preferr'd the two famous renowners[3] of *Beatrice* and *Laura* who never write but honour of them to whom they devote their verse, displaying sublime and pure thoughts, without transgression. And long it was not after, when I was confirm'd in this opinion, that he who would not be frustrate of his hope to write well hereafter in laudable things, ought him selfe to bee a true Poem, that is, a composition, and patterne of the best and honourablest things; not presuming to sing high praises of heroick men, or famous Cities, unlesse he have in himselfe the experience and the practice of all that which is praise-worthy.

[3] [Dante and Petrarch.]

JOHN MILTON

FROM

Paradise Lost

FROM BOOK III
[*1667*]

Hail holy Light, ofspring of Heav'n first-born,
Or of th' Eternal Coeternal beam
May I express thee unblam'd? since God is light,
And never but in unapproached light
Dwelt from Eternitie, dwelt then in thee,
Bright effluence of bright essence increate.
Or hear'st thou rather pure Ethereal stream,
Whose Fountain who shall tell? before the Sun,
Before the Heavens thou wert, and at the voice
Of God, as with a Mantle didst invest
The rising world of waters dark and deep,
Won from the void and formless infinite.
Thee I re-visit now with bolder wing,
Escap't the *Stygian* Pool, though long detain'd
In that obscure sojourn, while in my flight
Through utter and through middle darkness borne
With other notes then to th' *Orphean* Lyre
I sung of *Chaos* and *Eternal Night,*
Taught by the heav'nly Muse to venture down
The dark descent, and up to reascend,
Though hard and rare: thee I revisit safe,
And feel thy sovran vital Lamp; but thou
Revisit'st not these eyes, that rowle in vain
To find thy piercing ray, and find no dawn;
So thick a drop serene hath quencht thir Orbs,
Or dim suffusion veild. Yet not the more
Cease I to wander where the Muses haunt
Cleer Spring, or shadie Grove, or Sunnie Hill,
Smit with the love of sacred Song; but chief

Thee *Sion* and the flowrie Brooks beneath
That wash thy hallowd feet, and warbling flow,
Nightly I visit: nor somtimes forget
Those other two equal'd with me in Fate,
So were I equal'd with them in renown,
Blind *Thamyris* and blind *Mæonides,*
And *Tiresias* and *Phineus* Prophets old.[1]
Then feed on thoughts, that voluntarie move
Harmonious numbers; as the wakeful Bird
Sings darkling, and in shadiest Covert hid
Tunes her nocturnal Note. Thus with the Year
Seasons return, but not to me returns
Day, or the sweet approach of Ev'n or Morn,
Or sight of vernal bloom, or Summers Rose,
Or flocks, or heards, or human face divine;
But cloud in stead, and ever-during dark
Surrounds me, from the chearful wayes of men
Cut off, and for the Book of knowledg fair
Presented with a Universal blanc
Of Natures works to mee expung'd and ras'd,
And wisdome at one entrance quite shut out.
So much the rather thou Celestial light
Shine inward, and the mind through all her powers
Irradiate, there plant eyes, all mist from thence
Purge and disperse, that I may see and tell
Of things invisible to mortal sight.

1 [Thamyris, Thracian bard; Maeonides, Homer; Tiresias, the famous Theban soothsayer; Phineus, blind Thracian prophet, mentioned in Milton's Letter to Philaras.]

F R O M

Paradise Lost

THE VERSE
[*1668*]

The Measure is *English* Heroic Verse without Rime, as that of *Homer* in *Greek,* and of *Virgil* in *Latin;* Rime being no necessary Adjunct or true Ornament of Poem or good Verse, in longer Works especially, but the Invention of a barbarous Age, to set off wretched matter and lame Meeter; grac't indeed since by the use of some famous modern Poets, carried away by Custom, but much to thir own vexation, hindrance, and constraint to express many things otherwise, and for the most part worse then else they would have exprest them. Not without cause therefore some both *Italian* and *Spanish* Poets of prime note have rejected Rime both in longer and shorter Works, as have also long since our best *English* Tragedies, as a thing of it self, to all judicious ears, triveal and of no true musical delight; which consists onely in apt Numbers, fit quantity of Syllables, and the sense variously drawn out from one Verse into another, not in the jingling sound of like endings, a fault avoyded by the learned Ancients both in Poetry and all good Oratory. This neglect then of Rime so little is to be taken for a defect, though it may seem so perhaps to vulgar Readers, that it rather is to be esteem'd an example set, the first in *English,* of ancient liberty recover'd to Heroic Poem from the troublesom and modern bondage of Rimeing.

FROM

Samson Agonistes

OF THAT SORT OF DRAMATIC POEM
WHICH IS CALL'D TRAGEDY
[1671]

Tragedy, as it was antiently compos'd, hath been ever held the gravest, moralest, and most profitable of all other Poems: therefore said by *Aristotle* to be of power by raising pity and fear, or terror, to purge the mind of those and such like passions, that is to temper and reduce them to just measure with a kind of delight, stirr'd up by reading or seeing those passions well imitated. Nor is Nature wanting in her own effects to make good his assertion: for so in Physic things of melancholie hue and quality are us'd against melancholy, sowr against sowr, salt to remove salt humours. Hence Philosophers and other gravest Writers, às *Cicero, Plutarch* and others, frequently cite out of Tragic Poets, both to adorn and illustrate thir discourse. The Apostle *Paul* himself thought it not unworthy to insert a verse of *Euripides* into the Text of Holy Scripture, I *Cor.* 15. 33.[1] and *Paræus* commenting on the *Revelation,*[2] divides the whole Book as a Tragedy, into Acts distinguisht each by a Chorus of Heavenly Harpings and Song between. Heretofore Men in highest dignity have labour'd not a little to be thought able to compose a Tragedy. Of that honour *Dionysius* the elder was no less ambitious, then before of his attaining to the Tyranny. *Augustus Cæsar* also had begun his *Ajax,* but unable to please his own judgment with what he had begun, left it unfinisht. *Seneca* the Philosopher is by

1 [The proverbial "evil communications corrupt good manners" has been attributed both to Euripides and Menander.]
2 [*Operum Theologicorum* (1628), II, 1077. As translated in 1644, Pareus has u chapter "Touching the Forme of the Revelation."]

some thought the Author of those Tragedies (at lest the best of them) that go under that name. *Gregory Nazianzen* a Father of the Church, thought it not unbeseeming the sanctity of his person to write a Tragedy, which he entitl'd, *Christ suffering*.[3] This is mention'd to vindicate Tragedy from the small esteem, or rather infamy, which in the account of many it undergoes at this day with other common Interludes; hap'ning through the Poets error of intermixing Comic stuff with Tragic sadness and gravity; or introducing trivial and vulgar persons, which by all judicious hath bin counted absurd; and brought in without discretion, corruptly to gratifie the people. And though antient Tragedy use no Prologue,[4] yet using sometimes, in case of self defence, or explanation, that which *Martial* calls an Epistle; in behalf of this Tragedy coming forth after the antient manner, much different from what among us passes for best, thus much beforehand may be Epistl'd; that *Chorus* is here introduc'd after the Greek manner, not antient only but modern, and still in use among the *Italians*. In the modelling therefore of this Poem, with good reason, the Antients and *Italians* are rather follow'd, as of much more authority and fame. The measure of Verse us'd in the Chorus is of all sorts, call'd by the Greeks *Monostrophic,* or rather *Apolelymenon*,[5] without regard had to *Strophe, Antistrophe* or *Epod,* which were a kind of Stanza's fram'd only for the Music, then us'd with the Chorus that sung; not essential to the Poem, and therefore not material; or being divided into Stanza's or Pauses, they may be call'd *Allæostropha*.[6] Division into Act and Scene referring chiefly to the Stage (to which this work never was intended) is here omitted.

It suffices if the Whole Drama be found not produc't beyond the fift Act, of the style and uniformitie, and that commonly call'd the Plot, whether intricate or explicit, which is nothing indeed but such œconomy, or disposition of the fable as may stand best with verisimilitude and decorum; they only will best judge who are not unacquainted with *Æschulus, Sophocles,* and *Euripides,* the three Tragic Poets unequall'd yet by any, and

3 [Attributed during the Renaissance to Gregory Nazianzen, fourth-century Bishop of Constantinople.]
4 [I.e., a prose defense or explanation accompanying the play.]
5 [Transliterating a Greek term meaning "loose" or "free."]
6 [Having stanzas of varying form.]

the best rule to all who endeavour to write Tragedy. The circum-
scription of time wherein the whole Drama begins and ends, is
according to antient rule, and best example, within the space of
24 hours.

Sir Kenelm Digby

1603–65

One of those totally improbable figures who appear so frequently in
the period, Digby did—or tried to do, or represented himself as having
done—almost everything: discovered the need of plants for oxygen;
defeated in 1628 the combined French and Venetian fleets in the
harbor of Scanderoon; was ever desired of the ladies, most embarrass-
ingly, it seems, by Marie de Medicis; fought many men singlehanded
and successfully, for right was on his side; made a proper woman of
the famous Lady Venetia, reputed no mean task, though Digby held
it as a matter of recorded principle that a good man and lusty could
make an honest woman of a bawdy house; published a crotchety
attack on Browne's Religio Medici, as he was an expert who had himself produced treatises on the body and the immortality of the soul;
touted the "powder of sympathy," which could cure all wounds; and
wrote his "Memoirs" after the manner of the Greek romances, figur-
ing himself under the name "Theagenes."

Digby's criticism of Browne is theological rather than literary, but
besides the "Observations" (reprinted here) there exist in manuscript
another treatise on Spenser and one on the nature of poetry in general. Both these last are addressed to Thomas May and reveal Digby's
allegiance to the principles of neo-Platonism; neither possesses the
interest of the "Observations," which is unique in its explication of
ideas, its emphasis on detailed analysis. This early venture into explication of text and the history of ideas reveals, moreover, what is

*rarely revealed: that some Renaissance poetry was learnedly obscure
even to that convenient fiction of modern scholarship—The Renaissance Reader.*

With his characteristic sprezzatura, *Digby represents the "Observations" as the work of a few minutes, dashed off to oblige Sir Edward
Stradling; probably written in 1628, Digby revised and published it
while in prison in 1643; it is reprinted here from the edition of 1644.*

OBSERVATIONS

ON THE 22. *Stanza* IN THE 9TH

CANTO OF THE 2D. BOOK OF

SPENCERS FAERY QUEENE,

WRITTEN BY THE REQUEST

OF A FRIEND

[*1628?*]

My most honour'd Friend,

I am too well acquainted with the weaknesses of mine abilities
(far unfit to undergo such a Task as I have in hand) to flatter
my self with the hope I may either inform your understanding,
or do my self honour by what I am to write. But I am so desirous you should be possest with the true knowledge of what a
bent will I have upon all occasions to do you service, that obedience to your command weigheth much more with me, then the
lawfulnesse of any excuse can, to preserve me from giving you
in writing such testimonie of my ignorance and erring Phantasie
as I fear this will prove. Therefore without any more circumstance, I will, as I can, deliver to you in this paper, what th' other
day I discoursed to you upon the 22. Staffe of the ninth *Canto* in

the second Book of that matchlesse Poem, *The Faery Queen,*
written by our English *Virgil*; whose words are these:

> *The Frame thereof seem'd partly Circular,*
> *And part Triangular: O work divine!*
> *Those two the first and last proportions are;*
> *The one, imperfect, mortall, feminine;*
> *Th' other immortal, perfect, masculine;*
> *And twixt them both a Quadrate was the Base,*
> *Proportion'd equally by seven and nine;*
> *Nine was the Circle set in Heavens place,*
> *All which compacted made a goodly Diapase.*

In this Staffe the Author seems to me to proceed in a different
manner from what he doth elsewhere generally through his
whole Book. For in other places, although the beginning of his
Allegory or mysticall sense, may be obscure, yet in the processe
of it, he doth himself declare his own conceptions in such sort as
they are obvious to any ordinarie capacitie: But in this, he seems
onely to glance at the profoundest notions that any Science can
deliver us, and then on a sudden (as it were) recalling himself
out of an Enthusiasme, he returns to the gentle Relation of the
Allegoricall History he had begun, leaving his Readers to wander
up and down in much obscuritie, & to come within much danger
of erring at his Intention in these lines. Which I conceive to be
dictated by such a learned Spirit, and so generally a knowing
Soul, that were there nothing else extant of *Spencers* writing, yet
these few words would make me esteem him no whit inferiour to
the most famous men that ever have been in any age: as giving
an evident testimonie herein, that he was throughly verst in the
Mathematicall Sciences, in Philosophy, and in Divinity, to which
this might serve for an ample Theme to make large Commentaries upon. In my praises upon this subject, I am confident that
the worth of the Author will preserve me from this Censure, that
my Ignorance onely begets this Admiration, since he hath written nothing that is not admirable. But that it may appear I am
guided somewhat by my own Judgement (tho' it be a meane
one) and not by implicite Faith, and that I may in the best manner I can, comply with what you expect from me, I will no longer
hold you in suspense, but begin immediately, (tho' abruptly)

with the declaration of what I conceive to be the true sense of
this place, which I shall not go about to adorne with any plausible[1] discourses, or with Authorities and examples drawne from
others writings (since my want both of conveniency and learning would make me fall very short herein) but it shall be enough
for me to intimate mine own conceptions, and offer them up to
you in their own simple and naked form, leaving to your better
Judgement the examination of the weight of them, and after pe-
rusall of them, beseeching you to reduce[2] them and me if you
perceive us erring.

Tis evident that the Authors intention in this *Canto* is to describe the bodie of a man inform'd with a rationall soul, and in
prosecution of that designe he sets down particularly the severall
parts of the one and of the other: But in this *Stanza* he comprehends the generall description of them both, as (being joyned
together to frame a compleat Man) they make one perfect compound, which will the better appear by taking a survey of every
severall clause thereof by it self.

> *The Frame thereof seemd partly Circular,*
> *And part Triangular—*

By these Figures, I conceive that he means the mind and body
of Man; the first being by him compared to a Circle, and the
latter to a Triangle. For as a Circle of all Figures is the most
perfect, and includeth the greatest space, and is every way full
and without Angles, made by the continuance of one onely line:
so mans soul is the noblest and most beautifull Creature, that
God hath created, and by it we are capable of the greatest gifts
that God can bestow, which are Grace, Glory, and Hypostaticall
Union of the Humane nature to the Divine, and she enjoyeth
perfect freedome and libertie in all her Actions, and is made
without composition, which no Figures are that have Angles (for
they are caus'd by the coincidence of severall lines) but of one
pure substance which was by God breath'd into a Body made of
such compounded earth as in the preceding *Stanza* the Author
describes. And this is the exact Image of him that breathed it,
representing him as fully as tis possible for any creature which

---

1 [I.e., worthy of applause.]
2 [I.e., reform and correct.]

is infinitely distant from a Creator. For, as God hath neither beginning nor ending: so, neither of these can be found in a Circle, although that being made of the successive motion of a line, it must be supposed to have a beginning somewhere: God is compared to a Circle whose Center is every where, but his circumference no where:[3] But mans soul is a Circle, whose circumference is limited by the true center of it, which is onely God. For as a circumference doth in all parts alike respect that indivisible Point, and as all lines drawn from the inner side of it, do make right Angles within it, when they meet therein: so all the interiour actions of mans soul ought to have no other respective Point to direct themselves unto, but God; and as long as they make right Angles, which is, that they keep the exact middle of virtue, and decline not to either of the sides where the contrary vices dwell, they cannot fail, but meet in their Center. By the Triangular Figure he very aptly designes the body: for as the Circle is of all other Figures the most perfect and most capacious: so the Triangle is most imperfect, and includes least space. It is the first and lowest of all Figures; for fewer then 3 right Angles cannot comprehend and inclose a superficies, having but 3 angles they are all acute (if it be equilaterall) and but equall to 2 *right*; in which respect all other regular Figures consisting of more then 3 lines, do exceed it.

(May not these be resembled to the 3 great compounded Elements in mans bodie, to wit, Salt, Sulphur and Mercurie, which mingled together make the naturall heat and radicall moysture, the 2 qualities whereby man liveth?) For the more lines that go to comprehend the Figure, the more and the greater the Angles are, and the nearer it comes to the perfection and capacitie of a Circle. A Triangle is composed of severall lines, and they of Points, which yet do not make a quantitie by being contiguous to one another: but rather the motion of them doth describe the lines. In like manner the Body of man is compounded of the foure Elements which are made of the foure primarie qualities, not compounded of them (for they are but Accidents) but by

---

3 [This is the second of twenty-four definitions of God contained in the twelfth-century *Liber xxiv philosophorum*, attributed in the Renaissance to Hermes Trismegistus; but the idea also appears in Dionysius Areopagitica, Dante, Alanus, Ficino, Browne, and elsewhere. The definition lies behind the esthetics as well as the ethics of the period.]

their operation upon the first matter. And as a Triangle hath three lines, so a solid Body hath three dimensions, to wit, Longitude, Latitude and Profunditie. But of all bodies, Man is of the lowest rank, (as the Triangle is among Figures) being composed of the Elements which make it liable to alteration and corruption. In which consideration of the dignitie of bodies, I divide them by a generall division, into sublunarie (which are the elementated ones) and Æthereall, which are supposed to be of their own nature, incorruptible, and peradventure there are some other *species* of corporeall substances, which is not of this place to dispute.

O work divine!

Certainly of all Gods works, the noblest and perfectest is Man, and for whom indeed all others were done. For, if we consider his *soul*, it is the very Image of God. If his *bodie*, it is adornd with the greatest beautie and most excellent symmetry of parts, of any created thing: whereby it witnesseth the perfection of the Architect, that of so drossie mold is able to make so rare a fabrick: If his *operations*, they are free: If his *end*, it is eternall glory. And if you take *all together*, Man is a little world, an exact type of the great world, and of God himself. But in all this, me thinks, the admirablest work is the joyning together of the two *different* and indeed *opposite* substances in Man, to make one perfect compound; the *Soul* and the *Body*, which are of so contrary a nature, that their *uniting* seems to be a Miracle. For how can the one inform and work in the other, since there's no mean of operation (that we know of) between a spirituall substance and a corporeall? yet we see that it doth: as hard it is to find the true proportion betweene a Circle and a Triangle; yet, that there is a just proportion, and that they may be equall, *Archimedes* hath left us an ingenious demonstration; but in reducing it to a Probleme, it fails in this, that because the proportion between a crooked line and a straight one, is not known, one must make use of a Mechanick way of measuring the *peripherie* of the one, to convert it to the side of the other.

These two the first and last proportions are.

What I have already said concerning a Circle and a Triangle, doth sufficiently unfold what is meant in this verse. Yet twill not be amisse to speak one word more hereof in this place. All things that have existence, may be divided into three *Classes*; which are, either what is pure and simple in it self, or what hath a nature compounded of what is simple, or what hath a nature compounded of what is compounded. In continued quantitie this may be exemplified by a Point, a line, and a superficies in Bodies: and in numbers, by an unity, a Denary, and a Centenary. The first, which is onely pure & simple, like an indivisible point, or an unity, hath relation onely to the Divine nature: That point then moving in a sphericall manner (which serves to expresse the perfection of Gods actions) describes the Circles of our souls, and of Angels, and intellectuall substances, which are of a pure and simple nature, but receiveth that from what is so, in a perfecter manner, and that hath his, from none else. Like lines that are made by the flowing of points; or Denaries that are composed of Unities: beyond both which there is nothing. In the last place, Bodies are to be rankt, which are composed of the Elements: and they likewise suffer composition, and may very well be compared to the lowest of the Figures which are composed of lines, that owe their being to Points (and such are Triangles) or to Centenaries that are composed of Denaries, and they of Unities. But if we will compare these together by proportion, God must be left out, since there is as infinite distance betweene the Simplicitie and Perfection of his nature, and the composition and imperfection of all created substances, as there is between an indivisible Point and a continuate quantitie, or between a simple Unitie and a compounded number. So that onely the other two kinds of substance do enter into this consideration: and of them I have already proved, that mans Soul is of the one the noblest, (being dignified by hypostaticall Union above all other intellectuall substances) and his elementated Body, of the other the most low and corruptible. Whereby it is evident, that those two are the first and last Proportions, both in respect of their own Figure, and of what they expressed.

The one imperfect, Mortall, Feminine:
Th' other immortall, perfect, Masculine.

Mans Body hath all the proprieties[4] of imperfect matter. It is but the Patient: of it self alone, it can do nothing: it is liable to corruption and dissolution if it once be deprived of the form which actuates it, and which is incorruptible and immortall. And as the feminine Sex is imperfect, and receives perfection from the masculine: so doth the Body from the Soul, which to it is in lieu of a male. And as in corporall generations the female affords but grosse and passive matter, to which the Male gives active heat and prolificall vertue: so in spiritual generations (which are the operations of the minde) the body administers onely the Organs, which if they were not imployed by the Soul, would of them selves serve for nothing. And as therein a mutuall appetence between the Male and the Female, betweene matter and forme; So there is betweene the bodie and the soul of Man, but what ligament they have, our Author defineth not (and it may be Reason is not able to attaine to it) yet he tels us what is the foundation that this Machine rests on, and what keeps the parts together; in these words.

And twixt them both, a Quadrate was the Base.

By which Quadrate, I conceive, that he meaneth the foure principall humors in mans Bodie, *viz. Choler, Blood, Phleme,* and *Melancholy*: which if they be distempered and unfitly mingled, dissolution of the whole doth immediately ensue: like to a building which falls to ruine, if the foundation and Base of it be unsound or disordered. And in some of these, the vitall spirits are contained and preserved, which the other keep in convenient temper; and as long as they do so, the soul and bodie dwell together like good friends: so that these foure are the Base of the conjunction of the other two, both which he saith, are

Proportion'd equally by seven and nine.

In which words, I understand he meanes the influences of the superior substances (which governe the inferiour) into the two differing parts of Man; to wit, of the *Starres* (the most powerfull of which, are the seven Planets, into his body: and of the Angels

4 [I.e., properties—here and throughout Digby.]

divided into nine Hierarchies or Orders) into his soul: which in
his *Astrophel*, he saith is

> *By soveraigne choice from th' heavenly Quires select,*
> *And lineally deriv'd from Angels race.*

And as much as the one governe the Body, so much the other
do the Minde. Wherein is to be considered, that some are of
opinion, how at the instant of a childs conception, or rather
more effectually at the instant of his Birth, the conceived sperme
or tender Body doth receive such influence of the Heavens as
then raigne over that place, where the conception or birth is
made: And all the Starres or virtuall places of the celestiall
Orbes participating the qualities of the seven Planets (according to which they are distributed into so many Classes, or the
compounds of them) it comes to passe, that according to the
varietie of the severall Aspects of the one and of the other, there
are various inclinations and qualities in mens bodies, but all reduced to seven generall heads and the compounds of them,
which being to be varied innumerable wayes, cause as many
different effects, yet the influence of some one Planet continually predominating. But when the matter in a womans wombe
is capable of a soul to inform it, then God sendeth one from
Heaven into it.

> *Eternall God,*
> *In Paradise whilome did plant this Flower,*
> *Whence he it fetcht out of her native place,*
> *And did in Stock of earthly flesh inrace.*

And this opinion the Author more plainly expresses himself to
be of, in another work, where he saith:

> *There she beholds with high aspiring thought*
> *The cradle of her own Creation;*
> *Emongst the seats of Angels heavenly wrought . . .*

Which whether it have been created ever since the beginning
of the world, and reserv'd in some fit place till due time, or be
created on emergent occasion; no man can tell: but certain it is
that it is immortall, according to what I said before, when I

spake of the Circle which hath no ending, and an uncertain beginning. The messengers to conveigh which soul into the bodie, are the Intelligences which move the Orbes of Heaven, who according to their severall natures communicate to it severall proprieties: and they most, who are Governours of those Starres at that instant, who have the superioritie in the planetary aspects. Whereby it comes to passe, that in all inclinations there's much affinitie betweene the Soul and the Body, being that the like is betweene the Intelligences and the Starres, both which communicate their vertues to each of them. And these Angels, being, as I said before, of nine severall Hierarchies, there are so many principle differences in humane souls, which participate most of their proprieties, with whom in their descent they made the longest stay, and that had most active power to work on them, and accompanied them with a peculiar *Genius* (which is according to their severall Governments) like the same kind of water that running through various conduits wherein severall aromatike and odoriferous things are laid, do acquire severall kinds of tastes and smels. For it is supposed, that in their first Creation, all Souls are alike, and that their differing proprieties arive to them afterwards when they passe through the spheres of the governing Intelligences. So that by such their influence, it may truly be said, that

Nine was the Circle set in Heavens place.

Which verse, by assigning this office to the nine, and the proper place to the Circle, gives much light to what is said before. And for a further confirmation that this is the Authors opinion, read attentively the sixt *Canto* of the 3. Book, where most learnedly and at large he delivers the *Tenets* of this Philosophie; and for that, I commend to you to take particular notice of the 2d. and thirty two *Stanzaes:* as also the last of his *Epithalamion:* and survaying his works, you shall finde him a constant disciple of *Platoes* School.

All which compacted, made a goodly Diapase.

In Nature there is not to be found a more compleat and more exact Concordance of all parts, then that which is betweene the

compaction and conjunction of the Body and Soul of Man: Both
which although they consist of many and most different faculties and parts, yet when they keepe due time with one another,
they altogether make the most perfect Harmony that can be imagined. And as the nature of sounds, that consist of friendly
consonancies and accords, is to mingle themselves with one another, and to slide into the eare with much sweetnesse, where by
their unity they last a long time and delight it: where as contrar-
ily, discords continually jarre, and fight together, and will not
mingle with one another: but all of them striving to have the
victory, their reluctation and disorder gives a speedie end to
their sounds, which strike the Eare in a harsh and offensive
manner, and there die in the very beginning of their Conflict: In
like manner, when a mans Actions are regular, and directed towards God, they become like the lines of a Circle, which all meet
in the Center, then his musick is most excellent and compleat,
and all together are the Authors of that blessed harmony which
maketh him happie in the glorious vision of Gods perfections,
wherein the minde is filled with high knowledges and most
pleasing contemplations; and the senses, as it were, drowned in
eternall delight; and nothing can interrupt this Joy, this Happinesse, which is an everlasting Diapase: Whereas on the contrary, if a mans actions be disorderly, and consisting of discords,
(which is, when the sensitive part rebels and wrastles with the
Rationall, striving to oppresse it) then this musick is spoiled,
and instead of eternall life, pleasure and joy, it causeth perpetuall death, horrour, paine, and misery. Which infortunate estate
the Poet describes elsewhere; as in the conclusion of this Staffe
he intimates: the other happy one, which is the never-failing
Reward of such an obedient bodie, and ethereall and vertuous
minde, as he makes to be the seat of the bright virgin *Alma,* mans
worthiest inhabitant, *Reason. Her* I feele to speake within me,
and chide me for my bold Attempt, warning me to stray no further. For what I have said (considering how weakly it is said)
your Command is all the excuse that I can pretend. But since my
desire to obey that, may bee seene as well in a few lines, as in a
large Discourse, it were indiscretion in me to trouble you with
more, or to discover to you more of my Ignorance. I will onely
begge pardon of you for this blotted and interlined paper, whose

Contents are so meane that it cannot deserve the paines of a Transcription, which if you make difficulty to grant to it, for my sake, let it obtain it for having been yours.

And now I return to you also the Book that contains my Text, which yesterday you sent me, to fit this part of it with a Comment, which peradventure I might have performed better, if either I had afforded my selfe more time, or had had the conveniencie of some other books apt to quicken my Invention, to whom I might have been beholding for enlarging my understanding in some things that are treated here, although the Application should still have been my own: With these helps perhaps I might have dived further into the Authors Intention (the depth of which cannot be sounded by any that is lesse learned then he was). But I perswade my self very strongly, that in what I have said there's nothing contradictory to it, and that an intelligent and well learned man proceeding on my grounds might compose a worthie and true Commentarie on this Theme: Upon which I wonder how I stumbled, considering how many learned men have failed in the Interpretation of it, and have all at the first hearing, approved my opinion.

But it was Fortune that made me fall upon it, when first this *Stanza* was read to me for an indissoluble Riddle. And the same Discourse I made upon it, the first halfe quarter of an houre that I saw it, I send you here, without having reduced it to any better form, or added any thing at all unto it. Which I beseech you receive benignely, as coming from

> Your most affectionate Friend
> and humble Servant,
> *Kenelm Digby*

FINIS

William Drummond
of Hawthornden

1585–1649

*After attending Edinburgh, Drummond traveled extensively, then in
1610 became laird of Hawthornden; his retired life was thencefor-
ward devoted to reading widely, even in the lesser-known Continental
poets; to writing verse and prose, largely derivative; to speculations
on the tank and machine gun; and, in 1619, to the famous "Conversations" with Jonson. His poetry derives mainly from Petrarch and
Sidney, together with a host of smaller fry in the same tradition;
although he knew and appreciated certain aspects of Donne, it is not
surprising to find him, in the letter to Johnston, making an appeal
to "Nature" against the "Monsters" spawned by the wit of "Metaphysical" versifiers. Dryden was to express himself in much the same
manner toward the end of the century.*

*Arthur Johnston, who died in 1641, first described himself in print
as the King's physician in 1628; "To . . . Arthur Johnston, Physician to the King," reprinted here from the 1711 edition of Drummond's works, is undated, but the Letters accompanying it are mainly
from the 1620's.*

To his much honoured Friend Dr. Arthur Johnston, Physician to the KING

[c.1629]

It is more Praise-worthy in noble and excellent Things to know something, though little, than in mean and ignoble Matters to have a perfect Knowledge. Amongst all those rare Ornaments [of] the Mind of Man, *Poesy* hath had a most eminent Place, and been in high Esteem, not only at one Time, and in one Climate, but during all Times, and through all those Parts of the World, where any Ray of Humanity and Civility hath shined. So that she hath not unworthily deserved the Name of the Mistress of Humane Life, the Height of Eloquence, the Quintessence of Knowledge, the loud Trumpet of Fame, the Language of the Gods. There is not any Thing endureth longer: *Homer's Troy* hath out-lived many Republicks, and both the *Roman* and *Grecian* Monarchies; she subsisteth by her self; and after one Demeanor and Continuance her Beauty appeareth to all Ages. In vain have some Men of late (Transformers of every Thing) consulted upon her Reformation, and endeavoured to abstract her to *Metaphysical* Idea's, and *Scholastical* Quiddities, denuding her of her own Habits, and those Ornaments with which she hath amused the World some Thousand Years. *Poesy* is not a Thing that is yet in the finding and search, or which may be otherwise found out, being already condescended upon by all Nations, and as it were established *jure Gentium*, amongst *Greeks, Romans, Italians, French, Spaniards*. Neither do I think that a good Piece of *Poesy*, which *Homer, Virgil, Ovid, Petrarch, Bartas,*[1] *Ronsard,*

---

1 [Guillaume de Salluste Du Bartas (1544–90), author of the hexameral *Semaines. La Première Semaine* or *La Sepmaine* came out in 1578 and went through at least fifteen editions even before it was followed by the *Seconde Semaine* in 1584.]

Boscan,[2] *Garcilasso*[3] (if they were alive, and had that Language) could not understand, and reach the Sense of the Writer. Suppose these Men could find out some other new *Idea* like *Poesy*, it should be held as if Nature should bring forth some new *Animal*, neither Man, Horse, Lyon, Dog, but which had some Members of all, if they had been proportionably and by right Symmetry set together. What is not like the Ancients and conform to those Rules which hath been agreed unto by all Times, may (indeed) be something like unto *Poesy*, but it is no more *Poesy* than a Monster is a Man. Monsters breed Admiration at the First, but have ever some strange Loathsomness in them at last. I deny not but a Mulet is more profitable than some Horses, yet is it neither Horse nor Ass, and yet it is but a Mulet. There is a Tale told of a poor miserable Fellow accused of Bestality; and he at his Arraignment confessed, That it was not out of any evil Intention he had done it, but only to procreate a Monster, with which (having nothing to sustain his Life) he might win his Bread going about the Country. For the like Cause it may be thought these Men found out their new *Poesy* differing from the Matters, Manners, and Rules of former Ages; either they did not see the Way of *Poesy* or were afraid to enter it. The Verses of *Camillus Quernus* as they are imitated by *Strada*[4] seem very plausible[5] and to Admiration to some, but how far they are off right *Poesy* Children may guess. These Men's new Conceptions approach nearer his, than to the Majesty and Stateliness of the great Poets. The Contempt and Undervaluing of Verses hath made Men spare their Travel [6] in adorning them; but *Poesy*, as it hath overcome Ignorance, at last will overcome Envy and Contempt. This I have been bold to write unto you, not to give you any Instruction, but to manifest mine Obedience to your Request.

W. Drummond

2 [Juan Boscan Almogaver (1490?–1542), Catalan poet who adapted Italian meters to his Spanish poems.]
3 [Garcilaso de la Vega (1503–36), Spanish soldier and poet, whose verse was influenced by Italian models.]
4 [Camillo Querno (1470–1520), Italian poet; Famiano Strada (1572–1649), Italian man of letters probably best known for his *Prolusiones et paradigmata eloquentiae* (1617).]
5 [I.e., worthy of applause.]
6 [Travail or labor.]

Thomas Carew

1594/5–1639/40

*After attending Oxford and hesitating momentarily in the Middle
Temple, Carew entered the service of Sir Dudley Carleton, whom he
appears then to have slandered; the letters of the elder Carew, en-
treating forgiveness and reinstatement for his errant son, make up a
melancholy, unsuccessful series. But Carew's wit and person somehow recommended him to the Court, where his friends included
James Howell, Jonson, Suckling, George Sandys, Aurelian Townshend,
and William Davenant.*

Carew wrote a number of fine lyrics and a masque, Coelum Britan-
nicum, *but no formal literary criticism in prose. His commendatory
and elegiac verses are, however, remarkable for their sensitive appreciation of men so diverse as Davenant, Jonson, Sandys, and Donne.
"To Ben. Johnson," reprinted from Carew's Poems of 1640, forms
part of the controversy occasioned by Jonson's* New Inne, *acted in
1629, hissed from the stage, and truculently published in 1631;
Carew's poem, probably written in 1631 or '32, is notable for its san-
ity and mastery of tone. "An Elegie upon . . . Dr. John Donne,"
reprinted from Donne's Poems (1633), is referred to as early as 1632
and clearly influenced a number of the other elegies printed in 1633.
"To . . . Master Geo. Sands," reprinted from Carew's Poems (1640),
first appeared in* A Paraphrase upon the Divine Poems *(1638; colo-
phon 1637).*

To Ben. Johnson

Upon occasion of his Ode of defiance annext to his
Play of the new Inne

[*1631?*]

Tis true (deare *Ben:*) thy just chastizing hand
Hath fixt upon the sotted Age a brand
To their swolne pride, and empty scribbling due,
It can nor judge, nor write, and yet 'tis true
Thy commique Muse from the exalted line
Toucht by thy *Alchymist*, doth since decline
From that her Zenith, and foretells a red
And blushing evening, when she goes to bed,
Yet such, as shall out-shine the glimmering light
With which all stars shall guild the following night.
Nor thinke it much (since all thy Eaglets may
Endure the Sunnie tryall) if we say
This hath the stronger wing, or that doth shine
Trickt up in fairer plumes, since all are thine;
Who hath his flock of cackling Geese compar'd
With thy tun'd quire of Swans? or else who dar'd
To call thy births deformed? but if thou bind
By Citie-custome, or by *Gavell-kind*,[1]
In equall shares thy love on all thy race,
We may distinguish of their sexe, and place;
Though one hand form them, & though one brain strike
Soules into all, they are not all alike.
Why should the follies then of this dull age
Draw from thy Pen such an immodest rage
As seemes to blast thy (else-immortall) Bayes,

1 [Both legal jargon, having to do with laws of inheritance. By "Citie-custome" the inheritance is divided equally among wife, executors, and children; by "Gavell-kind" the division is equal among male children.]

When thine owne tongue proclaimes thy ytch of praise?
Such thirst will argue drouth. No, let be hurld
Upon thy workes, by the detracting world,
What malice can suggest; let the Rowte say,
The running sands, that (ere thou make a play)
Count the slow minutes, might a *Goodwin*[2] frame
To swallow when th'hast done thy ship-wrackt name.
Let them the deare expence of oyle upbraid
Suckt by thy watchfull Lampe, that hath betray'd
To theft the blood of martyr'd Authors, spilt
Into thy inke, whilst thou growest pale with guilt.
Repine not at the Tapers thriftie waste,
That sleekes thy terser Poems, nor is haste
Prayse, but excuse; and if thou overcome
A knottie writer, bring the bootie home;
Nor thinke it theft, if the rich spoyles so torne
From conquered Authors, be as Trophies worne.
Let others glut on the extorted praise
Of vulgar breath, trust thou to after dayes:
Thy labour'd workes shall live, when Time devoures
Th'abortive off-spring of their hastie houres.
Thou art not of their ranke, the quarrell lyes
Within thine owne Virge,[3] then let this suffice,
The wiser world doth greater Thee confesse
Then all men else, then Thy selfe onely lesse.

AN ELEGIE UPON THE DEATH OF THE
DEANE OF PAULS, DR. JOHN DONNE:
By *Mr. Tho: Carie*
[1632?]

Can we not force from widdowed Poetry,
Now thou art dead (Great DONNE) one Elegie
To crowne thy Hearse? Why yet dare we not trust
Though with unkneaded dowe-bak't prose thy dust,

2 [Goodwin Sands, off Ramsgate.]
3 [The area extending twelve miles around the King's court.]

Such as the uncisor'd [1] Churchman from the flower
Of fading Rhetorique, short liv'd as his houre,
Dry as the sand that measures it, should lay
Upon thy Ashes, on the funerall day?
Have we no voice, no tune? Did'st thou dispense
Through all our language, both the words and sense?
'Tis a sad truth; The Pulpit may her plaine,
And sober Christian precepts still retaine,
Doctrines it may, and wholesome Uses frame,
Grave Homilies, and Lectures, But the flame
Of thy brave Soule, that shot such heat and light,
As burnt our earth, and made our darknesse bright,
Committed holy Rapes upon our Will,
Did through the eye the melting heart distill;
And the deepe knowledge of darke truths so teach,
As sense might judge, what phansie could not reach;
Must be desir'd for ever. So the fire,
That fills with spirit and heat the Delphique quire,
Which kindled first by thy Promethean breath,
Glow'd here a while, lies quench't now in thy death;
The Muses garden with Pedantique weedes
O'rspred, was purg'd by thee; The lazie seeds
Of servile imitation throwne away;
And fresh invention planted, Thou didst pay
The debts of our penurious bankrupt age;
Licentious thefts, that make poëtique rage
A Mimique fury, when our soules must bee
Possest, or with Anacreons Extasie,
Or Pindars, not their owne; The subtle cheat
Of slie Exchanges, and the jugling feat
Of two-edg'd words, or whatsoever wrong
By ours was done the Greeke, or Latine tongue,
Thou hast redeem'd, and open'd Us a Mine
Of rich and pregnant phansie, drawne a line
Of masculine expression, which had good
Old Orpheus seene, Or all the ancient Brood
Our superstitious fooles admire, and hold
Their lead more precious, then thy burnish't Gold,
Thou hadst beene their Exchequer, and no more
They each in others dust, had rak'd for Ore.
Thou shalt yield no precedence, but of time,

1 [Uncut, unbarbered.]

And the blinde fate of language, whose tun'd chime
More charmes the outward sense; Yet thou maist claime
From so great disadvantage greater fame,
Since to the awe of thy imperious wit
Our stubborne language bends, made only fit
With her tough-thick-rib'd hoopes to gird about
Thy Giant phansie, which had prov'd too stout
For their soft melting Phrases. As in time
They had the start, so did they cull the prime
Buds of invention many a hundred yeare,
And left the rifled fields, besides the feare
To touch their Harvest, yet from those bare lands
Of what is purely thine, thy only hands
(And that thy smallest worke) have gleaned more
Then all those times, and tongues could reape before;
But thou art gone, and thy strict lawes will be
Too hard for Libertines in Poetrie.
They will repeale the goodly exil'd traine
Of gods and goddesses, which in thy just raigne
Were banish'd nobler Poems, now, with these
The silenc'd tales o'th' Metamorphoses
Shall stuffe their lines, and swell the windy Page,
Till Verse refin'd by thee, in this last Age,
Turne ballad rime, Or those old Idolls bee
Ador'd againe, with new apostasie;
Oh, pardon mee, that breake with untun'd verse
The reverend silence that attends thy herse,
Whose awfull solemne murmures were to thee
More then these faint lines, A loud Elegie,
That did proclaime in a dumbe eloquence
The death of all the Arts, whose influence
Growne feeble, in these panting numbers lies
Gasping short winded Accents, and so dies:
So doth the swiftly turning wheele not stand
In th'instant we withdraw the moving hand,
But some small time maintaine a faint weake course
By vertue of the first impulsive force:
And so whil'st I cast on thy funerall pile
Thy crowne of Bayes, Oh, let it crack a while,
And spit disdaine, till the devouring flashes
Suck all the moysture up, then turne to ashes.
I will not draw the envy to engrosse

All thy perfections, or weepe all our losse;
Those are too numerous for an Elegie,
And this too great, to be express'd by mee.
Though every pen should share a distinct part,
Yet art thou Theme enough to tyre all Art;
Let others carve the rest, it shall suffice
I on thy Tombe this Epitaph incise.

> *Here lies a King, that rul'd as hee thought fit*
> *The universall Monarchy of wit;*
> *Here lie two Flamens, and both those, the best,*
> *Apollo's first, at last, the true Gods Priest.*

To my worthy friend Master
GEO. SANDS, *on his translation of the Psalmes*
[*1637?*]

I Presse not to the Quire, nor dare I greet
The holy place with my unhallowed feet;
My unwasht Muse polutes not things Divine,
Nor mingles her prophaner notes with thine;
Here, humbly at the porch she stayes,
And with glad eares sucks in thy sacred layes.
So, devout penitents of Old were wont,
Some without dore, and some beneath the Font,
To stand and heare the Churches Liturgies,
Yet not assist the solemne exercise:
Sufficeth her, that she a lay-place gaine,
To trim thy Vestments, or but beare thy traine;
Though nor in tune, nor wing, she reach thy Larke,
Her Lyrick feet may dance before the Arke.[1]
Who knowes, but that her wandring eyes that run,
Now hunting Glow-wormes, may adore the Sun,
A pure flame may, shot by Almighty power
Into her brest, the earthy flame devoure.
My eyes, in penitentiall dew may steepe

[1] [2 Samuel vi. 13–14, where David dances before the Ark of God.]

That brine, which they for sensuall love did weepe.
So (though 'gainst Natures course) fire may be quencht
With fire, and water be with water drencht;
Perhaps my restlesse soule, tyr'de with persuit
Of mortall beauty, seeking without fruit
Contentment there, which hath not, when enjoy'd,
Quencht all her thirst, nor satisfi'd, though cloy'd;
Weary of her vaine search below, Above
In the first faire² may find th'immortall Love.
Prompted by thy example then, no more
In moulds of clay will I my God adore;
But teare those Idols from my heart, and write
What his blest Sprit, not fond Love shall indite;
Then, I no more shall court the verdant Bay,
But the dry leavelesse Trunke on *Golgotha;*
And rather strive to gaine from thence one Thorne,
Then all the flourishing wreathes by Laureats worne.

2 [I.e., God.]

Henry Reynolds

fl. 1628–32

A brief biographical sketch of Reynolds may have pretensions to completeness: he was the recipient, in 1627, of Drayton's "To my most dearely-loved friend Henery Reynolds Esquire, of Poets and Poesie"; in 1628 and 1632 he produced tales "imitated" from Anguillara's Ovid; he contributed to Lawes' Ayres and Dialogues; and in 1628 there appeared his Tasso's Aminta Englisht.

Mythomystes, dedicated to "Henry Lord Ma[l]trevers," was published undated but entered in the Stationers' Register 10 August 1632; and is reprinted here in entirety, with the exception of the dedication, an Appendix on the real reasons for Plato's having banished the poets, and the "annexed" tale of "Narcissus briefly mythologized." (Some remarks in the Appendix perhaps imply that the work circulated in manuscript before 1632: "The before-written Treatise of the dignity of the ould Poets and their Poesies, falling into the view of some not injudicious eyes. . . .") Reynolds' authorities are Philo, Reuchlin, Farra, and particularly Pico; partly as a result, Mythomystes, that extraordinary work, defines in unmistakable, if exaggerated, form the neo-Platonic and cabalistic tendencies that follow their subterranean courses throughout the period, and here intensify the grand debate between Ancients and Moderns.

Mythomystes

WHEREIN
A SHORT SURVAY
IS TAKEN OF THE
NATURE AND VALUE
OF TRUE POESY AND
DEPTH OF THE ANCIENTS
ABOVE OUR MODERNE
POETS
[*1632*?]

TO THE CANDID AND
INGENUOUS READER

*Looke not generous Reader (for such I write to) for more in the
few following leaves, then a plaine and simple verity; unadorned
at all with eloquution, or Rhetoricall phrase; glosses fitter perhaps to be set upon silken and thinne paradoxicall semblances,
then appertaining to the care of who desires to lay downe a
naked & unmasked Trueth. Nor expect heere an Encomium or
praise of any such thing as the world ordinarily takes Poësy for;
That same thing beeing (as I conceive) a superficiall meere out-
side of Sence, or gaye barke only (without the body) of Reason;
Witnesse so many excellent witts that have taken so much
paines in these times to defend her; which sure they would not
have done, if what is generally received now a dayes for Poësy,
were not meerely a faculty, or occupation of so little consequence, as by the lovers thereof rather to be (in their owne*

favour) excused, then for any good in the thing it selfe, to be
commended. Nor must thou heere expect thy solution, if thy curi-
osity invite thee to a satisfaction in any the under-Accidents, but
in meerely the Essentiall Forme, of true Poësy: Such I call the
Accidents or appendixes thereto, as conduce somewhat to the
Matter, and End, nothing to the reall Forme and Essence
thereof. And these accidents (as I call them) our commenders &
defenders of Poësy have chiefely, and indeed sufficiently in-
sisted, and dilated upon; and are first, those floures (as they are
called) of Rhetorick, consisting of their Anaphoras, Epistrophes,
Metaphors, Metonymyes, Synecdoches *and those their other po-*
tent Tropes and Figures; helpes, (if at all of use to furnish out
expressions with,) much properer sure, and more fitly belonging
to Poësy then Oratory; yet such helpes, as if Nature have not
beforehand in his byrth, given a Poët, all such forced Art will
come behind as lame to the businesse, and deficient, as the best-
taught countrey Morris dauncer with all his bells and napkins,
will ill deserve to be in an Inne of Courte at Christmas, tearmed
the thing they call a fine reveller. The other Accidents of Poësy,
and that are the greater part of the appurtenances thereof, in the
accoumpt of our Poëts of these times, are also heere utterly un-
mencioned; such as are, what sort of Poëme may admit the
blanke verse, what requires exacte rime; where the strong line (as
they call it) where the gentle, sortes best; what subject must have
the verse of so many feete, what of other; where the masculine
rime, where the feminine, and where the threesillabled (which
the Italians call their rime sdrucciole) *are to be used. These (I*
say) and the like Adjuncts of Poësy, (elsewhere amply dis-
coursed of by many curious witts) are not heere mencioned.
Only what I conceived fit to speake (and with what brevity I
could) of the Auncient Poëts in generall, and of the Forme and
reall Essence of true Poësy, considered meerely in its owne
worth and validity, without extrinsick and suppeditative orna-
ment at all, together with the paralell of their foyle (our Mod-
erne Poëts and Poësyes,) I have, (to the end to redeeme in
some parte, and vindicate that excellent Art from the injury it
suffers in the worlds generall misprizion and misconstruction
thereof,) heere touched, and but touched; the rather to awake
some abler understanding then my owne, to the pursute (if they

*please) of a theame (I conceive) well worthy a greater industry,
and happyer leisures then I my selfe possesse.*

I have thought upon the times wee live in; and am forced to
affirme the world is decrepit, and out of its age & doating estate,
subject to all the imperfections that are inseparable from that
wracke and maime of Nature, that the young behold with horror,
and the sufferers thereof lye under with murmur and languish-
ment. Even the generall Soule of this great Creature, whereof
every one of ours is a severall peece, seemes bedrid, as upon her
deathbed, and neere the time of her dissolution to a second better estate, and being: the yeares of her strength are past; and
she is now nothing but disease for the Soules health is no other
than meerely the knowledge of the Truth of things. Which
health, the worlds youth injoyed; and hath now[1] exchanged for
it, all the diseases of all errors, heresies, and different sects and
schismes of opinions and understandings in all matter of Arts,
Sciences, and Learnings whatsoever. To helpe on these diseases
to incurability, what age hath ever beene so fruitfull of liberty in
all kindes, and of all permission and allowance for this reason of
ours, to runne wildely all her owne hurtfullest wayes without
bridle, bound, or limit at all? For instance; what bookes have
wee of what ever knowledge, or in what mysteries soever, wisely
by our Aunatients (for avoiding of this present malady the world
is now falne into) couched, and carefully infoulded, but must
bee by every illiterate person without exception, deflowred and
broke open, or broke in pieces, because beyond his skill to unlocke them? Or what Law have we that provides for the restraint
of these myriads of hotheaded wranglers, & ignorant writers and
teachers, which, out of the bare priviledge of perhaps but puny
graduate in some University, will venter upon all, even the most
removed and most abstruse knowledges, as perfect understand-
ers and expounders of them, upon the single warrant of their
owne braine; or inventers of better themselves, than all Antiquity could deliver downe to them; out of the treasonous mint of
their owne imaginations? What havocke, what mischiefe to all
learnings, and how great a multiplicity of poysonous errours and

[1] *For the world hath lost his youth, and the times begin to waxe old.* 2 Esd.
cap. 14.

heresies must not of necessity hence ensue, and overspread the
face of all Truths whatsoever?

Among these heresies (to omit those in matter of Divinity, or
the right forme of worshipping God, which the Doctors of his
Church are fitter to make the subjects of their tongues and pens,
than I, a Layman, and all-unworthy the taske,) among, I say,
these, (if I may so call them) heresies, or ridiculous absurdities
in matter of humane letters, and their professors in these times,
I find none so grosse, nor indeed any so great scandall, or maime
to humane learning, as in the almost generall abuse, and violence offered to the excellent art of Poesye; first, by those learned
(as they thinke themselves) of our dayes, who call themselves
Poets; and next, by such as out of their ignorance, heede not how
much they prophane that high and sacred title in calling them
so.

From the number of these first mentioned, (for, for the last, I
will not mention them; nor yet say as a grave Father, and holy
one too, of certaine obstinate heretikes said; *Decipiantur in nom-
ine diaboli;*[2] but charitably wish their reformation, and cure of
their blindnesse;) from the multitude (I say) of the common
rimers in these our moderne times, and moderne tongues, I will
exempt some few, as of a better ranke and condition than the
rest. And first to beginne with *Spaine*. I will say it may justly
boast to have afforded (but many Ages since) excellent Poets, as
Seneca, the Tragedian, *Lucan*, and *Martiall* the Epigrammatist,
with others; and in these latter times, as diverse in Prose, some
good Theologians also in Rime, but for other Poesies in their
(now spoken) tongue, of any great name, (not to extoll their trifling, though extolled *Celestina*, nor the second part of their *Diana de Monte Maior*,[3] better much than the first; and these but
poeticke prosers neither,) I cannot say it affords many, if any at
all: The inclination of that people being to spend much more wit,
and more happily in those prose *Romances* they abound in, such
as their *Lazarillo, Don Quixote, Guzman*,[4] and those kind of *Cu-*

2 ["Let them be deceived in the name of the devil."]
3 [Fernando de Rojas' *Celestina* (1499) was Englished in 1631; Montemayor's
Diana, a pastoral romance, was published in English in 1598.]
4 [*Lazarillo de Tormes* (1553), the earliest example of the Spanish picaresque,
was Englished by David Rowland in 1586; Mateo Alemán's *Vida del Picaro
Guzmán de Alfarache* (1599) was translated by James Mabbe in 1623.]

enta's of their *Picaro's*, and *Gitanillas*, than in Rime. The *French* likewise, more than for a *Ronsart*, or *Des-Portes*, but chiefly their *Salust*,[5] (who may passe among the best of our modernes,) I can say little of. *Italy* hath in all times, as in all abilities of the mind besides, been much fertiler than either of these, in Poets. Among whom, (to omit a *Petrarch*, who though he was an excellent rimer in his owne tongue, and for his Latine *Africa* justly deserved the lawrell that was given him; yet was a much excellenter Philosopher in prose; and with him, a *Bembo, Dante, Ang: Politiano, Caporale, Pietro Aretino, Sannazaro, Guarini*,[6] and divers others, men of rare fancy all) I must preferre chiefely three; as the grave and learned *Tasso*, in his *Sette giorni*, (a divine worke) and his *Gierusalem liberata*, so farre as an excellent pile of meerely Morall Philosophy may deserve. Then, *Ariosto*, for the artfull woofe of his ingenious, though unmeaning fables; the best, perhaps, have in that kind beene sung since *Ovid*. And lastly, that smoothwrit *Adonis* of *Marino*,[7] full of various conception, and diversity of learning. The *Douche* I cannot mention, being a stranger to their minds, and manners; therefore I will returne home to my Countrey-men, and mother tongue: And heere, exempt from the rest, a *Chaucer*, for some of his poëms; chiefely his *Troylus* and *Cresside*. Then the generous and ingenious *Sidney*, for his smooth and artfull *Arcadia* (and who I could wish had choze rather to have left us of his pen, an Encomiasticke Poeme in honour, then prose-Apology in defence, of his favorite, the excellent Art of Poesy.) Next, I must approve the learned *Spencer*, in the rest of his Poëms, no lesse then his *Fairy Queene*, an exact body of the *Ethicke* doctrine: though some good judgments have wisht (and perhaps not without cause) that he had therein beene a little freer of his fiction, and not so close rivetted to his Morall; no lesse then many doe to *Daniells Civile warrs*, that it were (though otherwise a commendable worke) yet somwhat more than a true Chronicle history in rime; who, in other lesse laboured things, may have in-

5 [Guillaume de Salluste, sieur du Bartas (1544–90), author of the popular *Semaines*, was known in English through the versions of Joshua Sylvester.]
6 [Angelo Politian (1454–94), Florentine translator, critic, and poet; Cesare Caporali (1531–1601), writer of "mythological" satire; Pietro Aretino (1492–1556); Jacopo Sannazaro (1458–1530) wrote an early *Arcadia;* Baptista Guarini (1538–1612), author of *Pastor Fido* and rival of Tasso.]
7 [Giovanni Baptista Marino published the *Adone* in 1623.]

deed more happily, (how ever, always cleerely and smoothly) written. Wee have among us a late-writ *Polyolbion*, also and an *Agincourte*, wherin I will only blame their honest Authours[8] ill fate, in not having laid him out some happier Clime, to have given honour and life to, in some happier language. After these, (besides some late dead) there are others now living, drammaticke and liricke writers, that I must deservedly commend for those parts of fancy and imagination they possesse; and should much more, could wee see them somewhat more, force those gifts, and liberall graces of Nature, to the end shee gave them; and therewith, worke and constantly tire upon sollid knowledges; the which having from the rich fountes of our reverend Auncients, drawne with unwearied, and wholsomely imploied industries; they might in no lesse pleasing and profitable fictions than they have done (the very fittest conduit-pipes) derive downe to us the understanding of things even farthest remooved from us, and most worthy our speculation, and knowledge. But alas, such children of obedience, I must take leave to say, the most of our ordinary pretenders to Poesy now a dayes, are to their owne, and the diseased times ill habits, as the racke will not bee able to make the most advised among twenty of them confesse, to have farther inquired, or attended to more, in the best of their Authours they have chosen to read and study, than meerely his stile, phrase, and manner of expression; or scarce suffered themselves to looke beyond the dimension of their owne braine, for any better counsaile or instruction elsewhere. What can wee expect then of the Poems they write? Or what can a man mee thinks liken them more fitly to, than to *Ixion's* issue? for hee that with meerely a naturall veine, (and a little vanity of nature, which I can be content to allow a Poet) writes without other grounds of sollid learning, than the best of these ungrounded rimers understand or aime at, what does he more than imbrace assembled cloudes with *Ixion*, and beget only Monsters? This might yet be borne with, did not these people as confidently usurpe to themselves the title of Schollers, and learned men, as if they possest the knowledges of all the *Magi*, the wise East did ever breed; when, let me demand but a reason for secu-

8 [Michael Drayton.]

rity of my judgement in allowing them for such, they straite give mee to know they understand the *Greeke*, and *Latine*; and in conclusion, I discover, the compleate crowne of all their ambition is but to be stiled by others a good *Latinist* or *Grecian*, and then they stile themselves good Schollers. So would I too, had I not before hand beene taught to say: *Non quia Græca scias, vel calles verba Latina, Doctus es aut sapiens, sed quia vera vides;*[9] & besides, hapned to know a late travailing *Odcombian*[1] among us; that became (I know not for what mortaller sinne than his variety of language) the common scorne, and contempt of all the abusive witts of the time; yet possest both those languages in great perfection; as his eloquent orations in both toungs; (and uttered upon his owne head without prompting[2]) have ever sufficiently testified. Now, finding this to be the greater part of the Schollership these our Poets indeavour to have, and which many of them also have; I find with all, they sit downe as satisfied, as if their unfurnisht brests contained each one the learning and wisdome of an *Orpheus, Virgil, Hesiod, Pindarus,* and *Homer* altogether. When as, what have they else but the barke and cloathing meerely wherein their high and profound doctrines lay? Never looking farther into those their golden fictions for any higher sence, or any thing diviner in them infoulded & hid from the vulgar, but lulled with the mervellous expression & artfull contexture of their fables—*tanquam parvi pueri* (as one saies) *per brumam ad ignem sessitantes, aniles nugas fabellásque de Poëtis imbibunt, cum interim de utiliore sanctioréque sententia minime sunt solliciti.*[3]

I have staid longer, and rubde harder mee thinkes than needes, upon the sore of our now a day Poets. Let mee leave them, and looke backe to the never-enough honoured Auncients; and set them before our eyes, who no lesse deservedly wore the name of Prophets, and Privy-counsellors of the Gods (to use

9 ["You are not learned and wise because you may know Greek or may be well-versed in Latin but because you see the truth."]

1 [Thomas Coryate (1577?–1617), born at Odcombe, author of the *Crudities* (1611), which was accompanied by the *Odcombian Banquet.*]

2 *For they made him stand, and speake Greeke upon his head with his heeles upward.*

3 ["As little boys loiter by the fire through the winter, old women drink in the trifles and fables of poets, though in the meanwhile they remain not in the least concerned with more useful, more holy, thought."]

their owne phrase,[4] or Sonnes of the Gods, as *Plato*[5] calls them)
than Poets. To the end wee may, if in this declining state of the
world we cannot rectify our oblique one, by their perfect and
strait line, yet indeavour it: and in the meane time give the awe-
full reverence due to them, for the many regions of distance between their knowledges and ours. And this that wee may the
better doe, let us paralell them with the Poets (if I may so call
them) of our times, in three things only, and so carry along together their strait and our crooked line; for our better knowledge
of them, and reformation of our selves. In the first place then, let
us take a survay of their naturall inclination and propensenesse
to the acquisition of the knowledge of truth, by what is delivered
to us of them; as also, of their willing neglect, and aversion from
all worldly businesse and cogitations that might be hindrances in
the way to their desired end.

1. It is in humane experience found, as well as by all writers
determined, that the powerfullest of al the affects of the minde
is Love, and therefore the divine *Plato*[6] sayes, it is justly called
Roma; which among the Greeks, is force, potency, or vehe-
mence. Of this Love there be two kinds; Celestiall or Intellectuall; or else Carnall or Vulgar. Of both these kinds *Salomon* hath
spoken excellently; of the Vulgar, in his Proverbes as a Morall,
and in his Ecclesiastes as a Naturall Philosopher; and divine-like
of the divine and Intellectuall Love in his Canticle; for which it
is called among all the rest of the holy Scripture *Canticum canti-
corum,* as the most sacred and divine. The object of this Celestiall or Intellectuall Love, (for the other, or vulgar Love it concernes mee not to mention,) is the excellency of the Beauty of
Supernall and Intellectuall thinges: To the contemplation
whereof, rationall and wise Spirits are forcibly raised and lifted
aloft; yea lifted oftentimes so far (sayes *Plato*)[7] above mortal-
ity, as even—*in Deum transeunt,*[8] and so full fraught with the
delight and abondance of the pleasure they feele in those their
elevations, raptures, and mentall alienations (wherin the soule

---

4 *Hom. in Odiss.*
5 *De Repub. lib. 2.*
6 *In Phædro.*
7 *In Iöne.* [I.e., *Ion.*]
8 ["They are translated into God" (from Plato's *Ion*, probably by way of
Pico's or Ficino's commentary).]

remaines for a time quite seperated as it were from the body) do not only sing with the ingenious *Ovid: Est Deus in nobis, agitante calescimus illo,*[9] But in an Extaticke manner, and to use *Plato's*[1] phrase) *divino afflatu concitati,* cry out with the intraunced *Zoroaster—Ope thine eyes, ope them wide; raise and lift them aloft.* And of this, the excellent Prince *Jo: Picus-Mirandula,*[2] (in a discourse of his upon the doctrine of *Plato*) gives the reason; saying: *Such, whose understanding (being by Philosophicall studie refined and illuminated) knowes this sensible Beauty to bee but the image of another more pure and excellent, leaving the love of this, desire to see the other; and persevering in this elevation of the minde, arrive at last to that celestiall love; which although it lives in the understanding of the soule of every man, yet they only* (sayes he) *make use of it, and they are but few, who separating themselves wholy from the care of the body, seeme thence oftentimes extaticke, and as it were quite ravisht and exalted above the earth and all earthly amusements.* And farther, in another place[3] of that Treatise, adds that many with the fervent love of the beauty and excellence of intellectuall things, have beene so raized above all earthly considerations, as they have lost the use of their corporall eyes. *Homer* (sayes he) *with seeing the ghost of Achilles, which inspired him with that Poeticke fury, that who with understanding reades, shall find to containe in it all intellectuall contemplation, was thereby deprived* (or faigned to bee deprived) *of his corporall eye-sight,* as one that seeing all things above, could not attend to the heeding of triviall and meaner things below. And such rapture of the spirit, is exprest (saies he) *in the fable of Tyresias that Calimacus sings; who for having seene Pallas naked (which signifies no other than that Ideall beauty, whence proceeds all sincere wis-*

9 [Ovid, *Fasti* vi.5: "A God is in us, as he moves us we wax inspired."]
1 *In Iöne.* [In the *Ion* the poet is "quickened with divine afflatus."]
2 [Pico della Mirandola (1463–94), a brilliant syncretist who sought, in the manner of Ficino and the Florentine Academy, to reconcile Christianity with the arcane "wisdom of the ancients." The "discourse . . . upon . . . Plato," later referred to as "Treatise," is Pico's *Commento . . . Sopra Una Canzona de Amore . . . Seconde la Mente e Opinione de Platonici;* the three passages that Reynolds quotes in this paragraph may be found at III, 4 in the *Commento.* Pico's most famous work is the *Oration on the Dignity of Man.* A convenient modern edition, containing virtually all the materials on which Reynolds draws, is that of Eugenio Garin, *De Hominis Dignitate, Heptaplus, De Ente et Uno,* etc. (Florence, 1942).]
3 Fol. 507.

dome, and not cloathed or covered with corporall matter) be-
came sodainly blind, and was by the same Pallas made a
Prophet; so as that which blinded his corporall eyes, opened to
him the eyes of his understanding; by which he saw not only all
things past, but also all that were to come.

Loe, these, and such Spirits as these the learned *Picus*
speakes of, such were those of those Auncient Fathers of all
learning, and *Tyresia* like Prophets, as Poets: such their neglect
of the body, and businesse of the world! Such their blindnesse to
all things of triviall and inferiour condition; And such lastly
were those extaticke elevations; or that truly-*divinus furor* of
theirs, which *Plato*[4] speaking of sayes it is—*a thing so sacred,*
as—non sine maximo favore Dei comparari queat; cannot bee
attained to without the wonderfull favour of God. And which
selfe thing themselves ment in their fable of that beautifull *Gan-*
imede, they sing of, (which interpreted, is the Contemplation of
the Soule, or the Rationall part of Man) so deare to the God of
gods and men, as that he raiseth it up to heaven, there to powre
out to him (as they make him his cupbearer) the soveraigne
Nectar of Sapience and wisdome, the liquor he is onely best
pleased and delighted with. These were those fathers (as I lately
called them) and fountes of knowledge and learning; or nurses
of wisdome, from whose pregnant brests the whole world hath
suckt the best part of all the humane knowledge it it hath; And
from whose wise and excellent fables (as one our late Mythologians[5] truely notes) *All those were after them called Philosophers*
tooke their grounds and first *initia Philosophandi;* adding, that
their Philosophy was no other than meerely—*fabularum sensa*
ab involucris exuuiisque fabularum explicata—the senses and
meanings of fables taken out and seperated from their huskes
and involvements. With whom the excellent *Jo: Picus* (or rather
Phænix as wisemen[6] have named him) consenting, sayes in his
Apologia (speaking of the Poesies of *Zoroaster* and *Orpheus*)—

4 *In Iöne.* [*Ion.*]
5 *Nata: Comes.* [Natalis Comes, *Mythologiae, sive Explicationes Fabularum*
(1551), a popular Renaissance handbook.]
6 *Ang: Politianus,* (who likewise calls him—*Doctiorum omnium doctissimus,*)
["Most learned of all the learned." (And see previous note on Politian.)]
Pau: Jovius [Paulus Jovius or Paolo Giovio (1483–1552) wrote *Elogia Virorum*
Illustrium.], Baroaldus [Phillipo Beroaldo (1483–1505)], and our Sir *Tho:*
Moore, who (among infinite many others) hath voluminously write his praises,

*Orpheus apud Græcos fermè intiger; Zoroaster apud eos mancus,
apud Caldæos absolutior legitur. Ambo* (sayes he) *priscæ Sapientiæ patres & authores.*[7] Both of them fathers and authors of
the auncient Wisdome. With these also the most autenticke *Iamblicus,* the *Caldean,* who writes—*Pythagoras* had—*Orphicam
Theologiam tanquam exemplar, ad quam ipse suam effingeret
formaretque philosophiam;*[8] the Theology of *Orpheus* as his
coppy and patterne, by which hee formed and fashioned his philosophy. I will ad a word more of the before-cited *Picus;* who
thus far farther of *Orpheus* in particular sayes—*Secreta de Numeris doctrina, & quicquid magnum sublimèque habuit Græca
philosophia, ab Orphei institutis ut a primo fonte manavit,*[9] the
mysticall doctrine of Numbers, and what ever the Greeke philosophy had in it great and high, flowed all from the Institutions of
Orpheus, as from their first fount. And of the rest of his ranke
and fraternity, those *Sapientiæ patres, ac duces* (as *Plato*[1] calls
those old excellent Poets), I will conclude in generall, with the
testimony of first, the now-mentioned *Plato;* who sayes likewise
elsewhere[2] *Nihil aliud sunt quàm deorum interpretes;* they are
no other than the Interpreters of the gods. And in another place
that—their *præclara poemata non hominum sunt inventa, sed
cælestia munera.*[3] Their excellent Poëms are not the inventions of
men, but gifts and graces of heaven. And lastly with *Farra* the
learned *Alexandrian,* who speaking likewise of the old Poets,[4]
sayes—*Their fables are all full of most high Mysteries; and have
in them that splendor that is shed into the fancy and intellect,
ravisht, and inflamed with divine fury.* And in the same Trea-

---

7 [*Apology,* but see also *Oration on the Dignity of Man:* "Among the Greeks
Orpheus is read in a virtually complete text; Zoroaster is known only imperfectly, though among the Chaldeans he is read in a more complete text. Both
(sayes he) are fathers and authors of ancient wisdom." The *Oration,* intended
as an introduction to the public debate of Pico's "nine hundred theses," was
never delivered because of Papal disapproval. Pico, however, tried to justify the
"heretical" theses in a defense or *Apologia,* into which he incorporated almost
verbatim the second part of the *Oration.*]
8 [Again see Pico's *Oration on the Dignity of Man* (Reynolds himself translates
the passage in his text phrases).]
9 *In Apolog. fol.* 83. [*Apology,* but again see also the *Oration on the Dignity of
Man.* Reynolds' own translation follows the passage.]
1 ["The fathers and guides of wisdom."] *In Lyside.* [I.e., *Lysis.*]
2 *In Iöne.* [*Ion.*]
3 *In Phædro.*
4 *In Settena. Fol.* 320. [Alessandro Farra published *Settenario* in Venice in 1594.]

tise[5] makes this particular mention of some of them—*and in those times flourished Linus, Orpheus, Museus, Homer, Hesiod, and all the other most famous of that truly golden age.*

Now to apply this short view we have taken of these auncient Poets; whither there appeares ought in any our students, or writers of our times, be they Poets or Philosophers (I put them together, as who are, or should be both professors of but one, and the same learning, though by the one received and delivered in the apparell of verse, the other of prose,) that may in any degree of coherence suffer a paralell with either the Inclinations or Abilities of such as these before mentioned, I wish we could see cause to grant, but rather, that there is in them (for ought appeares) no such inclination to the love or search of any great or high truthes (for the Truthes sake, meerely) nor the like neglect of the world and blindnesse to the vanities thereof, in respect of it, nor lastly, any fruites from them, favouring of the like Industry, or bearing any shadow scarce of similitude with that of theirs, wee may positively affirme; as a truth no lesse obvious to every mans eye, than the lamentable cause and occasion thereof is to every mans understanding; which is the meane accoumpt, or rather contempt and scorne that in these dayes, all ungaining Sciences, & that conduce not immediately to worldly profit, or popular eminence, are held in the Poet especially.

> *Qual vaghezza di lauro, qual di mirto?*
> *Povera, e nuda vai filosofia,*
> *Dice la turba al vil guadagno intesa.*[6]

Whence it is, that much time spent in sollid contemplative studies is held vaine and unnecessary; and these slight flashes of ungrounded fancy, (ingenious Nothings, & meere imbroideries upon copwebbs) that the world swarmes with, (like sophisticate alchimy gold that will not abide the first touch, yet glitters more in the eye than the sadd weightyer true gold), are only laboured for and attended too; because they take best, and most please the corrupt tast and false appetite of the sordid and barbarous times

5 *fol.* 322.
6 [From Petrarch's "La gola e 'l sonno e 'oziose piume": "Is the love of laurel and mirtle gone? You go naked and poor, philosophy. The crowd, bent on vile lucre, has its say."]

wee live in. And yet to speake a troth, I cannot herein blame the diseased world so much, as I do the infelicity of that sacred Art of Poesy; which like the soveraigne prescriptions of a *Galen* or *Hypocrates*, ordered and dispensed by illiterate Empyricks or dogleeches, must needes (as the best phisicks ill handled) prove but so much variety of poyson instead of cure. And such are the mont'ibanke Rimers of the time, and so faulty, that have so much abused their prefession, and the world; and stucke so generall a scandall upon that excellent Physicke of the minde; with the poyson of their meritricious flatteries, and base servile fawning at the heeles of worldly wealth and greatnesse, as makes it abhorred of all men; and most, of those that are of most understanding. For indeed what can bee more contemptible, or breed a greater indignation in wise, and understanding minds, than to see the study of Wisdome made not only a mercinary, but vitious occupation. And that same—*pudicam Palladem*, (as a wise Author from the like resentment aptly saies) *deorum munere inter homines divers antem eiici, explodi exibilari; Non habere qui amet, qui faveat, nisi ipsa quasi prostans, & præfloratæ virginitatis accepta mercedula, maleparatum æs in amatoris arculam referat.*[7]

2. The second great disparity, that I find betweene those auncient Fathers of learning, and our moderne writers, is in the price and estimation they held their knowledges in. Which appeares in the care they tooke to conceale them from the unworthy vulgar; and which doth no lesse commend their wisdome, than conclude (by their contrary course) our Modernes, empty, and barren of any thing rare and pretious in them; who in all probability would not prostitute all they know to the rape and spoile of every illiterate reader, were they not conscious to themselves their treasor deserves not many locks to guard it under. But that I may not conclude upon a—*non concessum*,[8] for I remember I have heard it affirmed, (and by some too that the time calls Schollers), that the Auncients certainely spoke their meanings

7 [Pico's *Apology* and *Oration on the Dignity of Man:* "Chaste Pallas, sent among men as the gift of the gods, is thrown aside, hooted out, and hissed: not having anyone who loves her, who cherishes her, unless by prostituting herself, as it were, she puts the ill-gotten gains, accepted as the price of tarnished virginity, into the money-box of her lover."]
8 [A "nonconcession."]

as plaine as they could, and were the honester men for doing so;
and there may be more birds beside, of the same feather with
these; therefore I will in charity speake a word or two for these
peoples instruction; and in the meane betweene the whining
Heraclite, and over-rigid *Democritus* (as much as in me lyes)
comiter erranti monstrare viam.[1]

Let such then as are to learne whither to conceale their knowledges, was the intent and studied purpose of the Auncient Poets
all, and most of the auncient Philosophers also; let such I say,
know, that, when in the worlds youth & capabler estate, those
old wise *Ægyptian* Priests beganne to search out the Misteries of
Nature, (which was at first the whole worlds only divinity) they
devized, to the end to retaine among themselves what they had
found, (lest it should be abused and vilefied by being delivered
to the vulgar) certaine marks, and characters of things, under
which all the precepts of their wisdome were contained; which
markes they called *Hieroglyphicks* or sacred gravings. And more
then thus, they delivered little: or what ever it was, yet alwaies
dissimulanter, and in Enigma's and mysticall riddles, as their
following disciples also did. And this provizo of theirs, those
Images of *Sphynx* they placed before all their Temples did insinuate; and which they set for admonitions, that high and Mysticall matters should by riddles and enigmaticall knotts be kept
inviolate from the prophane Multitude. I will give instance of
one or two of them. The authentike testimony late cited (to other
purpose) by mee of *Orpheus,* and his learning, (viz. That he was
one of the *priscæ sapientiæ patres,* and that the *Secreta de numeris doctrina* and what ever the Greeke Philosophy had in it—
Magnum & sublime, did from his Institutions, *ut a primo fonte
manare,*[2]) hath these words immediately following—*Sed qui
erat veterum mos philosophorum, ita Orpheus suorum dog-
matum mysteria fabularum intexit involucris, & poetico vela-
mento dissimulavit; ut si quis legat illos Hymnos nihil subesse
credat præter fabellas nugàsque meracissimas*[3]—but as it was

1 ["willingly pointed out the way to one who had strayed."]
2 [Pico's *Apology,* but see also *Oration on the Dignity of Man:* "fathers of antique wisdom . . . arcane doctrine of numbers . . . great and sublime . . .
as from the original fountain flow."]
3 [Pico, *Apology,* but see also *Oration on the Dignity of Man;* the rest of the
sentence is Reynolds' translation of the passage.]

the manner of the Auncient Philosophers, so *Orpheus* within the foul[d]s and involuements of fables, hid the misteries of his doctrine; and dissembled them under a poeticke maske; so as who reades those hymnes of his, will not beleeve any thing to bee included under them, but meere tales and trifles. *Homer* likewise, by the same mouth positively averred to have included in his two Poems of *Iliads* and *Odisses*—*all intellectuall contemplation;* and which are called the Sun and Moone of the Earth, for the light they beare (as one well notes) before all Learning; (and of which *Democritus* speaking, (as *Farra*[4] the *Alexandrian* observes) sayes—*it was impossible but Homer, to have composed so wonderfull workes, must have been indued with a divine and inspired nature; who under a curious, and pleasing vaile of fable, hath taught the world how great and excellent the beauty of true wisdome is.* no lesse then *Ang: Politianus* who sayes— *Omnia in his, & ab his sunt omnia.*[5]) yet what appeares (I say) in these workes of *Homer* to the meere; or ignorant reader, at all of doctrine or document, or more, than two fictious impossible tales, or lyes of many men that never were, and thousands of deedes that never were done? Nor lesse cautious than these, were most of the Auncient Philosophers also. The divine *Plato* writing to a friend of his *de supremis substantius*—*Per ænigmata* (sayes he) *dicendum est: nesi epistola fortè ad aliorum pervenerit manus, quæ tibi scribimus, ab alius intelligantur* —we must write in enigma's and riddles; lest if it come to other hands; what wee write to thee, be understood by others. *Aristotle* of those his books, wherein he treates of Supernaturall things, sayes (as *Aulus Gellius* testifies)[6] that—*they were—editi, & non editi;* as much as to say, Mystically or enigmatically written; adding farther—*cognobiles iis tantum erunt qui nos audiunt*—they shall be only knowne to our hearers or disciples. And this closenesse *Pythagoras* also having learned of those his Masters, and taught it his disciples, he was made the Master of Silence. And who, as all the doctrines hee delivered were (after the manner of

---

4 *In Settena: fol.* 259. [See note 4, p. 235.]
5 *In Ambra.* [The "Ambra" is one of the four poems (including the famous "Nutricia") that make up Politian's *Sylvae,* literary criticism in hexameters (see also previous note on Politian, p. 229): "All things are in these, and from these all things are."]
6 *In Noct: Attic:* [I.e., in *Noctes Atticae* xx.5: "written, & not written."]

the *Hebrewes, Ægyptians,* and most auncient Poets,) layd downe
in enigmaticall and figurative notions, so one among other of his
is this—*Give not readily thy right hand to every one,* by which
Precept (sayes the profound *Iamblicus*)[7] that great Master adver-
tiseth that wee ought not to communicate to unworthy mindes,
and not yet practized in the understanding of occulte doctrines,
those misterious instructions that are only to bee opened (sayes
he) and taught to sacred and sublime wits, and such as have
beene a long time exercised and versed in them.

Now, from this meanes that the first auncients used, of delivering their knowledges thus among themselves by word of
mouth; and by successive reception from them downe to after
ages, That Art of mysticall writing by Numbers, wherein they
couched under a fabulous attire, those their verball Instructions,
was after, called *Scientia Cabalæ,* or the Science of reception:
Cabala among the *Hebrews* signifying no other than the Latine
receptio: A learning by the auncients held in high estimation
and reverence and not without great reason; for if God (as the
excellent *Jo: Picus*[8] rehearses)—*nihil casu, sed omnia per
suam sapientiam ut in pondere & mensura, ita in numero dis-
posuit;*[9] did nothing by chance, but through his wisdome disposed
all things as in weight and measure, so likewise in number;
(and which taught the ingenious *Saluste* to say, that,—

> *Sacred harmony*
> *And law of Number did accompany*
> *Th' allmighty most, when first his ordinance*
> *Appointed Earth to rest, and Heaven to daunce*)[1]

Well might *Plato*[2] consequently affirme that—*among all liberall
Arts, and contemplative Sciences, the chiefest and most divine
was the*—*Scientia numerandi.* and who likewise questioning
why Man was the wisest of Animalls, answers himselfe againe
(as *Aristotle* in his Problemes observes)—*quia numerare novit*
—because hee could number. no lesse than *Avenzoar* the *Baby-*

---

7 *In lib: de Mister:* [A Pythagorean work, only part of which survives.]
8 *In Apolog. fol.* 115. [The *Apology.*]
9 [*Cf.* the non-canonical Book of Wisdom 11:21.]
1 *Sigr. du Bertas* in his *Columnes.* [In Du Bartas' *Semaines* the "Columnes" appears in the second day of the second week. (See also note on Salluste on p.
229.)]
2 *In Epimenide.*

Ionian, whose frequent word by *Albumazars* report (as *Picus Mirandula*[3] notes) was—*eum omnia nosse qui noverat numerare* —that hee knowes all things that knowes number. But howsoever an Art thus highly cried up by the Auncients; Yet a Learning (I say) now more than halfe lost; or at least by such as possesse any limbe of it, rather talked of, than taught. *Rabanus* a great Doctor of the Christian Church only excepted, who hath writ a particular booke—*de Numerorum virtutibus.* by diverse others, as *Ambrose, Nazianzen, Origine, Augustine,* and many more, (as the learned *Jo: Picus* at large in his Apology showes) reverendly mentioned, but never published in their writings. And I am fully of opinion (which till I find reason to recant, I will not bee ashamed to owne) that the Ignorance of this Art, and the worlds mayme in the want, or not understanding of it, is insinuated in the Poets generally-sung fable of *Orpheus:* whom they faigne to have recovered his *Euridice* from Hell, with his Musick; that is Truth and Equity, from darkenesse of Barbarisme and Ignorance, with his profound and excellent Doctrines; but, that in the thicke caliginous way to the upper-earth, she was lost againe; and remaines lost to us, that read and understand him not, for want, meerely of the knowledge of that Art of Numbers that should unlocke and explane his Mysticall meanings to us.

This Learning of the *Ægyptians* (thus concealed by them, as I have shewed) being transferred from them to the *Greekes;* was by them from hand to hand delivered still in fabulous riddles among them; and thence downe to the *Latines.* Of which beades, the ingenious *Ovid* has made a curious and excellent chaine; though perhaps hee understood not their depth; as our wisest Naturalists doubt not to affirme, his other Contreymen *Lucretius,* and that more learned Scholler (I meane Imitater) of *Hesiod,* the singular *Virgil,* did; and which are the sinewes and marrow, no lesse than starres and ornaments of his incomparable Poems: And still by them, as by their masters before them, preserved with equall care, from the mischiefe of divulgation, or Prophanation: a vice by the Auncients in generall, no lesse than by *Moses* particularly, in the delivering of the Law (according to the opinions of the most learned, both Christian Divines, and

---

3 *In Apolog:* [The *Apology.*]

Jewish Rabines) with singular caution provided against and avoided. *Write* (said the Angell to *Esdras*)[4] *all these things that thou hast seene, in a booke, and hide them, and teach them only to the wise of the people, whose heartes thou knowest may comprehend and keep these secrets.* And since I late mentioned that great Secretary of God, *Moses,* to whose sacred pen as we cannot attribute too much, so, that wee may give the greater reverence to him, and consequently the greater credit to the authority of those Auncient followers and imitaters of his, or (that I may righter say, and not unreverently) those joint runners with him in the same example of closenesse, and care to conceale, I will speake a word or two of him. And upon the warrant of greater understandings than my owne, averre That it is the firme opinion of all ancient writers, which (as an indubitable troth), they do all with one mouth confirme, that the full and entire knowledge of all wisdome both divine & humane, is included in the five bookes of the *Mosaicke* law—*dissimulata autem, & occultata* (as the excellent *Jo: Picus* in his learned exposition[5] upon him sayes) *in literis ipsis, quibus dictiones legis contextæ sunt*—But hidden and disguized even in the letters themselves that forme the precepts of the Law. And the same *Picus,* in another discourse[6] of his upon the bookes of *Moses* more at large to the same purpose sayes—*Scribunt non modo celebres Hebræorum doctores* (whom afterwards he names,[7] as) *Rabi Eliazar, Rabi Moysis de Ægypto, Rabi Simeon Ben Lagis, Rabi Ismahel, Rabi Iodam, & Rabi Nachinan; sed ex nostris quoque Esdras, Hilarius, & Origines, Mosem non legem modo, quam quinque exaratam libris posteris reliquit, sed secretiorem quoque, & veram legis enarrationem in monte divinitus accepisse. Præceptum autem ei a Deo, ut legem quidem populo publicaret, legis autem interpretationem nec traderet literis nec invulgaret, sed ipse Jesu Nave tantum; tum ille, alliis deincèps sacerdotum primoribus, magna silentii religione revelaret*—[8] the most renowned and authentique not only among the Hebrew Doctors, as *Rabi Eliazar, Rabi Moyses de*

4 *Lib:* 2. *ca: 12; ver: 37.*
5 *In Heptap:* [In the *Heptaplus*—see note 2, p. 233.]
6 *In Apolog: fo:* 81. [The *Apology.*]
7 *Fo:* 116.
8 [Reynolds himself offers a close paraphrase of this and the following long passage from Pico.]

Ægypto, Rabi Symeon &c. but among ours also, *Esdras, Hillary,*
and *Origine,* doe write that *Moses* received from God upon the
mount not the Law only, which he hath left in five bookes exactly delivered to posterity, but the more hidden also, and true
explanation of the Law: But with all, was warned and com-
maunded by God, that as he should publish the Law to the People, so the interpretation thereof, he should neither commit to
letters nor divulge; but he to *Josua* only and *Josua* to the other
succeeding primaries among the Priests; and that, under a great
religion of secrecy; and concludes—*Et merito quidem; Nam
satis erat vulgaribus, & per simplicem historiam nunc Dei poten-
tiam, nunc in improbos iram, in bonos clementiam, in omnes
justitiam agnoscere, & per divina salutariàque præcepta, ad bene
beatèque vivendum & cultum relligionis institui; at misteria
secretiora, & sub cortice legis rudique verborum prætextu latitan-
tia altissimæ divinitatis arcana plebi palam facere, quid erat
aliud quàm dare sanctum canibus, & inter porcos spargere
margaritas;* and not without great reason; for it was enough for
the multitude to be by meerely the simple story, taught and made
to know, now the Power of God, now his Wrath against the
wicked, Clemency towards the good, and Justice to all; and by
divine and wholesome precepts instructed in the wayes of religion, and holy life. But those secreter Mysteries, and abstrusities
of most high divinity, hidden and concealed under the barke, and
rude cover of the words, to have divulged and layd these open to
the vulgar; what had it been other than to give holy things to
dogs, and cast pearles among swine? So he. And this little that I
have heere rehearsed (for in a thing so knowne to all that are
knowers, mee thinkes I have said rather too much than otherwise) shall serve for instance of *Moses* his mysticall manner of
writing. Which I have the rather done for instruction of some
ignorant, though stiffe opposers of this truth, that I have lately
met with; but chiefly in justification of those other wise Auncients of his, and succeeding times, Poets, and Philosophers,
that were no lesse carefull then *Moses* was, not to give—*Sanctum canibus,* (as before said) nor *inter porcos spargere margaritas.*[9]

9 [In Reynolds' translation (earlier): "holy things to dogs, and cast pearles
among swine."]

Now to go about to examine whither it appeares our Modernes (Poets especially, for I will exempt diverse late prose-writers), have any the like closenesse as before mentioned; were a worke sure as vaine and unnecessary, as it is a truth firme and unquestionable, that they possesse the knowledge of no such mysteries as deserve the use of any art at all for their concealing.

3. The last, and greatest disparity, and wherein above all others, the grossest defect and maime appeares, in our Modernes (and especially Poets) in respect of the Auncients; is their generall ignorance, even throughout all of them, in any the mysteries and hidden properties of Nature; which was an unconcerning Inquisition it appeares not in their writings they have at all troubled their heads with. Poets I said especially (and indeed only) for we have many Prose-men excellent naturall Philosophers in these late times; and that observe strictly that closenesse of their wise Masters the reverend Auncients; So as now a dayes our Philosophers are all our Poets, or what our Poets should bee; and our Poesies growne to bee little better than fardles of such small ware as those Marchants the French call pedlers, carry up and downe to sell; whissles, painted rattles, and such like *Bartholomew*-babyes;[1] for what other are our common uninstructing fabulous rimes, then amusements for fooles and children? But our Rimes (say they) are full of Morall doctrine; be it so. But why not delivered then in plaine prose, and as openly to every mans understanding, as it deserves to be taught, and commonly knowne by every one. The Auncients (say they) were Authors of Fables, which they sung in measured numbers, as we in imitation of them do. True: but sure enough their meanings were of more high nature, and more difficult to be found out, then any booke of Manners wee shall readily meete withall, affoordes; else they had not writ them so obscurely, or we should find them out more easily, and make some use of them: whereas not understanding nor seeking to understand them, we make none at all. Wee live in a myste, blind and benighted; and since our first fathers disobedience poysoned himselfe and his posterity, Man is become the imperfectest and most deficient Animall of all the field: for then he lost that Instinct that the Beast retaines; though with him the beast, and with it the whole vegitable and generall

1 [Kewpie dolls or puppets were sold at Bartholomew Fair.]

Terrene nature also suffered, and still groanes under the losse of their first purity, occasioned by his fall. What concernes him now so neerely as to attend to the cultivating or refining, & thereby advancing of his rationall part, to the purchase & regaining of his first lost felicity? And what meanes to conduce to this purchase, can there bee, but the knowledge first, and love next (for none can love but what hee first knowes) of his Maker, for whose love and service he was only made? And how can this blind, lame, and utterly imperfect Man, with so great a lode to boote of originall and actuall offence upon his back, hope to approach this supreme altitude, and immensity, which

> *In quella inaccessibil luce,*
> *Quasi in alta caligine s'asconde,*

(as an excellent Poetesse[2] discribes the inscrutable Beeing of God) but by two meanes only: the one, by laying his burden on him that on his Crosse bore the burthen of all our defectes, and interpositions betweene us and the hope of the vision of his blessed Essence face to face heereafter; and the other, by carefull searche of him here in this life (according to Saint *Paules* instruction[3]), in his works; who telles us—*those invisible things of God are cleerely seene, being understood by the things that are made;* or by the workes of his blessed hands? So as, betweene these two mayne and only meanes of acquiring here the knowledge, and hereafter the vision of him wherein all our present and future happinesse consists, what middle place (to descend to my former discourse) can these mens Morall Philosophy (trow we) challenge? which in its first Masters and teachers time, before there was any better divinity knowne, might well enough passe for a course kind of divinity; but however, such as one, as (with the leave of our Poets) needes no fiction to clothe or conceale it in. And therfore utterly unfit to bee the Subject of Poems: since it containes in it but the obvious restraints or impulsions of the Humane Sence and will, to or from what it ynly before-hand (without extrinsicke force or law) feeles and knowes it ought to shunne, or imbrace. The other two more re-

2 *La Sig:ra vitto: Colonna.* [Vittoria Colonna (1490–1547), from one of her *Rime di tre Gentildonne:* "In that inaccessible light, as if in an exalted fog it hides itself."]
3 *Rom: cap:* I. *ver:* 20.

mooved and harder lessons do certainely more in the affaire both of soule and body, concerne us. And these (if we be wise enough to love our selves so well), wee must seeke and take from the hands of their fittest teachers. As, in the first, we need goe no farther (though learned & wise Writers have made mention, and to high purpose, of a *Theologia Philosophica,* as they call some of the doctrines of the auncient Poets), then to the Doctors, and Doctrines of that Church that God dyed to plant, and which shall live till the worlds death. And for instruction in our next necessary Lesson, to wit, the Misteries of Nature, we must, if we will follow *Plato's* advice—*inquire of those* (and by them be directed) *who lived neerest to the time of the gods;* meaning the old wise Ethnicks: among whom, the best Masters were certainly most, if not all of them, Poets; and from whose fires (as I have formerly touched) the greatest part of all humane knowledges have taken their first light. Among these, I say, and not elsewhere (excepting the sacred Old Law only) must we search for the knowledge of the wise, and hidden wayes & workings of our great Gods handmaid, Nature. But alas who findes, or who seekes now adayes to finde them? Nay (what is more strange) there want not of these learned of our times, that will not bee intreated to admit those excellent Masters of knowledge to meane (if they allow them any meaning) scarce other at all, then meerely Morall doctrine.

I have knowne Latine and Greeke Interpreters of them in these times; men otherwise of much art, and such as able to render their Authors phrase to the height of their good, in our worse language; yet aske the most, as I have some of them, and I feare they will answere, as one (and the best) of our Greeke translators[4] hath ingenuously confest to mee, that for more then matter of Morality, hee hath discovered little in his Authors meanings. Yet my old good friend as well as I wish him, (and very well I wish him for those parts of Fancy, Industry, and meritorious Ability that are in him) must pardon mee that I affirme, it is not truer that there ever was such a thing as a *Musæus,* or *Hesiod,* or *Homer,* whom he has taught to speake excellent English; then it is, that the least part of the Doctrine (or their wisest expositors abuse mee, and other Ignorants with mee) that they

4 [George Chapman.]

meant to lay downe in those their wise, though impossible fables, was matter of Manners, but chiefly Nature: No lesse
then in the rest of those few before, and many after them, whom
all Antiquity has cried up for excellent Poets, and called their
works perfect Poems.

For proofe of which Truth; wee will first mention two or three
of the best of them; and to omit the multiplicity of lesse auten-
tike testimonies, that all Authors are full of, alledge only the
beforecited *Mirandula*, who speaking of that—*Magia naturalis,*
or naturall wisdome, or as he defines it[5]—*exacta & absoluta
cognitio omnium rerum naturalium*—the exact and absolute
knowledge of all naturall things (which the Aunciencts were
Masters of) sayes,[6] that in that Art (among some others he
mentions) *Praestitit Homerus,* Homer excelled; and who—*ut
omnes alias sapientias, ita hanc quoque; sub sui Ulyxis erroribus
dissimulavit*—as all other knowledges, so hath hiddenly layed
downe this also in his *Ulysses* his travailes. As likewise of *Orpheus*[7]—*Nihil efficacius Hymnis Orphei in naturali Magia, si
debita musica, animi intentio, & cæteræ circumstantiæ quas
nôrunt sapientes fuerint adhibitæ:* There is nothing of greater
efficacy then the hymnes of *Orpheus* in naturall Magick, if the
fitting musick, intention of the minde, and other circumstances
which are knowne to the wise, bee considered and applyed. And
againe[8]— *that they are of no lesse power in naturall magick,* or
to the understanding thereof, *then the Psalmes of David are in
the Caball,* or to understand the *Cabalistick* Science by. And
lastly, *Zoroaster;* who that he was a possessor likewise of that—
absoluta cognitio rerum Naturalium before mentioned, no lesse
then of that *Theologicall Philosophy* his expounders find in him,
may appeare by that Doctrine of his (in particular) of the—
Scala à Tartaro ad primum ignem,[9] which the learned *Jo: Picus*
interprets[1]— *Seriem naturarum universi à non gradu materiæ,
ad eum qui est super omnem gradum graduatè protensum*— the
series or concatenation of the universall Natures, from a no de-

---

[5] *In Apolog: fo:* 112. [The *Apology.*]
[6] *Ibid: fo:* 80. [See also *Oration on the Dignity of Man.*]
[7] *In Conclus.* [Pico's *Conclusiones.*]
[8] *Ibid:*
[9] ["A ladder from Tartarus to the first fire" (i.e., the ring of fire surrounding
the universe).]
[1] *In Conclu:* [Pico's *Conclusiones.*]

gree (as he speakes) of matter, to him that is above or beyond
all degree graduately extended; no lesse then by that Attribute
(in generall) given him by all the learned of all Ages; *viz:* that
he was one of the greatest (as first) of Naturall Magicians, or
Masters of the absolute knowledge of all Nature.

To omit (as I said) the Testimonies of an infinity of other
Authors in confirmation of the before-affirmed troth; who knowes
not, that most, if not all of those fables in all the rest of the
Auncients, of their gods and goddesses especially, with the affinities, entercourses, and commerces betweene themselves, and
with others; (of which, as *Homer,* that Greeke Oracle is abundantly full, so the rest, as a *Hesiod, Linus* the Master, and *Musæus* the Scoller of *Orpheus,* and (as we have said) *Zoroaster,*
and *Orpheus* himselfe, and all those most auncient, (if we may
beleeve their best expounders and relaters of most we have of
them, made the maine grounds and Subjects of their writings;)
who knowes not (I say) that most, if not all, of those their fables
of this kinde, and which have of all learned, in all ages, been
chiefely tearmed Poetick, & fittest matter for Poesy; have never
been by any wise expounder made to meane other then meerely
the Generation of the Elements, with their Vertues, and
Changes; the Courses of the Starres, with their Powers, and Influences; and all the most important Secrets of Nature, hanging
necessarily upon the knowledge of These; which could not suffer
so simple a Relation as the Ethick doctrine requires; because by
the vulgarity of Those, much mischiefe must in all reason ensue;
being (also) of those tenderer things, that are soonest pro-
phaned & vilefied by their cheapnesse; & This, cannot for the
generall benefit of mankinde be among the plainest of lessons
too commonly knowne and openly divulged to every body.

I will not deny but the Auncients mingled much doctrine of
Morality (yea, high Divinity also) with their Naturall Philosophy; as the late mentioned *Zoroaster* first; who hath divinely
sung of the Essence and attributes of God and was (as the
learned *Farra* avouches)[2]— *the first Author of that Religious
Philosophy, or Philosophical Religion, that was after followed &
amplified by Mercurius Trismegistus, Orpheus, Aglaophemus,
Pythagoras, Eudoxus, Socrates, Plato, &c.* And *Orpheus* next;

2 *In Settena: fo:* 57. [In the *Settenario.*]

who, as he writt particular bookes; of Astrology, first (as *Lucian*[3] tells us) of any man; as also of diseases and their cures; of the natures and qualities of the Elements; of the force of Love or agreement in Naturall things; and many more that we read of, besides his Hymnes which are perhaps the greatest part of what now remaines of him heere among us: so his expounders likewise find in him that *Theologia Philosophica* as they call it, which they give to *Zoroaster*. Witnesse Pausanias, who reports —*Orpheus multa humanæ politicæque vitæ utilia invenit: & universam Theologiam primus aperuit, & nefariorum facinorum expiationes excogitavit, &c.*[4] But let us heare how himselfe[5] sings; and which is by *Eusebius Pamphilus*, in his honour rehearsed.[6]

> *O you that vertue follow, to my sense*
> *Bend your attentive minds: Prophane ones hence.*
> *And thou Musæus, who alone the shine*
> *Highly contemplat'st of the formes divine,*
> *Learne my notes; which with th' inward eye behold,*
> *And untouch'd in thy sacred bosome hold.*
> *Incline thee by my safe-advizing verse*
> *To the high Author of this Universe.*
> *One only, all immortall, such is he;*
> *Whose Being I discover thus to thee;*
> *This alone-perfect, this eternall King*
> *Rais'd above all, created ev'ry thing,*
> *And all things governes, with the Spirit alone*
> *(Not otherwise) to be beheld, or knowne.*
> *From him no ill springs; there's no god but he.*
> *Thinke now, and looke about thee prudently;*
> *And better to discover him, loe I*
> *His tracts and footsteps upon earth, and high*
> *Strong hand behold, but cannot him descrie;*
> *Who (to an unimaginable height*
> *Rais'd) in darke clouds conceales him from my sight.*

3 *In Dialog: de Astrol:*
4 *In Bœotia:* ["Orpheus found many things useful to human and political life, and he was the first who unfolded all theology and devised atonements for nefarious deeds." *Cf.* Pausanias, *Boetia* xxx.4.]
5 *In Lib: de verbo sacre.*
6 *Lib:* 13. *de Præp: Evangel:* [Eusebius' *Praeparatio Evangelica* surveyed the philosophy and religion of the Greeks.]

Only a Caldean saw him;[7] and the grace
Hath now aloft to view him face to face.
His sacred right hand graspes the Ocean; and
Touch'd with it, the proud mountaines trembling stand
Ev'n from the deep rootes to their utmost height:
Nor feeles at all th' immensnesse of their weight,
He, who above the heav'n doth dwell, yet guides
And governes all that under heav'n abides.
O're all, through all doth his vast power extend;
Of th' Universe beginning, midds, & end.

And as these two divine Authors in particular, so likewise among
the rest of the Auncient Poets in generall, I will graunt they have
in their Poesies (as I have said) mingled much Morality with
their Ethick doctrines. As in their *Hercules, Theseus, Ulysses,*
Æneas, and other their Heröes they have given example of all
vertues; and punisht all vices; as pride and ambition, in their
Giants and *Titanes,* &c. Contempt of the gods, in their *Niobe,*
Arachne, Casseiope, Medusa, Amphion, Marsyas, the *Mineides,*
&c. murder, lust, covetise, and the rest, in their *Lycaon, Ixion,*
Sisyphus, Midas, Tantalus, Titius, &c. Yet questionlesse infinite
many more of their fables then these, (though even these and
the rest of this kind want not among our best Mythologians their
Physick, as well as Ethick meanings,) as all those of their gods
and goddesses, with their powers and digni[t]ies, and all passage
of affinity and commerce betweene themselves; and betweene
them and others, were (as I have said before) made to meane
meere matter of Nature; and in no possibility of Sense to bee
wrested to the doctrine of Manners, unlesse a man will (withall)
bee so inhumane as to allow all those riotts, rapes, murders,
adulteries, incestes, and those *nefaria* and *nefanda,* unnaturally-
seeming vices that they tell of them, to bee (litterally or Morally
taken) fit examples of Manners, or wholesome instructions for
the lives of men to be levelled and directed by.

Whereas, on the contrary side, (that I may instance some of
them) who can make that Rape of *Proserpine,* whom her mother
Ceres (that under the Species of Corne might include as well the
whole Genus of the Vegetable nature) sought so long for in the

[7] Meaning sure *Moses;* who the holy writ saies—*Saw God face to face.* unlesse
with *Eusebius,* we will have him meane the *Patriarke Abraham.*

earth, to meane other, then the putrefaction, and succeeding generation of the Seedes we commit to *Pluto,* or the earth? whome they make the God of wealth, calling him also *Dis-quasi dives*[8] (the same in Latine that *Pluto* is in Greeke) rich, or wealthy, because all things have their originall from the earth, and returne to the earth againe. Or what can *Jupiters* blasting of his beloved *Semele,* after his having defloured her, and the wrapping of his sonne he got on her (*Bacchus,* or wine) in his thigh after his production, meane other then the necessity of the Ayres heate to his birth, in the generation; and (after a violent pressure and dilaceration of his mother the Grape) the like close imprisoning of him also, in a fit vessell, till he gaine his full maturity, and come to be fit aliment?

After these two particular scandalous fables, and which I will call but inferiour speculations, yet necessary documents, because, of the Natures of Corne, and Wine, the *Sustentacula vitæ;*[9] To omit the Adultery of *Mars* and *Venus,* by which the Chymists will have meant the inseperability of those two Metals that carry their names; witnesse that exuberance of *Venus*—or copper which wee call *Vitriole,* that is seldome or never found without some mixture more or lesse of *Mars* or iron in it; as her husband *Vulcan,* or materiall fire findes and shewes the practitioners in Chymistry. And with this, other also of the like obviouser kinde of truths in Nature; as *Hebe's* stumbling and falling with the Nectar-bowle in her hand, and thereby discovering her hidden parts to the gods, as she served them at their boord; meaning the nakednesse of the trees and plants in Autumne, when all their leaves are falne from them by the downefall or departure of the *Spring,* which their *Hebe,* or *goddesse* of *youth* as the Auncients called her (because the Spring renewes and makes young all things) meanes. And with these, the Inceste of Mirrha with her father; meaning the Myrrh-tree, which the Sun (father of Plants) inflames, and making overtures in it, there flowes thence that odorous *Sabæan* gumme wee call Myrrhe, (meant by her child *Adonis,* which interpreted is sweet, pleasant, or delightfull.) To omit (I say) these, and the like trivialler

8 [I.e., the word "Dis," the name of the Roman god of the underworld, is "almost" the word "dives," or "rich," translating the Greek "Pluto."]
9 ["The supports of life."]

(though true) observations in Nature; and that carry also so foule a face to the eye; I would aske who can make those fights and contentions that the wise *Homer* faignes betweene his Gods and Goddesses to meane other then the naturall Contrariety of the Elements: and especially of the Fire and Water; which as they are tempered and reconciled by the aire, so *Juno* (which signifies the aëry region) reconciles, & accords the warring Gods. And next, what in generall those frequent, and no lesse scandalous brawles betweene *Jupiter* and (his wife and sister) *Juno,* can be made to meane other, then those Meteors occasioned by the upper and lower Region of the Ayres differing temperatures; Or what all those his unlawfull loves, his compressing so many *Dryads, Nayads,* and *Nereiads* (woodnymphes, and waternymphes) and the rest, can meane other then meerely the Fires power upon the Earth, and waters; (a study of a higher nature and vaster extente then the first alledged) and which *Jupiters* Inceste with his sister *Ceres* likewise meanes; and is the same with the tale of the contention of *Phaëton* which is *Incendium,* with the sonne of *Isis* which is *Terra.*

A Theame too infinite to pursue; and no lesse a fault heere, then (perhaps) a folly at all to mencion: For (besides the beeing a subject utterly unfit to suffer a mixture with a discourse of so light a nature as this of mine, where a slight touch at the generall mistake and abuse of Poesy in our times, was only intended) suppose a man should (wheras I have heere layd downe the faire sense of but two or three of the foulest of them) be at the paines of running through all the Fables of the Auncients, and out of them shew the reader, and leade him by the fingar as it were (who yet can discover nothing but matter of Manners in them) to the speculation of the entire Secret of our great God of Nature, in his miraculous fabrick of this World, (which, their god *Pan,* or the universall simple bodyes, and seedes of all Nature, gotten by *Mercury* or the divine Will, by which all things came to bee created meanes;) And (beginning with *Moses*) shew him how the Spirit of God first mooving upon the waters (a Mystery perhaps by few of our duller Modernes understood, though a *Thales Milesius,* or *Heraclius* the Ephesian, two Heathens, could instruct them) they faigne him under the name of *Jupiter,* by compressing *Latona* (meaning the shades or darkenesse of the first *Chäos*) to have begot on her, *Apollo* and *Diana,* which is the Sun and Moone, when he said— *fiat lux, & lux fuit,* and carry him along from this beginning to the end and compleate knowledge of all Nature, (which as *Moses* darkely, they no lesse darkely delivered;) Suppose (I say) a man should take this taske upon him, I would faine know who they are that would be perhaps, at least, that were, fit readers now a dayes of such a Treatise? Because what one of a million of our Scollers or writers among us, understands, or cares to be made understand scarse the lowest and triviallest of Natures wayes? much lesse seekes to draw (by wisely observing her higher and more hidden workings) any profitabler use or benefit from them, for their owne, or the publike good, then perhaps to make an Almanack, or a diving-bote to take butts or crabs under water with; or else some Douch water-bellowes, by rarefying water into a comprest ayre to blow the fire withall?

Whenas if they could, but from that poore step, learne the way to get a little higher up the right scale of Nature, and really indeed accord, and make a firme peace and agreement betweene all the discordant Elements; and (as the Fable of *Cupids* wrassle with *Pan,* and overcomming him, teaches them the beginning of all Natures productions are love and strife,) indeavour to irritate also, and force this *Pan,* or Simple Matter of things to his fit procreative ability, by an industrious and wise strife and colluctation with him; then they might perhaps do somewhat in Philosophy not unworth the talking of. No lesse then our common practitioners in Physick might better deserve their names then most of them do; (for to be a Physitian, what is it but to be a generall Naturalist, not meere transcriber and applyer of particular booke-*recipes*?) if they would but practise, by that Rule and Base of Nature the world was built upon, to make likewise and establish that Equality and concord betweene those warring Elements (which are the Complexions) in Mans body, that one exceed not an other in their Qualities: Or if they could but give better instance of their acquaintance with the wayes of Phylosophy, then in burdning and oppressing nature, rather then otherwise, as most of them doe, with their crude Vegetable and Minerall Physicks, for not understanding the necessity, (or though they did, yet not the Art) of exalting and bettering their natures, by correcting or remooving their in-bred imperfections, with that fit preparation that Nature teaches them.

The hidden workings of which wise Mistresse, could wee fully in all her wayes comprehend, how much would it cleare, and how infinitely ennoble our blind and groveling conditions, by exalting our understandings to the sight (as I have 'before toucht) of God, or— *those invisible things of God* (to use S. *Pauls* words once againe) *which are cleerely seene, being understood by the things that are made;* and thence instructing us, not sawcily to leap, but by the linkes of that golden chaine of *Homer,* that reaches from the foote of *Jupiters* throne to the Earthe, more knowingly, and consequently more humbly climbe up to him, who ought to bee indeed the only end and period of all our knowledge, and understanding; the which in us though but a small fainte beame of that our great blessed *Sun,* yet is that breath of life that he breathed into us, to draw us thereby (*fecisti nos Domine propter te;*[1] sayes the holy S. *Augustine*[2]) neerer to him, then all irrationall Animalls of his making; as a no lesse tenderly loving Father, then immense and omnipotent Creator.

To whom as wee cannot give too much love and reverence; so neither can wee with too wary hands approach his sacred Mysteries in Holy Writ. Howbeit I must (to returne home to my former discourse) in honour & just praise of the before mentioned wise Auncients (and with the premised befitting caution) not doubt to say, that as his Instructions in the holy Scripture, and especially in the old Law, must of necessity reach as far farther then the bare historicall trueth (though not in the same manner) as extends the difference in our selves betweene Nature alone, and Nature and Grace united; so likewise, that one, and a great portion of the doctrine of that part of holy Writ, the wise Ethnicks undoubtedly possest in all perfection; to wit, the knowledge of all Natures most high and hidden wayes and workings: and though far short in the safer part of wisdome, of their more inlightned successors, yet was the bare light (or rather fire) of nature in them, enough to draw them as high as Reason

1 ["You made us, Lord, for yourself."]
2 *In Confess:*

could help flesh and bloud to reach heaven with. Nay which is
more, were it not wide of my purpose (though it contradicts it
not) to conster them other then meere children of Nature, I
might perhaps gaine favour of some of our weaker persuaders in
their spirituall Cures (if to flanke and strengthen the divine letter with prophaner Authorities, be in this backward and incredu-
lous age, not irrequisite) by paralelling in the Historicall part I
meane chiefly, and as it lies, the Sacred letter and Ethnick
Poesyes together to a large extention: And beginning with
Moses, shew them, all those —*dii majorum gentium*[3] from *Sat-
urne* to *Deucalions* deluge, were but names for *Adam, Caine,
Lamech* and the rest of their successors to *Noahs* floud: Nor that
their *Rhæa* (or *Terra,* mother of all the Gods) and *Venus,* could
be other then *Moses* his *Eva* and *Noema.* What other can *Hesiod's Pandora*[4]— *the first and beautifullest of all women, by
whome all evils were dispersed and spred upon the Earth,* meane
then *Moses* his *Eve?* What can *Homers Ate,*[5] whom he calls the
first daughter of *Jupiter,* and a woman pernicious and harmefull
to all us mortalls; and in an other place tells how the wisest of
men was cosened and deceived by his wife; what can he I say,
meane in these women but *Eve?* What was the Poets *Bacchus*
but his *Noah,* or *Noachus,* first corrupted to *Boachus,* and after,
by remooving a letter, to *Bacchus;* who, (as *Moses* tels us of
Noah,) was the first likewise in their accompt, that planted the
vine, and taught men the use of wines soone after the universall
deluge? What can be plainer then that by their *Janus* they ment
Noah also, whome they give two faces to, for having seene both
the old and new world; and which, his name (in *Hebrew, Jain,*
or wine) likewise confirmes; *Noah* being (as we late alledged
Moses for witnesse) the first inventor of the use of wines? What
could they meane by their *Golden-Age,* when—

> *Nulli subigebant arva coloni;*
> > *Ipsaque tellus*
> *Omnia liberius, nullo poscente ferebat;*[6]

3 ["The gods of the greater nations."]
4 *Lib:* I. *Oper: & dier:*
5 *Ilia: lib:* 19.
6 [Vergil, *Georgics* i.125, 127–28: "No farmers subjugated the soil . . . . And
the earth brought forth more freely of herself when no one begged."]

But the state of Man before his Sin? and consequently by their Iron age, but the worlds infelicity, and miseries that succeeded his fall? when—

> *Luctus, & ultrices posuere cubilia curæ;*
> *Pallentesque habitant morbi, tristisque senectus,*
> *Et metus, & majesuada fames, & turpis egestas.*[7]

Lastly, (for I have too much already exceeded my commission) what can *Adonis horti* among the Poets meane other then *Moses* his *Eden*, or terrestriall Paradise? the Hebrew *Eden* being *Voluptas* or *Delitiæ*, whence the Greeke ἡδονή (or pleasure) seemes necessarily derived: The *Caldæans* and *Persians* (so I am tould) called it *Pardeis*, the Greeks, παράδεισος, the *Latines* altered the Greeke name to *Paradisus;* which as Eden, is (as, *Aulus Gellius* defines it) *Locus amænissimus, & voluptatis plenissimus;*[8] the which selfe thing the auncient both Poets and Philosophers certainely ment by their— *horti Hesperidum* likewise.

Now though we reverence *Moses* more (as we ought to doe) then these his condisciples, because inspired so far above them with the immediate spirit of Almighty God; yet ought we neverthelesse to reverence them, and the wisdome of their fables, however not understood by every body: his condisciples I call them, because they read bothe under their *Ægyptian* teachers one lesson; & were (as *Moses* of himselfe sayes) expert in the learning of the *Ægyptians:* yea many of them (and Poets all) were (to speake fitlyer) the teachers of that Learning themselves, and Masters therein no lesse then *Moses.* How can we then indeed attribute too much to their knowledges, though delivered out of wise consideration in riddles and fictious tales?

But alas (with shame enough may we speake it) so far are we now adayes from giving the due to them they deserve, as those their learned and excellent fables seeme rather read to be abused, then studied in these times; and even by people too that are, or would be accompted profound men.

---

[7] [*Aeneid* vi.274–76: "Grief and vengeful cares have made their bed; there live pale diseases and sorrowful old age, and fear, and hunger the cause of evil, and vile want."]

[8] *In Noc: Attic:* [I.e., *Noctes Atticae:* "A most pleasing place, and most full of delights." ("*Adonis horti*": Gardens of Adonis; "*horti Hesperidum*": Gardens of the Hesperides.)]

What child of learning or lover of Truth could abide to see great pretenders to learning among us, that doubt, and obstinately too, whether the pretious treasure of that wisdome of the Auncients, so carefully by them left sealed up to the use of their true Heires (the wise and worthy of their posterity) be any more indeed then a legacy of meere old wives tales to poyson the world with. If we will call this but ignorance, let us go farther; and suppose that a man[9] (nor unlearned one neither) shall have taken paines in foure or five fables of the Auncients to unfould and deliver us much doctrine and high meanings in them, which he calls their wisdome; and yet the same man in an other Treatise of his, shall say of those auncient Fables.— *I thinke they were first made, and their expositions devised afterward:* and a little after— *Of Homer himselfe, notwithstanding he was made a kind of Scripture by the latter Scooles of the Græcians, yet I should without any difficulty pronounce his fables had in his owne meaning no such inwardnesse, &c.* What shall we make of such willing contradictions, when a man to vent a few fancies of his owne, shall tell us first, they are the wisdome of the Auncients; and next, that those Auncient fables were but meere fables, and without wisdom or meaning, til their expositours gave them a meaning; & then, scornefully and contemptuously (as if all Poetry were but Play-vanity) shut up that discourse of his of Poetry, with— *It is not good to stay too long in the Theater.*

But let me not stick too long neither in this myre; nor seeme over-sensible of wrong to what can suffer none; for— *Veritas* (sayes the holy writ) *magna est, & prævalebit:*[1] and such are (nor lesse great and prevailing then truth it selfe) those before mentioned *Arcana* of our wise Auncients; which no Barbarisme I know can efface; nor all the dampes and thick fogs by dull & durty Ignorance breathed on them, darken at all, or hide from the quick eye of select and happier understandings; who know full well, the ripest fruites of knowledge grow ever highest; while the lower-hanging boughs (for every ones gripe) are either barren, or their fruite too sowre to be worth the gathering. And

9 [Francis Bacon in *De Sapientia Veterum* (1609); Reynolds goes on to speak next of the *Advancement of Learning* (1605).]
1 ["Truth is great and will prevail."]

among such may they ever rest, safe wrapt up in their huskes, and involvements: And let our writers write (if it can bee no better) and Rimers rime still after their accustomed and most accepted manner, and still captivate and ravish their like hearers. Though in my owne inclination, I could with much juster alacrety, then in person of the *Roman* Poet, with his— *Vilia miretur vulgus*,[2] or *Roman* Orator, with his—*Similes habent sua labra lactucas*[3] (while he laught to see a greedy Asse at his sutable thissles,) wish we might each one, according to the measure of his illumination, and by the direction of Gods two great bookes, that of his law first, and that of the Creature next, (wherein, to use the excellent *Jo: Picus* his phrase[4]— *leguntur magnalia Dei*— the wonderfull things of God are read) run on together in a safe and firme rode of Trueth: to the end that vindicating some part of our lost Heritage and Beatitude heere, we may thence (an advantage the holy *Maximus Tyrius*[5] sayes the more happy spirits have over others) arrive the lesse Aliens and strangers in the Land of our eternall Heritage, and Beatitude heereafter.

2 [Ovid, *Amores* i.15.35: "Let the vulgar crowd esteem the tawdry" (used by Shakespeare as part of the epigraph to *Venus and Adonis*).]
3 [St. Jerome (*Epistulae* vii) attributes the remark to M. Crassus who, when he observed an ass eating thistles, said: *similem habent labra lactucam*, "like lips, like lettuce" or "like meets like."]
4 *In Conclus:* [*Conclusiones.*]
5 *In Sermon:* [I.e., the *Sermones* of Maximus of Tyre, "Platonic" lecturer of the second century.]

George Herbert

1593–1633

Herbert was an exceptional student at Westminster and Cambridge, then an exemplary Public Orator to the university, and later M.P. for Montgomery. After a period of ill health, he married Jane Danvers and was appointed rector of Bemerton, near Salisbury, where he spent the remaining three years of his life. The years at Bemerton were taken up with parochial duties and intense literary activity. Besides producing A Priest to the Temple, *he translated, edited, and probably wrote most of the poems that make up* The Temple, *though it is quite possible that many of these "psalms" belong to the late 1620's or even earlier; the poems, which had long circulated in manuscript, were published posthumously by Nicholas Ferrar of Little Gidding. Although Herbert wrote no literary criticism as such, his poems bear witness again and again to the great critical question of the day: What has poetry to do with religion? Helicon with Jordan? Sometimes he confronts the problem directly, as in the "Jordan" poems, but often more allusively in poems like "The Collar" or "A Wreath."*

The poems reprinted here come from the 1633 edition of The Temple, *with one exception: "My God, where is that ancient heat . . ." is taken from Walton's* Life of Mr. George Herbert. *According to Walton, this poem (and another in the same vein) was composed at the age of seventeen and was sent to the poet's mother, Lady Magdalen Herbert, with a letter that read in part: "my meaning (dear Mother) is in these Sonnets, to declare my resolution to be, that my poor Abilities in Poetry shall be all, and ever consecrated to Gods glory; and I beg you to receive this as one testimony." This poem, written in the manner of Donne, reappears in* The Temple *as "Love" [II], drastically altered after the manner of the mature Herbert.*

"My God, where is that ancient heat towards thee"

[*c. 1610*]

My God, where is that ancient heat towards thee,
　　Wherewith whole showls of *Martyrs* once did burn,
　　Besides their other flames? Doth Poetry
Wear *Venus* Livery? only serve her turn?
Why are not *Sonnets* made of thee? and layes
　　Upon thine Altar burnt? Cannot thy love
　　Heighten a spirit to sound out thy praise
As well as any she? Cannot thy *Dove*
Out-strip their *Cupid* easily in flight?
　　Or, since thy wayes are deep, and still the same,
　　Will not a verse run smooth that bears thy name!
Why doth that fire, which by thy power and might
　　Each breast does feel, no braver fuel choose
　　Than that, which one day, *Worms* may chance refuse.

Love [II]

[*c. 1630?*]

Immortall Heat, O let thy greater flame
　　Attract the lesser to it: let those fires,
　　Which shall consume the world, first make it tame;
And kindle in our hearts such true desires,
As may consume our lusts, and make thee way.
　　Then shall our hearts pant thee; then shall our brain
　　All her invention on thine Altar lay,

And there in hymnes send back thy fire again:
Our eies shall see thee, which before saw dust;
   Dust blown by wit, till that they both were blinde:
   Thou shalt recover all thy goods in kinde,
Who wert disseized by usurping lust:
   All knees shall bow to thee; all wits shall rise,
   And praise him who did make and mend our eies.

Jordan [I]

[*c. 1630?*]

Who sayes that fictions onely and false hair
Become a verse? Is there in truth no beautie?
Is all good structure in a winding stair?
May no lines passe, except they do their dutie
   Not to a true, but painted chair?

Is it no verse, except enchanted groves
And sudden arbours[1] shadow course-spunne lines?
Must purling streams refresh a lovers loves?
Must all be vail'd, while he that reades, divines,
   Catching the sense at two removes?

Shepherds are honest people; let them sing:
Riddle who list, for me, and pull for Prime:[2]
I envie no mans nightingale or spring;
Nor let them punish me with losse of ryme,
   Who plainly say, *My God, My King.*

Jordan [II]

[*c. 1630?*]

When first my lines of heav'nly joyes made mention,
Such was their lustre, they did so excell,
That I sought out quaint words, and trim invention;

[1] [The allusion is to the element of surprise ("sudden") in gardening.]
[2] [In the card game Primero the player "pulls" a card to make himself "prime."]

My thoughts began to burnish, sprout, and swell,
Curling with metaphors a plain intention,
Decking the sense, as if it were to sell.

Thousands of notions in my brain did runne,
Off'ring their service, if I were not sped:
I often blotted what I had begunne;
This was not quick enough, and that was dead.
Nothing could seem too rich to clothe the sunne,
Much lesse those joyes which trample on his head.

As flames do work and winde, when they ascend,
So did I weave my self into the sense.
But while I bustled, I might heare a friend
Whisper, *How wide is all this long pretence!*
There is in love a sweetnesse readie penn'd:
Copie out onely that, and save expense.

A Wreath

[*c. 1630?*]

A wreathed garland of deserved praise,
Of praise deserved, unto thee I give,
I give to thee, who knowest all my wayes,
My crooked winding wayes, wherein I live,
Wherein I die, not live: for life is straight,
Straight as a line, and ever tends to thee,
To thee, who art more farre above deceit,
Then deceit seems above simplicitie.
Give me simplicitie, that I may live,
So live and like, that I may know thy wayes,
Know them and practise them: then shall I give
For this poore wreath, give thee a crown of praise.

Sir John Suckling

1609–42

After leaving Cambridge, apparently without a degree, and sojourn-
ing very briefly at Gray's Inn, Suckling traveled abroad for several
years and then took up his destined occupation, the life of an accom-
plished courtier. His love of courtly splendor—Aubrey calls him the
"greatest gallant of his time"—induced the wits to see a connection
between the extravagant costuming of his play Aglaura (1637–38)
and the equipage of the troop he led to Scotland during the first
Bishops' War (1639). The Account of Religion by Reason appeared
in 1640, the poems of Fragmenta Aurea in 1646, upon which this version of "A Sessions of the Poets" (apparently written 1637–38) is
based. (I have restored Stanza XVIII, deleted from the edition of 1646
because it glanced adversely at the Queen's courtiers, and have ven-
tured to rearrange and even to insert a couple of the suspended transitional words that emphasize Suckling's obvious effort to organize by
pairs of stanzas.)

The "Sessions," at bottom the old roll call of poets but renewed by
contact with Boccalini's Ragguagli di Parnaso, was one of many
essays in the kind. Suckling's reveals wit, though the text as we have
it does not display the poet's usual attention to meter and form; in
addition, it is a very private piece, being concerned not so much with
the world of letters as the literary environs of Viscount Falkland's
house at Tew, which is described in these terms by Clarendon: "His

house where he usually resided, (Tew, or Burford, in Oxfordshire,)
being within ten or twelve miles of the university, looked like the uni-
versity itself, by the company that was always found there."

A SESSIONS OF THE POETS
[*1637–38?*]

A session was held the other day,
And *Apollo* himself was at it (they say)
The Laurel that had been so long reserv'd,
Was now to be given to him best deserv'd.
           And
Therefore the wits of the Town came thither,
'T was strange to see how they flocked together,
Each strongly confident of his own way,
Thought to gain the Laurel away that day.

There *Selden,* and he sate hard by the chair;
Wenman[1] not far off, which was very fair;
Sands[2] with *Townsend,* for they kept no order;
Digby[3] and *Shillingsworth*[4] a little further:
           And
There was *Lucans* Translator[5] too, and he
That makes God speak so bigge in's Poetry;

1 [Sir Francis Wenman, first baronet of Caswell in Oxfordshire, of whom
Clarendon says: "He was a very good Latin scholar, but his ratiocination was
above his learning; and the sharpness of his wit incomparable."]
2 [George Sandys (1578–1644), translator of Ovid and the Psalms.]
3 [See headnote, p. 202.]
4 [William Chillingworth (1602–44), theologian, who with Wenman, Godolphin, Suckling, Waller, and other "wits" frequented the house of Lucius Cary,
Viscount Falkland, at Tew in Oxfordshire.]
5 [Thomas May (1595–1650) translated the *Pharsalia* in 1628.]

Selwin[6] and *Walter*,[7] and *Bartlets*[8] both the brothers;
Jack Vaughan[9] and *Porter*,[1] and divers others.

The first that broke silence was good old *Ben*,
Prepared before with Canary wine,
And he told them plainly he deserv'd the Bayes,
For his were calld Works, where others were but Plaies[2]
                    And
Bid them remember how he had purg'd the Stage
Of errors, that had lasted many an Age,
And he hopes they did not think the *silent Woman*,
The *Fox*, and the *Alchymist* out done by no man.

Apollo stopt him there, and bade him not go on,
'Twas merit, he said, and not presumption
Must carry't; at which *Ben* turned about,
And in great choler offer'd to go out:
                    But
Those that were there thought it not fit
To discontent so ancient a wit;
And therefore *Apollo* call'd him back agen,
And made him mine host of his own new Inne.

Tom Carew was next, but he had a fault
That would not well stand with a Laureat;
His Muse was hard bound, and th'issue of's brain
Was seldom brought forth but with trouble and pain.
                    And
All that were present there did agree,
A Laureat Muse should be easie and free,
Yet sure 'twas not that, but 'twas thought that his Grace
Consider'd he was well he had a Cup-bearers place.

Will. Davenant asham'd of a foolish mischance
That he had got lately travelling in *France*,[3]

6 [Untraced.]
7 [Evidently a misprint for Edmund Waller.]
8 [Untraced, though a William Bartlett was a "privy chamberman" with
Suckling.]
9 [Sir John Vaughan (1603–74), jurist and friend of Selden.]
1 [Endimion Porter (1587–1649), royalist and poet.]
2 [Even to collect and publish plays smacked of pretentiousness, so that the
folio *Works* of 1616 occasioned much derogatory comment.]
3 [William Davenant contracted the French disease and thereby lost his nose,
thus providing his contemporaries with the opportunity for endless merriment.]

Modestly hoped the handsomnesse of's Muse
Might any deformity about him excuse.
And
Surely the Company would have been content,
If they could have found any President;
But in all their Records either in Verse or Prose,
There was not one Laureat without a nose.

To *Will Bartlet* sure all the wits meant well,
But first they would see how his snow would fell:
Will smil'd and swore in their judgements they went lesse,
That concluded of merit upon successe.
Soe
Suddenly taking his place agen,
He gave way to *Selwin*, who streight stept in;
But alas! he had been so lately a wit,
That *Apollo* hardly knew him yet.

Toby Mathews[4] (pox on him) how came he there?
Was whispering nothing in some-bodies ear:
When he had the honour to be nam'd in Court,
But Sir, you may thank my Lady *Carleil* [5] for't:
For
Had not her care furnisht you out
With something of handsome, without all doubt
You and your sorry Lady Muse had been
In the number of those that were not let in.

In haste from the Court two or three came in,
And they brought letters (forsooth) from the Queen,
'Twas discreetly done too, for if th'had come
Without them, th'had scarce been let into the room.
And
This made a dispute; for 'twas plaine to be seene
Each man had a mind to gratify the Queene:
But *Apollo* himselfe could not thinke it fit;
There was difference, he sayd, betwixt fooling and wit.

Suckling next was call'd, but did not appear,
But strait one whisperd *Apollo* i' th' ear,

4 [Sir Toby Matthew (1577–1655), "likely for learning, memory, sharpness of
wit" (Harrington), courtier and writer.]
5 [Lucy Hay, Countess of Carlisle (1599–1660); Carew's "Lucinda."]

That of all men living, he cared not for't,
He loved not the Muses so well as his sport;
And
Prized black eyes, or a lucky hit
At bowls, above all the Trophies of wit;
But *Apollo* was angry, and publiquely said
'Twere fit that a fine were set upon's head.

Wat Montague[6] now stood forth to his tryal,
And did not so much as suspect a denial;
But witty *Apollo* asked him first of all
If he understood his own Pastoral.
For
If he could do it, 't would plainly appear
He understood more than any man there,
And did merit the Bayes above all the rest,
But the Mounsier was modest, and silence confest.

During these troubles in the Court was hid
One that *Apollo* soon mist, little *Cid;*[7]
And having spied him, call'd him out of the throng,
And advis'd him in his ear not to write so strong.

Murrey[8] was summon'd, but 't was urg'd that he
Was Chief already of another Company.

Hales[9] set by himself most gravely did smile
To see them about nothing keep such a coil;
Apollo had spied him, but knowing his mind
Past by, and call'd *Faulkland* [1] that sate just behind:
But
He was of late so gone with Divinity,
That he had almost forgot his Poetry,
Though to say the truth (and *Apollo* did know it)
He might have been both his Priest and his Poet.

---

[6] [Walter Montagu (1603?–77); his *The Shepherd's Paradise* (1629) was acted before Charles I.]
[7] [The poet Sidney Godolphin (1610–43).]
[8] [Perhaps William Murray, created Earl of Dysart in 1643.]
[9] [John Hales (1584–1656), fellow of Eton and member of the Falkland group; great admirer of Shakespeare.]
[1] [See note 4, page 264, and headnote.]

At length who but an Alderman did appear,
At which *Will. Davenant* began to swear;
But wiser *Apollo* bade him draw nigher,
And when he was mounted a little higher
He
Openly declared that the best signe
Of good store of wit's to have good store of coyn,
And without a Syllable more or lesse said,
He put the Laurel on the Aldermans head.

At this all the wits were in such a maze
That for a good while they did nothing but gaze
One upon another, not a man in the place
But had discontent writ in great in his face.
And
Onely the small Poets clear'd up again,
Out of hope as't was thought of borrowing,
But sure they were out, for he forfeits his Crown
When he lends any Poets about the Town.

Sir William Davenant
or D'Avenant

1606–68

Aubrey wryly alludes to the tale that Davenant was the natural son of Shakespeare, a story that occasioned less mirth among the wits than did the palpable fact of a nose marred by syphilis. Davenant wrote scores of plays and masques, served on sea and land during the Bishops' Wars and the civil war, and dedicated himself to the Royalist cause in Paris, 1646–50, with Cowley, Hobbes, Waller, and others. In 1660 he was granted one of the two theatrical patents.

Davenant's prolific but often pedestrian output seems to have led, in his time and ours, to an excessive amount of critical contempt. He was, in his own way, something of an innovator, writing the "operatic" Siege of Rhodes (1656) and enunciating for the first (and last) time in England a detailed theory of five-act epic—examples of which had begun to appear in England as early as Sidney's Old Arcadia and to disappear as late as Pope's five-act mock-epic "The Rape of the Lock." The selections from Discourse upon Gondibert offered here are important not merely because the preface occasioned Hobbes' Answer but also because Davenant anticipates something of French neoclassicism: the "Preface" to Gondibert is conveniently a transitional document, written in mid-century Paris by an Englishman concerned with the problem of "wit."

The text is the 1650 Paris edition, Discourse upon Gondibert. An Heroick Poem . . . With an Answer to it by Mr. Hobbs.

FROM

Discourse upon Gondibert

FROM

The Author's PREFACE
to his much honoured friend
MR. HOBBS
[1650]

SIR,

Since you have done me the honour to allow this Poem a daily examination as it was writing, I will presume, now it hath attain'd more length, to give you a longer trouble; that you may yield me as great advantages by censuring the Method, as by judging the Numbers in the matter. And because you shall passe through this new Building with more ease to your disquisition, I will acquaint you, what care I took of my materials ere I began to work.

. . . . .

I have now given you the accompt of such provisions as I made for this new Building; and you may next please (having examin'd the substance) to take a view of the form; and observe if I have methodically and with discretion dispos'd of the materi-

alls, which with some curiosity I had collected. I cannot discern
by any help from reading, or learned men, (who have been to
me the best and briefest Indexes of Books) that any Nation hath
in representment of great actions (either by *Heroicks* or *Dramat-
icks*) digested Story into so pleasant and instructive a method
as the English by their *Drama:* and by that regular species
(though narratively and not in Dialogue) I have drawn the body
of an Heroick Poem: In which I did not onely observe the Symmetry (proportioning five Books to five *Acts,* and *Canto's* to
Scenes, the *Scenes* having their number ever governed by occasion) but all the *shadowings, happy strokes, secret graces,* and
even the *drapery* (which together make the second beauty) I
have (I hope) exactly followed: and those compositions of second beauty, I observe in the *Drama* to be the under-walks, inter-
weaving, or correspondence of lesser design in *Scenes,* not the
great motion of the main plot, and coherence of the *Acts.*

Having described the outward frame, the large rooms within,
the lesser conveyances, and now the furniture; it were orderly to
let you examine the matter of which that furniture is made: But
though every owner who hath the Vanity to shew his ornaments
or hangings, must endure the curiosity, and censure of him that
beholds them; yet I shall not give you the trouble of inquiring
what is, but tell you of what I designed their substance, which is,
Wit: And *Wit* is the laborious, and the lucky resultances of
thought, having towards its excellence (as we say of the strokes
of Painting) as well a happinesse, as care. It is a Web consisting of the subtilest threads, and like that of the *Spider,* is consid-
erately woven out of our selves; for a *Spider* may be said to consider, not onely respecting his solemnesse and tacite posture
(like a grave scout in ambush for his Enemy) but because all
things done, are either from consideration or chance; and the
works of chance are accomplishments of an instant, having
commonly a dissimilitude; but hers are the works of time, and
have their contextures alike.

Wit is not onely the luck and labour, but also the dexterity of
the thought; rounding the world like the Sun with unimaginable
motion; and bringing swiftly home to the memory universall
surveyes. It is the Souls *Powder,* which when supprest (as forbidden from flying upward) blows up the restraint; and loseth

all force in a farther ascension towards Heaven (the region of God) and yet by nature is much lesse able to make any inquisition downward towards Hell, the Cell of the Devil; but breaks through all about it (as farre as the utmost it can reach) removes, uncovers, makes way for Light, where darknesse was inclosed, till great bodies are more examinable by being scattered into parcels; and till all that find its strength (but most of mankind are strangers to *Wit*, as *Indians* are to *Powder*) worship it for the effects, as derived from the Deity. It is in Divines Humility, Exemplarinesse, and Moderation: In States-men, Gravity, Vigilance, Benigne Complacency, Secrecy, Patience, and Dispatch. In Leaders of Armies; Valour, Painfulnesse, Temperance, Bounty, Dexterity in Punishing and Rewarding, and a sacred Certitude of Promise: It is in Poets a full comprehension of all recited in all these; and an ability to bring those comprehensions into action, when they shall so farre forget the true measure of what is of greatest consequence to humanity, (which are things righteous, pleasant, and usefull) as to think the delights of greatnesse equall to that of Poesie; or the Chiefs of any Profession more necessary to the World then excellent Poets. Lastly, though *Wit* be not the envy of ignorant Men, 'tis often of evil *Statesmen*, and of all such imperfect great spirits, as have it in a lesse degree then Poets: for though no man envies the excellence of that which in no proportion he ever tasted (as men cannot be said to envy the condition of Angels) yet we may say the devil envies the Supremacy of God, because he was in some degree partaker of his Glory.

That which is not, yet is accounted, *Wit*, I will but slightly remember; which seems very incident to imperfect youth and sickly age; Young men (as if they were not quite delivered from Child-hood whose first exercise is Language) imagine it consists in the Musick of words, and believe they are made wise by refining their speech above the vulgar Dialect: which is a mistake almost as great as that of the people, who think Oratours (which is a title that crowns at riper years those that have practised the dexterity of tongue) the ablest men; who are indeed so much more unapt for governing, as they are more fit for Sedition: and it may be said of them as of the Witches of *Norway*, who can sell a Storm for a *Doller*, which for ten thousand they cannot allay.

From the esteem of speaking they proceed to the admiration of what are commonly called *Conceits,* things that sound like the knacks or toyes of ordinary *Epigrammatists:* and from thence, after more conversation and variety of objects, grow up to some force of *Fancy;* Yet even then like young Hawks they stray and fly farre off; using their liberty as if they would ne're return to the Lure; and often go at check ere they can make a steddy view, and know their game.

Old men, that have forgot their first Child-hood, and are returning to their second, think it lies in *Agnominations,* and in a kind of an alike tinkling of words; or else in a grave telling of wonderfull things, or in comparing of times without a discover'd partiality; which they perform so ill by favouring the past, that, as 'tis observ'd, if the bodies of men should grow lesse, though but an unmeasurable proportion in seven years; Yet reckoning from the *Flood,* they would not remain in the stature of Frogs: so if States and particular persons had impair'd in Government, and increas'd in wickednesse, proportionably to what old Men affirm they have done, from their own infancy to their age; all publick Policy had been long since Confusion, and the congregated world would not suffice now to people a village.

The last thing they suppose to be *Wit,* is their bitter Morals, when they almost declare themselves Enemies to Youth and Beauty; by which Severity they seem cruel as *Herod* when he surpris'd the sleeping Children of *Bethleem:* For Youth is so farre from wanting Enemies, that it is mortally its own; so unpractis'd, that it is every where cozen'd more then a Stranger among *Jews;* and hath an infirmity of sight more hurtfull then Blindnesse to Blind men; for though it cannot chuse the way, it scorns to be led. And Beauty, though many call themselves her Friends, hath few but such as are false to her: Though the World sets her in a Throne, yet all about her (even her gravest Councellours) are Traytours, though not in conspiracy, yet in their distinct designes; and to make her certain not onely of distresse but ruine, she is ever pursu'd by her most cruel enemy, the great Destroyer, *Time.* But I will proceed no farther upon Old men, nor in recording mistakes; lest finding so many more, then there be Verities, we might believe we walk in as great obscurity as the Egyptians when Darknesse was their Plague. Nor will I presume to call the matter of which the Ornaments or Substantiall parts of this Poem are compos'd, *Wit;* but onely tell you my endeavour was, in bringing Truth (too often absent) home to mens bosomes, to lead her through unfrequented and new wayes, and from the most remote Shades; by representing Nature though not in an affected, yet in an unusuall dresse.

'Tis now fit, after I have given you so long a survey of the Building, to render you some accompt of the Builder; that you may know by what time, pains, and assistance I have already proceeded, or may hereafter finish my work: and in this I shall take occasion to accuse, and condemn, as Papers unworthy of light, all those hasty digestions of thought which were publish'd in my Youth; a sentence not pronounc'd out of melancholy rigour, but from a cheerfull obedience to the just authority of experience: For that grave mistresse of the World, *Experience* (in whose profitable Schoole those before the Flood stay'd long, but we like wanton Children come thither late, yet too soon are call'd out of it, and fetch'd home by Death) hath taught me, that the engendrings of unripe age become abortive, and deform'd; and that after obteining more years, those must needs prophecy with ill successe, who make use of their Visions in Wine; That when the antient Poets were valued as Prophets, they were long and painfull in watching the correspondence of Causes, ere they presum'd to foretell Effects: and that 'tis a high presumption to entertein a Nation (who are a Poets standing Guests, and require Monarchicall respect) with hasty provisions; as if a Poet might imitate the familiar dispatch of Faulconers, mount his *Pegasus,* unhood his *Muse,* and with a few flights, boast he hath provided a feast for a Prince. Such posting upon *Pegasus* I have long since forborn; and during my journey in this Work have mov'd with a slow place; that I might make my surveyes as one that travelled not to bring home the names, but the proportion and nature of things: and in this I am made wise by two great examples; for the friends of *Virgil* acknowledge he was many years in doing honour to *Æneas* (still contracting at night into a closer force the abundance of his morning strengths) and *Statius* rather seems to boast then blush, when he confesses he was twice Seven years in renowning the War between *Argos* and *Thebes.*

Next to the usefulnesse of Time (which here implies ripe

Age) I beleev'd pains most requisite to this undertaking: for though painfulnesse in Poets (according to the usuall negligence of our Nation in examining, and their diligence to censure) seems always to discover a want of naturall force, and is traduc'd, as if Poesie concern'd the world no more then Dancing; whose onely grace is the quicknesse and facility of motion; and whose perfection is not of such publick consequence, that any man can merit much by attaining it with long labour: yet let them consider, and they will find (nor can I stay long ere I convince them in the important use of Poesie) the naturall force of a Poet more apparent, by but confessing that great forces ask great labour in managing, then by an arrogant braving the world, when he enters the field with his undisciplin'd first thoughts: For a wise Poet, like a wise Generall, will not shew his strengths till they are in exact government and order; which are not the postures of chance, but proceed from Vigilance and Labour.

Yet to such painfull Poets some upbraid the want of extemporary fury, or rather *Inspiration;* a dangerous word, which many have of late successfully us'd; and *Inspiration* is a spirituall Fit, deriv'd from the antient Ethnick Poets, who then, as they were Priests, were States-men too, and probably lov'd Dominion; and as their well dissembling of inspiration begot them reverence then, equall to that which was payd to Lawes; so these who now professe the same fury, may perhaps by such authentick example pretend authority over the people; It being not unreasonable to imagine, they rather imitate the *Greek* Poets then the *Hebrew* Prophets, since the later were inspir'd for the use of others; and these, like the former, prophecy for themselves. But though the antient Poets are excus'd, as knowing the weak constitution of those Deities from whom they took their Priesthood; and the frequent necessity of dissembling for the ease of government; yet these (who also from the chief to the meanest are States-men and Priests, but have not the luck to be Poets) should not assume such saucy familiarity with a true God.

From the time and labour requir'd to my Poem, let me proceed to my Assistants; by which I shall not so much attest my own weaknesse, as discover the difficulties and greatness of such a work. For when *Solomon* made use of his Neighbours towards

his building, he lost no reputation, nor by demanding those aids
was thought a lesser Prince; but rather publish'd his Wisedome,
in rightly understanding the vast extent of his enterprise: who
likewise with as much glory made use of Fellers of wood, and
Hewers of Stone, as of learned Architects: Nor have I refrain'd
to be oblig'd to men of any science, as well mechanicall as liberall: Nor when Memory (from that various and plentifull stock,
with which all observers are furnish'd that have had diversity of
life) presented me by chance with any figure, did I lay it aside as
uselesse, because at that instant I was not skilfull to manage it
artfully; but I have staid and recorded such objects, till by consulting with right Masters I have dispos'd of them without mistake; It being no more shame to get Learning at that very time,
and from the same Text; when, and by which, we instruct
others; then for a forward Scout, discovering the Enemy, to save
his own life at a Passe, where he then teaches his Party to escape.

. . . Poesie, which (like contracted *Essences* seems the utmost
strength and activity of Nature) is as all good Arts, subservient
to Religion; all marching under the same Banner, though of
lesse discipline and esteem. And as Poesie is the best Expositour
of Nature (Nature being mysterious to such as use not to consider) so Nature is the best Interpreter of God; and more cannot
be said of Religion. And when the Judges of Religion (which are
the Chiefs of the Church) neglect the help of Moralists in re-
forming the People (and Poets are of all Moralists the most usefull) they give a sentence against the Law of Nature: For Nature performs all things by correspondent aids and harmony.
And 'tis injurious not to think Poets the most usefull Moralists;
for as Poesie is adorn'd and sublim'd by Musick, which makes it
more pleasant and acceptable; so morality is sweetned and made
more amiable by Poesie.

When neither Religion (which is our Art towards God) nor
Nature (which is Gods first Law to Man, though by Man least
study'd) nor when Reason (which is Nature, and made Art by
Experience) can by the Enemies of Poesie be sufficiently urg'd
against it; then some (whose frowardnesse will not let them quit

an evil cause) plead written Authority. And though such authority be a Weapon, that even in the Warre of Religion, distress'd
Disputers take up, as their last shift; yet here we would protest
against it, but that we find it makes a false defence, and leaves
the Enemy more open. This authority (which is but single too)
is from *Plato;* and him some have maliciously quoted; as if in his
feign'd Common-wealth he had banish'd all Poets. But *Plato*
saies nothing against Poets in generall; and in his particular
quarrel (which is to *Homer* and *Hesiod*) onely condemnes such
errours as we mention'd in the beginning of this *Preface,* when
we look'd upon the Antients. And those errours consist in their
abasing Religion, by representing the Gods in evill proportion,
and their *Heroes* with as unequal Characters; and so brought
Vices into fashion, by intermixing them with the Virtues of great
Persons. Yet even during this divine anger of *Plato,* he concludes
not against Poesie, but the Poems then most in request. . . .

.   .   .

And now, Sir, to end with the Allegory which I have so long
continu'd, I shall (after all my busie vanity in shewing and describing my new Building) with great quietnesse (being almost
as weary as your self) bring you to the Back-dore, that you may
make no review, but in my absence; and steal hastily from you,
as one who is ashamed of all the trouble you have receiv'd from,

    SIR,

                    Your most humble, and most
                        affectionate Servant,

                          Wil. D'avenant

From the Louvre
  in Paris,
January 2. 1650

Thomas Hobbes

1588–1679

After Oxford, Hobbes became a kind of tutor-companion in the Caven-dish family, a position he retained, with some interruptions, until the end of his life. His intellectual powers and wide-ranging interests appear to have been stimulated by his involuntary immersion (during the Royalist exile) in the cosmopolitan literary life of Paris, though there can be no doubt that his strictly rationalistic habits of mind, symbolized by his later addiction to Euclid, had been formed much ear-lier. His acquaintance included a large number of the influential men of his time: Descartes, Lord Herbert, Kenelm Digby, Waller, Davenant, Bacon, and many others. During his long life, taken up with a series of witty and ill-tempered controversies, he managed to find himself hated as well as respected; and his philosophical writings—ration-alistic, materialistic, nominalistic—were probably more influential, if we count negative as well as positive reactions, than any others of his time. Even the combined energies of the Cambridge Platonists proved insufficient to draw out Leviathan (1651) with a hook.

His abiding, if generally submerged, interest was literature; in his eighties he translated Homer. There occur throughout his philosoph-ical works important remarks on the nature of language, but his most extended theorizing about poetry appears in The Answer to Dave-nant's preface to Gondibert; the preface to Homer "Concerning the Vertues of an Heroique Poem," written a quarter of a century later, reveals little, if any, change in attitude. The Answer offers help in understanding the transition toward the rationalism of the Restoration, especially in the way Hobbes emphasizes "probability" and distinguishes between "wit" and "judgement." As for the doctrine of divine inspiration that was to serve Milton: "I can imagine no cause, but a reasonlesse imitation of custome . . . by which a man . . . loves rather to be thought to speak by inspiration, like a Bag-pipe."

The text: Discourse upon Gondibert. An Heroick Poem . . . With an Answer to it by Mr. Hobbs (*Paris, 1650*).

FROM

Discourse upon Gondibert

The ANSWER *of* MR. HOBBS
To S*r.* William D'Avenant's
PREFACE *before Gondibert*
[*1650*]

SIR,

If to commend your Poem, I should onely say (in generall terms) that in the choice of your Argument, the disposition of the parts, the maintenance of the Characters of your Persons, the Dignity and Vigour of your Expression you have performed all the parts of various experience, ready memory, clear judgement, swift and well govern'd fancy, though it were enough for the truth, it were too little for the weight and credit of my testimony. For I lie open to two Exceptions, one of an incompetent, the other of a corrupted Witnesse. Incompetent, because I am not a

Poet; and corrupted with the Honour done me by your PREFACE. The former obliges me to say something (by the way) of the Nature and differences of Poesie.

As Philosophers have divided the Universe (their subject) into three Regions, *Celestial, Aeriall,* and *Terrestriall;* so the Poets (whose work it is by imitating humane life, in delightfull and measur'd lines, to avert men from vice, and encline them to virtuous and honourable actions) have lodg'd themselves in the three Regions of Mankind, *Court, City,* and *Countrey* correspondent in some proportion, to those three Regions of the World. For there is in Princes and men of conspicuous power (antiently called *Heroes*) a lustre and influence upon the rest of men, resembling that of the Heavens; and an insincerenesse, inconstancy, and troublesome humour of those that dwell in populous Cities, like the mobility, blustring, and impurity of the Air; and a plainnesse, and (though dull) yet a nutritive faculty in rurall people, that endures a comparison with the Earth they labour.

From hence have proceeded three sorts of Poesie; *Heroick, Scommatick,*[1] and *Pastorall.* Every one of these is distinguish'd again in the manner of *Representation,* which sometimes is *Narrative,* wherein the Poet himself relateth, and sometimes *Dramatick,* as when the persons are every one adorned and brought upon the Theatre, to speak and act their own parts. There is therefore neither more nor lesse then six sorts of Poesie. For the Heroick Poem narrative (such as is yours) is called an *Epick Poeme;* The Heroick Poeme Drammatick, is *Tragedy.* The Scommatick Narrative, is *Satyre;* Drammatick is *Comedy.* The Pastorall narrative, is called simply *Pastorall* (antiently *Bucolick*) the same Dramatick, *Pastorall Comedie.* The Figure therefore of an Epick Poem, and of a Tragedy, ought to be the same, for they differ no more but in that they are pronounced by one, or many persons. Which I insert to justifie the figure of yours, consisting of five books divided into Songs or Cantoes, as five Acts divided into Scenes has ever been the approved figure of a Tragedy.

They that take for Poesie whatsoever is writ in Verse, will think this division imperfect, and call in Sonnets, Epigrammes,

1 [Scoffing, satirical.]

Eclogues, and the like pieces (which are but Essayes, and parts
of an entire Poeme) and reckon *Empedocles,* and *Lucretius*
(naturall Philosophers) for Poets, and the morall precepts of
Phocylides, Theognis, and the Quatrains of *Pybrach,*[2] and the
History of *Lucan,* and others of that kind amongst Poems; be-
stowing on such Writers for honour the name of Poets, rather
then of Historians or Philosphers. But the subject of a Poem is
the manners of men, not naturall causes; manners presented,
not dictated; and manners feigned (as the name of Poesie imports) not found in men. They that give entrance to Fictions
writ in prose, erre not so much, but they erre. For Poesie requireth delightfulnesse, not onely of fiction, but of stile; in which if
prose contend with Verse, it is with disadvantage (as it were) on
foot, against the strength and wings of *Pegasus.*

For Verse amongst the *Greeks* was appropriated antiently to
the service of their Gods, and was the Holy stile; the stile of the
Oracles; the stile of the Laws; and the stile of men that publickly
recommended to their Gods, the vows and thanks of the people;
which was done in their holy Songs called Hymns; and the Composers of them were called Prophets and Priests before the name
of Poet was known. When afterwards the majesty of that stile
was observed, the Poets chose it as best becoming their high invention. And for the Antiquity of Verse it is greater then the Antiquity of Letters. For it is certain *Cadmus* was the first that
(from *Phœnicia,* a countrey that neighboureth *Judea*) brought
the use of Letters into Greece. But the service of the Gods, and
the laws (which by measured Sounds were easily committed
to the memory) had been long time in use, before the arrivall of
Cadmus there.

There is besides the grace of stile, another cause why the
antient Poets chose to write in measured language, which is this.
Their Poems were made at first with intention to have them sung,
as well Epique, as Dramatique (which custome hath been long
time laid aside, but began to be revived in part, of late years in
Italy) and could not be made commensurable to the Voyce or
instruments, in Prose; the wayes and motions whereof are so

---

2 [Gui du Faur, seigneur de Pibrac (1529–84), *Cinquante quatrains con-
tenant préceptes et enseignements utiles pour la vie de l'homme, composés à
l'imitation de Phocylides, Epicharmus et autres poètes grecs* (Paris, 1574); the
quatrains were added to, and passed through many editions and translations.]

uncertain and undistinguished, (like the way and motion of a Ship in the Sea) as not onely to discompose the best Composers, but also to disappoint sometimes the most attentive Reader, and put him to hunt counter for the sense. It was therefore necessary for Poets in those times, to write in Verse.

The verse which the Greeks, and Latines (considering the nature of their own languages) found by experience most grave, and for an Epique Poem most decent, was their *Hexameter;* a Verse limited, not onely in the length of the line, but also in the quantity of the syllables. Instead of which we use the line of ten syllables, recompensing the neglect of their quantity, with the diligence of Rime. And this measure is so proper for an Heroick Poem, as without some losse of gravity and dignity, it was never changed. A longer is not farre from ill prose, and a shorter, is a kind of whisking (you know) like the unlacing, rather then the singing of a Muse. In an Epigramme or a Sonnet, a man may vary his measures, and seek glory from a needlesse difficulty, as he that contrived verses into the forms of an Organ, a Hatchet, an Egg, an Altar, and a pair of Wings; but in so great and noble a work as is an Epick Poeme, for a man to obstruct his own way, with unprofitable difficulties, is great imprudence. So likewise to chuse a needlesse and difficult correspondence of Rime, is but a difficult toy, and forces a man sometimes for the stopping of a chink to say somewhat he did never think; I cannot therefore but very much approve your *Stanza,* wherein the syllables in every verse are ten, and the Rime, Alternate.

For the choice of your subject you have sufficiently justified your self in your Preface. But because I have observed in *Virgil,* that the Honour done to *Æneas* and his companions, has so bright a reflection upon *Augustus Cesar,* and other great Romanes of that time, as a man may suspect him not constantly possessed with the noble spirit of those his *Heroes,* and believe you are not acquainted with any great man of the Race of *Gondibert,* I adde to your Justification the purity of your purpose, in having no other motive of your labour, but to adorn virtue, and procure her Lovers; then which there cannot be a worthier design & more becoming noble Poesie.

In that you make so small account of the example of almost all the approved Poets, antient and moderne, who thought fit in the beginning, and sometimes also in the progresse of their Poemes, to invoke a Muse, or some other Deitie, that should dictate to them, or assist them in their writings, they that take not the laws of Art, from any reason of their own, but from the fashion of precedent times, will perhaps accuse your singularity. For my part, I neither subscribe to their accusation, not yet condemne that Heathen custome, otherwise then as necessary to their false Religion. For their Poets were their Divines; had the name of Prophets; Exercised amongst the people a kind of Spirituall Authority; would be thought to speak by a Divine spirit; have their works which they writ in Verse (the Divine stile) passe for the word of God, and not of man; and to be harkened to with reverence. Do not our Divines (excepting the stile) do the same, and by us that are of the same Religion cannot justly be reprehended for it? Besides, in the use of the spirituall calling of Divines, there is danger sometimes to be feared, from want of skill, such as is reported of unskilfull Conjurers, that mistaking the rites and ceremonious points of their art, call up such spirits, as they cannot at their pleasure allay again; by whom storms are raised, that overthrow buildings, and are the cause of miserable wracks at Sea. Unskilfull Divines do oftentimes the like, For when they call unseasonably for *Zeal,* there appears a spirit of *Cruelty;* and by the like errour instead of *Truth* they raise *Discord;* instead of *Wisdome, Fraud;* instead of *Reformation, Tumult;* and *Controversie* instead of *Religion.* Whereas in the Heathen Poets, at least in those whose works have lasted to the time we are in, there are none of those indiscretions to be found, that tended to subversion or disturbance of the Commonwealths wherein they lived. But why a Christian should think it an ornament to his Poem, either to profane the true God, or invoke a false one, I can imagine no cause, but a reasonlesse imitation of custome; of a foolish custome; by which a man, enabled to speak wisely from the principles of nature, and his own meditation, loves rather to be thought to speak by inspiration, like a Bagpipe.

Time and education beget experience; Experience begets Memory; Memory begets Judgement and Fancy; Judgement begets the strength and structure, and Fancy begets the ornaments of a Poem. The Antients therefore fabled not absurdly, in mak-

ing memory the mother of the Muses. For memory is the World
(though not really, yet so as in a looking-glass) in which the
Judgement (the severer Sister) busieth her self in a grave and
rigid examination of all the parts of Nature, and in registring by
Letters, their order, causes, uses, differences and resemblances;
Whereby the Fancy, when any work of Art is to be performed,
findeth her materials at hand and prepared for use, and needs
no more then a swift motion over them, that what she wants,
and is there to be had, may not lye too long unespied. So that
when she seemeth to fly from one Indies to the other, and from
Heaven to Earth, and to penetrate into the hardest matter, and
obscurest places, into the future, and into her self, and all this in
a point of time; the voyage is not very great, her self being all
she seeks; and her wonderfull celerity, consisteth not so much in
motion, as in copious Imagery discreetly ordered, and perfectly
registred in the memory; which most men under the name of
Philosophy have a glimpse of, and is pretended to by many that
grossely mistaking her embrace contention in her place. But so
farre forth as the Fancy of man has traced the wayes of true
Philosophy, so farre it hath produced very marvellous effects to
the benefit of mankind. All that is beautifull or defensible in
building; or mervellous in Engines and Instruments of motion;
Whatsoever commodity men receive from the observation of the
Heavens, from the description of the Earth, from the account of
Time, from walking on the Seas; and whatsoever distinguisheth
the civility of *Europe*, from the Barbarity of the *American* sal-
vages, is the workmanship of Fancy, but guided by the Precep[t]s
of true Philosophy. But where these precepts fail, as they have
hitherto failed in the doctrine of Morall virtue, there the Architect (*Fancy*) must take the Philosophers part upon her self. He
therefore that undertakes an Heroick Poem (which is to exhibit
a venerable and amiable Image of Heroick virtue) must not
onely be the Poet, to place and connex,[3] but also the Philosopher,
to furnish and square his matter, that is, to make both body and
soul, colour and shadow of his Poem out of his own store: which
how well you have performed I am now considering.

Observing how few the persons be you introduce in the beginning, and how in the course of the actions of these (the number

3 [Tie or bind.]

increasing) after severall confluences, they run all at last into the two principall streams of your Poem, *Gondibert* and *Oswald,* me thinks the Fable is not much unlike the Theatre.[4] For so, from severall and farre distant Sources, do the lesser Brooks of *Lombardy,* flowing into one another, fall all at last into the two main Rivers, the *Po,* and the *Adice.* It hath the same resemblance also with a mans veins, which proceeding from different parts, after the like concourse, insert themselves at last into the two principall veins of the Body. But when I considered that also the actions of men, which singly are inconsiderable, after many conjunctures, grow at last either into one great protecting power, or into two destroying Factions; I could not but approve the structure of your Poem, which ought to be no other then such as an imitation of humane life requireth.

In the streams themselves I find nothing but setled Valour, clean Honour, calm Counsel, learned Diversion, and pure Love; save onely a torrent or two of Ambition, which (though a fault) hath somewhat Heroick in it, and therefore must have place in an Heroick Poem. To shew the Reader in what place he shall find every excellent picture of Virtue you have drawn, is too long. And to shew him one, is to prejudice the rest; yet I cannot forbear to point him to the Description of Love in the person of *Birtha,* in the seventh *Canto* of the second Book. There hath nothing been said of that subject neither by the Antient nor modern Poets comparable to it. Poets are Painters: I would fain see another Painter draw so true, perfect, and naturall a Love to the Life, and make use of nothing but pure lines, without the help of any the least uncomely shadow, as you have done. But let it be read as a piece by it self, and for in the almost equall heighth of the whole, the eminence of parts is Lost.

There are some that are not pleased with fiction, unless it be bold not onely to exceed the *work,* but also the *possibility* of nature: they would have impenetrable Armours, Inchanted Castles, invulnerable bodies, Iron men, flying Horses, and a thousand other such things which are easily feign'd by them that dare. Against such I defend you (without assenting to those that condemne either *Homer* or *Virgil*) by dissenting onely from those that think the Beauty of a Poem consisteth in the exorbi-

4 [Hobbes apparently has in mind the L. *Teatinus;* i.e., Italy.]

tancy of the fiction. For as truth is the bound of Historicall, so the Resemblance of truth is the utmost limit of Poeticall Liberty. In old time amongst the Heathens, such strange Fictions and Metamorphoses, were not so remote from the Articles of their Faith, as they are now from ours, and therefore we are not so unpleasant.[5] Beyond the actuall works of Nature a Poet may now go; but beyond the conceived possibility of Nature, never. I can allow a Geographer to make in the Sea, a fish or a ship, which by the scale of his Map would be two or three hundred miles long, and think it done for ornament, because it is done without the precincts of his undertaking; but when he paints an Elephant so, I presently apprehend it as ignorance, and a plain confession of *Terra incognita*.

As the description of great Men, and great Actions is the constant design of a Poet; so the Descriptions of worthy circumstances are necessary accessions to a Poem, and being well performed, are the Jewels and most precious ornaments of Poesie. Such in *Virgil*, are the Funeral games of *Anchises*. The Duel of *Æneas* and *Turnus*, &c. And such in yours, are *The Hunting. The Battel. The City Mourning. The Funeral. The House of Astragon. The Library. And the Temples*. Equal to his, or those of *Homer* whom he imitated.

There remains now no more to be considered but the Expression, in which consisteth the countenance and colour of a beautifull Muse; and is given her by the Poet out of his own provision, or is borrowed from others. That which he hath of his own, is nothing but experience and knowledge of Nature, and specially humane Nature; and is the true and naturall Colour. But that which is taken out of Books (the ordinary boxes of counterfeit Complexion) shews well or ill, as it hath more or lesse resemblance with the Naturall' and are not to be used (without examination) unadvisedly. For in him that professes the imitation of Nature, (as all Poets do) what greater fault can there be, then to bewray an ignorance of nature in his Poem; especially having a liberty allowed him, if he meet with any thing he cannot master, to leave it out?

That which giveth a Poem the true and naturall Colour, consisteth in two things, which are, *To know well;* that is, to have

5 [Indecorous.]

images of nature in the memory distinct and clear; and *To know much.* A sign of the first is perspicuity, property,[6] and decency; which delight all sorts of men, either by instructing the ignorant, or soothing the learned in their knowledge: A sign of the later is novelty of expression, and pleaseth by excitation of the mind; for novelty causeth admiration; and admiration, curiosity; which is a delightfull appetite of knowledge.

There be so many words in use at this day in the English tongue, that, though of magnifick sound, yet (like the windy blisters of a troubled water) have no sense at all; and so many others that lose their meaning by being ill coupled, that it is a hard matter to avoid them; for having been obtruded upon Youth in the Schools (by such as make it, I think, their businesse there, as 'tis exprest by the best Poet)

With terms to charm the weak and pose the wise.[7]

they grow up with them, and gaining reputation with the ignorant, are not easily shaken off.

To this palpable darknesse, I may also add the ambitious obscurity of expressing more then is perfectly conceived; or perfect conception in fewer words then it requires. Which Expressions, though they have had the honour to be called strong lines, are indeed no better then Riddles, and not onely to the Reader, but also (after a little time) to the Writer himself, dark and troublesome.

To the property[8] of Expression, I referre that clearnesse of memory, by which a Poet when he hath once introduced any person whatsoever, speaking in his Poem, maintaineth in him, to the end, the same Character he gave to him in the beginning. The variation whereof, is a change of pace that argues the Poet tired.

Of the Indecencies of an Heroick Poem, the most remarkable are those that shew disproportion either between the persons and their actions, or between the manners of the Poet and the Poem. Of the first kind, is the uncomelinesse of representing in great persons the inhumane vice of Cruelty, or the sordid vices

6 [Propriety.]
7 Gondib. 1 I. Cant. 5.
8 [Propriety.]

of Lust and Drunkennesse. To such parts as those, the Antient approved Poets thought it fit to suborn, not the persons of men, but of monsters and beastly Giants, such as *Polyphemus, Cacus,* and the *Centaurs.* For it is supposed, a Muse, when she is invoked to sing a song of that nature, should maidenly advise the Poet to set such persons to sing their own vices upon the stage; for it is not so unseemly in a Tragedy. Of the same kind it is to represent scurrility, or any action or language that moveth much laughter. The delight of an Epique Poem consisteth not in mirth but in admiration. Mirth and laughter is proper to Comedy and Satyre. Great persons that have their minds employed on great designs have not leisure enough to laugh, and are pleased with the contemplation of their own power and virtues, so as they need not the infirmities and vices of other men to recommend themselves to their own favour by comparison, as all men do when they laugh. Of the second kind, where the disproportion is between the Poet, and the persons of his Poem, one is in the Dialect of the Inferiour sort of People which is always different from the language of the Court. Another is to derive the Illustration of any thing, from such metaphors or comparisons as cannot come into mens thoughts, but by mean conversation, and experience of humble or evil Arts, which the persons of an Epick Poem cannot be thought acquainted with.

From *Knowing much,* proceedeth the admirable variety and novelty of metaphors and similitudes, which are not possibly to be lighted on in the compasse of a narrow knowledge. And the want whereof compelleth a Writer to Expressions that are either defac'd by time, or sullied with vulgar or long use. For the phrases of Poesie, as the airs of Musick, with often hearing become insipide; the Reader having no more sense of their force, then our Flesh is sensible of the bones that sustain it. As the sense we have of bodies, consisteth in change and variety of impression, so also do's the sense of language in the variety and changeable use of words. I mean not in the affectation of words newly brought home from travel, but in new (and withall, significant) translation to our purposes, of those that be already received, and in farre fetch't (but withall, apt, instructive, and comely) similitudes.

Having thus (I hope) avoided the first Exception, against the

Incompetency of my Judgement: I am but little moved with the second; which is, of being bribed by the honour you have done me, by attributing in your Preface somewhat to my Judgement. For I have used your Judgement no lesse in many things of mine, which coming to light will thereby appear the better. And so you have your bribe again.

Having thus made way for the admission of my Testimony, I give it briefly thus; I never yet saw Poem that had so much shape of Art, health of Morality, and vigour and beauty of Expression, as this of yours. And but for the clamour of the multitude that hide their Envy of the present, under a Reverence of Antiquity, I should say further, that it would last as long as either the *Æneid* or *Iliad*, but for one Disadvantage. And the Disadvantage is this: The languages of the Greeks and Romans (by their Colonies and Conquest) have put off flesh and bloud, and are become immutable, which none of the Modern Tongues are like to be. I honour Antiquity; but, that which is commonly called *old time*, is *young time*. The glory of Antiquity is due, not to the Dead, but to the Aged.

And now, whilst I think on't, give me leave with a short discord to sweeten the Harmony of the approaching close. I have nothing to object against your Poem; but, dissent onely from something in your Preface, sounding to the prejudice of Age. 'Tis commonly said, that old Age is a return to Child-hood. Which me thinks you insist on so long, as if you desired it should be beleeved. That's the Note I mean to shake a little. That saying, meant onely of the weakenesse of body, was wrested to the weakenesse of mind, by froward children, weary of the controlment of their parents, masters, and other admonitours. Secondly, the dotage and childishnesse they ascribe to Age, is never the effect of Time, but sometimes of the excesses of Youth, and not a returning to, but a continuall stay with Child-hood. For they that wanting the curiosity of furnishing their memories with the rarities of nature in their Youth, and passe their time in making provision onely for their ease and sensuall delight, are Children still, at what years soever; as they that coming into a populous city, never go out of their own Inne, are strangers still, how long soever they have been there. Thirdly, there is no reason for any man to think himself wiser to day then yesterday, which doth not equally convince he shall be wiser to morrow then to day.

Fourthly, you will be forced to change your opinion hereafter when you are old; and in the mean time you discredit all I have said before in your commendation, because I am old already. But no more of this.

I believe (Sir) you have seen a curious kind of perspective, where, he that looks through a short hollow pipe, upon a picture conteining diverse figures, sees none of those that are there painted, but some one person made up of their parts, conveighed to the eye by the artificiall cutting of a glasse. I find in my imagination an effect not unlike it from your Poem. The virtues you distribute there amongst so many noble Persons represent (in the reading) the image but of one mans virtue to my fancy, which is your own; and that so deeply imprinted, as to stay for ever there, and govern all the rest of my thoughts and affections in the way of honouring and serving you, to the utmost of my power, that am

SIR,

Your most humble, and
obedient Servant,

THOMAS HOBBS

January 10. 1650

FINIS

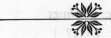

Andrew Marvell

1621–78

Educated at Cambridge, Marvell traveled widely before becoming tutor to the daughter of Lord Fairfax at Nun Appleton House, where it seems probable that he wrote much of his great lyric verse. In 1653, despite his reputation in some quarters as a "notable English Italo-Machavillian," he became tutor to a ward of Cromwell and secured Milton's enthusiastic recommendation of his abilities; after assisting Milton in the Latin secretaryship from 1657 to 1659, Marvell served conscientiously for the rest of his life as M.P. for Hull. Neither his satires nor pamphlets offer much in the way of literary criticism, but his lyric verse everywhere reveals a mind constantly intrigued with literary problems, especially that of genre and that of "decorum" in its widest sense.

"The Coronet," in which the poet criticizes the poem he is writing, perhaps dates from the early 1650's; it and "On . . . Paradise lost," which first came out in the second edition of the epic in 1674, are both reprinted from the Clark Library (Los Angeles, California) copy of the Miscellaneous Poems *that appeared posthumously in 1681.*

The Coronet

[*c. 1652?*]

When for the Thorns with which I long, too long,
  With many a piercing wound,
  My Saviours head have crown'd,
I seek with Garlands to redress that Wrong:
  Through every Garden, every Mead,
I gather flow'rs (my fruits are only flow'rs)
  Dismantling all the fragrant Towers
That once adorn'd my Shepherdesses head.
And now when I have summ'd up all my store,
  Thinking (so I my self deceive)
  So rich a Chaplet thence to weave
As never yet the king of Glory wore:
  Alas I find the Serpent old
  That, twining in his speckled breast,
  About the flow'rs disguis'd does fold,
  With wreaths of Fame and Interest.
Ah, foolish Man, that would'st debase with them,
And mortal Glory, Heavens Diadem!
But thou who only could'st the Serpent tame,
Either his slipp'ry knots at once untie,
And disentangle all his winding Snare:
Or shatter too with him my curious frame:
And let these wither, so that he may die,
Though set with Skill and chosen out with Care.
That they, while Thou on both their Spoils dost tread,
May crown thy Feet, that could not crown thy Head.

On Mr. Milton's *Paradise lost*
[1674]

When I beheld the Poet blind, yet bold,
In slender Book his vast Design unfold,
Messiah Crown'd, *Gods* Reconcil'd Decree,
Rebelling *Angels,* the Forbidden Tree,
Heav'n, Hell, Earth, Chaos, All; the Argument
Held me a while misdoubting his Intent,
That he would ruine (for I saw him strong)
The sacred Truths to Fable and old Song,
(So *Sampson* groap'd the Temples Posts in spight)
The World o'rewhelming to revenge his Sight.

Yet as I read, soon growing less severe,
I lik'd his Project, the success did fear;
Through that wide Field how he his way should find
O're which lame Faith leads Understanding blind;
Lest he perplext the things he would explain,
And what was easie he should render vain.

Or if a Work so infinite he spann'd,
Jealous I was that some less skilful hand
(Such as disquiet alwayes what is well,
And by ill imitating would excell)
Might hence presume the whole Creations day
To change in Scenes, and show it in a Play.[1]

Pardon me, *mighty Poet,* nor despise
My causeless, yet not impious, surmise.
But I am now convinc'd, and none will dare
Within thy Labours to pretend a Share.
Thou hast not miss'd one thought that could be fit,
And all that was improper dost omit:
So that no room is here for Writers left,
But to detect their Ignorance or Theft.

That Majesty which through thy Work doth Reign
Draws the Devout, deterring the Profane.
And things divine thou treats of in such state
As them preserves, and Thee inviolate.
At once delight and horrour on us seize,

1 [An allusion to Dryden's *The State of Innocence;* see note 2 below.]

Thou singst with so much gravity and ease;
And above humane flight dost soar aloft,
With Plume so strong, so equal, and so soft.
The *Bird* nam'd from that *Paradise* you sing
So never Flags, but alwaies keeps on Wing.

Where couldst thou Words of such a compass find?
Whence furnish such a vast expense of Mind?
Just Heav'n Thee, like *Tiresias*, to requite,
Rewards with *Prophesie* thy loss of Sight.

Well might thou scorn thy Readers to allure
With tinkling Rhime, of thy own Sense secure;
While the *Town-Bays* writes all the while and spells,
And like a Pack-Horse tires without his Bells.
Their Fancies like our bushy Points appear,
The Poets tag them;[2] we for fashion wear.
I too transported by the *Mode* offend,
And while I meant to *Praise* thee, must Commend.
Thy verse created like thy *Theme* sublime,
In Number, Weight, and Measure,[3] needs not *Rhime*.

[2] [Aubrey records: "Jo: Dreyden Esq Poet Laureate, who very much admires him: & went to him to have leave to putt his Paradise-lost into a Drama: in Rhyme M Milton received him civilly, & told him he would give him leave to tagge his verses." Clothing was fastened with "Points," which might be conservatively "tagged" or adorned with "bushy" tassels.]

[3] [An allusion to the apocryphal Wisdom of Solomon 11:21 (*omnia in mensura et numero et pondere disposuisti*): "thou hast disposed all in measure and number and weight." The verse lies behind much of Renaissance literary theory and practice.]

Abraham Cowley

1618–67

Educated at Westminster and Cambridge, Cowley became a fellow in 1640 but left to attend the court at Oxford in 1643, then spent some ten years in France with the exiles, serving as secretary to the Queen and as a royalist agent. After the Restoration he retired to Barn Elms and Chertsey, where he occupied himself with books and the writing of his poetry and essays.

Educated like Milton and Jonson in the older traditions of Renaissance humanism, Cowley produced in his youth Poetical Blossoms (1633), influenced by Spenser; The Mistress (1647), influenced by Donne, occasioned the condemnation of Dr. Johnson; Davideis (1656) anticipates Milton in the attempt to write Christian epic; the Pindarique Odes, published in the Poems of 1656, testify, through the learned and extensive annotation, not only to Cowley's link with the past but also to the need, at mid-century, to interpret the past to the present; and, finally, the late essays share the urbane ease of the Restoration. Cowley is something of a literary barometer, finely sensitive to the pressures of the age; there is even an ode "To the Royal Society," celebrating Bacon as the "Moses" of the scientific land.

The "Preface" may be dated 1656, the time of the publication of "The Muse" and "Of Wit"; but the poems were probably written earlier. The texts are reprinted from The Works of 1668.

FROM

Poems

THE PREFACE *of the Autor*
[*1656*]

At my return lately into *England,* I met by great accident (for such I account it to be, that any Copy of it should be extant any where so long, unless at his house who printed it) a *Book* entituled, *The Iron Age,* and published under *my name,* during the time of my absence. I wondred very much how one who could be so *foolish* to write so ill Verses, should yet be so *Wise* to set them forth as another *Mans* rather than his *own;* though perhaps he might have made a better choice, and not fathered the *Bastard* upon such a person, whose stock of Reputation is, I fear, little enough for maintenance of his own numerous *Legitimate Off-spring* of that kind. It would have been much less injurious, if it had pleased the *Author* to put forth some of my Writings under his *own name,* rather than his own under *mine:* He had been in that a more pardonable Plagiary, and had done less wrong by *Robbery,* than he does by such a *Bounty;* for no body can be *justified* by the *Imputation* even of anothers *Merit;* and our own course *Cloathes* are like to become us better, than those of another mans, though never so *rich:* but these, to say the truth, were so *beggarly,* that I my self was ashamed to *wear* them. It was in vain for me, that I avoided censure by the concealment of my own writings, if my reputation could be thus *Executed in Effigie;* and impossible it is for any good *Name* to be in safety, if the malice of *Witches* have the power to consume and destroy it in an *Image* of their own making. This indeed was so ill made, and so *unlike*, that I hope the *Charm* took no effect. So that I esteem my self less prejudiced by it, than by that which has been done to me since, almost in the same kinde, which is the publication of some things of mine without my consent or knowledge, and those so mangled and imperfect, that I could neither with honour acknowledge, nor with honesty quite disavow them. Of which sort, was a *Comedy* called *The Guardian*, printed in the year 1650. but made and acted before the *Prince*, in his passage through *Cambridge* towards *York*, at the beginning of the late unhappy War; or rather neither *made* nor *acted*, but *rough-drawn* onely, and *repeated;* for the haste was so great, that it could neither be *revised* or *perfected* by the *Author*, nor *learned without-Book* by the *Actors*, nor set forth in any measure tolerably by the *Officers* of the *College*. After the *Representation* (which, I confess, was somewhat of the *latest*) I began to look it over, and changed it very much, striking out some whole parts, as that of the *Poet* and the *Souldier;* but I have lost the *Copy*, and dare not think it deserves the pains to write it again, which makes me omit it in this publication, though there be some things in it which I am not ashamed of, taking the excuse of my age and small experience in humane conversation when I made it. But as it is, it is only the hasty *first-sitting* of a *Picture*, and therefore like to resemble me accordingly. From this which has hapned to my self, I began to reflect on the fortune of almost all *Writers*, and especially *Poets*, whose *Works* (commonly printed after their deaths) we finde stuffed out, either with *counterfeit pieces*, like *false Money* put in to fill up the *Bag*, though it adde nothing to the *sum;* or with such, which though of their own *Coyn*, they would have called in themselves, for the baseness of the *Allay:* whether this proceed from the indiscretion of their *Friends*, who think a vast *heap* of Stones or Rubbish a better *Monument*, than a little *Tomb* of *Marble*, or by the unworthy avarice of some *Stationers*, who are content to diminish the value of the *Author*, so they may encrease the price of the *Book;* and like *Vintners* with sophisticate mixtures, spoil the whole vessel of wine, to make it yield more *profit*. This has been the case with *Shakespear*, *Fletcher*, *Johnson*, and many others; part of whose *Poems* I should take the boldness to prune and lop away, if the care of replanting them in print did belong to me, neither would I make any scruple to cut off from some the unnecessary young *Suckers,* and from others the old withered *Branches;* for *a great Wit* is no more tyed to live in a *Vast Volume,* than in a *Gigantick Body;* on the contrary, it is commonly more vigorous the less space it animates. And as *Statius* says of little *Tydeus,*

Totos infusa per artus
Major in exiguo regnabat corpore virtus.[1]

I am not ignorant, that by saying this of others, I expose my self to some *Raillery,* for not using the same severe discretion in my own case, where it concerns me nearer: But though I publish here, more than in strict wisdom I ought to have done, yet I have supprest and cast away more than I *publish;* and for the ease of my self and others, have *lost,* I believe too, more than *both.* And upon these considerations I have been perswaded to overcome all the just repugnances of my own *modesty,* and to produce these *Poems* to the light and view of the World; not as a thing that I approved of in it self, but as a less evil, which I chose rather than to stay till it were done for me by some body else, either surreptitiously before, or avowedly after my death: and this will be the more excusable, when the *Reader* shall know in what respects he may look upon me as a *Dead,* or at least a *Dying Person,* and upon my *Muse* in this action, as appearing, like the *Emperor Charls the Fifth,* and *assisting* at her own *Funeral.*

For to make my self absolutely dead in a *Poetical* capacity, my resolution at present, is never to exercise any more that faculty. It is, I confess, but seldom seen that the *Poet* dyes before the *Man;* for when we once fall in love with that bewitching *Art,* we do not use to court it as a *Mistress,* but marry it as a *Wife,* and take it for better or worse, as an *Inseparable Companion* of our whole life. But as the *Mariages* of *Infants* do but rarely prosper, so no man ought to wonder at the diminution or decay of my

[1] [*Thebaid* i.416–17: "Infused throughout all his limbs, greater strength ruled in a small body."]

affection to *Poesie;* to which I had contracted my self so much
under *Age,* and so much to my own prejudice in regard of those
more profitable matches which I might have made among the
richer Sciences. As for the *Portion* which this brings of *Fame,* it
is an *Estate* (if it be any, for men are not oftner deceived in their
hopes of *Widows,* than in their opinion of, *Exegi monumentum
ære perennius*[2]) that hardly ever comes in whilst we are *Living*
to enjoy it, but is a *fantastical kind of Reversion to our own
selves:* neither ought any man to envy *Poets* this posthumous
and imaginary happiness, since they find commonly so little in
present, that it may be truly applyed to them, which S. *Paul*
speaks of the first *Christians, If their reward be in this life, they
are of all men the most miserable.*

And if in quiet and flourishing times they meet with so small
encouragement, what are they to expect in rough and troubled
ones? if *Wit* be such a *Plant,* that it scarce receives heat enough
to preserve it alive even in the *Summer* of our cold *Clymate,* how
can it choose but wither in a long and a sharp *winter?* a warlike,
various, and a tragical age is best to *write of,* but worst to *write
in.* And I may, though in a very unequal proportion, assume that
to my self, which was spoken by *Tully* to a much better person,
upon occasion of the *Civil Wars* and Revolutions in his time, *Sed
in te intuens, Brute, doleo, cuius in adolescentiam per medias
laudes quasi quadrigis vehentem transversa incurrit misera
fortuna Reipublicæ.*[3]

Neither is the present constitution of my *Mind* more proper
than that of the *Times* for this exercise, or rather divertisement.
There is nothing that requires so much serenity and chearful-
ness of *Spirit;* it must not be either overwhelmed with the cares
of *Life,* or overcast with the *Clouds of Melancholy* and *Sorrow,*
or shaken and disturbed with the storms of injurious *Fortune;* it
must like the *Halcyon,* have *fair weather* to breed in. The *Soul*
must be filled with bright and delightful *Idea's,* when it undertakes to communicate delight to others; which is the main end of

2 [Horace's proud boast (*Odes* iii.30) that in his verse he had built himself a
monument more enduring than bronze.]
3 [Cicero, *Brutus* xcvii: "But in considering you I am sad, Brutus, whose
youth, when moving in triumph in the midst of honors, has been thwarted
by the unhappy fate of the republic."]

Poesie. One may see through the stile of *Ovid. de Trist.* the humbled and dejected condition of *Spirit* with which he wrote it; there scarce remains any footsteps of that *Genius,*

> *Quem nec Jovis ira, nec ignes, &c.*[4]

The *cold* of the Countrey had strucken through all his faculties, and benummed the very *feet* of his *Verses.* He is himself, methinks, like one of the *Stories* of his *own Metamorphosis;* and though there remain some weak *resemblances* of *Ovid* at *Rome;* It is but as he says of *Niobe,*

> *In vultu color est sine sanguine, lumina mœstis*
> *Stant inmota genis; nihil est in Imagine vivum,*
> *Flet tamen—*[5]

The truth is, for a man to write well, it is necessary to be in good humor; neither is *Wit* less eclipsed with the unquietness of *Mind,* than *Beauty* with the *Indisposition* of *Body.* So that 'tis almost as hard a thing to be a *Poet* in despight of *Fortune,* as it is in despight of *Nature.* For my own part, neither my obligations to the *Muses,* nor expectations from them are so great, as that I should suffer my self on no considerations to be *divorced;* or that I should say like *Horace,*

> *Quisquis erit vitæ, Scribam, color.*[6]

I shall rather use his words in another place,

> *Vixi Camænis nuper idoneus,*
> *Et militavi non sine gloriâ,*
> *Nunc arma defunctúmq; bello*
> *Barbiton hic paries habebit.*[7]

4 [*Metamorphoses* xv.871: "Whom neither the ire of Jove, nor fire, etc." (Cowley misquotes slightly.)]
5 [*Metamorphoses* vi.304–05, 310: "In expression she is pale and bloodless, her eyes immobile in the sad face, nothing is alive in the picture—yet she weeps."]
6 [*Satires* ii.1.59: "Whatever the conditions of my life, I will write."]
7 [*Odes* iii.26: "Recently I lived fit for the Muses, and fought not without glory; now this wall shall have my arms and lyre, finished with war." (Cowley adapts, substituting "Muses" for "girls.")]

And this resolution of mine does the more befit me, because my desire has been for some years past (though the execution has been accidentally diverted) and does still vehemently continue, to retire my self to some of our *American Plantations,* not to seek for *Gold,* or inrich my self with the traffick of those parts (which is the end of most men that travel thither; so that of *these Indies* it is truer than it was of the former,

Improbus extremos currit Mercator ad Indos
Pauperiem fugiens—)[8]

But to forsake this world for ever, with all the *vanities* and *Vexations* of it, and to bury my self there in some obscure retreat (but not without the consolation of *Letters* and *Philosophy*)

Oblitúsq; meorum, obliviscendus & illis.[9]

As my former *Author* speaks too, who has inticed me here, I know not how, into the *Pedantry* of this heap of *Latine Sentences.* And I think *Doctor Donnes Sun Dyal in a grave* is not more useless and ridiculous than *Poetry* would be in that *retirement.* As this therefore is in a true sense a kind of *Death* to the *Muses,* and a real *literal quitting* of this *World:* So, methinks, I may make a just claim to the undoubted priviledge of *Deceased Poets,* which is to be read with more *favor,* than the *Living;*

Tanti est ut placeam tibi, Perire.[1]

Having been forced for my own necessary *justification* to trouble the *Reader* with this long Discourse of the *Reasons* why I trouble him also with all the rest of the *Book,* I shall only add somewhat concerning the several Parts of it, and some other pieces, which I have thought fit to reject in this publication: As

8 [Horace, *Epistles* i.1.45, goes: *impiger extremos curris mercator ad Indos,/ per mare pauperiem fugiens,* which Cowley changes slightly to read: "The bad merchant runs to the farthest Indies fleeing poverty."]
9 [Horace, *Epistles* i.11.9: "Forgetting my friends, I ought also to be forgotten by them."]
1 [Martial, *Epigrams* viii.69 reads "tanti non est, ut placeam tibi, perire," i.e., "it is not worth it to die in order to please you." Cowley adapts: "It is worth dying to please you."]

first, all those which I wrote at *School* from the age of ten years, till after fifteen; for even so far backward there remain yet some *traces* of me in the little *footsteps* of a *child;* which though they were then looked upon as *commendable extravagances* in a *Boy* (men setting a value upon *any kind* of *fruit* before the usual *season* of it) yet I would be loth to be bound now to read them all over *my self;* and therefore should do ill to expect that patience from *others.* Besides, they have already past through several *Editions,* which is a longer *Life* than used to be enjoyed by *Infants* that are born before the ordinary *terms.* They had the good fortune then to find the world so *indulgent* (for considering the time of their production, who could be so hard-hearted to be *severe?*) that I scarce yet apprehend so much to be censured for *them,* as for not having made *advances* afterwards proportionable to the speed of my *setting out,* and am obliged too in a manner by Discretion to conceal and suppress them, as *Promises* and *Instruments* under my own hand, whereby I stood *engaged* for more then I have been able to *perform;* in which truly, if I have failed, I have the real excuse of the *honestest* sort of *Bankrupts,* which is, to have been made *Unsolvable,* not so much by their own *negligence* and *ill-husbandry,* as by some notorious accidents and publick disasters. In the next place, I have cast away all such pieces as I wrote during the time of the late troubles, with any relation to the differences that caused them; as among others, *three Books of the Civil War itself,* reaching as far as the first *Battel* of *Newbury,* where the succeeding *misfortunes* of the *party* stopt the *work.*

As for the ensuing Book, it consists of four parts: The first is a *Miscellanie* of several Subjects, and some of them made when I was very young, which it is perhaps *superfluous* to tell the *Reader;* I know not by what chance I have kept *Copies* of them; for they are but a very few in comparison of those which I have lost, and I think they have no extraordinary virtue in them, to deserve more care in preservation, than was bestowed upon their *Brethren;* for which I am so little concerned, that I am ashamed of the *arrogancy* of the *word,* when I said, *I had lost them.*

The *Second,* is called, *The Mistress,* or *Love-Verses;* for so it is, that *Poets* are scarce thought *Free-men* of their *Company,* without paying some duties, and obliging themselves to be true to *Love*. Sooner or later they must all pass through that *Tryal*, like some *Mahumetan Monks*, that are bound by their Order, once at least, in their life, to make a *Pilgrimage* to *Meca*,

In furias ignémq; ruunt; Amor omnibus idem.[2]

But we must not always make a judgment of their *manners* from their *writings* of this kind; as the *Romanists* uncharitably do of *Beza*,[3] for a few lascivious *Sonnets* composed by him in his youth. It is not in this sense that *Poesie* is said to be a kind of *Painting*; it is not the *Picture* of the *Poet*, but of *things* and *persons* imagined by him. He may be in his own practice and disposition a *Philosopher*, nay a *Stoick*, and yet speak sometimes with the softness of an amorous *Sappho*.

Feret & rubus asper Amomum.[4]

He professes too much the use of *Fables* (though without the malice of deceiving) to have his testimony taken even against himself. Neither would I here be misunderstood, as if I affected so much gravity; as to be ashamed to be thought really in *Love*. On the contrary, I cannot have a good opinion of any man who is not at least capable of being so. But I speak it to excuse some expressions (if such there be) which may happen to offend the severity of supercilious *Readers*; for much *Excess* is to be allowed in *Love*, and even more in *Poetry*; so we avoid the two unpardonable vices in both, which are *Obscenity* and *Prophaneness*, of which I am sure, if my *words* be ever guilty, they have ill represented my *thoughts* and *intentions*. And if, notwithstanding all this, the lightness of the matter here displease any body; he may find wherewithall to content his more serious inclinations in the weight and height of the ensuing *Arguments*.

For as for the *Pindarick Odes* (which is the third part) I am in great doubt whether they will be understood by most *Readers*; nay, even by very many who are well enough acquainted with

2 [Vergil, *Georgics* iii.244: "They rush into passions and fires; Love is the same for all."]
3 [Théodore de Bèze (1519–1605), the religious reformer, attempted to suppress the *Juvenilia* he had written before the age of twenty.]
4 [Vergil, *Eclogues* iii.89: "And may the rough bramble bear cardamon."]

the common Roads, and ordinary Tracks of *Poesie*. They either
are, or at least were meant to be, of that kind of *Stile* which
Dion. Halicarnasseus calls, Μεγαλοφυὲς καὶ ἡδὺ μετὰ δεινότητος,[5] and
which he attributes to *Alcæus:* The digressions are many, and
sudden, and sometimes long, according to the fashion of all
Lyriques, and of *Pindar* above all men living. The *Figures* are
unusual and *bold,* even to *Temeritie,* and such as I durst not
have to do withall in any other kind of *Poetry:* The *Numbers* are
various and irregular, and sometimes (especially some of the
long ones) seem harsh and uncouth, if the just measures and
cadencies be not observed in the *Pronunciation.* So that almost
all their *Sweetness* and *Numerosity* (which is to be found, if I
mistake not, in the roughest, if rightly repeated) lies in a manner
wholly at the *Mercy* of the *Reader.* I have briefly described the
nature of these Verses, in the *Ode* entituled, *The Resurrection:*
And though the *Liberty* of them may incline a man to believe
them easie to be composed, yet the undertaker will find it otherwise.

> *Ut sibi quivis*
> *Speret idem, multum sudet frustráq, laboret*
> *Ausus idem——.*[6]

I come now to the last Part, which is *Davideis,* or an *Heroical
Poem* of the *Troubles of David;* which I designed into *Twelve
Books;* not for the *Tribes* sake,[7] but after the *Pattern* of our Master *Virgil;* and intended to close all with that most Poetical and
excellent *Elegie* of *Davids* on the death of *Saul* and *Jonathan:*
For I had no mind to carry him quite on to his *Anointing* at
Hebron, because it is the custom of *Heroick Poets* (as we see by
the examples of *Homer* and *Virgil,* whom we should do ill to
forsake to imitate others) never to come to the full end of their
Story; but onely so near, that every one may see it; as men commonly play not out the game, when it is evident that they can
win it, but lay down their *Cards,* and take up what they have

5 [Cowley compresses Helicarnassus (*De veterum scriptorum censura* ii.8):
"Grand in nature, combining sweetness with sublimity."]
6 [Horace, *Ars Poetica* 240–42: "so that anyone may hope for the same success,
may sweat much, and yet work in vain in attempting it."]
7 [I.e., for the sake of the twelve tribes of Israel.]

won. This, I say, was the *whole Design*, in which there are many noble and fertile Arguments behind; as, The barbarous cruelty of *Saul* to the *Priests* at *Nob*, the several flights and escapes of *David*, with the manner of his living in the *Wilderness*, the *Funeral* of *Samuel*, the love of *Abigal*, the sacking of *Ziglag*, the loss and recovery of *Davids* wives from the *Amalekites*, the *Witch* of *Endor*, the War with the *Philistines*, and the *Battel* of *Gilboa;* all which I meant to interweave upon several occasions, with most of the illustrious *Stories* of the *Old Testament*, and to embellish with the most remarkable *Antiquities* of the *Jews*, and of other Nations before or at that *Age*. But I have had neither *Leisure* hitherto, nor have *Appetite* at present to finish the work, or so much as to revise that part which is done with that care which I resolved to bestow upon it, and which the *Dignity* of the *Matter* well deserves. For what worthier *subject* could have been chosen among all the *Treasuries* of past times, than the *Life* of this young *Prince;* who from so small beginnings, through such infinite troubles and oppositions, by such miraculous virtues and excellencies, and with such incomparable variety of wonderful actions and accidents, became the greatest *Monarch* that ever sat on the most *famous* Throne of the whole Earth? whom should a *Poet* more justly seek to *honour*, than the highest Person who ever *honoured* his Profession? whom a *Christian Poet*, rather than the *man after Gods own heart*, and the man who had that sacred pre-eminence above all other *Princes*, to be the best and mightiest of that Royal Race from whence *Christ* himself, according to the flesh disdained not to descend? When I consider this, and how many other bright and magnificent subjects of the like nature, the *Holy Scripture* affords and *proffers*, as it were, to *Poesie*, in the wise managing and illustrating whereof, the *Glory* of God Almighty might be joyned with the singular utility and noblest delight of *Mankind;* It is not without grief and indignation that I behold that *Divine Science* employing all her inexhaustible riches of *Wit* and *Eloquence*, either in the wicked and beggerly *Flattery* of great persons, or the unmanly *Idolizing* of *Foolish Women*, or the wretched affection of scurril *Laughter*, or at best on the confused antiquated *Dreams* of senseless *Fables* and *Metamorphoses*. Amongst all holy and consecrated things which the *Devil* ever stole and alienated from the service of the *Deity*, as *Altars, Temples, Sacrifices, Prayers,* and the like; there is none that he so universally, and so long usurpt, as *Poetry.* It is time to recover it out of the *Tyrants* hands, and to restore it to the *Kingdom* of *God,* who is the *Father* of it. It is time to *Baptize* it in *Jordan,* for it wil never become clean by bathing in the *Water* of *Damascus.* There wants, methinks, but the *Conversion* of *That,* and the *Jews,* for the accomplishment of the *Kingdom of Christ.* And as men before their receiving of the *Faith,* do not without some carnal reluctancies, apprehend the *bonds* and *fetters* of it, but find it afterwards to be the truest and greatest *Liberty:* It will fare no otherwise with this *Art,* after the *Regeneration* of it; it will meet with wonderful variety of new, more beautiful, and more delightful *Objects;* neither will it want *Room,* by being *confined to Heaven.* There is not so great a *Lye* to be found in any *Poet,* as the vulgar conceit of men, that *Lying* is *Essential* to good *Poetry.* Were there never so wholesome *Nourishment* to be had (but alas, it breeds nothing but *Diseases*) out of these boasted *Feasts* of *Love* and *Fables;* yet, methinks, the unalterable continuance of the *Diet* should make us *Nauseate* it: For it is almost impossible to serve up any *new Dish* of that kind. They are all but the *Cold-meats* of the *Antients,* new-heated, and new set forth. I do not at all wonder that the old *Poets* made some rich crops out of these grounds; the heart of the *Soil* was not then wrought out with continual *Tillage:* But what can we expect now, who come a *Gleaning,* not after the first *Reapers,* but after the very *Beggars?* Besides, though those mad stories of the *Gods* and *Heroes,* seem in themselves so ridiculous; yet they were then the *whole Body* (or rather *Chaos*) of the *Theologie* of those times. They were believed by all but a few *Philosophers,* and perhaps some *Atheists,* and served to good purpose among the *vulgar,* (as pitiful things as they are) in strengthening the authority of *Law* with the terrors of *Conscience,* and expectation of certain rewards, and unavoidable punishments. There was no other *Religion,* and therefore *that* was better then *none at all.* But to us who have no need of them, to us who deride their *folly,* and are wearied with their *impertinencies,* they ought to appear no better arguments for *Verse,* then those of their worthy *Successors,* the *Knights Errant.* What can we imagine more proper for the ornaments of *Wit* or

Learning in the story of *Deucalion*, than in that of *Noah*? why
will not the actions of *Sampson* afford as plentiful matter as the
Labors of Hercules? why is not *Jephta's Daughter* as *good a
woman* as *Iphigenia*? and the friendship of *David* and *Jonathan*
more worthy celebration, than that of *Theseus* and *Perithous*?
Does not the passage of *Moses* and the *Israelites* into the *Holy
Land*, yield incomparably more Poetical variety, then the voyages of *Ulysses* or *Æneas*? Are the obsolete thread-bare tales of
Thebes and *Troy*, half so stored with great, heroical and supernatural actions (since *Verse* will needs *find* or *make* such) as
the wars of *Joshua*, of the *Judges*, of *David* and divers others?
Can all the *Transformations* of the *Gods* give such copious hints
to flourish and expatiate on, as the true *Miracles* of *Christ*, or of
his *Prophets*, and *Apostles*? what do I instance in these few particulars? All the *Books* of the *Bible* are either already most admirable, and exalted pieces of *Poesie*, or are the best *Materials* in
the world for it. Yet, though they be in themselves so proper to
be made use of for this purpose; None but a good *Artist* will
know how to do it: neither must we think to cut and polish *Dia-
monds* with so little pains and skill as we do *Marble*. For if any
man design to compose a *Sacred Poem*, by only turning a story
of the *Scripture*, like Mr. *Quarles's*, or some other godly matter,
like Mr. *Heywood of Angels*, into *Rhyme*;[8] He is so far from
elevating of *Poesie*, that he only *abases Divinity*. In brief, he who
can write a *prophane Poem well*, may write a *Divine one better*;
but he who can do that but ill, will do this much worse. The
same fertility of *Invention*, the same wisdom of *Disposition*; the
same *Judgment* in observance of *Decencies*; the same lustre and
vigor of *Elocution*; the same modesty and majestie of *Number*;
briefly the same kind of *Habit*, is required to both; only this
latter allows better *stuff*, and therefore would look more deform-
edly, if *ill drest* in it. I am far from assuming to my self to have
fulfilled the duty of this weighty undertaking: But sure I am,
that there is nothing yet in our *Language* (nor perhaps in *any*)
that is in any degree answerable to the *Idea* that I conceive of it.
And I shall be ambitious of no other fruit from this weak and
imperfect attempt of mine, but the opening of a way to the cour-

8 [Francis Quarles, *Job Militant* (1624); Thomas Heywood, *Hierarchy of the
Blessed Angels* (1635).]

age and industry of some other persons, who may be better able
to perform it throughly and successfully.

ODE:

Of Wit

[*before 1656*]

1

Tell me, O tell, what kind of thing is *Wit,*
    Thou who *Master* art of it.
For the *First matter* loves *Variety* less;
Less *Women* love't, either in *Love* or *Dress.*
    A thousand different shapes it bears,
    Comely in thousand shapes appears.
Yonder we saw it plain; and here 'tis now,
Like *Spirits* in *a Place,* we know not *How.*

2

London that vents of *false Ware* so much store,
    In no *Ware* deceives us more.
For men led by the *Colour,* and the *Shape,*
Like *Zeuxes Birds* fly to the painted *Grape;*
    Some things do through our Judgment pass
    As through a *Multiplying Glass.*
And sometimes, if the *Object* be too far,
We take a *Falling Meteor* for a *Star.*

3

Hence 'tis a *Wit* that greatest *word* of *Fame*
    Grows such a common Name.
And *Wits* by our *Creation* they become,
Just so, as *Tit'lar Bishops* made at *Rome.*
    'Tis not a *Tale,* 'tis not a *Jest*
    Admir'd with *Laughter* at a feast,
Nor florid *Talk* which can that *Title* gain;
The *Proofs* of *Wit* for ever must remain.

4

'Tis not to force some lifeless *Verses* meet
    With their five gowty feet.
All ev'ry where, like *Mans*, must be the *Soul*,
And *Reason* the *Inferior Powers* controul.
    Such were the *Numbers* which could call
    The *Stones* into the *Theban* wall.[1]
Such *Miracles* are ceast; and now we see
No *Towns* or *Houses* rais'd by *Poetrie*.

5

Yet 'tis not to adorn, and gild each part;
    That shows more *Cost*, than *Art*.
Jewels at *Nose* and *Lips* but ill appear;
Rather than *all things Wit*, let *none* be there.
    Several *Lights* will not be seen,
    If there be nothing else between.
Men doubt, because they stand so thick i'th'skie,
If those be *Stars* which paint the *Galaxie*.

6

'Tis not when two like words make up one noise;
    Jests for *Dutch Men*, and *English Boys*.
In which who finds out *Wit*, the same may see
In *An'grams* and *Acrostiques Poetrie*.
    Much less can that have any place
    At which a *Virgin* hides her face,
Such *Dross* the *Fire* must purge away; 'tis just
The *Author blush*, there where the *Reader* must.

7

'Tis not such *Lines* as almost crack the *Stage*
    When *Bajazet* begins to rage.
Nor a tall *Meta'phor* in the *Bombast way*,
Nor the dry chips of short lung'd *Seneca*.
    Nor upon all things to obtrude,
    And force some odd *Similitude*.
What is it than, which like the *Power Divine*
We only can by *Negatives* define?

---

[1] [The music of Amphion raised the walls of Thebes.]

8

In a true piece of *Wit* all things must be,
Yet all things there *agree*.
As in the *Ark*, joyn'd without force or strife,
All *Creatures* dwelt; all *Creatures* that had *Life*.
Or as the *Primitive Forms* of all
(If we compare great things with small)
Which without *Discord* or *Confusion* lie,
In that strange *Mirror* of the *Deitie*.

9

But *Love* that moulds *One Man* up out of *Two*,
Makes me forget and injure you.
I took *you* for *my self* sure when I thought
That you in any thing were to be *Taught*.
Correct my error with thy Pen;
And if any ask me then,
What thing right *Wit*, and height of *Genius* is,
I'll onely shew your *Lines*, and say, 'Tis This.

The Muse
[*before 1656*]

1

(1) Go, the rich *Chariot* instantly prepare;
The *Queen*, my *Muse*, will take the air;
Unruly *Phansie* with strong *Judgment* trace,
Put in the nimble-footed *Wit*,
Smooth-pac'ed *Eloquence* joyn with it,
Sound *Memory* with young *Invention* place,
Harnest all the *winged race*.
Let the *Postillion Nature* mount, and let
The *Coachman Art* be set.
And let the airy *Footmen* running all beside,
Make a long row of *goodly pride*.
Figures, *Conceits*, *Raptures*, and *Sentences*[1]
In a well-worded, *dress*.

---

[1] [I.e., apothegms.]

And *innocent Loves*, and *pleasant Truths*, and *usefull Lies*,
　　In all their gaudy *Liveries*.
　　Mount, glorious *Queen*, thy *travelling Throne*,
　　　And bid it to put on;
　　For *long*, though *cheerful*, is the *way*,
And *Life*, alas, allows but one ill *winters Day*.

2

Where never *Foot* of *Man*, or *Hoof* of *Beast*,
　　The passage prest,
(1) Where never *Fish* did *fly*,
And with short silver *wings* cut the low liquid *Sky*.
(2) Where *Bird* with painted *Oars* did nere
Row through, the trackless *Ocean* of the *Air*.
　　Where never yet did pry
　　The busie *Mornings* curious *Sky*:
The *Wheels* of thy bold *Coach* pass quick and free;
　　And all's an *open Road* to *Thee*.
(3) Whatever *God* did *Say*,
Is all thy plain and smooth, uninterrupted *way*.
Nay ev'n beyond his *works* thy *Voyages* are known,
　　Thou'hast thousand *worlds* too of thine *own*.
Thou speakst, great *Queen*, in the same *stile* as *He*,
And a *New world* leaps forth when *Thou* say'st, *Let it Be*.

3

(1) Thou fadom'est the deep *Gulf* of *Ages* past,
　　And canst pluck up with ease
　　The *years* which thou dost please,
Like shipwrackt *Treasures* by rude *Tempests* cast
　　Long since into the *Sea*,
Brought up again to *light* and publique *Use* by Thee.
　　Nor dost thou onely *Dive* so low,
　　　But *Fly*
With an unwearied *Wing* the other way on high,
(2) Where *Fates* among the *Stars* do grow;
There into the close *Nests* of *Time* do'st peep,
　　And there with piercing *Eye*,
Through the firm *shell*, and the thick *White* do'st spie,
　　Years to come a forming lie,
[3] Close in their *sacred Secondine* sleep,
　　Till *hatcht* by the *Suns* vital heat

Which o're them yet does *brooding* set
They *Life* and *Motion* get,
And *ripe* at last with vigorous might
Break through the *Shell*, and take their everlasting *Flight*.

4

And sure we may
The same too of the *Present* say,
If *Past,* and *Future Times* do thee obey.
Thou stopst this *Current,* and dost make
This running *River* settle like a *Lake,*
(1) Thy certain hand holds fast this slippery *Snake.*
The *Fruit* which does so quickly wast,
Men scarce can see it, much less *tast,*
Thou *Comfitest*² in *Sweets* to make it *last.*
This shining piece of *Ice*
(2) Which melts so soon away
With the *Suns* ray,
Thy *Verse* does solidate and *Chrystallize,*
Till it a lasting *Mirror* be.
Nay thy *Immortal Rhyme*
Makes this one short *Point* of *Time,*
(3) To fill up half the *Orb* of *Round Eternity.*

NOTES

1

(1) *Pindar* in the 6. *Olymp.* has a *Phansie* somewhat of
this kind: where he says, Ὦ Φίντις ἀλλὰ ζεῦξον ἤδή μοι σθένος ἡμιόνων
ᾗ ταχος ὄφρα κελεύθῳ τ'ἐν καθαρᾷ βάσομεν ὄκχον. *Sed,* Ô *Phinty,*
junge iam mihi robur Mularum *quibus celeritas est, ut viâ purâ*
ducamus currum. Where by the Name of *Phintis* he speaks to his
own Soul. O, my *Soul,* join me the strong and swift *Mules* together, that I may drive the *Chariot* in this fair way. Some make
φιντν to be a Dialect for φίλης: as if he should say, Oh my *friend:*
Others (whom I rather believe) take it for the proper Name of
some famous *Chariot-driver.* The *Aurea Carm.* use the same *Met-*
aphor, Ἡνίοχον γνώμην στήσας καθὐπερθεν ἀρίστην. *Aurigâ supernè*
constitutâ optimâ ratione; Making right Reason the *Chariot-*

² [Preservest.]

driver of the *Soul. Porphyrius* calls the *Spirits,* ῎Οχημα τῆς ψυχῆς
The *Chariot* of the Soul.

2

(1) For *Fins* do the same Office to *Fish,* that *Wings* do to
Birds; and the *Scripture* it self gives authority to my calling the
Sea the *Low Sky;* where it says, *Gen.* 1.6 *Let there be a Firma-
ment in the midst of the waters, and let it divide the waters from
the waters.*

(2) This *Metaphor* was used by the ancient *Poets,* Virg. *Æn.* I.

> *Volat ille per aera magnum Remigio alarum.*

And elsewhere *Lucret.* before him, *L.*6.

> *Remigii oblitæ pennarum.*

Ovid in his Epistle *applies* the same to *Mens Arms.*

> *Remis ego corporis utar.*
> I'll use the *Bodies Oars.*

(3) *Whatsoever God made;* for his saying, *Let it be,* made all
things. The meaning is, that *Poetry* treats not only of all things
that are, or can be but makes *Creatures* of her own, as *Centaurs,
Satyrs, Fairies,* &c. makes *persons* and *actions* of her own, as in
Fables and *Romances,* makes *Beasts, Trees, Waters,* and other
irrational and insensible things to act above the possibility of
their natures, as to *understand* and *speak,* nay makes what *Gods*
it pleases too without *Idolatry,* and varies all these into unnumer-
able *Systemes,* or *Worlds* of Invention.

3

(1) That is, The subject of *Poetry* is all *Past, Future* and
Present Times; and for the *Past,* it makes what choice it pleases
out of the *wrack* of *Time* of things that it will save from *Oblivion.*

(2) According to the vulgar (but false) opinion of the *Influence* of the *Stars* over mens *actions* and *Fortunes.* There is no
difficulty, I think, in the *Metaphor* of making a *year* to come like
an *Egg* that is not yet *hatcht,* but a *brooding.*

(3) The thin *Film* with which an *Infant* is covered in the *womb*, so called, because it *follows* the *Child*. In Latine *Secundæ*, as in the 9. Epistle of *Seneca*, where he says most admirably. *Sed ut ex barbâ capillos detonsos negligimus, ita divinus ille animus egressurus hominem quo receptaculum suum referatur, ignis illud exurat, an feræ distrahant, an terra contegat non magis ad se pertinere judicat quam Secundas ad editum infantem.*[3]

4

(1) A *Snake* with the *Tail* in the mouth of it, was the ancient *Hieroglyphick* of the year.

(2) Because the course of the *Sun* seems to consume *Time*, as the Beams of it do *Ice*.

(3) There are two sorts of *Eternity;* from the *Present backwards* to *Eternity*, and from the *Present forwards*, called by the Schoolmen *Æternitas à parte ante*, and *Æternitas à parte post*. These two make up the whole *Circle* of *Eternity*, which the *Present Time* cuts like a *Diameter*, but Poetry makes it extend to all *Eternity to come*, which is the *Half-Circle*.

3 [Actually *Epistulae Morales* xcii, where Seneca's full version reads: "But just as we take no notice of clippings from hair or beard, so also the divine soul, when it is ready to depart from the body, considers the end of its mortal receptacle (whether consumed by fire, shut up in stone, covered over by earth, or torn apart by wild animals) to be of no greater importance to it than the after-birth or 'secondine' to a new-born babe."]

Thomas Sprat

1635–1713

Educated at Oxford, Sprat later became Bishop of Rochester and Dean of Westminster. He was a close friend of Cowley and edited the poet's works, to which was prefaced "An Account of the Life and Writings of Mr. Abraham Cowley" that reveals Sprat's talent for alert, tolerant criticism. But it was in his double role as historian of the Royal Society and member of its committee for improving the English language that Sprat exerted the greatest influence. Sprat used the History *to popularize "Baconian" ideals of language and to urge the founding of an "English Academy" that would, presumably, "reform" English speech along scientific and utilitarian lines. Thus, the change (discussed in the Introduction) in the older view of Nature appears explicitly in Sprat: "Nature has only form'd [witty poets] to be pleas'd with its irregularities," whereas the "real* Philosophers" *contemplate the "Order and Beauty" of Nature and its "beautiful Works."*

The two selections reprinted here are from the second and third parts of The History of the Royal-Society of London *(1667).*

The History of the Royal–Society
[1667]

FROM [THE SECOND PART]

. . . There is nothing of all the works of Nature, so inconsider-able, so remote, or so fully known; but, by being made to reflect on other things, it will at once enligten them, and shew it self the clearer. Such is the dependance amongst all the orders of crea-tures; the inanimate, the sensitive, the rational, the natural, the artificial: that the apprehension of one of them, is a good step towards the understanding of the rest: And this is the highest pitch of *humane reason;* to follow all the links of this chain, till all their secrets are open to our minds; and their works advanc'd, or imitated by our hands. This is truly to command the world; to rank all the *varieties,* and *degrees* of things, so orderly one upon another; that standing on the top of them, we may perfectly be-hold all that are below, and make them all serviceable to the quiet, and peace, and plenty of Man's life. And to this happiness, there can be nothing else added: but that we make a second advantage of this *rising ground,* thereby to look the nearer into heaven: An ambition, which though it was punish'd in the *old World,* by an *universal Confusion;* when it was manag'd with *impiety,* and *insolence:* yet, when it is carried on by that *humil-ity* and *innocence,* which can never be separated from true knowledg; when it is design'd, not to *brave* the Creator of all things, but to *admire* him the more: it must needs be the utmost perfection of *humane Nature.*

Sect. XX
Their manner of Discourse

Thus they have directed, judg'd, conjectur'd upon, and improved *Experiments.* But lastly, in these, and all other businesses, that have come under their care; there is one thing more, about which the *Society* has been most sollicitous; and that is, the manner of their *Discourse:* which, unless they had been very watchful to keep in due temper, the whole spirit and vigour of their *Design,* had been soon eaten out, by the luxury and redundance of *speech.* The ill effects of this superfluity of talking, have already overwhelm'd most other *Arts* and *Professions;* insomuch, that when I consider the means of *happy living,* and the causes of their corruption, I can hardly forbear recanting what I said before; and concluding, that *eloquence* ought to be banish'd out of all *civil Societies,* as a thing fatal to Peace and good Manners. To this opinion I should wholly incline; if I did not find, that it is a Weapon, which may be as easily procur'd by *bad* men, as *good:* and that, if these should onely cast it away, and those retain it; the *naked Innocence* of vertue, would be upon all occasions expos'd to the *armed Malice* of the wicked. This is the chief reason, that should now keep up the Ornaments of speaking, in any request: since they are so much degenerated from their original usefulness. They were at first, no doubt, an admirable Instrument in the hands of *Wise Men:* when they were onely employ'd to describe *Goodness, Honesty, Obedience;* in larger, fairer, and more moving Images: to represent *Truth,* cloth'd with Bodies; and to bring *Knowledg* back again to our very senses, from whence it was at first deriv'd to our understandings. But now they are generally chang'd to worse uses: They make the *Fancy* disgust the best things, if they come sound, and unadorn'd: they are in open defiance against *Reason;* professing, not to hold much correspondence with that; but with its Slaves, *the Passions:* they give the mind a motion too changeable, and bewitching, to consist with *right practice.* Who can behold, without indignation, how many mists and uncertainties, these specious *Tropes* and *Figures* have brought on our Knowledg? How many rewards, which are due to more profitable, and difficult *Arts,* have been still snatch'd away by the easie vanity of *fine speaking*? For now I am warm'd with this just Anger, I cannot with-hold my self, from betraying the shallowness of all these seeming Mysteries; upon which, *we Writers,* and *Speakers,* look so bigg. And, in few words, I dare say; that of all the Studies of men, nothing may be sooner obtain'd, than this vicious abundance of *Phrase,* this trick of *Metaphors,* this volubility of *Tongue,* which makes so great a noise in the World. But I spend words in vain; for the evil is now so inveterate, that it is hard to know whom to *blame,* or where to begin to *reform.* We all value one another so much, upon this beautiful deceipt; and labour so long after it, in the years of our education: that we cannot but ever after think kinder of it, than it deserves. And indeed, in most other parts of Learning, I look on it to be a thing almost utterly desperate in its cure: and I think, it may be plac'd amongst those *general mischiefs;* such, as the *dissention* of Christian Princes, the *want of practice* in Religion, and the like; which have been so long spoken against, that men are become insensible about them; every one shifting off the fault from himself to others; and so they are only made bare common places of complaint. It will suffice my present purpose, to point out, what has been done by the *Royal Society,* towards the correcting of its excesses in *Natural Philosophy;* to which it is, of all others, a most profest enemy.

They have therefore been most rigorous in putting in execution, the only Remedy, that can be found for this *extravagance:* and that has been, a constant Resolution, to reject all the amplifications, digressions, and swellings of style: to return back to the primitive purity, and shortness, when men deliver'd so many *things,* almost in an equal number of *words.* They have exacted from all their members, a close, naked, natural way of speaking; positive expressions; clear senses; a native easiness: bringing all things as near the Mathematical plainness, as they can: and preferring the language of Artizans, Countrymen, and Merchants, before that, of Wits, or Scholars.

And here, there is one thing, not to be pass'd by; which will render this establish'd custom of the *Society,* well nigh everlasting: and that is, the general constitution of the minds of the *English*. I have already often insisted on some of the prerogatives of *England;* whereby it may justly lay claim, to be the Head of a *Philosophical league,* above all other Countries in *Europe:* I have urg'd its scituation, its present Genius, and the disposition of its Merchants; and many more such *arguments* to incourage us, still remain to be us'd: But of all others, this, which I am now alledging, is of the most weighty, and important consideration. If there can be a true character given of the *Universal Temper* of any Nation under Heaven: then certainly this must be ascrib'd to our Countrymen: that they have commonly an unaffected sincerity; that they love to deliver their minds with a sound simplicity; that they have the middle qualities, between the reserv'd subtle southern, and the rough unhewn Northern people: that they are not extreamly prone to speak: that they are more concern'd, what others will think of the strength, than of the fineness of what they say: and that an universal modesty possesses them. These Qualities are so conspicuous, and proper to our Soil; that we often hear them objected to us, by some of our neighbour Satyrists, in more disgraceful expressions. For they are wont to revile the *English*, with a want of familiarity; with a melancholy dumpishness; with slowness, silence, and with the unrefin'd sullenness of their behaviour. But these are only the reproaches of partiality, or ignorance: for they ought rather to be commended for an honourable integrity; for a neglect of circumstances, and flourishes; for regarding things of *greater* moment, more than *less;* for a scorn to deceive as well as to be deceiv'd: which are all the best indowments, that can enter into a *Philosophical Mind*. So that even the position of our climate, the air, the influence of the heaven, the composition of the English blood; as well as the embraces of the Ocean, seem to joyn with the labours of the *Royal Society*, to render our Country, a Land of *Experimental knowledge*. And it is a good sign, that Nature will reveal more of its secrets to the English, than to others; because it has already furnish'd them with a Genius so well proportion'd, for the receiving, and retaining its mysteries.

FROM [THE THIRD PART]

Sect. XXXV
*Experiments will be
beneficial to our
wits and Writers*

To this address which I have made to our *Nobility*, and *Gentry*, I will add as an appendix another benefit of *Experiments*, which perhaps it will scarce become me to name amidst so many matters of greater weight: and that is, that their discoveries will be very serviceable to the *Wits*, and *Writers* of this, and all future *Ages*. But this I am provok'd to mention by the consideration of the present *Genius* of the *English Nation;* wherein the study of *Wit*, and humor of *Writing* prevails so much, that there are very few conditions, or degrees, or Ages of Men who are free from its infection. I will therefore declare to all those whom this Spirit has possess'd, that their is in the *Works of Nature* an inexhaustible Treasure of *Fancy*, and *Invention*, which will be reveal'd proportionably to the increas of their *Knowledge*.

To this purpose I must premise, that it is requir'd in the best, and most delightful *Wit;* that it be founded on such images which are generally known, and are able to bring a strong, and a sensible impression on the *mind*. The several subjects from which it has bin rays'd in all Times, are the *Fables*, and *Religions* of the *Antients*, the *Civil Histories* of all *Countries*, the *Customs* of *Nations*, the *Bible*, the *Sciences*, and *Manners* of *Men*, the several *Arts* of their hands, and the works of *Nature*. In all these, where there may be a resemblance of one thing to another, as there may be in all, there is a sufficient Foundation for *Wit*. This in all its kinds has its increases, heigths, and decays, as well as all other human things: Let us then examin what Parts of it are already exhausted, and what remain new, and untouch'd, and are still likely to be farther advanc'd.

The *Wit* of the *Fables* and *Religions* of the *Ancient World* is well-nigh consum'd: They have already serv'd the *Poets* long enough; and it is now high time to dismiss them; especially seing they have this peculiar *imperfection*, that they were only *Fictions* at first: whereas *Truth* is never so well express'd or amplify'd, as by those Ornaments which are *Tru* and *Real* in themselves.

The *Wit* which is rais'd from *Civil Histories,* and the Customs of *Countries,* is solid and lasting: The *Similitudes* it affords are substantial, and equal to the minds of men, being drawn from themselves and their own actions. Of this the wittiest Nations have always made the greatest use; their writings being adorn'd with a *Wit* that was free of their own *Cities,* consisting of *Examples,* and *Apothegms,* and *Proverbs,* derived from their *Ancestors.* This I allege, because this kind is scarce yet begun in the *English Language;* though our own *Civil History* abounds as much as any other, with great *Examples* and memorable Events, which may serve for the ornament of Comparison.

The Manners and Tempers, and Extravagances of men are a standing and eternal foundation of *Wit:* This if it be gather'd from particular *Observations,* is call'd *Humor:* And the more particular they are, they are still the pleasanter. In this kind I may well affirm that our *Nation* excells all others, as our *Dramatic Poetry* may witness.

The *Wit* that may be borrow'd from the *Bible* is magnificent; and as all the other Treasures of *Knowledge* it contains, inexhaustible. This may be us'd and allow'd without any danger of prophaness. The *Ancient Hethens* did the same: They made their *Divine Ceremonies* the chief Subjects of their *Fancies:* By that means their *Religions* had a more awful impression, became more popular, and lasted longer in force than else they would have done. And why may not *Christianity* admit the same thing, if it be practis'd with *sobriety* and *reverence*? What irreligion can there be in applying some *Scripture-expressions* to *Natural things*? Why are not the one rather exalted and purifi'd, than the other defil'd by such applications? The very *Enthusiasts* themselves, who are wont to start at such *Wit* as *Atheistical,* are more guilty of its excesses than any other sort of men: For whatever they allege out of the *Historical, Prophetical,* or *Evangelical Writings,* and apply it to themselves, their Enemies, or their Country, though they call it the mind of *God,* yet it is nothing else but *Scripture-comparison* and *Similitude.*

The *Sciences* of mens brains are none of the best Materials for this kind of *Wit.* Very few have happily succeeded in *Logical,*

Metaphysical, Grammatical, nay even scarce in *Mathematical Comparisons;* and the reason is, because they are most of them conversant about things remov'd from the Senses, and so cannot surprise the *fancy* with very obvious, or quick, or sensible delights.

The *Wit* that is founded on the *Arts* of mens hands is masculine and durable: It consists of *Images* that are generally observ'd, and such visible things which are familiar to mens minds. This therefore I will reckon as the first sort, which is still improvable by the advancement of *Experiments*.

And to this I will add the *Works of Nature,* which are one of the best and most fruitful Soils for the growth of *Wit.* It is apparent, that the defect of the *Antients* in *Natural Knowledge* did also streighten[1] their *Fancies:* Those few things which they knew, they us'd so much, and appli'd so often, that they even almost wore them away by their using. The sweetness of Flowers, and Fruits, and Herbs, they had quite devour'd: They had tir'd out the *Sun,* and *Moon,* and *Stars* with their Similitudes, more than they fancy them to be wearied by their daily journeys round the *Hevens.*

It is now therefore seasonable for *Natural Knowledge* to come forth, and to give us the *understanding* of new *Virtues* and *Qualities* of things; which may relieve their fellow-creatures, that have long born the burden alone, and have long bin vex'd by the imaginations of *Poets.* This charitable assistance *Experiments* will soon bestow. The Comparisons which these may afford will be intelligible to all, becaus they proceed from things that enter into all mens Senses. These will make the most vigorous impressions on mens *Fancies,* becaus they do even touch their *Eyes,* and are neerest to their *Nature.* Of these the variety will be infinit; for the particulars are so, from whence they may be deduc'd: These may be always new and unsullied, seing there is such a vast number of *Natural* and *Mechanical things,* not yet fully known or improv'd, and by consequence not yet sufficiently apply'd.

The use of *Experiments* to this purpose is evident, by the wonderful advantage that my Lord *Bacon* receiv'd from them. This excellent Writer was abundantly recompenc'd for his Noble La-

1 [I.e., limit.]

bors in that *Philosophy,* by a vast Treasure of admirable *Imaginations* which it afforded him, wherewith to express and adorn his thoughts about other matters. But I will not confine this *Observation* to one single *Author,* though he was one of the first and most artificial Managers of this way of *Wit.* I will venture to declare in general of the *English Tongue,* That as it contains a greater stock of *Natural* and *Mechanical Discoveries,* so it is also more inrich'd with beautiful *Conceptions,* and inimitable *Similitudes,* gather'd from the *Arts* of mens hands, and the *Works of Nature,* than ever any other *Language* could produce.

And now I hope what I have here said will prevail somthing with the *Wits* and *Railleurs* of this *Age,* to reconcile their Opinions and Discourses to these *Studies:* For now they may behold that their Interest is united with that of the *Royal Society;* and that if they shall decry the promoting of *Experiments,* they will deprive themselves of the most fertil Subject of *Fancy:* And indeed it has bin with respect to these terrible men, that I have made this long digression. I acknowledge that we ought to have a great dread of their power: I confess I believe that *New Philosophy* need not (as *Cæsar*) fear the pale, or the melancholy, as much as the humorous, and the merry: For they perhaps by making it ridiculous, becaus it is *new,* and becaus they themselves are unwilling to take pains about it, may do it more injury than all the Arguments of our severe and frowning and dogmatical *Adversaries.*

But to gain their good will, I must acquaint them, That the Family of the *Railleurs* is deriv'd from the same Original with the *Philosophers.* The Founder of *Philosophy* is confess'd by all to be *Socrates;* and he also was the famous Author of all *Irony.* They ought therefore to be tender in this matter, wherein the honor of their *Common Parent* is concern'd: it becomes them to remember, that it is the fault, and not the excellence of *Wit,* to defile its own Nest, and not to spare its own Friends and Relations, for the sake of a jest.

The truth is, The Extremes of *Raillery* are more offensive than those of *Stupidity:* It is a work of such a tender and subtil spirit, that it cannot be decently perform'd by all pretenders to it: Nor does it always agree well with the Temper of our *Nation;* which as it has a greater corage than to suffer *derision,* so it has a firmer virtu than to be wholly taken up about deriding of others. Such men are therefore to know, That all things are capable of abuse from the same *Topicks* by which they may be commended; they are to consider, That Laughter is the easiest and the slendrest fruit of *Wit;* they are to understand, That it proceeds from the observation of the *deformity* of things; but that there is a nobler and more masculine pleasure, which is rais'd from beholding their *Order* and *Beauty:* From thence they may conclude, how great the difference is between them, and the real *Philosophers:* For while *Nature* has only form'd them to be pleas'd with its irregularities and monsters, it has given the other the delight of knowing and studying its most *beautiful Works.*

In plain terms, a universal abuse of every thing, though it may tickle the fancy never so much, is *inhuman madness;* as one of the *Ancients* well expresses it, who calls such mirth *humanis Bacchari rebus.*[2] If all things were made the subjects of such humour, all worthy designs would soon be laugh'd out of the World; and for our present sport, our *Posterity* would become barbarous. All good Enterprises ought to find assistance when they are begun, applaus when they succeed, and even pity and prais if they fail. The true *Raillery* should be a defence for *Good* and *Virtuous Works,* and should only intend the derision of extravagant, and the disgrace of vile and dishonourable things. This kind of *Wit* ought to have the nature of *Salt,* to which it is usually compar'd; which preserves and keeps sweet the good and the sound parts of all Bodies, and only frets, dries up, and destroys those humors which putrify and corrupt.

2 ["to make insane sport of (all) things human."]

John Wilmot, Earl of Rochester

1647–80

Educated first at home by the clergyman Giffard and then at Burford Grammar School, the precocious Rochester was able to enter Wadham College, Oxford, at the time of the Restoration. When he came to court at the age of eighteen, his favorite authors were "Boileau among the French, and Cowley among the English Wits." Reputed a good husband and landlord in the country, he was at court the "prince of all the devils of the Town." Rochester is a fine but careless poet, capable in "Satyr upon Mankind" and "Upon Nothing" of satirical grandeur, in many poems of marvelous ribaldry, and in verses like those of the "Young Lady to her Ancient Lover" of profoundly moving wit. His "A Session of the Poets," reprinted from Poems on Several Occasions *(1680), is more lively and more "public" than Suckling's effort in the same genre; although Rochester's authorship has been doubted, it seems probable that he composed the poem, as one ms. suggests, in 1676/7.*

A Session of the POETS
[1676/7]

Since the *Sons* of the *Muses*, grew num'rous, and loud,
For th'appeasing so factious, and clam'rous a Crowd;
Apollo, thought fit in so weighty a cause,
T'Establish a Govornment, *Leader,* and *Laws.*
The hopes of the *Bays,* at this summoning call,
Had drawn 'em together, the *Devil* and all;
All thronging and listning, they gap'd for the Blessing,
No *Presbyter Sermon,* had more crowding, and pressing.
   In the *Head* of the *Gang J[ohn] D[ryden]*, appear'd,
That Antient grave *Wit,* so long lov'd, and fear'd;
But *Apollo,* had heard a Story 'ith' *Town,*
Of his quitting the *Muses,* to wear the black *Gown;*
And so gave him leave now his *Poetry's* done,
To let him turn *Priest,* now *R[eeve]*, is turn'd *Nun.*[1]
   This Reverend *Author* was no sooner set by,
But *Apollo,* had got gentle *George,* in his Eye;
And frankly confest, of all Men that writ,
There's none had more fancy, sense, Judgement, & *Wit.*
But 'th' crying Sin, idleness, he was so harden'd,
That his long Seav'n years silence, was not to be pardon'd.[2]
   Brawny *W[ycherley]*, was the next Man shew'd his Face,
But *Apollo,* e'ne thought him too good for the Place;
No *Gentleman Writer,* that office shou'd bear
'Twas a *Trader* in *Wit,* the *Lawrel* shou'd wear,
As none but a *Citt,* e're makes a *Lord Maior.*
   Next into the Crowd, *Tom S[hadwell]*, does wallow,
And Swears by his *Guts,* his *Paunch,* and his *Tallow,*

---

1 [Anne Reeves, an actress rumored to have been Dryden's mistress, turned nun around 1675.]
2 ["Gentle George" Etherege produced the *Man of Mode* (1675/6) some seven years after *She Wou'd if She cou'd* (1667/8).]

'Tis he that alone best pleases the Age,
Himself, and his *Wife* have supported the *Stage*.
Apollo, well pleas'd with so bonny a *Lad,*
T'oblige him, he told him he shou'd be huge glad,
Had he half so much *Wit,* as he fancy'd he had.
How ever to please so *Jovial* a *Wit,*
And to keep him in humor, *Apollo,* thought fit,
To bid him drink on, and keep his Old Trick,
Of railing at *Poets,* and shewing his *Prick*.

N[at] L[ee], stept in next, in hopes of a *Prize,*
Apollo, remember'd he had hit once in Thrice;
By the Rubyes in's Face, he cou'd not deny,
But he had as much Wit, as *Wine* cou'd supply;
Confest that indeed he had a *Musical Note,*
But sometimes strain'd so hard, that he rattled i'th' Throat;
Yet owning he had *Sense,* t'encourage him for't,
He made him his *Ovid* in *Augustus's Court*.[3]

Poet S[ettle], his *Tryal,* was the next came about,
He brought him an *Ibrahim,* with the Preface torn out;[4]
And humbly desir'd, he might give no offence;
God damme, cryes S[hadwell], he cannot write sense,
And Ballocks cry'd *Newport,*[5] I hate that dull *Rogue;*
Apollo, consid'ring he was not in vogue,
Wou'd not trust his dear *Bays,* with so modest a *Fool,*
And bid the great *Boy,* shou'd be sent back to *School,*

Tom O[tway], came next, *Tom S[hadwell's]*, dear *Zany,*
And swears for *Heroicks,* he writes best of any;
Don *C[arlos]*,[6] his Pockets so amply had fill'd,
That his *Mange* was quite cur'd, and his *Lice,* were all kill'd.
But *Apollo,* had seen his Face on the *Stage,*
And prudently did not think fit to engage,
The scum of a *Play-house,* for the Prop of an *Age*.

In the numerous Herd, that encompast him round
Little starcht *Jonny C[rowne]*,[7] at his Elbow he found,
His *Crevat-string,* new Iron'd, he gently did stretch,

3 [Nathaniel Lee wrote *Gloriana, or the Court of Augustus Caesar,* in which "Ovid" is represented as the lover of Julia, the Emperor's daughter.]
4 [Settle's *Ibrahim, the Illustrious Bassa* was printed with a preface attacking Shadwell.]
5 [An associate of Killigrew and a member of that racy group known as "The Ballers."]
6 [A heroic tragedy by Otway.]
7 ["Starch" Johnny Crowne, a minor literary figure (*c.* 1640–1712) who began his career with the romance of *Pandion and Amphigenia;* Rochester got him a commission to write a masque, *Calisto,* for Charles II.]

His Lilly white hand out, the *Lawrel* to reach;
Alledging that he had most right to the *Bays,*
For writing *Romances,* and shiting of *Plays.*
Apollo, rose up, and gravely confest,
Of all *Men* that writ, his *Tallent* was best:
For since pain, and dishonor, *Mans* life only damn,
The greatest felicity, *Mankind* can claim,
Is to want sense of smart, and be past sense of shame:
And to perfect his *Bliss,* in *Poetical Rapture,*
He bid him be dull to the end of the *Chapter.*

 The *Poetess Afra,*[8] next shew'd her sweet face,
And swore by her *Poetry,* and her black *Ace,*
The *Lawrel,* by a double right was her own,
For the *Plays* she had writ, and the *Conquests* she had won:
Apollo, acknowledg'd 'twas hard to deny her,
Yet to deal franckly, and ingeniously[9] by her,
He told her [the] *Conquests,* and *Charmes* [were] pretence,
She ought to have pleaded a *Dozen* years since.
Anababaluthu[1] put in for a share,
And little *Tom Essences Author,*[2] was there.
Nor cou'd D[*urfey*], forbear for the *Lawrel* to stickle,
Protesting he had had the *Honor* to tickle,
The *Eares* of the *Town,* with his dear *Madam Fickle.*[3]

 With other pretenders, whose names I'd rehearse,
But that they're too long to stand in my *Verse.*
Apollo, quite tir'd with their tedious *Harrangue,*
Finds at last *Tom* B[*etterton's*],[4] face in the gang,
And since *Poets,* without the kind *Play'rs,* may hang;
By his own light, he solemnly swore,
That in search of a *Laureat,* he'd look out no more.
A general murmur ran quite through the *Hall,*
To think that the *Bays,* to an *Actor,* shou'd fall,
But *Apollo,* to quiet, and pacifie all;
E'ne told 'em to put his desert to the Test,
That he had made *Plays,* aswel as the best;

---

8 [Aphra Behn (1640–89), poetess, dramatist, and "novelist."]
9 [I.e., ingenuously.]
1 [One ms. substitutes for these nonsense syllables "At last, Mamamouche," alluding to Edward Ravenscroft's adaptation, entitled *Mamamouchi,* of Molière's *Bourgeois Gentilhomme.*]
2 [Rawlins, perhaps Thomas Rawlins, wrote *Tom Essence, or the Modish Wife* in 1676.]
3 [Thomas Durfey or D'Urfey (1653–1723) produced *Madame Fickle* in 1676.]
4 [Betterton (1635?–1710) was an author as well as an actor.]

And was the greatest wonder, the *Age* ever bore,
For of all the *Play-Scriblers*, that e're writ before,
His wit, had most worth, and most modesty in't,
For he had writ *Plays*, yet ne're came in print.

John Dryden
1631–1700

Educated at Westminster and Cambridge, Dryden wrote one poem in the "metaphysical" manner, the elegy on Hastings, and then went on to become the most influential "neoclassic" poet and critic of the century. Partly because of its conversational style and pragmatic approach, his criticism has acquired a higher reputation than that of any of his contemporaries; Dryden rarely seeks to legislate, and most of his criticism, seemingly secreted by his plays and poems, consists of explanation and persuasive self-justification. Even Of Dramatick Poesie *(1668), his one work of criticism* qua *criticism, is cast in the form of a dialogue, allowing Dryden to maintain a degree of anonymity and to avoid absolute commitment. Instead of repeating this venture into formal criticism as such, he chose to write over a period of thirty-six years three classical lives and some twenty-five prefaces to his own works—so many subtle examples of self-justification that the satiric portrayal of "Bayes" in* The Rehearsal *(1672) cuts uneasily close: "I have printed above a hundred sheets of paper, to insinuate the plot into the boxes." Influenced by Hobbes and the aims of the Royal Society, impressed and rather nonplussed by Rymer, Dryden nevertheless derived his flexible neoclassicism mainly from Corneille and modified it in the direction of his own pragmatic and tentative aims. There is perhaps no more characteristic statement in his critical prose than the adieu to rhyme and espousal of blank verse in the* preface to **All for Love**: *"Not that I condemn my former way, but that this is more proper to my present purpose."*

The pieces reprinted here provide clear testimony of Dryden's mixed attitude toward the principles of neoclassicism: his respect for The Rules and his dismay at their rigid application. "The Authors Apology for Heroique Poetry; and Poetique Licence" is the preface to The State of Innocence, and the Fall of Man *and is reprinted from the edition of 1677;* The State of Innocence, *Dryden's attempt to "tag" the "verses" of* Paradise Lost *for opera, was written before 1674, but the "Apology" evidently belongs to 1677. The "Heads of an Answer to Rymer," reprinted here from Tonson's 1711 edition of Beaumont and Fletcher, was later incorporated by Dryden into his "The Grounds of Criticism in Tragedy" (prefixed to* Troilus and Cressida *in 1679), a longer but far less candidly direct response to Rymer. Jacob Tonson accounts for the "Heads" in this manner: "In the Year 1677, Mr. Rymer (now Historiographer Royal) publish'd* The Tragedies of the last Age *consider'd, in a Letter to* Fleetwood Shepherd, Esq; *In this Treatise he Criticises upon* Rollo *Duke of* Normandy, The Maids Tragedy, *and* The King and no King; *all three written by our Authors, and the most taking Plays then Acted. He has there endeavour'd to the utmost the exposing their Failings, without taking the least Notice of their Beauties; Mr. Rymer sent one of his Books as a Present to Mr. Dryden, who on the Blank Leaves, before the Beginning, and after the End of the Book, made several Remarks, as if he design'd an Answer to Mr. Rymer's Reflections; they are of Mr. Dryden's own Hand Writing, and may be seen at the Publisher's of this Book; 'tis to be wish'd he had put his last Hand to 'em, and made the Connection closer, but just as he left them be pleas'd to take them here* verbatim *inserted."*

The Authors Apology for HEROIQUE POETRY;

and POETIQUE LICENCE

[*1677*]

To satisfie the Curiosity of those who will give themselves the
trouble of reading the ensuing POEM, I think my self oblig'd to
render them a Reason, why I publish an OPERA which was never
acted. In the first place I shall not be asham'd to own, that my
chiefest Motive, was the Ambition which I acknowledg'd in the
Epistle. I was desirous to lay at the feet of so Beautiful and Excellent a Princess,[1] a Work which I confess was unworthy her,
but which I hope she will have the goodness to forgive. I was also
induc'd to it in my own defence: many hundred Copies of it
being dispers'd abroad, without my knowledge or consent: so
that every one gathering new faults, it became at length a Libel
against me; and I saw, with some disdain, more nonsence than
either I, or as bad a Poet, could have cram'd into it, at a Months
warning, in which time 'twas wholly Written, and not since
Revis'd. After this, I cannot without injury to the deceas'd Author of *Paradice Lost,* but acknowledge that this POEM has receiv'd its entire Foundation, part of the Design, and many of the
Ornaments, from him. What I have borrow'd, will be so easily
discern'd from my mean Productions, that I shall not need to
point the Reader to the places: And, truly, I should be sorry, for
my own sake, that any one should take the pains to compare
them together: The Original being undoubtedly, one of the
greatest, most noble, and most sublime POEMS, which either this
Age or Nation has produc'd. And though I could not refuse the
partiality of my Friend,[2] who is pleased to commend me in his

1 [Mary, Duchess of York.]
2 [Nathaniel Lee, whose complimentary verses precede *The State of Innocence.*]

Verses, I hope they will rather be esteem'd the effect of his love to me, than of his deliberate and sober judgment. His Genius is able to make beautiful what he pleases: Yet, as he has been too favorable to me, I doubt not but he will hear of his kindness from many of our Contemporaries. For, we are fallen into an Age of Illiterate, Censorious, and Detracting people, who thus qualified, set up for Critiques.

In the first place I must take leave to tell them, that they wholly mistake the Nature of Criticism, who think its business is principally to find fault. Criticism, as it was first instituted by *Aristotle*, was meant a Standard of judging well. The chiefest part of which is to observe those Excellencies which should delight a reasonable Reader. If the Design, the Conduct, the Thoughts, and the Expressions of a POEM, be generally such as proceed from a true Genius of Poetry, the Critique ought to pass his judgement in favor of the Author. 'Tis malicious and unmanly to snarl at the little lapses of a Pen, from which *Virgil* himself stands not exempted. *Horace* acknowledges that honest *Homer* nods sometimes: He is not equally awake in every Line: But he leaves it also as a standing Measure for our judgments,

> *Non, Ubi plura nitent in Carmine, paucis*
> *Offendi maculis, quas aut incuria fudit*
> *Aut humana parùm cavit Natura.*[3]

And *Longinus*, who was undoubtedly, after *Aristotle*, the greatest Critique amongst the *Greeks*, in his twenty seventh Chapter περὶ ὑψοῦς,[4] has judiciously preferr'd the sublime Genius that sometimes erres, to the midling or indifferent one which makes few faults, but seldome or never rises to any Excellence. He compares the first to a Man of large possessions, who has not leisure to consider of every slight expence, will not debase himself to the management of every trifle: particular summs are not layd out or spar'd to the greatest advantage in his Oeconomy:

---

3 [Horace, *Ars Poetica* 351–53: "When there are many beauties in a poem, I will not be the one to find fault with a few blemishes that lack of care occasioned or human weakness has failed to avoid."]

4 [*On the Sublime*, attributed to "Longinus," had been translated earlier in the Renaissance but failed to exert any marked influence until the eighteenth century.]

but are sometimes suffer'd to run to waste, while he is only careful of the Main. On the other side, he likens the Mediocrity of
Wit, to one of a mean fortune, who manages his store with extream frugality, or rather parsimony: but who with fear of running into profuseness, never arrives to the magnificence of living. This kind of Genius writes, indeed correctly. A wary man he
is in Grammar; very nice as to Solæcism or Barbarism, judges to
a hair of little decencies, knows better than any Man what is not
to be written: and never hazards himself so far as to fall: but
plods on deliberately, and, as a grave Man ought, is sure to put
his staff before him; in short, he sets his heart upon it; and with
wonderful care makes his business sure: that is, in plain English, neither to be blam'd, nor prais'd.—I could, sayes my Author, find out some blemishes in *Homer:* and am perhaps, as
naturally inclin'd to be disgusted at a fault as another Man: But,
after all, to speak impartially, his faillings are such, as are only
marks of humane frailty: they are little Mistakes, or rather Neg-
ligences, which have escap'd his pen in the fervor of his writing;
the sublimity of his spirit carries it with me against his careles-
ness: And though *Apollonius* his *Argonautes,* and *Theocritus,*
his *Eidullia,* are more free from Errors, there is not any Man of
so false a judgment, who would choose rather to have been *Apollonius* or *Theocritus,* than *Homer.*

'Tis worth our consideration, a little to examine how much
these *Hypercritiques* of English Poetry, differ from the opinion
of the Greek and Latine Judges of Antiquity: from the *Italians*
and *French* who have succeeded them; and, indeed, from the
general tast and approbation of all Ages. Heroique Poetry, which
they contemn, has ever been esteem'd, and ever will be, the
greatest work of humane Nature: In that rank has *Aristotle*
plac'd it, and *Longinus* is so full of the like expressions, that he
abundantly confirms the others Testimony. *Horace* as plainly delivers his opinion, and particularly praises *Homer* in these
Verses.

Trojani Belli Scriptorem, Maxime Lolli,
Dum tu declamas Romæ, præneste relegi:

Qui quid sit pulchrum, quid turpe, quid utile, quid non,
Plenius ac melius Chrysippo & Crantore dicit.[5]

And in another place modestly excluding himself, from the
number of Poets, because he only writ Odes and Satyres, he tells
you a Poet is such an one,

Cui mens Divinior, atque os
Magna Sonaturum.[6]

Quotations are superfluous in an establish'd truth: otherwise I
could reckon up amongst the Moderns, all the *Italian* Commen-
tators on *Aristotle*'s Book of Poetry; and amongst the *French*, the
greatest of this Age, *Boileau* and *Rapin:* the latter of which is
alone sufficient, were all other Critiques lost, to teach anew the
rules of writing. Any Man who will seriously consider the nature
of an Epique Poem, how it agrees with that of Poetry in general,
which is to instruct and to delight; what actions it describes, and
what persons they are chiefly whom it informs, will find it a
work which indeed is full of difficulty in the attempt, but admirable when 'tis well performed. I write not this with the least
intention to undervalue the other parts of Poetry: for Comedy is
both excellently instructive, and extreamly pleasant: Satyre
lashes Vice into Reformation, and humor represents folly, so as
to render it ridiculous. Many of our present Writers are eminent
in both these kinds, and particularly the Author[7] of the *Plain
Dealer*, whom I am proud to call my Friend, has oblig'd all honest and vertuous Men, by one of the most bold, most general,
and most useful Satyres which has ever been presented on the
English Theater. I do not dispute the preference of Tragedy; let
every Man enjoy his tast: but 'tis unjust, that they who have not
the least notion of Heroique writing, should therefore condemn
the pleasure which others receive from it, because they cannot

5 [*Epistles* i.2.1–4: "While you, Lollius Maximus, declaim in Rome, at
Praeneste I have reread the writer of the Trojan War, who reveals more
plainly and better than Chrysippus and Crantor what is fair, what foul, what
is useful and what not."]
6 [*Satires* i.4.43–44: "whose soul is more divine and whose mouth will speak
great things."]
7 [William Wycherley's comedy *The Plain Dealer* was published in 1677.]

comprehend it. Let them please their appetites in eating what they like: but let them not force their dish on all the Table. They who would combat general Authority, with particular Opinion, must first establish themselves a reputation of understanding better, than other men. Are all the flights of Heroique Poetry, to be concluded bombast, unnatural, and meer madness, because they are not affected with their Excellencies? 'Tis just as reasonable as to conclude there is no day, because a blind Man cannot distinguish of Light and Colours? ought they not rather, in modesty, to doubt of their own judgments, when they think this or that expression in *Homer, Virgil, Tasso,* or *Milton's Paradice,* to be too far strain'd, than positively to conclude, that 'tis all fustian, and meer nonsense? 'Tis true, there are limits to be set betwixt the boldness and rashness of a Poet; but he must understand those limits who pretends to judge, as well as he who undertakes to write: and he who has no liking to the whole, ought in reason to be excluded from censuring of the parts. He must be a Lawyer before he mounts the Tribunal: and the Judicature of one Court too, does not qualifie a man to preside in another. He may be an excellent Pleader in the *Chancery,* who is not fit to rule the *Common Pleas.* But I will presume for once to tell them, that the boldest strokes of Poetry, when they are manag'd Artfully, are those which most delight the Reader.

Virgil and *Horace,* the severest Writers of the severest Age, have made frequent use of the hardest Metaphors, and of the strongest Hyperboles: And in this case the best Authority is the best Argument. For generally to have pleas'd, and through all ages, must bear the force of Universal Tradition. And if you would appeal from thence to right Reason, you will gain no more by it in effect, than First, to set up your Reason against those Authors; and Secondly, against all those who have admir'd them. You must prove why that ought not to have pleas'd, which has pleas'd the most Learn'd, and the most Judicious: and to be thought knowing, you must first put the fool upon all Mankind. If you can enter more deeply, than they have done, into the Causes and Ressorts of that which moves pleasure in a Reader, the Field is open, you may be heard: but those Springs of humane Nature are not so easily discover'd by every superficial

Judge: It requires Philosophy as well as Poetry, to sound the depth of all the Passions; what they are in themselves, and how they are to be provok'd: and in this Science the best Poets have excell'd. *Aristotle* rais'd the Fabrique of his Poetry, from observation of those things, in which *Euripides, Sophocles,* and *Æschylus* pleas'd: He consider'd how they rais'd the Passions, and thence has drawn rules for our Imitation. From hence have sprung the Tropes and Figures, for which they wanted a name, who first practis'd them, and succeeded in them. Thus I grant you, that the knowledge of Nature was the Original Rule; and that all Poets ought to study her; as well as *Aristotle* and *Horace* her Interpreters. But then this also undeniably follows, that those things which delight all Ages, must have been an imitation of Nature; which is all I contend. Therefore is Rhetorick made an Art: therefore the Names of so many Tropes and Figures were invented: because it was observ'd they had such and such an effect upon the Audience. Therefore *Catachreses* and *Hyperboles* have found their place amongst them; not that they were to be avoided, but to be us'd judiciously, and plac'd in Poetry, as heightnings and shadows are in Painting, to make the Figure bolder, and cause it to stand off to sight.

> *Nec retia Cervis*
> *Ulla, dolum meditantur;*[8]

sayes *Virgil* in his *Eclogues:* and speaking of *Leander* in his *Georgiques,*

> *Cæcâ nocte natat serus freta, quem super, ingens*
> *Porta tonat Cœli; & scopulis illisa reclamant*
> *Æquora:* [9]

In both of these you see he fears not to give Voice and Thought to things inanimate.

Will you arraign your Master *Horace,* for his hardness of Expression, when he describes the death of *Cleopatra?* and sayes

8 [v.60–61: "Nets meditate no snare for the stag."]
9 [iii.260–62: "He swims the straits, late in the dark night. Heaven's great portal thunders above him, and the waves, dashing upon the cliffs, echo the cry."]

she did *Asperos tractare serpentes, ut atrum corpore combiber-
et venenum?*[1] because the Body in that action, performs what is
proper to the mouth?

As for *Hyperboles,* I will neither quote *Lucan,* nor *Statius,*
Men of an unbounded imagination, but who often wanted the
Poyze of Judgement. The Divine *Virgil* was not liable to that ex-
ception; and yet he describes *Polyphemus* thus:

> *Graditurque per æquor
> Iam medium; nec dum fluctus latera ardua tinxit.*[2]

In imitation of this place, our Admirable *Cowley* thus paints
Goliah.

> *The Valley, now, this Monster seem'd to fill;
> And we, methought, look'd up to him from our Hill.*[3]

Where the two words *seem'd,* and *methought,* have mollify'd the
Figure: and yet if they had not been there, the fright of the *Israelites* might have excus'd their belief of the Giants Stature.

In the *8th* of the *Æneids,* *Virgil* paints the swiftness of *Camilla*
thus:

> *Illa vel intactæ segetis per summa volaret
> Gramina, nec teneras cursu læsisset aristas;
> Vel Mare per medium, fluctu suspensa tumenti,
> Ferret iter, celeres nec tingeret æquore plantas.*[4]

You are not oblig'd, as in History, to a literal belief of what the
Poet says; but you are pleas'd with the Image, without being
couzen'd by the Fiction.

Yet even in History, *Longinus* quotes *Herodotus* on this occasion of *Hyperboles.* The *Lacedemonians,* says he, at the

---

[1] [*Odes* i.37.26–28: "handle fierce snakes, so that her body might imbibe black
vernom."]
[2] [*Aeneid* iii.664–65: "He strides through the midst of the sea, nor have the
waves wet his mighty sides."]
[3] [*Davideis,* III, 385–86.]
[4] [*Aeneid* vii.808–11: "She might have flown over the highest ears of unmown
corn, nor bruised the tender ears in her flight; or swept over the open sea
suspended above the rising waves, nor dipped her swift feet in the water."]

straights of *Thermopylæ,* defended themselves to the last ex-
tremity: and when their Arms fail'd them, fought it out with
their Nails and Teeth: till at length, (the *Persians* shooting continually upon them) they lay buried under the Arrows of their
enemies. It is not reasonable, (continues the *Critique*) to believe
that Men could defend themselves with their Nails and Teeth
from an arm'd multitude: nor that they lay buried under a pile
of Darts and Arrows; and yet there wants not probability for the
Figure: because the *Hyperbole* seems not to have been made for
the sake of the description; but rather to have been produc'd
from the occasion.

'Tis true, the boldness of the Figures are to be hidden, sometimes by the address of the Poet; that they may work their effect
upon the Mind, without discovering the Art which caus'd it. And
therefore they are principally to be us'd in passion; when we
speak more warmly, and with more precipitation than at other
times: for then, *Si vis me flere dolendum est primùm ipsi tibe,*[5]
the Poet must put on the Passion he endeavours to represent: A
man in such an occasion is not cool enough, either to reason
rightly, or to talk calmly. Aggravations are then in their proper
places, Interogations, Exclamations, Hyperbata, or a disorder'd
connection of discourse, are graceful there, because they are
Natural. The summ of all depends on what before I hinted, that
this boldness of expression is not to be blam'd; if it be manag'd
by the coolness and discretion, which is necessary to a Poet.

Yet before I leave this subject, I cannot but take notice how
dis-ingenuous[6] our Adversaries appear: All that is dull, insipid,
languishing and without sinews in a Poem, they call an imitation of Nature: they onely offend our most equitable Judges,
who think beyond them; and lively Images and Elocution, are
never to be forgiven.

What Fustian, as they call it, have I heard these Gentlemen
find out in Mr. *Cowley*'s Odes? I acknowledge my self unworthy

5 [Horace, *Ars Poetica* 102–03: "If you want me to weep, you yourself must
first feel grief."]
6 [Intolerant of *ingenium* or genius.]

to defend so excellent an Author; neither have I room to do it here: onely in general I will say, that nothing can appear more beautiful to me, than the strength of those Images which they condemn.

Imaging is, in it self, the very heighth and life of Poetry. 'Tis, as *Longinus* describes it, a Discourse, which, by a kind of Enthusiasm, or extraordinary emotion of the Soul, makes it seem to us, that we behold those things which the Poet paints, so as to be pleas'd with them, and to admire them.

If Poetry be imitation, that part of it must needs be best, which describes most lively our Actions and Passions; our Virtues and our Vices; our Follies and our Humors: for neither is Comedy without its part of Imaging: and they who do it best, are certainly the most excellent in their kind. This is too plainly prov'd to be denied: but how are Poetical Fictions, how are Hippocentaures and Chymæras, or how are Angels and immaterial Substances to be Imag'd? which some of them are things quite out of Nature: others, such whereof we can have no notion? this is the last refuge of our Adversaries; and more than any of them have yet had the wit to object against us. The answer is easie to the first part of it. The fiction of some Beings which are not in Nature, (second Notions as the Logicians call them) has been founded on the conjunction of two Natures, which have a real separate Being. So *Hippocentaures* were imagin'd, by joyning the Natures of a Man and Horse together; as *Lucretius* tells us, who has us'd this word of Image oftner than any of the Poets.

> *Nam certé ex vivo, Centauri non fit Imago,*
> *Nulla fuit quoniam talis natura animaì:*
> *Verùm ubi equi atque hominis, casu, convenit imago,*
> *Hærescit facilè extemplo, &c.*[7]

The same reason may also be alledg'd for *Chymæra*'s and the rest. And Poets may be allow'd the like liberty, for describing

[7] [*De Rerum Natura* iv. 739–42: "For certainly the picture of a centaur is not drawn from life, since in nature there never existed such an animal. But if by chance the images of a horse and a man are fitted together, they quickly and easily hold fast to life."]

things which really exist not, if they are founded on popular belief: of this nature are Fairies, Pigmies, and the extraordinary
effects of Magick: for 'tis still an imitation, though of other
mens fancies: and thus are *Shakespeare's Tempest,* his *Mid-
summer nights Dream,* and *Ben. Johnson's Masque of Witches*[8]
to be defended. For Immaterial Substances we are authoriz'd by
Scripture in their description: and herein the Text accommo-
dates it self to vulgar apprehension, in giving Angels the like-
ness of beautiful young men. Thus, after the Pagan Divinity, has
Homer drawn his Gods with humane Faces: and thus we have
notions of things above us, by describing them like other beings
more within our knowledge.

  I wish I could produce any one example of excellent imaging
in all this Poem:[9] perhaps I cannot: but that which comes nearest it, is in these four lines, which have been sufficiently can-
vas'd by my well-natur'd Censors.

> *Seraph* and *Cherub, careless of their charge,*
> *And wanton, in full ease now live at large:*
> *Unguarded leave the passes of the Sky;*
> *And all dissolv'd in Hallelujahs lye.*

  I have heard (sayes one of them) of Anchove's dissolv'd in
Sauce; but never of an Angel in Hallelujahs. A mighty *Witty-
cism,* (if you will pardon a new word!) but there is some difference between a Laugher and a Critique. He might have Bur-
lesqu'd *Virgil* too, from whom I took the Image. *Invadunt urbem,
somno vinoque sepultam.*[1] A Cities being buried is just as proper
an occasion, as an Angels being dissolv'd in Ease, and Songs of
Triumph. Mr. *Cowley* lies as open too in many places:

> *Where there vast Courts the Mother Waters keep,* &c.[2]

for if the mass of Waters be the Mothers, then their Daughters,
the little streams, are bound in all good manners, to make Cour-

---

8 [*The Masque of Queens.*]
9 [I.e., in *The State of Innocence.*]
1 [*Aeneid* ii.265: "They invade the city, buried in sleep and wine."]
2 [*Davideis,* I, 79.]

tesie to them, and ask them Blessing. How easie 'tis to turn into ridicule, the best descriptions, when once a man is in the humor of laughing, till he wheezes at his own dull jest! but an Image which is strongly and beautifully set before the eyes of the Reader, will still be Poetry, when the merry fit is over: and last when the other is forgotten.

I promis'd to say somewhat of *Poetique Licence*, but have in part anticipated my discourse already. *Poetique Licence* I take to be the Liberty, which Poets have assum'd to themselves in all ages, of speaking things in Verse, which are beyond the severity of Prose. 'Tis that particular character, which distinguishes and sets the bounds betwixt *Oratio soluta*,[3] and *Poetry*. This, as to what regards the thought, or imagination of a Poet, consists in Fiction: but then those thoughts must be express'd; and here arise two other branches of it: for if this *Licence* be included in a single word, it admits of Tropes: if in a Sentence or Proposition, of Figures: both which are of a much larger extent, and more forcibly to be us'd in Verse than Prose. This is that Birthright which is deriv'd to us from our great Forefathers, even from *Homer* down to *Ben*, and they who would deny it to us, have, in plain terms, the Foxes quarrel to the Grapes; they cannot reach it.

How far these Liberties are to be extended, I will not presume to determine here, since *Horace* does not. But it is certain that they are to be varied, according to the Language and Age in which an Author writes. That which would be allow'd to a *Grecian* Poet, *Martial* tells you, would not be suffer'd in a *Roman*. And 'tis evident that the *English*, does more nearly follow the strictness of the latter, than the freedoms of the former. Connection of Epithetes, or the conjunction of two words in one, are frequent and elegant in the *Greek*, which yet Sir *Philip Sidney*, and the Translator of *Du Bartas*,[4] have unluckily attempted in the *English*; though this I confess, is not so proper an Instance of *Poetique Licence*, as it is of variety of *Idiom* in Languages.

3 [I.e., prose, or speech free of meter, as distinct from *oratio poemata*.]
4 [Joshua Sylvester (1563–1618), whose collected edition of *Bartas His Devine Weekes, and Workes* appeared in 1605.]

Horace a little explains himself on this subject of *Licentia Poetica;* in these Verses,

> *Pictoribus atque Poetis*
> *Quidlibet audendi, semper fuit æqua potestas:*
> *Sed non, ut placidis coeant immitia, non ut*
> *Serpentes avibus geminentur, Tygribus Hædi.*[5]

He would have a Poem of a piece: not to begin with one thing and end with another: he restrains it so far, that Thoughts of an unlike Nature, ought not to be joyn'd together: That were indeed to make a Chaos. He tax'd not *Homer*, nor the Divine *Virgil*, for interesting their gods in the Wars of *Troy* and *Italy;* neither had he now liv'd, would he have tax'd *Milton*, as our false Critiques have presum'd to do, for his choice of a supernatural Argument: but he would have blam'd my Author, who was a *Christian*, had he introduc'd into his Poem Heathen Deities, as *Tasso* is condemn'd, by *Rapin* on the like occasion: and as *Camoens*, the Author of the *Lusiads*, ought to be censur'd by all his Readers, when he brings in *Bacchus* and Christ into the same Adventure of his Fable. From that which has been said, it may be collected, that the definition of Wit (which has been so often attempted, and ever unsuccessfully by many Poets,) is only this: That it is a propriety of Thoughts and Words; or in other terms, Thought and Words, elegantly adapted to the Subject. If our Critiques will joyn issue on this Definition, that we may *convenire in aliquo tertio*,[6] if they will take it as a granted Principle, 'twill be easie to put an end to this dispute: No man will disagree from anothers judgement, concerning the dignity of Style, in Heroique Poetry: but all reasonable Men will conclude it necessary, that sublime Subjects ought to be adorn'd with the sublimest, and (consequently often) with the most figurative expressions. In the mean time I will not run into their fault of imposing my opinions on other men, any more than I would my Writings on their tast: I have onely laid down, and that superficially enough, my present thoughts; and shall be glad to be taught better, by those who pretend to reform our Poetry.

5 [*Ars Poetica* 9–10, 12–13: "Painters and poets have always shared equal rights in audacious undertakings, but not so that the savage should mate with the tame, nor that serpents should couple with birds, lambs with tigers."]
6 [I.e., resolve upon agreement by introducing a third principle.]

HEADS OF AN ANSWER TO RYMER
[1677]

He who undertakes to Answer this Excellent Critick of Mr.
Rymer, in behalf of our *English* Poets against the *Greek*, ought
to do it in this manner.

Either by yielding to him the greatest part of what he contends for, which consists in this, that the Μῦθος (*i.e.*) the Design
and Conduct of it is more conducing in the *Greeks*, to those Ends
of Tragedy which *Aristotle* and he propose, namely, to cause
Terror and Pity; yet the granting this does not set the *Greeks*
above the *English* Poets.

But the Answerer ought to prove two things; First, That the
Fable is not the greatest Master-Piece of a Tragedy, tho' it be the
Foundation of it.

Secondly, That other Ends, as suitable to the Nature of Tragedy, may be found in the *English*, which were not in the *Greek*.

Aristotle places the Fable first; not *quoad dignitatem, sed
quoad fundamentum;*[1] for a Fable never so Movingly contriv'd,
to those Ends of his, Pity and Terror, will operate nothing on
our Affections, except the Characters, Manners, Thoughts and
Words are suitable.

So that it remains for Mr. *Rymer* to prove, That in all those, or
the greatest part of them, we are inferior to *Sophocles* and *Euripides:* And this he has offer'd at in some measure, but, I think, a
little partially to the Ancients.

To make a true Judgment in this Competition, between the
Greek Poets and the *English* in Tragedy, Consider,

    I. How *Aristotle* has defin'd a Tragedy.

   II. What he assigns the End of it to be.

  III. What he thinks the Beauties of it.

  IV. The Means to attain the End propos'd. Compare the *Greek*
       and *English* Tragick Poets justly and without Partiality,
       according to those Rules.

Then, Secondly, consider, whether *Aristotle* has made a just

---

1 [Not "according to worth but priority."]

Definition of Tragedy, of its Parts, of its Ends, of its Beauties; and whether he having not seen any others but those of *Sophocles, Eurypides,* &c. had or truly could determine what all the Excellencies of Tragedy are, and wherein they consist.

Next show in what ancient Tragedy was deficient; for Example, in the narrowness of its Plots, and fewness of Persons, and try whether that be not a Fault in the *Greek* Poets; and whether their Excellency was so great, when the Variety was visibly so little; or whether what they did was not very easie to do.

Then make a Judgment on what the *English* have added to their Beauties: as for Example, not only more Plot, but also new Passions; as namely, that of Love, scarce touch'd on by the Ancients, except in this one Example of *Phædra,* cited by Mr. *Rymer,* and in that how short they were of *Fletcher.*

Prove also that Love, being an Heroique Passion, is fit for Tragedy, which cannot be deny'd; because of the Example alledged of *Phædra:* And how far *Shakespear* has outdone them in Friendship, &c.

To return to the beginning of this Enquiry, consider if Pity and Terror be enough for Tragedy to move, and I believe upon a true definition of Tragedy, it will be found that its Work extends farther, and that it is to reform Manners by delightful Representation of Human Life in great Persons, by way of Dialogue. If this be true, then not only Pity and Terror are to be mov'd as the only Means to bring us to Virtue, but generally Love to Virtue, and Hatred to Vice, by shewing the Rewards of one, and Punishments of the other; at least by rendring Virtue always amiable,[2] though it be shown unfortunate; and Vice detestable, tho' it be shown Triumphant.

If then the Encouragement of Virtue, and Discouragement of Vice, be the proper End of Poetry in Tragedy: Pity and Terror, tho' good Means, are not the only: For all the Passions in their turns are to be set in a Ferment; as Joy, Anger, Love, Fear, are to be used as the Poets common Places; and a general Concernment for the principal Actors is to be rais'd, by making them appear such in their Characters, their Words and Actions, as will Interest the Audience in their Fortunes.

And if after all, in a large Sense, Pity comprehends this Con-

2 [Worthy of love.]

cernment for the Good, and Terror includes Detestation for the Bad; then let us consider whether the *English* have not answer'd this End of Tragedy, as well as the Ancients, or perhaps better.

And here Mr. *Rymer*'s Objections against these Plays are to be impartially weigh'd; that we may see whether they are of weight enough to turn the Ballance against our Country-men.

'Tis evident those Plays which he arraigns have mov'd both those Passions in a high Degree upon the Stage.

To give the Glory of this away from the Poet, and to place it upon the Actors, seems unjust.

One Reason is, because whatever Actors they have found, the Event has been the same, that is, the same Passions have been always mov'd: which shows, that there is something of Force and Merit in the Plays themselves, conducing to the Design of Raising those two Passions: And suppose them ever to have been excellently acted, yet Action only adds Grace, Vigour, and more Life upon the Stage, but cannot give it wholly where it is not first. But Secondly, I dare appeal to those who have never seen them acted, if they have not found those two Passions mov'd within them; and if the general Voice will carry it, Mr. *Rymer*'s Prejudice will take off his single Testimony.

This being matter of Fact, is reasonably to be Established by this Appeal: As if one Man say 'tis Night, when the rest of the World conclude it to be Day, there needs no further Argument against him that it is so.

If he urge, that the general Taste is deprav'd; his Arguments to prove this can at best but evince, that our Poets took not the best way to raise those Passions; but Experience proves against him, that those Means which they have us'd, have been successful, and have produc'd them.

And one Reason of the Success is, in my Opinion, this, that *Shakespear* and *Fletcher* have written to the Genius of the Age and Nation in which they liv'd: For tho' Nature, as he objects, is the same in all Places, and Reason too the same; yet the Climate, the Age, the Dispositions of the People to whom a Poet writes, may be so different, that what pleas'd the *Greeks*, would not satisfie an *English* Audience.

And if they proceeded upon a Foundation of truer Reason to please the *Athenians*, than *Shakespear* and *Fletcher* to please the

English, it only shows that the *Athenians* were a more judicious People: But the Poet's business is certainly to please the Audience.

Whether our *English* Audience have been pleas'd hitherto with Acorns, as he calls it, or with Bread, is the next Question; that is, whether the Means which *Shakespear* and *Fletcher* have us'd in their Plays to raise those Passions before-named, be better applied to the ends by the *Greek* Poets than by them; and perhaps we shall not grant him this wholly. Let it be yielded that a Writer is not to run down with the Stream, or to please the People by their own usual Methods, but rather to reform their Judgments: It still remains to prove that our Theater needs this total Reformation.

The Faults which he has found in their Designs, are rather wittily aggravated in many places, than reasonably urg'd; and as much may be return'd on the *Greeks*, by one who were as witty as himself.

Secondly, They destroy not, if they are granted, the Foundation of the Fabrick, only take away from the Beauty of the Symmetry: For Example: The faults in the Character of the *King and no King*,[3] are not, as he makes them, such as render him detestable; but only Imperfections which accompany human Nature, and for the most part excus'd by the Violence of his Love; so that they destroy not our Pity or Concernment for him. This Answer may be applied to most of his Objections of that kind.

And *Rollo*[4] committing many Murders, when he is answerable but for one, is too severely arraign'd by him; for it adds to our Horror and Detestation of the Criminal: And Poetique Justice is not neglected neither, for we stab him in our Minds for every Offence which he commits; and the point which the Poet is to gain upon the Audience, is not so much in the Death of an Offender, as the raising an Horror of his Crimes.

That the Criminal should neither be wholly Guilty, nor wholly Innocent, but so participating of both, as to move both Pity and Terror, is certainly a good Rule; but not perpetually to be observed, for that were to make all Tragedies too much alike;

3 [By Beaumont and Fletcher, first printed 1619.]
4 [In *The Bloody Brother; or, Rollo* (1639) by Fletcher (and, possibly, Massinger and Jonson).]

which Objection he foresaw, but has not fully answered.

To conclude therefore, if the Plays of the Ancients are more correctly Plotted, ours are more beautifully written; and if we can raise Passions as high on worse Foundations, it shows our Genius in Tragedy is greater, for in all other parts of it the *English* have manifestly excell'd them.

For the Fable it self, 'tis in the *English* more adorn'd with Episodes, and larger than in the *Greek* Poets, consequently more diverting; for, if the Action be but one, and that plain, without any Counterturn of Design or Episode (*i.e.*) Under-plot, how can it be so pleasing as the *English,* which have both Under-plot, and a turn'd Design, which keeps the Audience in Expectation of the Catastrophe? whereas in the *Greek* Poets we see through the whole Design at first?

For the Characters, they are neither so many nor so various in *Sophocles* and *Euripides,* as in *Shakespear* and *Fletcher;* only they are more adapted to those ends of Tragedy which *Aristotle* commends to us; Pity and Terror.

The Manners flow from the Characters, and consequently must partake of their Advantages and Disadvantages.

The Thoughts and Words, which are the fourth and fifth Beauties of Tragedy, are certainly more Noble and more Poetical in the *English* than in the *Greek,* which must be proved by comparing them somewhat more Equitably than Mr. *Rymer* has done.

After all, we need not yield that the *English* way is less conducing to move Pity and Terror; because they often shew Virtue oppress'd, and Vice punish'd; where they do not both or either, they are not to be defended.

That we may the less wonder why Pity and Terror are not now the only Springs on which our Tragedies move, and that *Shakespear* may be more excus'd, *Rapin* confesses that the *French* Tragedies now all run upon the *Tendre,* and gives the Reason, because Love is the Passion which most Predominates in our Souls,[5] and that therefore the Passions represented become in-

---

[5] [*Réflexions sur la poétique d'Aristote* (1674), a work Dryden appears to have read with care, though here he misrepresents Rapin, who is actually attacking this kind of tragedy (in Ch. XX of the second part of the English translation).]

sipid, unless they are conformable to the Thoughts of the Audience; but it is to be concluded, that this Passion works not now among the *French* so strongly, as the other two did amongst the Ancients: Amongst us, who have a stronger Genius for Writing, the Operations from the Writing are much stronger; for the raising of *Shakespear*'s Passions are more from the Excellency of the Words and Thoughts, than the Justness of the Occasion; and if he has been able to pick single Occasions, he has never founded the whole reasonably, yet by the Genius of Poetry, in Writing he has succeeeded.

The Parts of a Poem, Tragique or Heroique, are,

    I. The Fable it self.

   II. The Order or Manner of its Contrivance, in relation of the parts to the whole.

  III. The Manners, or Decency of the Characters in Speaking or Acting what is proper for them, and proper to be shewn by the Poet.

  IV. The Thoughts which express the Manners.

   V. The Words which express those Thoughts.

In the last of these *Homer* excels *Virgil, Virgil* all other ancient Poets, and *Shakespear* all Modern Poets.

For the second of these, the Order; the meaning is, that a Fable ought to have a beginning, middle, and an end, all just and natural, so that that part which is the middle could not naturally be the beginning or end and so of the rest; all are depending one on another, like the links of a curious Chain.

If Terror and Pity are only to be rais'd; certainly this Author follows *Aristotle's* Rules, and *Sophocles* and *Euripedes's* Example; but Joy may be rais'd too, and that doubly, either by seeing a wicked Man Punish'd, or a good Man at last Fortunate; or perhaps Indignation, to see Wickedness prosperous, and Goodness depress'd: both these may be profitable to the end of Tragedy, Reformation of Manners; but the last improperly, only as it begets Pity in the Audience; tho' *Aristotle*, I confess, places Tragedies of this kind in the second Form.

And, if we should grant that the *Greeks* perform'd this better; perhaps it may admit a Dispute whether Pity and Terror are either the Prime, or at least the Only Ends of Tragedy.

'Tis not enough that *Aristotle* has said so, for *Aristotle* drew his Models of Tragedy from *Sophocles* and *Euripides;* and if he had seen ours, might have chang'd his Mind.

And chiefly we have to say (what I hinted on Pity and Terror in the last Paragraph save one) that the Punishment of Vice, and Reward of Virtue, are the most Adequate ends of Tragedy, because most conducing to good Example of Life; now Pity is not so easily rais'd for a Criminal (as the Ancient Tragedy always Represents his chief Person such) as it is for an Innocent Man and the Suffering of Innocence and Punishment of the Offender, is of the Nature of *English* Tragedy; contrary in the *Greek,* Innocence is unhappy often, and the Offender escapes.

Then we are not touch'd with the Sufferings of any sort of Men so much as of Lovers; and this was almost unknown to the Antients; so that they neither administred Poetical Justice (of which Mr. *Rymer* boasts) so well as we, neither knew they the best common Place of Pity, which is Love.

He therefore unjustly blames us for not building upon what the Antients left us, for it seems, upon consideration of the Premises, that we have wholly finished what they begun.

My Judgment on this Piece is this; that it is extreamly Learned; but that the Author of it is better Read in the *Greek* than in the *English* Poets; that all Writers ought to Study this Critick as the best Account I have ever seen of the Ancients; that the Model of Tragedy he has here given, is Excellent, and extream[ly] Correct; but that it is not the only Model of all Tragedy; because it is too much circumscrib'd in Plot, Characters, &c. and lastly, that we may be taught here justly to Admire and Imitate the Antients, without giving them the Preference, with this Author, in Prejudice to our own Country.

Want of Method, in this Excellent Treatise, makes the Thoughts of the Author sometimes obscure.

His Meaning, that Pity and Terror are to be mov'd, is that they are to be mov'd as the Means conducing to the Ends of Tragedy, which are Pleasure and Instruction.

And these two Ends may be thus distinguish'd. The chief End of the Poet is to please; for his immediate Reputation depends on it.

The great End of the Poem is to Instruct, which is perform'd by making Pleasure the Vehicle of that Instruction: For Poetry is an Art, and all Arts are made to Profit.

The Pity which the Poet is to Labour for, is for the Criminal, not for those, or him, whom he has murder'd, or who have been the Occasion of the Tragedy: The Terror is likewise in the Punishment of the same Criminal, who if he be represented too great an Offender, will not be pitied; if altogether Innocent, his Punishment will be unjust.

Another Obscurity is where he says, *Sophocles* perfected Tragedy, by introducing the third Actor; that is, he meant three kinds of Action, one Company singing, or speaking, ano[ther] Playing on the Musick, a third Dancing.

Rapin attributes more to the *Dictio*, that is, to the Words and Discourses of a Tragedy, than *Aristotle* has done, who places them in the last Rank of Beauties; perhaps only last in Order, because they are the last Product of the Design of the Disposition or Connexion of its Parts, of the Characters, of the Manners of those Characters, and of the Thoughts of proceeding from those Manners.

Rapin's Words are Remarkable:

'Tis not the admirable Intrigue, the surprizing Events, and extraordinary Incidents that make the Beauty of a Tragedy, 'tis the Discourses, when they are Natural and Passionate.[6]

So are *Shakespear*'s.

6 [*Réflexions* (Ch. XXI of the second part of the English translation).]

Joseph Glanvill

1636–80

---

*Educated at Oxford, Glanvill later became rector of the Abbey Church,
Bath, and other benefices. He attacked scholastic philosophy in* The
Vanity of Dogmatizing *(1661) and dogmatically defended his belief
in witches in* Sadducismus Triumphatus *(1666). Although the movement toward simplicity and clarity in the pulpit is perennial and
owes its force in the seventeenth century to a variety of forces besides
that of the new science, it seems significant that Glanvill should,
with an emphasis appropriate to an original fellow of the Royal Society, denominate "plainness," in opposition to the "conceited" manner of the metaphysical sermonizers, the "first Rule, and Character
of Preaching." "I shall," he promises plainly, "handle the* Rules of
Preaching *under these four Heads. It ought to be* plain, practical,
methodical, affectionate." *The first "Head" is offered here from the
edition licensed in 1677 and printed the following year; it is reprinted
from the copy held by Butler Library, Columbia University, New York
City.*

An Essay concerning Preaching

[1677]

Plainness is a Character of great latitude, and stands in opposition, First to *hard words*. Secondly, to *deep* and *mysterious notions*. Thirdly, to *affected Rhetorications*, and Fourthly, to *Phantastical Phrases*.

1. The Preacher should use *plain words:* so the end, *Edifica-
tion,* requires. He that affects hard ones, speaks in an unknown
tongue, and is a *Barbarian* to his Auditors; they hear the sound,
but are not edified: of all the vanities of Speech, there is none
more contemptible than this, and none is more exploded among
the wise; not only in preaching, but in all matters of solemn
discourse and ordinary conversation. It is commonly the Error of
the Youth; and may be pardon'd to such, in Moral, and Philosophical subjects: but in *Men,* set apart to instruct the people in
thing of spiritual, and eternal concernment, 'tis not to be indured. If you here ask me, *What I mean by hard words?* I will
presume that you cannot think I intend to condemn all that are
borrow'd from the *Greek, Latin,* or other more modern languages:
No, the *English* is a mixt speech, made up of divers tongues, and
we cannot speak without using forreign words: So that those
that talk of *pure English,* if they mean *unmixt,* by it, dream of
Chimæra's: our Language hath in all Ages been inlarging by the
Introduction of borrow'd words, which when they are once
brought into common use, they may be spoken without blame of
affectation: yea there is sometimes vanity, and affectation in

avoiding them: You know a great instance of this in a late
Writer,[1] who to shun the Latinisms of *immensity, eternity, pene-
trability,* &c. useth these, *all-placeness, all-timeness, thorow-
fareness,* and abundance such like. This *English* is far more un-
intelligible, than that *Latin,* which custom of speech hath made
easie, and familiar. I therefore blame not all forreign words, provided common usage hath made them free of our language: and
when we have not native ones that do as well express what we
would say: but to affect outlandish words that have not yet receiv'd the publick stamp, and especially to do it, when the ordinary *English* will represent the thing as well; These are the hard
words I condemn, and this is a vanity I think extreamly repre-
hensible in a Preacher. Besides which, I note by way of further
limitation, and for more clearness, that I blame not all words
that are not understood by the meer vulgar: every Art, every
Profession, every Subject hath proper terms, which are of hard,
and harsh sound to those that understand not those matters re-
spectively; but are easie and familiar to such as know them. And
in Divinity there are frequent occasions of using reasons, and
illustrations taken from the Philosophy, and nature of things; as
particularly in the discourses concerning the *Being* and *Attributes* of *God,* the *Immortality* of the *Soul,* and a future life;
about *Enthusiasm* and *Fanatical* pretences to the *Spirit:* These,
and divers other main subjects of Religion, that are fit, and necessary to be spoken to, sometimes, especially among hearers of
more advanced understandings, cannot be treated of without using words which the meer common sort cannot comprehend:
and yet as long as they are such, as are known, and frequently
used, in those subjects, 'twere humour and ignorance to interdict
them. But then, I would caution here, that the Preacher should
not employ more terms of art than need: Yea he should always
avoid them when they are not necessary; that is, when more
generally known expressions will explain the thing as well. And
this further I would advise, that you deal not much on such arguments among common hearers: These are strong meat, babes
must have milk, and simpler diet.

[1] [Nathaniel Fairfax (1637–90), *A Treatise of the Bulk and Selvedge of the
World* (1674): "Only tis like there is one thing which I may be blam'd for by
many; and that is a kind of shiness all along of those borrowed words & gay-
nesses, that Englishmen have pickt and cull'd from other Tongues. . . ."]

To this head of hard words I may refer another vanity, which is an affected use of scraps of *Greek* and *Latin,* things of no Service to the vulgar, by whom they are not understood; and by the wise they are now generally despised. I suppose I need not caution you, in more words, against this antiquated pedantry, which is worn out every where, except in some remote, and dark corners, where mean spirits seek the admiration of the ignorant by such low, and little devices. Indeed, in solemn assemblies of knowing and learn'd men, the Authority of the ancients may properly be cited in their own words, when they serve to confirm or illustrate some doubted truth; but to do it frequently in common and vulgar matters, among ordinary hearers, is affected folly, that signifieth nothing, but the weakness, and vanity of him that doth it.

2. Preaching should be plain, in opposition to deep and mysterious notions: We should not trouble our pulpits with Hypotheses of Philosophy or the heights of speculative Theology. The generality are not capable of much Theory: those are matters fit for the schools of learning, and the thoughts of deep, considering men. Much mischief is faln on Religion by reason of the transgression of this Rule: mysterious, notional preaching hath put many conceited people upon medling with what they can never well understand, and so hath fill'd them with air, and vanity, and made them proud, phantastical, and troublesome; disobedient to their Governours, and contemptuous to their betters. True knowledge indeed humbleth; but the conceited image of it, knowledge *falsly so call'd,* puffeth up, and is an instrument of mischief.

3. Plainness may be opposed to affected Rhetorick, and in this sense, too, Preaching should be plain: *Not in the inticing words of mans wisdome,* or *excellency of speech* (as the Apostle speaks) *viz.* not like the Orators, and Rhetoricians of those times, who coveted the glory of being accounted eloquent; and when they were praised, they had their reward: but our ends are far greater, and nobler, and so we should speak *not as pleasing men, but God;* with that seriousness and gravity as becomes those that design to *persuade men,* in the matters that relate to the glory of God, and their own present, and future well-being: for which purposes a manly unaffectedness, and simplicity of

speech is most proper. There is a bastard kind of eloquence that is crept into the Pulpit, which consists in affectations of wit and finery, flourishes, metaphors, and cadencies: This may be pardon'd to young men, in their first Essays of Preaching, but is by no means to be used by an exercised and constant Preacher: for the meer common sort heed not those things, and the wise despise them; so that all the praise that is aim'd at is lost, except it be among some phantastical, and unjudicious hearers; and on those, they have usually no other effect but that they entertain and tickle their phancies for the present, without making any impression upon their minds, or affections: And this is a very low End for a Minister of God, who is to *beseech men in* Christ's *stead.* If we would acquit our selves as such, we must not debase our great, and important message by those vanities of conceited speech: plainness is for ever the best eloquence; and 'tis the most forcible: so that our study should be to represent what we have to deliver in proper and easie expressions; neglecting and despising all starchedness of set, and affected speaking.

4. Plainness of preaching implies also the avoiding of phantastical phrases. There are some that place the power, and spirituality of Preaching in these; and reckon that there is something of extraordinary grace, and force in them: so that if a man represents the truths of the Gospel in simplicity and plainness, that shall go for dull morality; but the same things set off by conceited, fashionable phrases shall be most rare, and spiritual Divinity. Thus if you teach men to believe *Christ's* Doctrines, to obey his Laws, to trust to his promises, and to conform to his Example; these shall be counted dull, dry, and unedifying things that no-ways affect or move: but if you tell the people, that they must roll upon *Christ,* close with *Christ,* get into *Christ,* get a saving interest in the Lord *Christ:* O, this is savoury, this precious, this is spiritual teaching indeed; whereas if any thing more be meant by those phrases; than what the other plain expressions intend, it is either falshood, or non-sense. If therefore you would be a taking popular Preacher, here is your way; but if you would (as I hope you design) be a solid and honest one, you must avoid such odd, and foolish affectations. For by the use, and delight in such, ignorant people are blown up into an apprehension of their extraordinary knowledge, and acquaintedness

with the mysteries of the Gospel, when as indeed they know
nothing; and when they hear such phrases, they are pleased with
their sound, but have no meaning or knowledge of any thing
convey'd by them, and though this be vulgarly accounted plain
preaching; yet in truth it is the most difficult; and for the most
part neither teachers, nor hearers understand it.

Thus I have described to you the first Rule, and Character of
Preaching, it should be PLAIN.

Samuel Butler

1612–80

Son of a farmer, Butler was educated at Worcestershire free school and briefly attended Cambridge, then entered the service of Elizabeth, Countess of Kent. He next became clerk to several Puritan justices of the peace, a series of experiences that were presumably transmuted into the satiric art of Hudibras *(Part I, 1663; Part II, 1664; Part III, 1668). Neither Butler's acerbic wit nor the popularity of* Hudibras *gained him preferment, and it seems he died in poverty.*

The amusing invective "Upon Critics"—Butler can rhyme "Latin" with "Cat in"—was provoked by Thomas Rymer's attack on Beaumont and Fletcher in The Tragedies of the Last Age *(1677) and was therefore written between 1677 and 1680; it offers astringent testimony to the peculiarly English opposition to rigid application of neoclassical principles.*

The text is based on the Thyer edition of 1827, but of course I have also made use of Spingarn and Lamar, both of whom had access to the mss. in the British Museum.

UPON
CRITICS
WHO JUDGE OF
MODERN PLAYS
PRECISELY BY THE
RULES OF THE ANTIENTS
[1678?]

Who ever wil Regard Poetique Fury,
When it is once found Idiot by a Jury?
And evry Peart, & Arbitrary Fool
Can all Poetique Licence over-Rule?
Assume a Barbrous Tyranny, to Handle
The Muses, worse then Ostro-goth, or Vandal?
Make 'em submit to verdict & Report
And stand (or Fall) to th' orders of a Court.
Much lesse, Be sentenc'd by the Arbitra[r]y
Proceedings of a Witles Plagiary
That forge's old Records, & Ordinances
Against the Right & Property of Fancys
More False, & Nice, then weighing of the weather
To th' Hundredth Atom, of the lightest Feather,
Or measuring of Aire upon Pernassus
With Cilinders of Torricellian Glasses;[1]
Reduce all Tragedy by Rules of Art
Back, to its Antique Theater, a Cart,
And make 'em hence forth keep the beaten Roades
Of Reverend Choruses, & Episodes;
Reforme & Regulate a Puppet-Play
According to the tru & antient way:

1 [Evangelista Torricelli invented the barometer in 1643.]

That not an Actor shal Presume to Squeek
Unless he hav a Licence for't, in Greek;
Nor Whittington[2] Henceforward, sel his Cat in
Plaine vulgar English, without Mewing Latin:
No Pudding shalbe sufferd to be witty
Unles it be in Order to Raise Pitty;
Nor Devil in the Puppet-play, b'allowd
To Rore & Spit fire, but to fright the Crowd,
Unless some God, or Dev'l chance t' have Piques
Against an Antient Family of Greeks;
Others may have Leave to tremble, & take warning,
How such a Fatal Progeny th' are Born in.
For none but such for Tragedy are fitted
That have been Ruind only to be Pittyd;
And only those held Proper to Deterre
Wh' have had th' Il Luck, against their wils to erre.
Whence only such as are of Midling Sizes
Between Morality and venial vices
Are Qualifyd to be Destroyd by Fate
For other Mortals to take warning at.
    As if the Antique Laws of Tragedy
Did with our own Municipall agree
And servd like Cobwebs but t' insnare the weake
And give Diversion to the Great to break;
To make a lesse Delinquent to be brought
To Answer for a Greater Persons Fault
And suffer all the worst, the worst Approver
Can, to excuse, & save himself, Discover.
    No longer shal Dramatiques be confind
To draw tru Images, of al Mankinde,
To Punish in Effigie Criminals,
Reprieve the Innocent, & hang the False;
But a Club-Law [to] execute, & kill,
For nothing, whom so ere they Please, at will:
To terrify Spectators from committing
The Crimes they did, & sufferd for, unwitting.
    These are the Reformations of the Stage,
Like other Reformations of the Age:
On Purpose to Destroy all wit & sense
As th' other did all Law, & Conscience.

2 [The popular legend of Whittington (d. 1423) and his cat was made into a
play as early as 1605. Butler, inveterate quibbler, may also have wanted us to
remember another Whittington, who co-edited a Latin *Vulgaria.*]

No better then the Laws of British Plays
Confirmd in th' Antient good King Howels Days
Who made a Gen'ral Councel Regulate
Mens catching women by the—you know what,
And set down in the Rubrick, at what time
It should be counted Legal, when a Crime;
Declare when 'twas, & when 'twas not a sin
And on what days it went out, or came in.
   An English Poet should be tryd b' his Peres
And not by Pedants, & Philosophers
Incompetent to Judge Poetique Fury,
As Butchers are forbid to b' of a Jury;
Beside the most Intollerable wrong
To try their Matter in a Forrain Tongue
By Forrain Jury men, like Sophocles
Or Tales falser then Euripides;
When not an English Native dares appear
To be a witnes for the Prisoner,
When all the Laws they use t' Arraigne, & try
The Innocent & wrongd Delinquent by
Were made b' a Forraine Laweyer[3] & his Pupils
To put an End to all Poetique Scruples,
And by th' Advice of Virtuosi-Tuscans
Determind al the Doubts of Socks & Buskins;
Gave Judgment on all Past & Future Plays,
As is Apparent by Speronys[4] Case,
Which Lope Vega first began to steale,
And after him the French Filew Corniele;[5]
And since our English Plagiarys Nim[6]
And steal Their farfet Criticismes, from him,
And, by an Action falsly layd of Trover,[7]
The Lumber, for their Proper Goods Recover;
Enough to furnish al the Lewd Impeachers
Of witty Beumonts Poetry, & Fletchers,
Who, for a few Misprisons of wit,
Are chargd by those, who ten times worse commit;

3 [Aristotle.]
4 [Sperone Speroni (1500–88), critic of Tasso and writer of a "classical" tragedy that occasioned great controversy. (But Lope's *Arte Nuevo* [1609] does not
seem to be indebted to Speroni nor can it be regarded as advocating the Rules.)]
5 [Pickpocket Corneille.]
6 [Filch, pilfer.]
7 [Legal action pursued to recover the value of property used illegally by
someone else.]

And for Misjudging some unhappy scenes
Are censurd for't, with more unlucky sense;
When all their worst miscarriages Delight
And please more then the Best, that Pedants write.

Sir William Soames

1645?–86?

Virtually all that is known of Soames (Soame?), Sheriff of Suffolk in the 1670's, derives from a puff written by Dryden's publisher, Jacob Tonson: "This translation of M. Boileau's Art of Poetry was made in the year 1680 by Sir William Soame of Suffolk, Baronet; who, being very intimately acquainted with Mr. Dryden, desired his revisal of it. I saw this manuscript lie in Mr. Dryden's hand for above six months, who made very considerable alterations in it, particularly the beginning of the Fourth Canto; and it being his opinion that it would be better to apply the poem to English writers than to keep the French names, as it was first translated, Sir William desired that he would take the pains to make that alteration; and accordingly, that was done by Mr. Dryden. The poem was first published in the year 1683. Sir William was after sent ambassador to Constantinople, in the reign of King James, but died in the voyage." Soames appears to have died in Malta in 1686.

Nicolas Boileau-Despréaux (1636–1711) studied law at the Sorbonne but came to devote himself entirely to literature, writing satires, translating Longinus, and producing the Art Poétique. Friend of Molière and Racine, he was involved in the literary arguments of his time and became one of the most influential proponents of neoclassicism.

It would be difficult to exaggerate the importance of Soames' work. First of all, it points directly to the French influence of the Restora-

tion; second, it involves Dryden; and lastly it must be viewed not merely as a translation but as a critical document in its own right, for the two translators have managed to acclimatize Boileau, emphasizing distinctively English concerns as well as substituting English for French names. Pope was not too proud, in writing An Essay on Criticism, *to borrow from the Soames-Dryden translation of Boileau.*

Canto I and Canto IV are reprinted here from the edition of 1710 (first edition 1683); the two omitted cantos are concerned with generic criticism of the pastoral, ode, epigram, tragedy, epic, and so on.

FROM

Art of Poetry

[*1680*]

CANTO I

Rash Author, 'tis a vain presumptuous Crime
To undertake the Sacred Art of Rhyme;
If at thy Birth the Stars that rul'd thy Sence
Shone not with a Poetic Influence:
In thy strait Genius thou wilt still be bound,
Find *Phœbus* deaf, and *Pegasus* unsound.
     You then, that burn with the desire to try
The dangerous Course of charming Poetry;
Forbear in frutless Verse to lose your time,
Or take for Genius the desire of Rhyme:
Fear the allurements of a specious Bait,
And well consider your own Force and Weight.

Nature abounds in Wits of every kind,
And for each Author can a Talent find:
One may in Verse describe an Amorous Flame,
Another sharpen a short Epigram:
Waller a Hero's mighty Acts extol;
Spencer Sing *Rosalind* in Pastoral:
But Authors that themselves too much esteem,
Lose their own Genius, and mistake their Theme;
Thus in times past *Dubartas*[1] vainly Writ,
Allaying Sacred Truth with trifling Wit,
Impertinently, and without delight,
Describ'd the *Israelites* Triumphant Flight,
And following *Moses* o'er the Sandy Plain,
Perish'd with *Pharaoh* in th' *Arabian* Main.
    What-e're you write of Pleasant or Sublime,
Always let sense accompany your Rhyme:
Falsely they seem each other to oppose;
Rhyme must be made with Reason's Laws to close:
And when to conquer her you bend your force,
The Mind will Triumph in the Noble Course;
To Reason's yoke she quickly will incline,
Which, far from hurting, renders her Divine:
But, if neglected, will as easily stray,
And master Reason, which she should obey.
Love Reason then: and let whate'er you Write
Borrow from her its Beauty, Force, and Light.
Most Writers, mounted on a resty Muse,
Extravagant, and Senceless Objects chuse;
They Think they err, if in their Verse they fall
On any thought that's Plain, or Natural:
Fly this excess; and let *Italians* be
Vain Authors of false glitt'ring Poetry.
All ought to aim at Sence; but most in vain
Strive the hard Pass, and slipp'ry Path to gain:
You drown, if to the right or left you stray;
Reason to go has often but one way.
Sometimes an Author, fond of his own Thought,
Pursues his Object till it's over-wrought:
If he describes a House, he shews the Face,
And after walks you round from place to place;

---

1 Dubartas *Translated by* Sylvester. [*Bartas His Devine Weekes and Workes
translated . . . by Joshua Sylvester* (collected edition 1605).]

Here is a *Vista*, there the Doors unfold,
Balcone's here are ballustred with Gold;
Then counts the Rounds and Ovals in the Halls,
The Festoons, Freezes, and the Astragals:[2]
Tir'd with his tedious Pomp, away I run,
And skip'd o'er twenty Pages to be gone.
Of such Descriptions the vain Folly see,
And shun their barren Superfluity.
All that is needless carefully avoid,
The Mind once satisfi'd, is quickly cloy'd:
He cannot Write, who knows not to give o'er;
To mend one Fault, he makes a hundred more:
A Verse was weak, you turn it much too strong,
And grow Obscure, for fear you should be Long.
Some are not Gaudy, but are Flat and Dry;
Not to be low, another soars too high.
Would you of every one deserve the Praise?
In Writing, vary your Discourse and Phrase;
A frozen Style, that neither Ebs or Flows,
Instead of pleasing, makes us gape and doze.
Those tedious Authors are esteem'd by none
Who tire us, Humming the same heavy Tone.
Happy, who in his Verse can gently steer,
From Grave, to Light; from pleasant, to Severe:
His Works will be admir'd where-ever found,
And oft with Buyers will be compass'd round.
In all you Write, be neither Low nor Vile:
The meanest Theme may have a proper Style.
　　The dull Burlesque appear'd with impudence,
And pleas'd by Novelty, in Spite of Sense.
All, except trivial points, grew out of date;
Parnassus spoke the Cant of *Billingsgate:*
Boundless and Mad, disorder'd Rhyme was seen:
Disguis'd *Apollo* chang'd to *Harlequin.*
This Plague, which first in Country Towns began,
Cities and Kingdoms quickly over-ran;
The dullest Scriblers some Admirers found,
And the *Mock-Tempest* [3] was a while renown'd:
But this low stuff the town at least despis'd,

---

2 *Verse of* Scudery. [Not Mlle. but Georges de Scudéry; *Alaric* (1654), **Book III.**]
3 *The* Mock-Tempest, *a Play* [acted at Drury Lane in 1674], *written by Mr.* [Thomas] Duffet.

And Scorn'd the Folly that they once had priz'd;
Distinguish'd Dull, from Natural and Plain,
And left the Villages to *Fleckno's* Reign.
Let not so mean a Style your muse debase;
But learn from *Butler*[4] the Buffooning grace:
And let Burlesque in Ballads be employ'd;
Yet noisy Bumbast carefully avoid,
Nor think to raise (tho' on *Pharsalia's* Plain)
Millions of mourning Mountains of the Slain:[5]
Nor, with *Dubartas*, bridle up the Floods,
And Perriwig with Wool the bald-pate Woods,[6]
Chuse a just Style; be Grave without constraint,
Great without Pride, and Lovely without Paint:
Write what your Reader may be pleas'd to hear:
And, for the Measure, have a careful Ear.
On easy Numbers fix your happy choice;
Of jarring Sounds avoid the odious noise:
The fullest Verse and the most labour'd Sense,
Displease us, if the Ear once take offence.
Our ancient Verse, (as homely as the Times,)
Was rude, unmeasur'd, only Tagg'd with Rhimes:
Number and Cadence, that have since been Shown,
To those unpolish'd Writers were unknown.
Fairfax[7] was He, who, in that Darker Age,
By his just Rules restrain'd Poetic Rage:
Spencer did next in Pastorals excel,
And taught the Noble art of Writing well:
To stricter Rules the Stanza did restrain,
And Found for Poetry a richer Vein.
Then *D'Avenant* came; who, with a new found Art,
Chang'd all, spoil'd all, and had his way apart:
His haughty Muse all others did despise,
And thought in Triumph to bear off the Prize,
Till the Sharp-sighted Critics of the Times

4 *Hudebrass.*
5 Verse of *Brebeuf.* [From Georges de Brébeuf's translation (1654) of Lucan's *Pharsalia*, Book VII.]
6Verse of *Dubartas.* [*Devine Weekes and Workes*, translated by Joshua Sylvester: from the Second Week, First Day, Part Four.]
7 [Edward] *Fairfax* in his Translation of *Godfrey* of Bullen. [Translated from Tasso and published in 1600. Dryden in *Preface to the Fables* says: "Spenser and Fairfax both flourished in the reign of Queen Elizabeth; great masters in our language, and who saw much farther into the beauties of our numbers than those who immediately followed them. Milton was the poetical son of Spenser, and Mr. Waller of Fairfax. . . ."]

In their Mock-*Gondibert* [8] expos'd his Rhimes;
The Laurels he pretended did refuse,
And dash'd the hopes of his aspiring Muse.
This head-strong Writer, falling from on high,
Made following Authors take less Liberty.
Waller came last, but was the first whose Art
Just Weight and Measure did to Verse impart;
That of a well-plac'd Word could teach the force,
And shew'd for Poetry a nobler Course:
His happy Genius did our Tongue Refine,
And easy Words with pleasing Numbers joyn:
His Verses to good method did apply,
And chang'd harsh Discord to Soft Harmony.
All own'd his Laws; which, long approv'd and try'd,
To present Authors now may be a *Guide*.
Tread boldly in his Steps, secure from Fear,
And be, like him, in your Expressions clear.
If in your Verse you drag, and Sense delay,
My Patience tires, my Fancy goes astray,
And from your vain Discourse I turn my mind,
Nor search an Author troublesome to find.
There is a kind of Writer pleas'd with Sound,
Whose Fustian head with clouds is compass'd round,
No Reason can disperse 'em with its Light:
Learn then to Think, e'er you pretend to Write,
As your Idea's clear, or else obscure,
Th' Expression follows perfect, or impure:
What we conceive, with ease we can express;
Words to the Notions flow with readiness.
  Observe the Language well in all you write,
And swerve not from it in your loftiest flight.
The smoothest Verse, and the exactest Sense
Displease us, if ill *English* give offence:
A barb'rous Phrase no Reader can approve;
Nor Bombast, Noise, or Affectation Love.
In short, without pure Language, what you Write,
Can never yield us profit, or Delight.
Take time for thinking; never work in hast;
And value not your self for writing fast.

[8] [Probably the reference is to *Certain Verses written by several of the Author's Friends, to be Reprinted in the Second Edition of Gondibert* (1653). These (mocking) "Friends" were less than friendly.]

A rapid Poem, with such fury writ,
Shews want of Judgment, not abounding Wit.
More pleas'd we are to see a River lead
His gentle Streams along a flow'ry Mead,
Than from high Banks to hear loud Torrents roar,
With foamy Waters on a Muddy Shore.
Gently make hast, of Labour not afraid;
A hundred times consider what you've said:
Polish, repolish, every Colour lay,
And sometimes add; but oft'ner take away.
'Tis not enough, when swarming Faults are writ,
That here and there are scatter'd Sparks of Wit;
Each Object must be fix'd in the due place,
And diff'ring parts have Corresponding Grace:
Till by a curious Art dispos'd we find
One perfect whole, of all the pieces joyn'd.
Keep to your Subject close, in all you say;
Nor for a sounding Sentence ever stray.
The publick Censure for your Writings fear,
And to your self be Critic most severe.
Fantastic Wits their darling Follies love;
But find You faithful Friends that will reprove,
That on your Works may look with careful Eyes,
And of your Faults be zealous Enemies:
Lay by an Author's Pride and Vanity,
And from a Friend a Flatterer descry,
Who seems to like, but means not what he says:
Embrace true Counsel, but suspect false Praise.
A Sycophant will every thing admire;
Each Verse, each Sentence sets his Soul on Fire:
All is Divine! there's not a Word amiss!
He shakes with Joy, and weeps with Tenderness;
He over-pow'rs you with his mighty Praise.
Truth never moves in those impetuous ways:
A Faithful Friend is careful of your Fame,
And freely will your heedless Errors blame;
He cannot pardon a neglected Line,
But Verse to Rule and Order will confine,
Reproves of words the too affected noise;
Here the Sense flags and repetition cloys:
Your Fancy tires and your Discourse grows vain,
Your Terms improper; make them just and plain.

Thus 'tis a faithful Friend will freedom use;
But Authors, (partial to their Darling Muse,)
Think to protect it they have just pretence,
And at your Friendly Counsel take offence.
Said you of this, that the Expression's flat?
Your Servant, Sir; you must excuse me that,
He answers you. This word has here no grace,
Pray leave it out: That, Sir, 's the proper'st Place.
This Turn I like not: 'Tis approv'd by all.
Thus, resolute not from a fault to fall,
If there's a Syllable of which you doubt,
'Tis a sure Reason not to blot it out.
Yet still he says you may his Faults confute,
And over him your pow'r is absolute:
But of his feign'd Humility take heed;
'Tis a Bait lay'd, to make you hear him read:
And when he leaves you, happy in his Muse,
Restless he runs some other to abuse.
And often finds; for in our scribling times
No Fool can want a Sot to praise his Rhymes:
The flattest work as ever, in the Court,
Met with some Zealous *Ass* for its support:
And in all times a forward, Scribling Fop
Has found some greater Fool to cry him up.

CANTO IV

In *Florence* dwelt a Doctor of Renown,
The Scourge of God, and Terror of the Town,
Who all the Cant of Physick had by heart,
And never murder'd but by Rules of Art.
The public Mischief was his private Gain;
Children their slaughter'd Parents sought in vain:
A Brother here his poyson'd Brother wept;
Some bloodless dy'd, and some by *Opium* slept.
Colds, at his Presence, would to Frenzies turn;
And Agues, like malignant Fevers, burn.
Hated, at last, his Practice gives him o'er:
One Friend, unkill'd by Drugs, of all his Store,
In his new Country-house affords him place,
'Twas a rich Abbot, and a Building Ass:

Here first the Doctor's Talent came in play,
He seems inspir'd, and talks like *Wren* or *May:*[9]
Of this new Portico condemns the Face,
And turns the Entrance to a better place;
Designs the Stair-case at the other end.
His Friend approves, does for his Mason send,
He comes; the Doctor's Arguments prevail.
In short, to finish this our hum'rous Tale,
He *Galen's* dang'rous Science does reject,
And from ill Doctor turn good Architect.

   In this Example we may have our part:
Rather be Mason, ('tis an useful Art!)
Than a dull Poet; for that Trade accurst,
Admits no mean betwixt the Best and Worst.
In other Sciences, without Disgrace
A Candidate may fill a second place;
But Poetry no medium can admit,
No Reader suffers an indiff'rent Wit:
The ruin'd Stationers against him baul,
And *Herringman*[1] degrades him from his Stall.
Burlesque, at least our Laughter may excite;
But a cold Writer never can delight.
The *Counter-Scuffle*[2] has more Wit and Art,
Than the stiff formal Stile of *Gondibert*.
Be not effected with that empty praise
Which your vain Flatterers will sometimes raise,
And when you read, with Ecstasie will say,
The finish'd Piece! The admirable Play!
Which when expos'd to Censure and to Light,
Cannot indure a Critic's piercing sight.
A hundred Authors Fates have been foretold,
And *Sh——le's*[3] Works are printed, but not sold.
Hear all the World; consider every Thought;
A Fool by chance may stumble on a Fault:

9 *The King's Architects.* [Sir Christopher Wren (1632–1723) designed St. Paul's. "May" refers not to Thomas but to Baptist May (1629–98), who worked with Wren on Windsor Castle and in so many other ways made himself useful to Charles II that Pepys called him "court pimp."]
1 [Henry Herringman, bookseller, was Dryden's own publisher before Jacob Tonson.]
2 [A burlesque poem printed by Dryden in his *Miscellanies*, Vol. III.]
3 [Evidently Shadwell (*c.* 1642?–92), who constantly quarreled with Dryden and who had suggested that Dryden was a journeyman-hack for Herringman (see note 1, above). But of course Shadwell's works were not only printed—they sold.]

Yet, when *Apollo* does your Muse inspire,
Be not impatient to expose your Fire;
Nor imitate the *Settles*[4] of your Times,
Those Tuneful Readers of their own dull Rhymes,
Who seize on all th' Acquaintance they can meet,
And stop the Passengers that walk the Street;
There is no Sanctuary you can chuse
For a Defence from their pursuing Muse.
I've said before, Be patient when they blame;
To alter for the better is no Shame.
Yet yield not to a Fool's Impertinence:
Sometimes conceited Sceptics void of Sence,
By their false Taste condemn some finish'd part,
And blame the noblest flights of Wit and Art.
In vain their fond Opinions you deride,
With their lov'd Follies they are satisfy'd;
And their weak Judgment, void of Sence and Light,
Thinks nothing can escape their feeble sight:
Their dang'rous Counsels do not cure, but wound; ⎫
To shun the Storm, they run your Verse aground, ⎬
And thinking to escape a Rock, are drown'd. ⎭
Chuse a sure Judge to Censure what you write,
Whose Reason leads, and Knowledge gives you light,
Whose steady hand will prove your faithful Guide,
And touch the darling Follies you would hide:
He, in your doubts, will carefully advise,
And clear the Mist before your feeble Eyes.
'Tis he will tell you, to what noble height
A generous Muse may sometimes take her flight;
When, too much fetter'd with the Rules of Art,
May from her stricter Bounds and Limits part:
But such a perfect Judge is hard to see,
And every Rhymer knows not Poetry;
Nay some there are, for writing Verse extol'd,
Who know not *Lucan's* Dross from *Virgil's* Gold.

    Would you in this great Art acquire Renown:
Authors, observe the Rules I here lay down.
In prudent Lessons every where abound;
With pleasant, joyn the useful and the sound:
A sober Reader, a vain Tale will slight;
He seeks as well Instruction, as Delight.

---

[4] [Elkanah Settle (1648–1724), writer of rhyming tragedies.]

Let all your Thoughts to Virtue be confin'd,
Still off'ring noble Figures to our Mind:
I like not those loose Writers, who employ
Their guilty Muse, good Manners to destroy;
Who with false Colours still deceive our Eyes,
And show us Vice dress'd in a fair Disguise.
Yet do I not their sullen Muse approve
Who from all modest Writings banish Love;
That strip the Play-house of its chief Intrigue,
And make a Murderer of *Roderigue*:[5]
The lightest Love, if decently exprest,
Will raise no Vicious Motions in our Brest.
Dido in vain may weep, and ask relief;
I blame her Folly, whil'st I share her Grief.
A Virtuous Author, in his Charming Art,
To please the Sense needs not corrupt the Heart;
His heat will never cause a guilty Fire:
To follow Virtue then be your desire.
In vain your Art and Vigor are exprest;
Th' obscene Expression shows th' infected Breast.
But above all, base Jealousies avoid,
In which detracting Poets are employ'd:
A noble Wit dares lib'rally commend;
And scorns to grudge at his deserving Friend.
Base Rivals, who true Wit and Merit hate,
Caballing still against it with the Great,
Maliciously aspire to gain Renown
By standing up, and pulling others down.
Never debase your self by Treacherous ways,
Nor by such abject Methods seek for praise:
Let not your only bus'ness be to write;
Be Virtuous, Just, and in your Friends delight.
'Tis not enough your Poems be admir'd;
But strive your Conversation be desir'd:
Write for immortal Fame; nor ever chuse
Gold for the Object of a gen'rous Muse.
I know a noble Wit may, without Crime,
Receive a lawful Tribute for his time:
Yet I abhor those Writers, who despise
Their Honor; and alone their Profit prize:

5 *The Cid. Translated into* English. [Corneille's drama was translated by
Joseph Rutter as early as 1637, but of course Dryden, who had read the
Frenchman closely, needed no help.]

Who their *Apollo* basely will degrade,
And of a noble Science, make a Trade.
Before kind [6] Reason did her Light display,
And Government taught Mortals to obey,
Men, like wild Beasts, did Nature's Laws pursue,
They fed on Herbs, and drank from Rivers drew,[7]
Their Brutal force, on Lust and Rapine bent,
Committed Murders without Punishment:
Reason at last, by her all conquering Arts,
Reduc'd these Savages, and tun'd their Hearts;
Mankind from Bogs, and Woods, and Caverns calls,
And Towns and Cities fortifies with Walls:
Thus fear of Justice made proud Rapine cease,
And shelter'd Innocence by Laws and Peace.
   These Benefits from Poets we receiv'd,
From whence are rais'd those Fictions since believ'd,
That *Orpheus,* by his soft Harmonious strains
Tam'd the fierce Tygers of the *Thracian* Plains;
Amphion's Notes, by their melodious pow'rs,
Drew Rocks and Woods, and rais'd the *Theban* Tow'rs:
These Miracles from Numbers did arise,
Since which, in Verse Heav'n taught his Mysteries,
And by a Priest, possess'd with Rage Divine,
Apollo spoke from his Prophetick Shrine.
Soon after *Homer* the old Heroes prais'd,
And noble Minds by great Examples rais'd;
Then *Hesiod* did his *Grӕcian* Swains incline
To till the Fields, and prune the bounteous Vine.
Thus useful Rules were by the Poets aid,
In easy Numbers, to rude Men convey'd,
And pleasingly their Precepts did impart;
First charm'd the Ear, and then ingag'd the Heart:
The Muses thus their Reputation rais'd,
And with just Gratitude in *Greece* were prais'd.
With Pleasure Mortals did their Wonders see,
And sacrific'd to their Divinity:
But Want, at last base Flatt'ry entertain'd,
And old *Parnassus* with this Vice was stain'd;
Desire of Gain dazling the Poets Eyes,
Their Works were fill'd with fulsome Flatteries,

6 [Natural.]
7 [Muddy or turbid.]

Thus needy Wits a vile Revenue made,
And Verse became a mercenary Trade.
Debase not with so mean a Vice thy Art:
If Gold must be the Idol of thy Heart,
Fly, fly, th' unfruitful *Heliconian* strand,
Those Streams are not enrich'd with Golden Sand:
Great Wits, as well as Warriours, only gain
Laurels and Honors for their Toil and Pain:
But, what? an Author cannot live on Fame,
Or pay a Reck'ning with a lofty Name:
A Poet to whom Fortune is unkind,
Who when he goes to Bed has hardly din'd;
Takes little pleasure in *Parnassus* Dreams,
Or relishes the *Heliconian* Streams.
Horace had Ease and Plenty when he writ, ⎤
And free from Cares for Money or for Meat, ⎬
Did not expect his Dinner from his Wit. ⎦
'Tis true; but Verse is cherish'd by the Great,
And now none famish who deserve to eat:
What can we fear, when Virtue, Arts, and Sence,
Receive the Stars propitious Influence;
When a sharp-sighted Prince, by early Grants
Rewards your Merits, and prevents your Wants?
Sing then his Glory, Celebrate his Fame;
Your Noblest Theme is his immortal Name.
Let mighty *Spencer* raise his reverend Head,
Cowley and *Denham* start up from the dead;
Waller his Age renew, and Off'rings bring,
Our Monarch's⁸ praise let bright-ey'd Virgins sing;
Let *Dryden* with new Rules our Stage refine,
And his great Models form by this Design:
But where's a second *Virgil*, to Rehearse
Our Hero's Glories in his Epic Verse?
What *Orpheus* sing his Triumphs o'er the Main,
And make the Hills and Forests move again;
Show his bold Fleet on the *Batavian* Shore,
And *Holland* trembling as his Cannons roar;
Paint *Europe's* Balance in his steady hand, ⎤
Whilst the two Worlds in Expectation stand ⎬
Of Peace or War, that wait on his Command? ⎦

---

⁸ [Charles II allied himself with the French against the Dutch and made peace in 1674, matters to which Soames (Dryden?) alludes in the following lines.]

But, as I speak, new Glories strike my Eyes,
Glories, which Heav'n it Self does give, and prize,
Blessings of Peace; that with their milder Rays
Adorn his Reign, and bring *Saturnian* Days:
Now let Rebellion, Discord, Vice, and Rage,
That have in Patriots Forms debauch'd our Age,
Vanish, with all the Ministers of Hell;
His Rays their poys'nous Vapors shall dispel:
Tis he alone our Safety did create,
His own firm Soul secur'd the Nation's Fate,
Oppos'd to all the *boutfeaus*[9] of the State.
Authors, for Him your great indeavours raise;
The loftiest Numbers will but reach his praise.
For me, whose Verse in Satyr has been bred,
And never durst Heroic Measures tread;
Yet you shall see me, in that famous Field
With Eyes and Voice, my best Assistance yield;
Offer you Lessons, that my Infant Muse
Learnt, when she *Horace* for her Guide did chuse:
Second your Zeal with Wishes, Heart, and Eyes,
And afar off hold up the glorious Prize.
But pardon too, if, Zealous for the Right,
A strict Observer of each Noble Flight,
From the fine Gold I separate th' Allay,
And show how hasty Writers sometimes stray:
Apter to blame, than knowing how to mend;
A sharp, but yet a necessary Friend.

FINIS

9 [Incendiaries or firebrands.]

Wentworth Dillon,
Earl of Roscommon

1633?–85

Educated by tutors, first in England and then (after the fall of Strafford) in France, Dillon succeeded to the earldom in 1649, though he did not return to England until after the Restoration. Roscommon's gentlemanly interest in literature extended so far as an attempt to form a literary academy on the Continental model, consisting of himself, Halifax, and Lord Maitland; the meetings of this noble triumvirate were on occasion attended by others, including Dryden. But Roscommon's reputation rests neither on his organizing ability nor even on his original poems. He is important as a critic, primarily for the influential and representative criticism of "An Essay on Translated Verse," which while recognizing the power of Milton enunciates the principles of poetic diction that appealed to the age of Queen Anne.

"An Essay," reprinted here from Tonson's edition of 1711, first appeared in 1684 without the "Miltonic imitation" that was added in 1685.

AN
ESSAY
ON
TRANSLATED VERSE
[*1684*]

Happy that Author, whose correct Essay[1]
Repairs so well our Old *Horatian* way;
And happy you, who (by propitious Fate)
On great *Apollo's* sacred Standard wait,
And with strict Discipline instructed right,
Have learn'd to *use* your Arms before you *fight*.
But since the *Press,* the *Pulpit* and the *Stage,*
Conspire to censure and expose our Age:
Provok'd, Too far, we resolutely must,
To the few Virtues that we have, be just.
For who have long'd, or who have labour'd more ⎫
To search the Treasures of the *Roman* Store;   ⎬
Or dig in *Grecian Mines* for *purer Ore;*   ⎭
The noblest Fruits Transplanted in our Isle
With early Hope, and fragrant Blossoms smile.
Familiar *Ovid* tender Thoughts inspires,
And *Nature* seconds all his soft *Desires:*
Theocritus does now to *Us* belong;
And *Albion's Rocks* repeat his *Rural Song.*
Who has not heard how *Italy* was blest,
Above the *Medes,* above the wealthy *East?*
Or *Gallus* Song, so tender, and so true,
As ev'n *Lycoris* might with Pity view!

---

[1] *Essay on Poetry* [1682], *Written by the E.[arl] of M.[ulgrave] now D.[uke] of B.[uckinghamshire.]*

When *Mourning Nymphs* attend their *Daphni's Herse,*
Who does not *Weep,* that *Reads* the *moving Verse!*
But hear, oh hear, in what exalted Strains
Sicilian Muses through these happy Plains,
Proclaim *Saturnian* Times, our own *Apollo* reigns.

When *France* had breath'd, after intestine Broils,
And Peace and Conquest crown'd her foreign Toils,
There (cultivated by a Royal Hand)
Learning grew fast, and spread, and blest the Land;
The choicest Books, that *Rome,* or *Greece* have known,
Her excellent *Translators* made her own:
And *Europe* still considerably gains,
Both by their good *Example* and their *Pains.*
From hence our gen'rous Emulation came,
We undertook, and we perform'd the same.
But now, *We* shew the World a nobler Way,
And in *Translated Verse,* do more than *They.*
Serene, and clear, harmonious *Horace* flows,
With Sweetness not to be exprest in *Prose.*
Degrading *Prose* explains his Meaning ill,
And shews the *Stuff,* but not the Workman's Skill.
I (who have serv'd him more than twenty Years)
Scarce know my Master as he there appears.[2]
Vain are our *Neighbours Hopes,* and *Vain* their Cares,
The *Fault* is more their *Languages,* than theirs.
'Tis courtly, florid, and abounds in Words;
Of softer Sound than ours perhaps affords.
But who did ever in *French Authors* see
The Comprehensive, *English Energy?*
The weighty *Bullion* of *One Sterling Line,*
Drawn to *French Wire,* would thro' whole *Pages* shine.
I speak my *private,* but *impartial Sense,*
With *Freedom,* and (I hope) without *Offence:*
For I'll recant, when *France* can shew me *Wit,*
As strong as *Ours,* and as *succinctly writ.*
'Tis true, *Composing* is the *Nobler* Part,
But good *Translation* is no *easie* Art,
For tho' *Materials* have long since been found,

2 [In André Dacier's translation into French prose, which began appearing in 1681.]

Yet both your *Fancy*, and your *Hands* are *bound;*
And by *improving* what was writ *before;*
Invention Labours *less*, but *Judgment, more.*

The Soil intended for *Pierian Seeds*
Must be well *purg'd*, from *rank Pedantick Weeds.*
Apollo starts, and all *Parnassus* shakes,
At the rude rumbling *Baralipton*[3] makes.
For none have been with *Admiration*, read,
But who (beside their *Learning*) were *Well-bred.*

The first great Work, (a Task perform'd by few)
Is, that *your self* may to *your self* be *true:*
No *Masque*, no *Tricks*, no *Favour*, no *Reserve;*
Dissect your Mind, examine ev'ry *Nerve.*
Whoever *vainly* on his *Strength* depends,
Begins like *Virgil*, but like *Mævius*,[4] *ends.*
That Wretch (in spight of his forgotten Rhimes)
Condemn'd to live to all succeeding Times,
With *pompous Nonsense* and a *bellowing Sound*
Sung *lofty Illium, tumbling* to the *Ground.*
And (if my Muse can through past Ages see)
That *noisie, nauseous, gaping Fool* was *he;*
Exploded, when with universal Scorn,
The *Mountains labour'd* and a *Mouse* was *born.*

Learn, learn, *Crotona's* brawny Wrestler cries,
Audacious Mortals, and be *timely* wise!
'Tis I that call, remember *Milo's End,*
Wedg'd in that Timber, which he strove to *rend.*

Each Poet with a *different Talent* writes,
One *Praises*, one *Instructs*, another *Bites.*
Horace did ne'er aspire to *Epick Bays,*
Nor lofty *Maro*[5] stoop to *Lyrick Lays.*
Examine how your *Humour* is inclin'd,
And which the *ruling Passion* of your Mind;

3 [A "mode" in logic. Evidently a glance at what Drummond called "*Scholasti-cal* Quiddities" in verse; perhaps in particular a glance at the "Quiddities" of Donne, since Roscommon's "*rank Pedantic Weeds*" comes from Carew's elegy on Donne.
4 [A poetaster who by incurring the displeasure of Vergil and Horace suc-ceeded in immortalizing himself ignominiously.]
5 [Vergil.]

Then, seek a *Poet* who *your* Way does bend,
And chuse an *Author* as you chuse a *Friend*.
United by this *Sympathetick Bond*,
You grow *familiar, intimate,* and *fond;*
Your *Thoughts,* your *Words,* your *Stiles,* your *Souls* agree,
No longer his *Interpreter,* but *He.*

With how much Ease is a *young Muse betray'd,*
How *nice* the *Reputation* of the *Maid?*
Your *early, kind, paternal* Care appears,
By *chast Instruction* of her *tender Years.*
The *first Impression* in her *Infant* Breast
Will be the *deepest,* and should be the best.
Let not Austerity breed servile *Fear,*
No *wanton* Sound offend her *Virgin-Ear.*
Secure from *foolish Pride's affected State,*
And *specious Flatt'ry's more pernicious Bait,*
Habitual Innocence adorns her *Thoughts,*
But your Neglect must answer for her *Faults.*

Immodest Words admit of no Defence;
For want of *Decency,* is want of *Sense.*
What mod'rate *Fop* wou'd rake the *Park,* or *Stews,*
Who among Troops of *faultless Nymphs* may chuse?
Variety of *such* is to be found;
Take then a Subject, *proper* to expound:
But *Moral, Great,* and worth a *Poet's Voice,*
For Men of *Sense despise a trivial Choice:*
And such *Applause* it must expect to meet,
As wou'd some Painter, busie in a Street,
To Copy *Bulls* and *Bears,* and ev'ry *Sign*
That calls the *staring Sots* to *nasty Wine.*

Yet 'tis not all to have a Subject *Good,*
It must *Delight* us when 'tis *understood.*
He that brings *fulsome Objects* to my View,
(As many *Old* have done, and many *New*)
With *nauseous Images* my Fancy fills,
And all goes down like *Oxymel* of *Squils.*[6]
Instruct the list'ning World how *Maro* sings
Of *useful Subjects,* and of *lofty Things.*

6 [Sirup of sea-onion, a Galenic "remedy."]

These will such true, such bright *Idea's* raise,
As merit *Gratitude,* as well as *Praise:*
But *foul Descriptions* are *offensive* still,
Either for being *Like,* or being *Ill.*
For who, without a *Qualm,* hath ever look'd
On *Holy Garbage,* tho' by *Homer Cook'd?*
Whose *rayling Heroes,* and whose *wounded Gods,*
Make some suspect, He *Snores,* as well as *Nods.*
But I offend—*Virgil* begins to *frown,*
And *Horace* looks with *Indignation* down;
My blushing Muse with *conscious*[7] *Fear* retires,
And whom *They like, Implicitly Admires.*

On *sure Foundations* let your *Fabrick Rise,*
And with attractive *Majesty* surprise,
Not by affected, *meritricious Arts,*
But strict *harmonious Symetry* of *Parts.*
Which through the *Whole* insensibly must pass,
With vital Heat to animate the Mass.
A *pure,* an *active,* an *auspicious Flame,*
And *bright* as *Heav'n,* from whence the *Blessing* came;
But few, oh few Souls, præordain'd by *Fate,*
The Race of *Gods,* have reach'd that *envy'd Height.*
No *Rebel-Titan's sacrilegious Crime,*
By heaping Hills on Hills can *thither climb.*
The grizly *Ferry-man of Hell* deny'd
Æneas Entrance, 'till he knew his *Guide;*
How justly then will Impious Mortals fall,
Whose *Pride* wou'd soar to *Heav'n* without a *Call?*

Pride (of all others the most *dang'rous* Fault,)
Proceeds from want of *Sense,* or want of *Thought.*
The Men, who *labour* and *digest* things *most,*
Will be much apter to *despond,* than *boast.*
For if your Author be *profoundly good,*
'Twill cost you *dear* before he's *understood.*
How many Ages since has *Virgil* writ?
How few are they who understand him *yet?*
Approach his Altars with *religious Fear,*
No *vulgar Deity* inhabits *there:*
Heav'n shakes not more at *Jove's Imperial Nod,*

7 [Shameful, guilty.]

Than *Poets* shou'd before their *Mantuan God.*
Hail mighty *Maro!* may that Sacred Name
Kindle *my Breast* with *thy cœlestial Flame;*
Sublime Ideas, and *apt Words* infuse.
The *Muse* instruct *my Voice,* and *Thou* inspire the *Muse!*

What I have instanc'd only in the *best,*
Is, in proportion true of All the *rest.*
Take Pains the *genuine* Meaning to explore;
There *sweat,* there *strain,* tug the laborious *Oar:*
Search *ev'ry Comment* that your Care can find,
Some here, some there, may hit the Poet's *Mind;*
Yet be not blindly guided by the *Throng;*
The Multitude is always in the *Wrong.*
When Things appear *unnatural* or *hard,*
Consult your *Author,* with *Himself* compar'd;
Who knows what Blessing *Phœbus* may bestow,
And future Ages to your Labour owe?
Such Secrets are not easily found out,
But once Discover'd, leave no Room for Doubt.
Truth stamps *Conviction* in your Ravish'd Breast,
And *Peace* and *Joy* attend the glorious Guest.

Truth still is *One; Truth* is Divinely *bright,*
No cloudy *Doubts* obscure her *Native Light;*
While in your *Thoughts* you find the *least* Debate,
You may *Confound,* but *never* can *Translate.*
Your *Stile* will this thro' all Disguises show,
For none *Explain,* more clearly than they *Know.*
He only proves he *Understands* a Text,
Whose *Exposition* leaves it *unperplex'd.*
They who too faithfully on *Names* insist,
Rather Create than *Dissipate* the *Mist;*
And grow *Unjust* by being *over nice,*
(For *Superstitious Virtue* turns to *Vice.*)
Let *Crassus's* Ghost, and *Labienus* tell
How twice in *Parthian* Plains their *Legions* fell.
Since *Rome* hath been so Jealous of her Fame,
That few know *Pacorus* or *Monæses* Name.[8]

Words in One Language Elegantly us'd,
Will hardly in another be excus'd.

8 *Hor. l. 3. Od. 6.* [Horace, *Odes*, iii.6.]

And some that *Rome* admir'd in *Cæsar's* Time,
May neither suit *Our Genius* nor our *Clime.*
The *Genuine Sense, intelligibly* told,
Shews a *Translator* both *Discreet* and *Bold.*

   Excursions are *inexpiably Bad;*
And 'tis much safer to leave out than *Add.*
Abstruse and Mystick Thoughts you must express ⎤
With painful Care, but seeming Easiness; ⎬
For Truth shines brightest thro' the plainest Dress. ⎦
Th' *Ænean Muse*, when she appears in *State,*
Makes all *Jove's Thunder* on her *Verses* wait,
Yet writes sometimes as soft and moving Things
As *Venus* speaks, or *Philomela* sings.
Your Author always will the best advise,
Fall when *He* falls, and when *He Rises, Rise.*
Affected *Noise* is the most *wretched* Thing,
That to *Contempt* can *Empty Scriblers* bring.
Vowels and *Accents, regularly plac'd,*
On *even Syllables* (and still the *Last*)
Tho' gross innumerable *Faults* abound,
In spight of Nonsense, never *fail* of *Sound.*
But this is meant of *even Verse* alone,
As being most harmonious and most known:
For if you will unequal Numbers try,
There Accents on odd *Syllables* must lye.
Whatever Sister of the Learned Nine
Does to your Suit a willing Ear incline,
Urge your Success, deserve a lasting Name,
She'll Crown a *Grateful* and a *Constant Flame.*
But if a wild *Uncertainty* prevail,
And turn your *veering Heart* with ev'ry Gale,
You lose the *Fruit* of all your *former Care,*
For the sad *Prospect* of a *Just Despair.*

   A *Quack* (too scandalously mean to name)
Had, by *Man-Midwifry*, got *Wealth*, and *Fame;*
As if *Lucina* had forgot her *Trade,*
The *Lab'ring Wife* invokes *his surer Aid.*
Well-season'd Bowls the Gossips Spirits raise,
Who while she Guzzles, chats the *Doctor's* Praise.
And largely, what she wants in *Words*, supplies,

With *Maudlin-Eloquence* of *trickling Eyes.*
But what a thoughtless *Animal* is *Man,*
(How very *Active* in his own *Trepan!*)
For greedy of *Physicians* frequent *Fees,*
From *Female Mellow Praise* He takes Degrees;
Struts in a new *Unlicens'd Gown,* and then,
From *saving Women* falls to *killing Men.*
Another Such had left the *Nation Thin,*
In spight of all the *Children* he brought in.
His *Pills* as thick as *Hand Granadoes* flew,
And where they *fell,* as certainly they *slew.*
His *Name* struck ev'ry where as great a *Damp*
As *Archimedes* through the *Roman Camp.*
With this, the *Doctor's Pride* began to *Cool;*
For *Smarting soundly* may *convince* a Fool.
But now *Repentance* came too late, for *Grace;*
And meagre *Famine* star'd him in the Face.
Fain wou'd he to the *Wives* be reconcil'd,
But found no *Husband* left to *own a Child.*
The *Friends,* that *got* the Brats, were poison'd too;
In this sad case what cou'd our *Vermin* do?
Worry'd with *Debts* and past all *Hope* of *Bail,*
Th' unpity'd Wretch lyes *Rotting* in a *Jail.*
And there with *Basket-Alms,* scarce kept *Alive,*
Shews how *mistaken Talents* ought to *Thrive.*

    I pity, from my Soul, Unhappy Men,
Compell'd by *Want* to *prostitute* their *Pen;*
Who must, like *Lawyers,* either *starve* or *plead,*
And *follow,* right or wrong, where *Guineas lead;*
But you, *Pompilian, wealthy, pamper'd Heirs,*
Who to your *Country* owe your *Swords* and *Cares,*
Let no vain Hope your easie Mind seduce,
For *Rich Ill Poets* are without *Excuse.*
'Tis very Dang'rous, *Tampring* with a *Muse,*
The *Profit's small,* and you have *much* to *lose;*
For, tho' *true Wit* adorns your *Birth,* or *Place,*
Degen'rate Lines *degrade* th' *attainted Race.*
No Poet any *Passion* can Excite;
But what they feel transport them when they write.
Have you been led through the *Cumæan Cave,*
And heard th' Impatient Maid *Divinely Rave?*

I hear her now; I see her Rowling *Eyes*;
And panting; *Lo!* the *God*, the *God* she cries;
With *Words*, not *Hers*, and more than *human Sound*,
She makes th' obedient *Ghosts* peep trembling thro' the Ground.
But tho' we *must obey* when *Heav'n commands*,
And Man in vain the *Sacred Call withstands*,
Beware *what Spirit* rages in your Breast;
For ten Inspir'd ten thousand are possest.
Thus make the *proper Use* of each *Extream*,
And *write* with *Fury*, but *correct* with *Phleam.*[9]
As when the chearful Hours too freely pass,
And sparkling Wine smiles in the tempting Glass,
Your *Pulse* advises, and begins to beat
Thro' ev'ry swelling Vein a *loud Retreat:*
So when a *Muse propitiously invites*,
Improve her Favours, and *indulge* her Flights;
But when you find that vigorous Heat *abate*,
Leave off, and for *another Summons* wait.
Before the *Radiant Sun*, a *Glimmering Lamp*;
Adult'rate Metals to the *Sterling Stamp*,
Appear not *meaner*, than *meer human Lines*,
Compar'd with those whose *Inspiration shines*:
These, nervous, bold; those, languid and *remiss*;
There, Cold salutes; but *here*, a *Lover's Kiss.*
Thus have I seen a rapid, headlong Tide,
With foaming Waves the Passive *Soan* divide,
Whose lazy Waters without Motion lay,
While he, with eager Force, urg'd his Impetuous Way.

The *Privilege* that Ancient Poets claim, ⎤
Now turn'd to *License* by too *just* a Name, ⎬
Belongs to none but an *Establish'd Fame*, ⎦
Which *scorns* to *Take* it——[1]
Absurd Expressions, crude, abortive Thoughts,
All the lewd *Legion* of *Exploded Fau'ts*,
Base Fugitives to that *Asylum* fly,
And Sacred *Laws* with *Insolence* defy.
Not thus our *Heroes* of the *former* Days,
Deserv'd and *Gain'd* their never-fading *Bays*;

9 [Phlegm, in the old physiology, could imply calmness and coolness.]
1 [A witty "Comment to the Sense": Roscommon takes the poetic "license" of
a Vergilian half-line.]

For I mistake, or far the greatest Part
Of what some call *Neglect,* was *study'd Art.*
When *Virgil* seems to *Trifle* in a Line,
'Tis like a *Warning-piece,* which gives the *Sign*
To *wake* your *Fancy,* and *prepare* your *Sight,*
To reach the noble Height of some *unusual Flight.*
I lose my Patience, when, with *sawcy Pride,*
By *untun'd Ears* I hear *His Numbers* try'd.
Reverse of *Nature!* shall *such Copies* then
Arraign th' *Originals* of *Maro*'s Pen!
And the *rude Notions* of *Pedantick Schools*
Blaspheme the Sacred *Founder* of *Our Rules!*

The Delicacy of the nicest Ear
Finds nothing *harsh,* or out of *Order* There.
Sublime or *Low, Unbended* or *Intense,*
The *Sound* is still a *Comment* to the *Sense.*

A skilful *Ear,* in *Numbers* shou'd preside,
And all *Disputes* without *Appeal* decide.
This Ancient Rome, and *Elder Athens* found,
Before *mistaken Stops debauch'd* the *Sound.*

When, by Impulse from Heav'n, *Tyrtæus* Sung,
In drooping Soldiers a new Courage sprung;
Reviving Sparta now the Fight maintain'd,
And what *Two Gen'rals Lost,* a *Poet Gain'd.*
By secret Influence of Indulgent Skies,
Empire and *Poesie Together* rise.
True Poets are the *Guardians* of a *State,*
And when *They fail,* portend approaching *Fate.*
For that which *Rome* to *Conquest* did Inspire,
Was not the *Vestal,* but the *Muses Fire;*
Heav'n joins the *Blessings:* No *declining* Age
E'er felt the *Raptures* of *Poetick Rage.*

Of many Faults, *Rhyme* is (perhaps) the *Cause;*
Too *strict* to *Rhyme,* we slight more useful *Laws.*
For *That,* in *Greece* or *Rome,* was never *known,*
Till by *Barbarian* Deluges *o'erflown:*
Subdu'd, Undone, They did at last *Obey,*
And change their *Own* for their *Invaders* way.

I grant that from some *Mossie, Idol Oak,*
In *Double Rhymes* our *Thor* and *Woden* spoke;
And by Succession of unlearned Times,
As *Bards began,* so *Monks Rung on* the *Chimes.*

But now that *Phœbus* and the *sacred Nine,*
With all their Beams on our blest Island shine,
Why should not *We* their *ancient Rites restore,*
And *be,* what *Rome* or *Athens* were *Before?*

Have we forgot how Raphael's *Num'rous Prose*[2]
Led our exalted Souls thro' heav'nly Camps,
And mark'd the ground where proud Apostate Thrones
Defy'd Jehovah! Here, *'twixt Host and Host,*
(A narrow but a dreadful Interval)
Portentous Sight! before the Cloudy Van
Satan with vast and haughty Strides advanc'd,
Came tow'ring arm'd in Adamant and Gold.
There bellowing Engines, with their fiery Tubes,
Dispers'd Æthereal Forms, and down they fell
By thousands, Angels on Arch-Angels rowl'd;
Recover'd, to the Hills they ran, they flew,
Which (with their pond'rous load, Rocks, Waters, Woods
From their firm Seats torn by the shaggy Tops,
They bore like Shields before them thro' the Air,
'Till more incens'd they hurl'd 'em at their Foes.
All was Confusion, Heav'ns Foundations shook,
Threatning no less than Universal Wrack,
For Michael's *Arm main Promontories flung,*
And over-prest whole Legions weak with Sin;
Yet they Blasphem'd and struggled as they lay,
'Till the great Ensign of Messiah *blaz'd,*
And (arm'd with Vengeance) God's Victorious Son
(Effulgence of Paternal Deity)
Grasping ten thousand Thunders in his Hand
Drove th' old Original Rebels headlong down,
And sent them flaming to the vast Abyss.

O may I live to hail the Glorious Day,
And sing loud *Pæans* thro' the crowded Way,

2 An Essay on Blanc Verse, out of *Paradise Lost,* Book VI.

When in Triumphant State the *British* Muse,
True to her self, shall barb'rous Aid refuse,
And in the *Roman* Majesty appear,
Which none know better, and none come so near.

Francis Atterbury

1662–1732

Educated at Westminster and Oxford, Atterbury took holy orders in 1687 and in 1713 succeeded Thomas Sprat as Bishop of Rochester and Dean of Westminster. He was throughout his career a vigorous controversialist; having early acquired the seventeenth-century habit of confusing politics and religion, he wrote Anglican apologetics with the usual tincture of royalism. As a preacher he was one who might, according to Steele in the Tatler, *"pass the criticism of Longinus." After translating Dryden's "Absalom and Achitophel" into Latin in 1682, he published in 1684 an* Anthologia *of his own Latin verse. Atterbury, who was an intimate of Pope, Gay, Arbuthnot, and Prior, figures as Apollo, the chief of the Christ Church wits, in Swift's* Battle of the Books.*

It would be a mistake to suppose "The Preface" merely a puff: Atterbury voices the Augustan idea of progress in poetry—that poets from the time of Chaucer worked to file and polish the mother tongue, until perfection was finally attained in the refinements of Waller's "Beauty and Numbers." "The Preface" is reprinted from the edition of 1693, which includes The Second Part of Mr. Waller's Poems, *known originally as* The Maid's Tragedy With some other Pieces *(licensed 1689, printed 1690). Though unsigned, "The Preface" is usually attributed to Atterbury, partly on the basis of Jacob Tonson's claim that "Dr. Atterbury borrow'd" the "Manuscript Copy" and "took upon him to print."*

FROM

Waller's *Poems*

THE PREFACE

[*1690*]

The Reader need be told no more in commendation of these Poems, than that they are Mr. *Waller*'s: A Name that carries every thing in it, that's either Great or Graceful in Poetry. He was indeed the Parent of *English* Verse, and the first that shew'd us our Tongue had Beauty and Numbers in it. Our Language owes more to him than the *French* does to *Cardinal Richlieu*, and the whole Academy. A Poet cannot think of him, without being in the same rapture *Lucretius* is in, when *Epicurus* comes in his way.

> *Tu pater & rerum inventor, Tu patria nobis*
> *Suppeditas præcepta: Tuesque ex Inclyte, chartis*
> *Floriferis ut Apes in sallibus omnia libant,*
> *Omnia Nos itidem depascimur aurea dicta:*
> *Aurea, perpetua semper dignissima vita.*[1]

The Tongue came into his hands, like a rough Diamond; he polish'd it first, and to that degree that all Artists since him have admired the Workmanship, without pretending to mend it. *Sucklyn* and *Carew*, I must confess, wrote some few things smoothly enough, but as all they did in this kind was not very consider-

1 [*De Rerum Natura* iii.9–13: "Thou, father and discoverer of truths, thou dost give us paternal advice; as bees sip all sweets in flowery meadows, so in thy writings, glorious one, we feed upon all golden words, golden and most worthy of perpetual life."]

able, so 'twas a little later than the earliest pieces of Mr. *Waller*. He undoubtedly stands first in the List of Refiners, and for ought I know, last too; for I question whether in *Charles* the Second's Reign, *English* did not come to its full perfection; and whether it has not had its *Augustean Age*, as well as the *Latin*. It seems to be already mix'd with Foreign Languages, as far as its purity will bear; and, as Chymists says of their *Menstruums*,[2] to be quite sated with the Infusion. But Posterity will best judge of this—In the mean time, 'tis a surprizing Reflection, that between what *Spencer* wrote last, and *Waller* first, there should not be much above twenty years distance: and yet the one's Language, like the Money of that time, is as currant now as ever; whilst the other's words are like old Coyns, one must go to an Antiquary to understand their true meaning and value. Such advances may a great Genius make, when it undertakes any thing in earnest!

Some Painters will hit the chief Lines, and master strokes of a Face so truly, that through all the differences of Age, the Picture shall still bear a Resemblance. This Art was Mr. *Waller*'s; he sought out, in this flowing Tongue of ours, what parts would last, and be of standing use and ornament; and this he did so successfully, that his Language is now as fresh as it was at first setting out. Were we to judge barely by the wording, we could not know what was wrote at twenty, and what at fourscore. He complains indeed of a Tyde of words that comes in upon the *English* Poet, o'reflows whate're he builds: but this was less his case than any mans, that ever wrote; and the mischief on't is, this very complaint will last long enough to confute it self. For though *English* be mouldring Stone, as he tells us there, yet he has certainly pick'd the best out of a bad Quarry.

We are no less beholding to him for the new turn of Verse, which he brought in, and the improvement he made in our Numbers. Before his time, men Rhym'd indeed, and that was all: as for the harmony of measure, and that dance of words, which good ears are so much pleas'd with, they knew nothing of it. Their *Poetry* then was made up almost entirely of monosyllables; which, when they come together in any cluster, are certainly the most harsh untunable things in the World. If any man doubts of this, let him read ten lines in *Donne*, and he'll be

2 [Solvents.]

quickly convinc'd. Besides, their Verses ran all into one another, and hung together, throughout a whole Copy,[3] like the *hook't Attoms*, that compose a Body in *Des Cartes*. There was no distinction of parts, no regular stops, nothing for the Ear to rest upon—But as soon as the Copy began, down it went, like a Larum, incessantly; and the Reader was sure to be out of Breath, before he got to the end of it. So that really Verse in those days was but down-right Prose, tagg'd with Rhymes. Mr. *Waller* remov'd all these faults, brought in more Polysyllables, and smoother measures; bound up his thoughts better, and in a cadence more agreeable to the nature of the Verse he wrote in: So that where-ever the natural stops of that were, he contriv'd the little breakings of his sense so as to fall in with 'em. And for that reason, since the stress of our Verse lyes commonly upon the last Syllable, you'll hardly ever find him using a word of no force there. I would say if I were not afraid the Reader would think me too nice, that he commonly closes with Verbs, in which we know the Life of Language consists.

Among other improvements, we may reckon that of *his Rhymes*. Which are always good, and very often the better for being *new*. He had a fine Ear, and knew how quickly that Sense was cloy'd by the same round of chiming Words still returning upon it. 'Tis a decided Case by the great Master of Writing. *Quæ sunt ampla & Pulchra, diu placere possunt; quæ lepida & concinna,* (amongst which Rhyme must, whether it will or no, take its place) *cito satietate adficiunt aurium sensum fastidiosissimum.*[4] This he understood very well, and therefore, to take off the danger of a Surfeit that way, strove to please by Variety, and new sounds. Had he carried this Observation (among others) as far as it would go, it must, methinks, have shown him the incurable fault of this jingling kind of Poetry, and have led his later judgment to blank Verse. But he continu'd an obstinate Lover of Rhyme to the very last: 'Twas a Mistress, that never appear'd unhandsome in his Eyes, and was courted by him long after *Sa-*

3 [A composition, as in "a copy of verses."]
4 [The "great master of writing" is of course Cicero, and the passage comes from *Rhetorica ad Herrenium* (iv.23.32), a work the Renaissance attributed to Cicero: "the great and beautiful are able to please over a long period of time, but what is merely pretty and neat quickly affects that most fastidious sense of the ears with satiety."]

charissa[5] was forsaken. He had rais'd it, and brought it to that perfection we now enjoy it in: And the Poet's temper (which has always a little vanity in it) would not suffer him ever to slight a thing, he had taken so much pains to adorn. My Lord *Roscommon*[6] was more impartial: No man ever Rhym'd truer and evener than he; yet he is so just as to confess, that 'tis but a Trifle, and to wish the Tyrant dethron'd, and blank Verse set up in its room. There is a third person,[7] the living Glory of our English Poetry, who has disclaim'd the use of it upon the Stage, tho no Man ever employ'd it there so happily as He. 'Twas the strength of his Genius that first brought it into credit in Plays; and 'tis the force of his Example that has thrown it out agen. In other kinds of writing it continues still; and will do so, till some excellent Spirit arises, that has leisure enough, and resolution to break the charm, and free us from the *troublesome bondage of Rhyming*.[8]

As Mr. *Milton* very well calls it, and has prov'd it as well, by what he has wrote in another way. But this is a thought for times at some distance; the present Age is a little too Warlike: It may perhaps furnish out matter for a good Poem in the next, but 'twill hardly encourage one now: Without Prophesying, a Man may easily know, what sort of Lawrels are like to be in request?

Whilst I am talking of Verse, I find my self, I don't know how, betray'd into a great deal of Prose. I intended no more than to put the Reader in mind, what respect was due to any thing that fell from the Pen of Mr. *Waller*. I have heard his last Printed Copies, which are added in the several Editions of his Poems, very slightly spoken of; but certainly they don't deserve it. They do indeed discover themselves to be his last, and that's the worst we can say of 'em. He is there *Iam Senior: Sed cruda Deo viridisque Senectus*.[9] The same censure perhaps will be past on the

---

5 [Lady Dorothy Sidney provided the "inspiration" for a number of Waller's early poems. The poet and the lady, then both older in years, are reported to have had the following exchange: When will you write such beautiful verses to me again? When your Ladyship is as young and as handsome again.]
6 [Wentworth Dillon, Earl of Roscommon (1633?–85), brought out the "Essay on Translated Verse" in 1684, to which in 1685 he added a passage in Miltonic blank verse.]
7 [Dryden vacillated on the question of rhyme.]
8 [From Milton's attack on rhyme in "The Verse" appended to *Paradise Lost*.]
9 [Vergil, *Aeneid* vi.304: "Now old, but the old age of a god remains strong and green."]

pieces of this second part. I shall not so far engage for 'em, as to pretend they are all equal to whatever he wrote in the vigour of his Youth. Yet they are so much of a piece with the rest, that any Man will at first sight know 'em to be Mr. *Waller*'s. Some of 'em were wrote very early, but not put into former Collections, for reasons obvious enough, but which are now ceas'd. The Play[1] was alter'd, to please the Court: 'Tis not to be doubted who sat for the two Brothers Characters, 'Twas agreeable to the sweetness of Mr. *Waller*'s Temper, to soften the rigour of the Tragedy, as he expresses it; but whether it be so agreeable to the Nature of Tragedy it self, to make every thing come off easily, I leave to the Criticks. In the Prologue, and Epilogue, there are a few Verses that he has made use of upon another occasion. But the Reader may be pleased to allow that in him, that has been allowed so long in *Homer* and *Lucretius*. Exact Writers dress up their thoughts so very well always, that when they have need of the same sense, they can't put it into other words, but it must be to its prejudice. Care has been taken in this Book to get together every thing of Mr. *Waller*'s, that's not put into the former Collection; so that between both, the Reader may make the set compleat.

It will perhaps be contended after all, that some of these ought not to have been Publish'd: And Mr. *Cowly*'s decision will be urg'd, that a neat Tomb of Marble is a better Monument, than a great Pile of Rubbish, &c. It might be answer'd to this, that the Pictures and Poems of great Masters have been always valu'd, tho the last hand weren't put to 'em. And I believe none of those Gentlemen that will make the objection would refuse a Sketch of *Raphael*'s or one of *Titian*'s draughts of the first sitting.

I might tell 'em too, what care has been taken by the Learned, to preserve the Fragments of the Ancient Greek and Latin Poets: There has been thought to be a Divinity in what they said, and therefore the least pieces of it have been kept up and reverenc'd, like Religious reliques. And I am sure, take away the *mille anni*,[2] and Impartial reasoning will tell us, there is as much due

1 [*The Maid's Tragedy* by Beaumont and Fletcher, first printed in 1619.]
2 ["thousand years."]

to the Memory of Mr. *Waller,* as to the most celebrated names of Antiquity.

But to wave the dispute now of what *ought* to have been done; I can assure the Reader, what *would* have been had this Edition been delay'd. The following Poems were got abroad, and in a great many hands: It were vain to expect that amongst so many admirers of Mr. *Waller,* they should not meet with one fond [3] enough to Publish 'em. They might have staid indeed, till by frequent transcriptions they had been corrupted extreamly, and jumbled together with things of another kind: But then they would have found their way into the World. So 'twas thought a greater piece of kindness to the Author, to put 'em out; whilst they continue genuine and unmix'd; and such, as he himself, were he alive, might own.

[3] [Foolish.]

Charles Gildon

1665–1724

Gildon, first a Catholic and later a deist but always a Royalist, was a professional man of letters whose vocational manner earned him a place in the Dunciad. *Literary criticism was ever one of his major concerns; toward the end of his life he even attempted a* Complete Art of Poetry (1718) *and a* Laws of Poetry (1721). (Green's Spleen *acknowledges the contribution in 1737: "Gildon sells/ Poetic buckets for dry wells.") Gildon's earlier endeavors were less ambitious, less grandly legislative. The "Vindications" of Cowley, Waller, and Milton (the last may not have been written by Gildon but by a certain "J. J.") are reprinted from* Miscellaneous Letters and Essays (1694), *a collection that harbors letters to ladies and "To my Honour'd, Ingenious and Learned Friend, Dr. Midgely, about* SLEEP *and its medicinal Property." A number of literary items are certainly by Gildon himself and serve to suggest his habitual stance: "An Essay at a Vindication of Love in Tragedies, against Rapin and Mr. Rymer"; "An Apology for Poetry"; and "Some Reflections on Mr. Rymer's Short View of Tragedy, and an Attempt at a Vindication of Shakespear, in an Essay directed to John Dryden Esq." Gildon's most congenial role is that of "vindicator," and in this he doubtless typifies much of the educated opinion of the time: combining respect for the Ancients with affection for the Moderns, he conserves the past while defending the present against the rigidities of Rymer and the strict application of Frenchified Rules.*

An ESSAY *at a Vindication of the* LOVE-VERSES *of*
COWLEY *and* WALLER, *&c.*
In Answer to the Preface of a Book Intituled,
LETTERS AND VERSES AMOROUS AND GALLANT.
Directed to
Mr. CONGREVE
[*1693?*]

As in my two former Critical Discourses of this Book against Mr. *Rymer*'s SHORT VIEW OF TRAGEDY,[1] a Zeal for the Honour of my Country in its greatest Ornaments, her Poets, Engag'd me; so here I cannot help challenging the same Pretence, since I can't suppose them deficient in LOVE, without derogating from the *Justness* of their Characters. But I must confess I have not the same hopes of Success in this; for there I had to do with an *impotent Opiniator;* but here with a Gentleman[2] of a great deal of *Wit* and fine *Sense*. There I address'd to Parties already sensible of the Justice of my Cause; here to one who is prepossess'd

---

1 ["Some Reflections on Mr. Rymer's Short View of Tragedy, and an Attempt at a Vindication of Shakespear, in an Essay directed to John Dryden Esq." and "An Essay at a Vindication of Love in Tragedies, against Rapin and Mr. Rymer"—both printed in Gildon's *Miscellaneous Letters and Essays* (London, 1694).]
2 [William Walsh. In the Preface to his *Letters and Poems, Amorous and Gallant* (1692), Walsh appeals to the principle of continuity in human nature to establish the superiority of the Ancients over the Moderns: "The second Part of this Collection consists of Amorous Verses. Those who are conversant with the Writings of the Antients, will observe a great difference between what they, and the Moderns have published on this Subject. The occasions upon which the Poems of the former are written, are such as happen to every Man almost that is in Love; and the Thoughts such, as are natural for every Man in love to think. The Moderns on the other hand have sought out for Occasions, that none meet with, but themselves; and fill their Verses with . . . forc'd Conceits, far-fetch'd Similes, and shining Points. . . ."]

of the contrary. But on the other hand I have the greater satisfaction here of being Worsted by one whose *Wit* can better defend an *Error,* than I the *Truth;* and I'm of Opinion, that 'tis a nobler Fate to fall by the Hand of an Hero, than Conquer a *Dastard Pretender.* And tho' my Prudence might be call'd in Question by this Attempt, yet my generous Ambition will merit a *Magnis tamen excidit Ausis.*[3] One thing I must possess you of in my favour, that my unhappy Circumstances allow me not time to use all the Caution I ought, or search all the Reasons might be urg'd in this noble Cause; so that I am not only *Viribus,* but *Opibus impar.*[4] However, I hope the Design will gain me the Opinion of a *Good English Man,* if my Performance shou'd not attain that of a *good Critic,* which will sufficiently compensate my trouble; for I shou'd be prouder to be thought a Zealot for the Glory as well as Interest of my Country, than the greatest Wit, and most Learned Arguer.

I shall never deny the Ancients their just Praise of the Invention of *Arts* and *Sciences;* but I cannot without contradicting my own Reason, allow them the Perfecters of 'em so far that they must be our uncontroverted Patterns and Standard: For our Physicians have found the Prescripts of *Hippocrates* very Defective: And as in Physic, so in Poetry, there must be a regard had to the Clime, Nature, and Customs of the People; for the Habits of the Mind as well as those of the Body, are influenc'd by them; and LOVE with the other Passions vary in their *Effects* as well as *Causes,* according to each Country and Age; nay, according to the very Constitution of each Person affected. This makes me hope, that the Ingenious Author of the *Letters and Verses Amorous and Gallant,* guides himself by a fallacious Rule, when he makes the Ancients the Standard of the Excellence of the Moderns (or indeed when by exalting *those,* he wholly deprives *these* of all Honour) in LOVE VERSES. His Charge is reducible to these two Heads, *viz.* The *Occasions* and the *Performances.* He will have it, that *the Occasions on which their Poems are written are sought out, and that none meet with 'em but themselves, whilst those of the Ancients are such as happen almost to e'ry Man in Love.* Next, *That the Verses of the Moderns, are fill'd with*

3 ["But he falls in great attempts."]
4 [Not only "in abilities" but "in resources unequal."]

Thoughts that are indeed SURPRIZING *and* GLITTERING, *but not* TENDER, PASSIONATE, *or* NATURAL *for e'ry Man in* LOVE *to think*. This is the sum of his Charge against 'em; of which in the Order I've plac'd 'em. First, As for the *Occasions*; I cannot remember any Subject chosen by either *Cowly* or *Waller*, (for we've nothing to do here with *Petrarch* a Foreigner) that seems to be sought out, or unnatural for a Man in Love to choose; and if some of 'em do not happen to e'ry Man in Love, they are yet on an equal Bottom with the Ancients, many of whose *Subjects* or *Occasions,* are far from happening to all Lovers, as none who can pretend to any knowledge of their Writings can deny. *Corinna's* Parrot dy'd, and *Ovid* writes its Funeral Elegy; but sure none will contend that this is an Accident common to all Ladies who have Lovers, and those Poets too. *Catullus* addresses one Copy of Verses to the very Sparrow of *Lesbia,* and in another deplores its Death. A great many Lovers may have Mistresses who never take a Voyage during their Amour, and yet *Ovid* has an Elegy *ad Amicam Navigantem;*[5] and so may ten thousand true Lovers, especially such as are Poets, never venture on any other Billows, but the Frown of their Fair ones; and yet *Propertius* toss'd in another Storm, Writes to *Cynthia* upon it. And indeed to reduce the *Subjects* or *Occasions* of LOVE-VERSES to any particular Standard, is highly Irrational, and must only be the effect of want of Consideration, for the various Circumstances and Fortunes of the Lovers must diversifie and alter the *Occasions* of writing to their Mistresses: So that there is no Occasion that is General, and that can reach all Men in Love, but the Cruelty of their Mistresses on their first Addresses, (that is, their not immediate Compliance) for Jealousie is not Universal, or at least to extend to the Beating of her a Man Loves; yet *Ovid* Writes *ad Amicam quam verberaverat.*[6] I must confess, I can't see the least Reason why the *Name* and *Gloves* of a Mistress, with *the Place of her Birth,* are not as just *Occasions* to Write on as the Ring given to a Mistress, or her Parrot or Sparrow; or a great many more I might enumerate out of the Ancients. A true Lover thinks e'ry thing that belongs to her he Loves, worthy his Thoughts; and the more our Modern Poets extend their Reflec-

[5] ["To a 'Friend' Making a Voyage," *Amores* i.11.]
[6] ["To a 'Friend' Whom he had Beaten," *Amores* i.7.]

tions beyond the Ancients in this, so much the greater Lovers they shew themselves. But the *Place of one's Mistress's Birth* is not only worthy a Lover's Thoughts, but even an *Universal Occasion*, since no Lover but must meet with that Occurrence in whatever fair one he adores, among all the beauteous Daughters of *Eve*.

By what has been said, Sir, 'tis evident that our Moderns are not inferiour to the Ancients, in their Judgment in chusing *Occasions* on which they write to their Mistresses: Or, That this Ingenious Gentleman has either through Want of Advertence, or out of Design expressed himself *ambiguously*, or at least not with that *Clearness* that is requisite to a conclusive Argument; which cannot be excused when the Honour and Merit of such great Men as *Cowley* and *Waller* is concerned; nay, the Honour of our Country.

I come now to the Second Accusation, which is, that *the Moderns fill their Verses with Thoughts* surprising *and* glittering, *but not natural for e'ry Man in Love to think.* This lies under the same Fault as the other does, of being too general to be of any Force, it either condemns all that the Moderns have wrote, it casts off e'ry Thought in their Love-Verses as not tender and passionate, or does nothing at all, for it instances no particular. I'm confident the ingenious[7] Gentleman will have so much Candor, as to confess that there are a great many very tender and soft Thoughts, and passionate Expressions in *Cowley's* Mistress, as in this one, that now occurrs to my Mind: *Then like some wealthy Island thou shalt lie,* &c. but if there be some, nay, a great many tender, soft, and passionate thoughts in our Moderns, then is this general charge not at all conclusive against 'em. Besides, *Thoughts natural to a Man in* Love, is an obscure Expression, it conveys no clear Idea of any thing to the Mind; or, what is fully as erroneous, it seems to level the Thoughts of all Mankind, but it cannot be doubted, but that in the very same Circumstances the Thoughts of different Men will be various, and more or less Excellent and Noble, as the Wit, Judgment, Fancy, and the other Qualities of the Mind of the Person affected, are more or less Excellent and perfect: And I am confident your ingenious Friend (whom I honour for his Wit, tho I

7 [Ingenuous—here and below.]

differ from his Opinion) will allow me, That one of Mr. *Cowley*'s Genius wou'd no more have the Thoughts of a Fop, a Beau, a Tinker, a Shepherd, or any other ignorant and *unelevated* Mechanic, in Love, than out of it. *Again,* Thoughts *surprizing,* and *glittering* without particular Instances of 'em, as they prove nothing, so can they not be well answer'd, for an Instance would have made us apprehend what he takes for *surprizing* and *glittering*; but without that, or any Definition, we wander in the dark, and I can at best but only ghess at his meaning. If by *Thoughts surprizing,* and *glittering* he means *extraordinary* and *uncommon,* I'm apt to think he will allow them very natural to Mr. *Cowley* or Mr. *Waller* in any Circumstance. A Man that is us'd to a good Habit of thinking, cannot be without extraordinary Thoughts, on what concerns him so near as the Heart of his Mistress. *Lastly,* As to *far-fetch'd Similes,* 'tis an Expression very *obscure* and *ambiguous*; and I must acknowledge my self wholly to seek in his Meaning, if a *Simile* be just, and hold an exact Analogy to the thing 'tis applied to, and of the thing 'tis designed to heighten, I presume it cannot come into the Number of the *farfetch'd,* and when-ever the Gentleman will please to instance in Particulars in either *Cowley* or *Waller,* I engage to fellow them with those that are full as faulty, even according to his own Definition, let that be what it will, (for I suppose it can't be much amiss from so accurate a Pen.) And till then I may supersede any particular Defence in this. Besides, 'tis not to be supposed, that the Verses written by Lovers are the *Extempore* Result of a sudden Gust of Passion, like the Inspirations of the *Delphic* Prophetess; for I'm confident he'll agree with me that the Excuse of Love will not free a Poet, that lets them pass so from the Censure of *Boileau*

> *Un sot en ecrivant, fait tout avec plaisir*
> *I'll na point en ses vers l'ambarras de Choisir.*[8]

A Poetizing Lover, must be allow'd not to be absolutely out of his Wits, and that 'tis possible for him to study, and consider what he says in so solemn a Manner to his Mistress.

[8] ["A fool when writing does everything with delight: there is nowhere in his verse the inconvenience of choice." From Satire II: "A Molière: Accord de la Rime et de la Raison."]

After this bold Assertion without Proof, he advances to examine which are in the right, the Ancients or the Moderns; the Rule of our Judgment in this, he justly makes the End the Poet aims at, *viz. The obtaining the Love of his Mistress*, tho I cannot see why he should suppose that contrary to, or inconsistent with getting *Fame* and *Admiration*, since Admiration is a certain Step to Love. When I read Mr. *Dryden*'s Works, I cannot help Loving him. If I should not love and respect him and any other Poet that thinks well, and expresses his Thoughts nobly, I should sin against my Reason. *Ovid* urges his Fame and Reputation as a Motive for his Mistress's Love, and if that can move a Man of Sense, why should we think the Effect wou'd not be the same on a Woman of Sense, and Generosity? And indeed, in e'ry one but an absolute dull, insipid Fool, which no Lover can think his Mistress.

The End of Love-Verses being the gaining the fair ones Heart, he proceeds to the best means of obtaining that End, *viz. The convincing her that you love her*. I must deny this Assertion too, for tho *Love* in the Severity of Justice require *Love*; yet is that an Argument that ought not always to prevail, since 'tis a Plea that's common to a great many, for so the fair one ought to surrender to 'em all; a Liberty no Lover would willingly allow his Mistriss on any Consideration whatever. But how often does Experience tell us, that this *best Way* fails? Or indeed, how seldom does it hit? *Admiration* is the only just, and unquestioneable Parent of Love; for the Senses or the Mind must be first won with some Perfection, either real or imaginary. Whatever therefore can ravish Fame from the envious censorious World, may justly be suppos'd able to give *Admiration* to a Mistress. Nor is this inconsistent with the *true and lively Representation of the Pains, and Thoughts attending the Passion of Love;* for sure the Advantage of *Art* in Poems cannot destroy the *End* which is not to be obtain'd in Painting without it, *viz.* a *lively Representation of Nature. Similes*, fine *Thoughts*, and *shining Points*, if they be just, and good, must certainly give a greater Idea of any Pain, than a bare and unpolished Rhime, without Beauty or Grace. *This* gives us a *weak*, a *faint*, an *unmoving* View of the Pain; *That* sets it close to us, magnifies and enlarges it: *This* gives it you as the reverse end of a Prospective Glass does Objects, *That* as the right

end of it; so that if a Representation of our Pain be the Path
to Success, *Art* will be no ill Help and guide in it; unless
we'll suppose that our Mistress would be more sensibly touched
with a *Grubstreet* Ballad, than a Copy of Verses by a *Cowley* or a
Waller. But indeed, the Pain a Lover feels cannot be truely, and
with Life represented without *Similes*, as is evident from the
very Nature of the Mind, when in Pain: For 'tis an universal
Measure of our Judgment of things to compare them with something else; and the Mind in expressing its Pains endeavours to
make it known in its full Greatness: to give therefore the greater
Image of it, it generally seeks out something by a Comparison of
which it hopes to obtain that End; Comparison being the only
Distinction of Degrees of things. This makes it narrowly in these
Circumstances, regard and observe that Train of *Ideas* that continually pass before it, to call out such as are most proper for its
purpose: For *'tis evident,* (as Mr. *Lock* remarks) *to any one that
will but observe what passes in his own Mind, that there is a
Train of Ideas constantly succeeding one another in his Understanding, as long as he's awake.* An Assertion therefore of an
Ingenious Friend of mine, to the Prejudice of the Moderns,
against *Similes* in the Expression of the Passions of Love and
Grief, is contrary to the very Nature of the Mind. For let any
Man endeavour to retain any particular Idea firmly and without
Alteration, he will find it not in his Power to do it any considerable time, such a necessary Succession and Variation of Ideas
(the Origin of Similes) is there in the human Mind. But because
'tis said that *'tis the nature of Grief to confine the Soul, straiten
the Imagination, and extremely lessen the Number of its Objects,* I shall only oppose the Assertion of this Gentleman (whom
I have always allow'd a Man of great Wit and Sense) with an
Observation of Mr. *Le Clerk,*[9] (whom I'm sure no Man that
knows his Works, will deny to be one of the best Philosophers of
the Age) in the 6*th. Chapter* of his *Ontologie* and the 4*th. Paragraph,* he has to this purpose—"This being so, we observe that
the time seems short to those who spend it in Mirth, or any
Employment they perform with Pleasure and Desire; but on the

---

9 [Jean Leclerc (1657–1736) corresponded with Locke and wrote *An Account
of the Life and Writings of John Locke Esq.* Gildon probably read the edition
of the *Ontologia* published in London in 1692.]

contrary, Tedious and Irksome to the Unfortunate, and those that are in Pain, or to those that are against their Wills, oblig'd to some troublesome Business. For we keep the Idea that is Gratefull and Pleasant to us, as long without Variation as we are able, and thus by the viewing of the fewer Ideas, the time we spend in Pleasure and Content, seems the shorter; whilst on the contrary, our Minds endeavour to drive away a troublesome Idea, and strive to substitute some others in its room; Turning, Winding, Changing, Adding and Diminishing it, as the uneasie inquietude Prompts. Thus the time seems longer than it wou'd do else, by that vast and numerous Train of Ideas, which, as I may say, shew themselves *en passant* to the Mind, with an incredible Rapidity and Swiftness." From this just and rational Observation of Mr. *Le Clerk* 'tis evident, That Similes are not so unnatural in expression of Grief or Pain, as some Ingenious Gentlemen contend: For the Mind (especially that which is us'd to an Expression of its self in Allegory and Similes) will easily in this Number of Ideas, meet with some that will answer the End, the Mind is born to with so much Impatience and Desire: For 'tis here also evident, That Grief multiplies nor lessens the Number of the Objects of the Mind.

From what has been said 'twill appear, That *Similes* cannot be an unnatural Expression of this Passion, or any Effects of it. I shall therefore proceed to those few particular Instances the Author of the *Preface* gives, by which he draws a short Parallel betwixt the Ancients and the Moderns. *I am pleas'd,* says he, *with* Tibullus, *when he says, he cou'd live in a Desart with his Mistress, where never any Humane Foot-steps appear'd, because I doubt not but he really thinks what he says: But I confess, I can hardly forbear Laughing, when* Petrarch *tells us he cou'd live without any other Sustenance than his Mistresses Looks.* I confess, I must ev'n here dissent from him too; for if you go to the Rigor or Severity of the Reason of both Expressions, they are equally impossible, and in Impossibilities as well as Infinites, there are no Degrees. For I can see no greater Probability of Living in a Desart where there were no Humane Foot-steps, than on the Looks of a Mistress only; unless like *Nebuchadnezzar,* he wou'd feed on the Leaves of the Trees, and Grass of the Ground if there were any; which is not very kind to hope his Mistress wou'd comply with. But supposing it impossible, is there any Necessity of a Lovers saying nothing that exceeds the Bounds of *Possibility*? especially in Poetry, where Hyperbole's are justifiable almost to Extravagance. That certainly wou'd be most unnatural of all, for the Thoughts of a Man really in Love, are naturally Extravagant ev'n to Impossibilities; tho *possunt quia posse videntur*.[1] The very Definition of this Passion in Ethics, shews it violent and exorbitant. But we may in favour of *Petrarch* and Mr. *Cowley*, (who make use of the same Thought) say that they mean the Dyet of their Love, is a Look of their Mistress.

I must confess, I'm extremely supriz'd to find your Ingenious Friend an Advocate for that which wou'd make all the Sir *Courtly*'s Compositions of the *Nation*, the Standard of good Verses; when he himself is really so well qualify'd to write like *Cowley* and *Waller*, and has by his own Practice in those Verses that are Publish'd, better confuted his Preface, than all I can pretend to say.

To Mr. T[HOMAS?] S[OUTHERNE?]

in Vindication of

Mr. MILTON's *Paradise lost*

[1694]

SIR,
You will pardon me, I am confident, tho' in Opposition to your Thoughts, I positively declare my self extreamly well pleas'd with that part of Mr. *Milton*'s most excellent Poem, to which you discover the least Inclination:Those *Antient*, and consequently *less Intelligible* Words, Phrases, and Similes, by which he frequently, and *purposedly* affects to express his Meaning, in my Opinion do well suit with the *Venerable Antiquity*, and *Sublime Grandeur* of his Subject. And how much soever some *Unthinking* have Condemn'd this his Choice, *You*, who have Maturely weigh'd, how

---

1 ["they are possible because they seem to be possible."]

much deeper an Impression *less us'd,* (so they be what you will grant his always are) *Significant words,* make on a *Readers* fancy, than such as are *more common;* (you I say) must pay a vast deference to Mr. *Milton's* great *Judiciousness* in this particular, no less than to his *entire Manage* of every part of that *Charming Poem,* in which upon every Occasion he discovers himself a perfect, unimitable *Master of Language.* Here are you forc'd to give a profound Attention to the *Universal Creator,* speaking like *that Almighty,* who by the *Fiat* of his Mouth made all things, and yet so *Gracious* are All his *Expressions,* as if he valued himself more on his *Good Will to Man,* than on his *Prerogative* over him: There, shall you read *Man,* addressing himself *Submissively* like a *Creature,* who owes his Being to a better, wiser, and higher power, and yet not so *Abjectly,* but you will easily perceive him to be *Lord* of the whole Creation. *Elsewhere,* you may see an *Angel* discovering himself, not a Little *Man's Superior* by Creation, in *Place* and *Power* more, but in *Knowledge* most of all. In *another place,* behold *Woman,* appearing *Inferiour* to both these, and yet more *Ambitious* than either, but then *softer,* much in her *Make* and *Manners,* than her *rougher Spouse,* whom *down right Sincerity,* and unaffected plainness, seem mostly to Delight. Nor can I now forget with what *vast complacency* we have oft together read the most *Natural, Lively,* yet (as their Sexes) different Descriptions, our first *Parents,* separately make of their own Apprehensions of themselves, at their *first finding* themselves *Living Creatures.* Nay, the very *fallen Angels* are much Honour'd above the best of their deserts, by the *Amazing Relation,* we there meet with of their *Ambition, Malice, Inveteracy,* and *Cunning;* and never was *Scene,* so livelily shown, as that of his *Pandæmonium* in the first Book. Once more, and you are no less astonisht at his *Description,* than he makes the *Angels,* to be at the Report of their Adversaries Thund'ring Fire-works. And yet, if his Matter requires a *Meaner Style,* how much soever he speaks *Loftily* at one time, at another does, even to a *Miracle,* suit his *Speech* to his *Subject.* This (I well know) has been censur'd in him for *Servile creeping;* but if 'tis well *consider'd,* upon what *proper Occasion* he thus *humbles* his Style, 'twill be *Accounted,* (as really it is) his *Great Commendation:* But in praise of Mr. *Milton's* admirable Dexterity in this his *Matchless Performance*, since All I can say must come exceeding short of his *due Merit*, that I bring not my self under the Correction of that known saying, *Præstat de Carthagine tacere quam pauca dicere*.[1] I shall venture to add no more but this; tho' the Composing such a *compleat Poem* on such, a no less *Obscure*, than *weighty* Subject, was a *Task* to be perform'd by Mr. *Milton* only, yet 'tis not out of doubt, whether *himself* had ever been able so to Sing of *Unrevealed Heavenly Mysteries*, had he not been altogether depriv'd of his *Outward Sight*, and thereby made capable of such *continued Strenuous, Inward Speculations*: as he who has the use of his *Bodily Eyes*, cannot possibly become possest with. *This* however must be Granted, as indubitably true; The *bountiful Powers* above, did more than make him amends for their taking away his Sight, by so *Illumining* his Mind, as to enable him *most compleatly* to sing of *Matchless Beings, Matchless Things*, before *unknown* to, and even *unthought* of by the whole Race of Men; thus rewarding him for a *Temporary Loss*, with an *Eternal Fame*, of which *Envy* it self shall not be able ever to deprive this *best of Poems*, or its most *Judicious Author*.

> *In this Faith I Subscribe my self,*
> S I R,
> *Yours, &c.*

[1] ["It is better to keep quiet than to speak little of Carthage."]

George Granville, Baron Lansdowne

1667–1735

Educated in France and at Cambridge, Granville held public office for many years. In 1715–17 he was imprisoned in the Tower on suspicion of Jacobitism and fell permanently from favor. His plays were acted at Drury Lane, and he wrote poetry that received high praise from Pope. "Upon unnatural Flights in Poetry," first published in 1701 in one of Charles Gildon's miscellanies, is reprinted from The Genuine Works in Verse and Prose of 1732 *(Tonson's editions of 1712, 1721, and 1726 lack the "Explanatory Annotations on the Foregoing Poem"). Granville's verse-essay is in large part imitated from Bouhours'* La Manière de bien penser dans les Ouvrages d'Esprit *(1687); even the prose annotations owe much to the same source. Writing just after the close of the seventeenth century, Granville records something of the congenial reception French neoclassicism had found in various quarters of Augustan England.*

ESSAY

Upon unnatural Flights in POETRY

[*1701*]

As when some Image of a charming Face
In living Paint, an Artist tries to trace,
He carefully consults each beauteous Line,
Adjusting to his Object, his Design,
We praise the Piece, and give the Painter Fame,
But as the just Resemblance speaks the Dame.
Poets are Limners of another kind,
To copy out Ideas in the Mind;
Words are the Paint by which their Thoughts are shown,
And Nature sits, the Object to be drawn;
The written Picture we applaud, or blame,
But as the due Proportions are the same.
　Who driven with ungovernable Fire,
Or void of Art, beyond these Bounds aspire,
Gigantick Forms, and monstrous Births alone
Produce, which Nature shockt, disdains to own.
By true Reflexion I would see my Face,
Why brings the Fool a Magnifying-Glass?
(1) "But Poetry in Fiction takes delight,
　　And mounting in bold Figures out of sight,
　　Leaves Truth behind, in her audacious Flight:
　　Fables and Metaphors that always lye,
　　And rash Hyperboles that soar so high,
　　And every Ornament of Verse must die."
Mistake me not: No Figures I exclude,
And but forbid Intemperance, not Food.
Who would with care some happy Fiction frame,
So mimicks Truth, it looks the very same;
Not rais'd to force, or feign'd in Nature's Scorn,

But meant to grace, illustrate, and adorn.
Important Truths still let your Fables hold,
And moral Mysteries with Art unfold.
Ladies and Beaux to please, is all the Task,
But the sharp Critick will Instruction ask.
(2) As Veils transparent cover, but not hide,
Such Metaphors appear when right apply'd;
When thro' the Phrase we plainly see the Sense,
Truth, where the Meaning's obvious, will dispense;
The Reader what in Reason's due, believes,
Nor can we call that false, which not deceives.
(3) Hyperboles, so daring and so bold,
Disdaining Bounds, are yet by Rules control'd;
Above the Clouds, but still within our Sight,
They mount with Truth, and make a tow'ring Flight,
Presenting things impossible to view,
They wander thro' incredible to True:
Falshoods thus mix'd, like Metals are refin'd,
And Truth, like Silver, leaves the Dross behind.
Thus Poetry has ample Space to soar,
Nor needs forbidden Regions to explore:
Such Vaunts as his, who can with Patience read,
Who thus describes his Hero slain and dead:
(4) "Kill'd as he was, insensible of Death,
He still fights on, and scorns to yield his Breath." [1]
The noisy Culverin o'ercharg'd, lets fly,
And burst unaiming in the rended Sky:
Such frantick Flights are like a Mad-man's Dream,
And Nature suffers in the wild Extreme.
The captive Canibal weigh'd down with Chains,
Yet braves his Foes, reviles, provokes, disdains,
Of Nature fierce, untameable, and proud,
He grins Defiance at the gaping Croud,
And spent at last, and speechless as he lies,
With Looks still threatning, mocks their Rage, and dies.
This is the utmost Stretch that Nature can,
And all beyond is fulsom, false, and vain.
Beauty's the Theme; some Nymph divinely fair
Excites the Muse: Let Truth be even there:
As Painters flatter, so may Poets too,

---

[1] Ariosto. [Bouhours, from whom Granville apparently took the lines, mistakenly attributes this couplet, from Berni's recasting of Boiardo's *Orlando Innamorato*, to Ariosto.]

But to Resemblance must be ever true.
(5) "The Day that she was born, the CYPRIAN Queen
    Had like t'have dy'd thro' Envy and thro' Spleen;
    The Graces in a hurry left the Skies
    To have the Honour to attend her Eyes;
    And Love, despairing in her Heart a Place,
    Would needs take up his Lodging in her Face." [2]
Tho' wrote by great CORNEILLE, such Lines as these,
Such civil Nonsense sure could never please.
WALLER, the best of all th' inspir'd Train,
To melt the Fair, instructs the dying Swain.

(6) The ROMAN Wit,[3] who impiously divides
His Hero, and his Gods to diff'rent Sides,
I would condemn, but that, in spight of Sense
Th' admiring World still stands in his Defence.
How oft, alas! the best of Men in vain
Contend for Blessings which the worst obtain!
The Gods, permitting Traitors to succeed,
Become not Parties in an impious Deed:
And by the Tyrant's Murder, we may find
That CATO and the Gods were of a Mind.

Thus forcing Truth with such prepost'rous Praise,
Our Characters we lessen, when we'd raise:
Like Castles built by magick Art in Air,
That vanish at Approach, such Thoughts appear;
But rais'd on Truth, by some judicious Hand,
As on a Rock they shall for Ages stand.

(7) Our King[4] return'd, and banish'd Peace restor'd,
The Muse ran mad to see her exil'd Lord;
On the crack'd Stage the Bedlam Heroes roar'd,
And scarce could speak one reasonable Word;
DRYDEN himself, to please a frantick Age,
Was forc'd let his Judgment stoop to Rage,[5]
To a wild Audience he conform'd his Voice,
Comply'd to Custom, but not err'd by Choice:
Deem then the Peoples, not the Writer's Sin,
ALMANSOR's Rage, and Rants of MAXIMIN;
That Fury spent in each elaborate Piece,
He vies for Fame with ancient ROME and GREECE.

2 Corneille. [The "Cyprian Queen" is Venus.]
3 Lucan.
4 *King* Charles II.
5 [I.e., poetic "rage." See my Preface; and compare "Fury," below.]

First MULGRAVE rose, ROSCOMMON next,[6] like Light,
To clear our Darkness, and to guide our Flight;
With steady Judgment, and in lofty Sounds,
They gave us Patterns, and they set us Bounds;
The STAGIRITE and HORACE laid aside,
Inform'd by them, we need no foreign Guide:
Who seek from Poetry a lasting Name,
May in their Lessons learn the Road to Fame;
But let the bold Adventurer be sure
That every Line the Test of Truth endure;
On this Foundation may the Fabrick rise,
Firm and unshaken, till it touch the Skies.
  From Pulpits banish'd, from the Court, from Love,
Forsaken Truth seeks Shelter in the Grove;
Cherish, ye Muses! the neglected Fair,
And take into your Train th' abandon'd Wanderer.

EXPLANATORY ANNOTATIONS
ON THE
FOREGOING POEM.

(1) The *Poetick World* is nothing but Fiction; *Parnassus,*
Pegasus, and the *Muses,* pure Imagination and Chimæra: But
being however a System universally agreed on, all that has or
may be contrived or invented upon this Foundation, according to
Nature, shall be reputed as Truth; but whatsoever shall diminish
from, or exceed the just Proportions of Nature, shall be rejected
as false, and pass for Extravagance; as Dwarfs and Giants, for
Monsters.

(2) When *Homer,* mentioning *Achilles,* terms him a Lion,
this is a Metaphor, and the Meaning is obvious and true, tho' the
literal Sense be false, the Poet intending thereby to give his
Reader some Idea of the Strength and Fortitude of his Hero. Had
he said, that Wolf, or that Bear, this had been false, by presenting an Image not conformable to the Nature and Character of a
Hero, &c.

(3) *Hyperboles* are of diverse sorts, and the manner of introducing them is different: Some are as it were naturalized and
established by a customary way of Expression; as when we say,

6 *Earl of* Mulgrave's *Essay upon Poetry; and Lord* Roscommon's *upon Translated Verse.*

such a one's as swift as the Wind, whiter than Snow, or the like. *Homer* speaking of *Nereus*, calls him, Beauty it self;[1] *Martial* of *Zoilus*, Lewdness it self.[2] Such Hyperboles lye indeed, but deceive us not; and therefore *Seneca* terms them Lyes that readily conduct our Imagination to Truths, and have an intelligible Signification, tho' the Expression be strain'd beyond Credibility.[3] Custom has likewise familiarized another way for Hyperboles, for Example, by Irony; as when we say of some infamous Woman, She's a civil Person, where the Meaning's to be taken quite opposite to the Letter. These few Figures are mentioned only for Example sake; it will be understood that all others are to be used with the like Care and Discretion.

(4) I needed not to have travelled so far for an extravagant Flight; I remember one of *British* Growth of the like Nature:

> *See those dead Bodies hence convey'd with Care,*
> *Life may perhaps return—with change of Air.*

But I choose rather to correct gently, by foreign Examples, hoping that such as are conscious of the like Excesses will take the Hint, and secretly reprove themselves. It may be possible for some Tempers to maintain Rage and Indignation to the last Gasp; but the Soul and Body once parted, there must necessarily be a Determination of Action.

> *Quodcunque ostendis mihi sic incredulus odi.*[4]

I cannot forbear quoting on this Occasion, as an Example for the present Purpose, two noble Lines of *Jasper Main*'s, in the Collection of the *Oxford* Verses printed in the Year 1643, upon the Death of my Grandfather Sir *Bevil Granville*, slain in the heat of Action at the Battle of *Landsdowne*. The Poet, after having described the Fight, the Soldiers animated by the Example of their Leader, and enraged at his Death, thus concludes,

> *Thus he being slain, his Action fought anew,*
> *And the Dead conquer'd, whilst the Living slew.*

---

1 [*Iliad* ii.671.]
2 [*Epigrams* xi.92.]
3 [*De Benficiis* vii.23.]
4 [Horace, *Ars Poetica* 188: "Whatever you show me of this kind, I discount and hate."]

This is agreeable to Truth, and within the Compass of Nature: It is thus only that the Dead can act.

> (5) *Le jour qu'elle nâquit, Venus bien qu'Immortelle,*
> *Pensa mourir de honte, en la voyant si belle,*
> *Les graces a l'envi descendirent des Cieux*
> *Pour avoir l'honeur d'accompagner ses yeux,*
> *Et l'Amour, qui ne pût entrer dans son courage,*
> *Voulut obstinément loger sur son Visage.*

This is agreeable to Truth, and within the Compass of Nature: It *neille*; civil, to be sure, and polite as any thing can be. Let any Body turn over *Waller*, and he will see how much more naturally and delicately the *English* Author treats the Article of Love, than this celebrated *Frenchman*. I would not however be thought by any derogatory Quotation to take from the Merit of a Writer whose Reputation is so universally and so justly established in all Nations; but as I said before, I rather choose, where any Failings are to be found, to correct my own Countrymen by foreign Examples, than to provoke them by Instances drawn from their own Writings. *Humanum est errare.*[5] I cannot forbear one Quotation more from another celebrated *French* Author. It is an Epigram upon a Monument for *Francis* the first King of *France*, by way of Question and Answer, which in *English* is *verbatim* thus,

> *Under this Marble, who lies buried here?*
> Francis *the Great, a King beyond compare.*
> *Why has so great a King, so small a Stone?*
> *Of that great King here's but the Heart alone.*
> *Then of this Conqueror here lies but part?*
> *No—here he lies* all—*for he was all* Heart.

The Author was a *Gascon*, to whom I can properly oppose no body so well as a *Welchman*, for which purpose I am farther furnished from the forementioned Collection of *Oxford* Verses, with an Epigram by *Martin Lluellin* upon the same Subject, which I remember to have heard often repeated to me when I was a Boy. Besides, from whence can we draw better Examples than from the very Seat and Nursery of the *Muses*?

[5] ["To err is human"—a proverbial phrase, anticipating l. 525 of Pope's *Essay on Criticism*.]

Thus slain, thy valiant Ancestor[6] did lie,
When his one Bark a Navy did defy;
When now encompass'd round, he Victor stood,
And bath'd his Pinnace in his conquering Blood,
Till all the purple Current dry'd and spent,
He fell, and made the Waves his Monument.
Where shall the next fam'd Granville's *Ashes stand?*
Thy Grandsire's fills the Sea, and thine the Land.

I cannot say the two last Lines, in which consists the Sting or Point of the Epigram, are strictly conformable to the Rule herein set down; the Word Ashes, metaphorically, can signify nothing but Fame; which is meer Sound, and can fill no Space either of Land or Sea: The *Welchman* however must be allow'd to have out-done the *Gascon.* The Fallacy of the *French* Epigram appears at first Sight; but the *English* strikes the Fancy, suspends and dazles the Judgment, and may perhaps be allow'd to pass under the Shelter of those daring Hyperboles, which by presenting an obvious Meaning, make their way, according to *Seneca,* through the Incredible to True.

(6) *Victrix Causa Deis placuit, sed Victa Catoni.*[7] The Consent of so many Ages having establish'd the Reputation of this Line, it may perhaps be Presumption to attack it; but it is not to be supposed that *Cato,* who is described to have been a Man of rigid Morals and strict Devotion, more resembling the Gods, than Men, would have chosen any Party in opposition to those Gods whom he profest to adore. The Poet would give us to understand, that his Hero was too righteous a Person to accompany the Divinities themselves in an unjust Cause; but to represent a mortal Man to be either wiser or juster than the Deity, may shew the Impiety of the Writer, but add nothing to the Merit of the Hero; neither Reason nor Religion will allow it, and it is impossible for a corrupt Being to be more excellent than a divine: Success implies Permission, and not Approbation; to place the Gods always on the thriving Side, is to make them Partakers of all Successful Wickedness: To judge right, we must wait for the

6 *Sir* Richard Granville, *Vice-Admiral of* England, *in the Reign of Queen* Elizabeth, *maintain'd a Fight with his single Ship against the whole Armada of* Spain, *consisting of fifty three of their best Men of War.*
7 [Lucan, *Pharsalia* i.128: "The victor had the gods on his side, but the vanquished had Cato."]

Conclusion of the Action; the Catastrophe will best decide on which side is Providence, and the violent Death of *Cæsar* acquits the Gods from being Companions of his Usurpation.

Lucan was a determin'd Republican, no wonder he was a Freethinker.

(7) Mr. *Dryden* in one of his Prologues[8] has these two Lines:

> *He's bound to please, not to write well, and knows*
> *There is a Mode in Plays, as well as Cloaths.*

From whence it is plain where he has exposed himself to the Criticks; he was forced to follow the Fashion to humour an Audience, and not to please himself. A hard Sacrifice to make for present Subsistence, especially for such as would have their Writings live as well as themselves. Nor can the Poet whose Labours are his daily Bread, be deliver'd from this cruel Necessity, unless some more certain Encouragement can be provided than the bare uncertain Profits of a Third Day,[9] and the Theatre be put under some more impartial Management than the Jurisdiction of the Players. Who write to live, must unavoidably comply with their Taste by whose Approbation they subsist; some generous Prince, or Prime Minister like *Richlieu,* can only find a Remedy. In his Epistle Dedicatory to the *Spanish Friar,* this incomparable Poet thus censures himself:

"I remember some Verses of my own, *Maximin* and *Almanzor,* which cry Vengeance upon me for their Extravagance, *&c.* All I can say for those Passages, which are I hope not many, is, that I knew they were bad enough to please, even when I wrote them; but I repent of them among my Sins: And if any of their Fellows intrude by chance into my present Writings, I draw a Stroke over those *Dalilah's* of the Theatre, and am resolved I will settle my self no Reputation by the Applause of Fools: 'Tis not that I am mortified to all Ambition, but I scorn as much to take it from half-witted Judges, as I should to raise an Estate by cheating of Bubbles: Neither do I discommend the lofty Style in Tragedy, which is pompous and magnificent; but nothing is truly sublime, that is not just and proper."

8 [To *The Rival Ladies* (1664).]
9 [The author received no profit from the proceeds of the first two nights.]

This may stand as an unanswerable Apology for Mr. *Dryden*, against his Criticks: And likewise for an unquestionable Authority to confirm those Principles which the foregoing Poem pretends to lay down, for nothing can be just and proper but what is built upon Truth.

Appendix

Samuel Johnson
on Metaphysical Wit

FROM *The Life of Cowley* (1779)

Wit, like all other things subject by their nature to the choice of man, has its changes and fashions, and at different times takes different forms. About the beginning of the seventeenth century appeared a race of writers that may be termed the metaphysical poets; of whom, in a criticism on the works of Cowley, it is not improper to give some account.

The metaphysical poets were men of learning, and to shew their learning was their whole endeavour; but, unluckily resolving to shew it in rhyme, instead of writing poetry they only wrote verses, and very often such verses as stood the trial of the finger better than of the ear; for the modulation was so imperfect, that they were only found to be verses by counting the syllables.

If the father of criticism has rightly denominated poetry τέχνη μιμητική, *an imitative art*, these writers will, without great wrong, lose their right to the name of poets; for they cannot be said to have imitated any thing; they neither copied nature nor life; neither painted the forms of matter, nor represented the operations of intellect.

Those however who deny them to be poets, allow them to be wits. Dryden confesses of himself and his contemporaries, that they fall below Donne in wit, but maintains that they surpass him in poetry.

If Wit be well described by Pope, as being, "that" which has been often thought, but was never before so "well expressed," they certainly never attained, nor ever sought it; for they endeavoured to be singular in their thoughts, and were careless of their diction. But Pope's account of wit is undoubtedly erroneous: he depresses it below its natural dignity, and reduces it from strength of thought to happiness of language.

If by a more noble and more adequate conception that be considered as Wit, which is at once natural and new, that which, though not obvious is, upon its first production, acknowledged to be just; if it be that, which he that never found it wonders how he missed; to wit of this kind the metaphysical poets have seldom risen. Their thoughts are often new, but seldom natural; they are not obvious, but neither are they just; and the reader, far from wondering that he missed them, wonders more frequently by what perverseness of industry they were ever found.

But Wit, abstracted from its effects upon the hearer, may be more rigorously and philosophically considered as a kind of *discordia concors;* a combination of dissimilar images, or discovery of occult resemblances in things apparently unlike. Of wit, thus defined, they have more than enough. The most heterogeneous ideas are yoked by violence together; nature and art are ransacked for illustrations, comparisons, and allusions; their learning instructs, and their subtilty surprises; but the reader commonly thinks his improvement dearly bought, and, though he sometimes admires, is seldom pleased.

From this account of their compositions it will be readily inferred, that they were not successful in representing or moving the affections. As they were wholly employed on something unexpected and surprising, they had no regard to that uniformity of sentiment which enables us to conceive and to excite the pains and the pleasure of other minds: they never enquired what, on any occasion, they should have said or done; but wrote rather as beholders than partakers of human nature; as Beings looking upon good and evil, impassive and at leisure; as Epicurean deities making remarks on the actions of men, and the vicissitudes of life, without interest and without emotion. Their courtship was void of fondness and their lamentation of sorrow. Their wish was only to say what they hoped had been never said before.

Nor was the sublime more within their reach than the pathetick; for they never attempted that comprehension and expanse of thought which at once fills the whole mind, and of which the first effect is sudden astonishment, and the second rational admiration. Sublimity is produced by aggregation, and littleness by dispersion. Great thoughts are always general, and consist in positions not limited by exceptions, and in descriptions not descending to minuteness. It is with great propriety that Subtlety, which in its original import means exility of particles, is taken in its metaphorical meaning for nicety of distinction. Those writers who lay on the watch for novelty could have little hope of greatness; for great things cannot have escaped former observation. Their attempts were always analytick; they broke every image into fragments; and could no more represent by their slender conceits and laboured particularities, the prospects of nature, or the scenes of life, than he, who dissects a sun-beam with a prism, can exhibit the wide effulgence of a summer noon.

What they wanted however of the sublime, they endeavoured to supply by hyperbole; their amplification had no limits; they left not only reason but fancy behind them; and produced combinations of confused magnificence, that not only could not be credited, but could not be imagined.

Yet great labour, directed by great abilities, is never wholly lost: if they frequently threw away their wit upon false conceits, they likewise sometimes struck out unexpected truth: if their conceits were far-fetched, they were often worth the carriage. To write on their plan, it was at least necessary to read and think. No man could be born a metaphysical poet, nor assume the dignity of a writer, by descriptions copied from descriptions, by imitations borrowed from imitations, by traditional imagery, and hereditary similes, by readiness of rhyme, and volubility of syllables.

In perusing the works of this race of authors, the mind is exercised either by recollection or inquiry; either something already learned is to be retrieved, or something new is to be examined. If their greatness seldom elevates, their acuteness often surprises; if the imagination is not always gratified, at least the powers of reflection and comparison are employed; and in the mass of materials which ingenious absurdity has thrown together, genuine wit and useful knowledge may be sometimes found, buried perhaps in grossness of expression, but useful to those who know their value; and such as, when they are expanded to perspicuity, and polished to elegance, may give lustre to works which have more propriety though less copiousness of sentiment.

This kind of writing, which was, I believe, borrowed from Marino and his followers, had been recommended by the example of Donne, a man of very extensive and various knowledge, and by Jonson, whose manner resembled that of Donne more in the ruggedness of his lines than in the cast of his sentiments.

When their reputation was high, they had undoubtedly more imitators, than time has left behind. Their immediate successors, of whom any remembrance can be said to remain, were Suckling, Waller, Denham, Cowley, Cleiveland, and Milton. Denham and Waller sought another way to fame, by improving the harmony of our numbers. Milton tried the metaphysick style only in his lines upon Hobson the Carrier. Cowley adopted it, and excelled his predecessors, having as much sentiment, and more musick. Suckling neither improved versification, nor abounded in conceits. The fashionable style remained chiefly with Cowley; Suckling could not reach it, and Milton disdained it.

CRITICAL REMARKS are not easily understood without examples; and I have therefore collected instances of the modes of writing by which this species of poets, for poets they were called by themselves and their admirers, was eminently distinguished.

As the authors of this race were perhaps more desirous of being admired than understood, they sometimes drew their conceits from recesses of learning not very much frequented by common readers of poetry. Thus Cowley on *Knowledge:*

> The sacred tree midst the fair orchard grew;
> The phœnix Truth did on it rest,
> And built his perfum'd nest,
> That right Porphyrian tree which did true logick shew.
> Each leaf did learned notions give,
> And th' apples were demonstrative:
> So clear their colour and divine,
> The very shade they cast did other lights outshine.

· · ·

Thus *Donne* shews his medicinal knowledge in some encomiastick verses:

> In every thing there naturally grows
> A Balsamum to keep it fresh and new,
> If 'twere not injur'd by extrinsique blows;
> Your youth and beauty are this balm in you.
> But you, of learning and religion,
> And virtue and such ingredients, have made
> A mithridate, whose operation
> Keeps off, or cures what can be done or said.

Though the following lines of Donne, on the last night of the year, have something in them too scholastick, they are not inelegant:

> This twilight of two years, not past nor next,
> Some emblem is of me, or I of this,
> Who, meteor-like, of stuff and form perplext,
> Whose what and where in disputation is,
> If I should call me any thing, should miss.
>
> I sum the years and me, and find me not
> Debtor to th' old nor creditor to th' new,
> That cannot say, my thanks I have forgot,
> Nor trust I this with hopes; and yet scarce true
> This bravery is, since these times shew'd me you.
>   DONNE

Yet more abstruse and profound is *Donne's* reflection upon Man as a Microcosm:

> If men be worlds, there is in every one
> Something to answer in some proportion
> All the world's riches: and in good men, this
> Virtue, our form's form, and our soul's soul is.

· · ·

Who but Donne would have thought that a good man is a telescope?

Though God be our true glass, through which we see
All, since the being of all things is he,
Yet are the trunks, which do to us derive
Things in proportion fit, by perspective
Deeds of good men; for by their living here,
Virtues, indeed remote, seem to be near.

. . .

In forming descriptions, they looked out not for images, but for conceits. Night has been a common subject, which poets have contended to adorn. Dryden's Night is well known; Donne's is as follows:

Thou seest me here at midnight, now all rest.
Time's dead low-water; when all minds divest
To-morrow's business, when the labourers have
Such rest in bed, that their last church-yard grave,
Subject to change, will scarce be a type of this,
Now when the client, whose last hearing is
To-morrow, sleeps; when the condemned man,
Who when he opes his eyes, must shut them then
Again by death, although sad watch he keep,
Doth practise dying by a little sleep,
Thou at this midnight seest me.

It must be however confessed of these writers, that if they are upon common subjects often unnecessarily and unpoetically subtle; yet where scholastick speculation can be properly admitted, their copiousness and acuteness may justly be admired. What Cowley has written upon Hope shews, an unequalled fertility of invention:

Hope, whose weak being ruin'd is,
  Alike if it succeed, and if it miss;
Whom good or ill does equally confound,
And both the horns of Fate's dilemma wound.
  Vain shadow, which dost vanish quite,
  Both at full noon and perfect night!
The stars have not a possibility
  Of blessing thee;
If things then from their end we happy call,
'Tis Hope is the most hopeless thing of all.

Hope, thou bold taster of delight,
Who, whilst thou should'st but taste, devour'st it quite!
Thou bring'st us an estate, yet leav'st us poor,
By clogging it with legacies before!
  The joys which we entire should wed,
  Come deflower'd virgins to our bed;
Good fortunes without gain imported be,
  Such mighty custom's paid to thee:
For joy, like wine, kept close does better taste:
If it take air before, its spirits waste.

To the following comparison of a man that travels, and his wife that stays at home, with a pair of compasses, it may be doubted whether absurdity or ingenuity has the better claim:

> Our two souls therefore, which are one,
>   Though I must go, endure not yet
> A breach, but an expansion,
>   Like gold to airy thinness beat.
>
> If they be two, they are two so
>   As stiff twin-compasses are two,
> Thy soul, the fixt foot, makes no show
>   To move, but doth, if th' other do.
>
> And though it in the centre sit,
>   Yet when the other far doth roam,
> It leans, and hearkens after it,
>   And grows erect, as that comes home.
>
> Such wilt thou be to me, who must
>   Like th' other foot, obliquely run.
> Thy firmness makes my circle just,
>   And makes me end where I begun.
>   DONNE

In all these examples it is apparent, that whatever is improper or vitious, is produced by a voluntary deviation from nature in pursuit of something new and strange; and that the writers fail to give delight, by their desire of exciting admiration.

Selected Bibliography

ANTHOLOGIES

Joel E. Spingarn's *Critical Essays of the Seventeenth Century* (3 vols., 1908–09), with scholarly notes and an excellent introduction, remains the standard work in the field. For the earlier and later periods, well-edited material may be found in G. Gregory Smith, *Elizabethan Critical Essays* (2 vols., 1904), and Scott Elledge, *Eighteenth-Century Critical Essays* (2 vols., 1961). H. H. Adams and B. Hathaway have edited *Dramatic Essays of the Neoclassical Age* (1950). Allan H. Gilbert's *Literary Criticism: Plato to Dryden* (1940) is particularly valuable for translations from important Continental critics.

HISTORY OF CRITICISM

The most comprehensive treatment of the period appears in J. W. H. Atkins, *English Literary Criticism: The Renascence* (2nd ed., 1951) and *English Literary Criticism: 17th and 18th Centuries* (1951), but many will find the appropriate sections of William K. Wimsatt and Cleanth Brooks, *Literary Criticism: A Short History* (1957), more incisive and stimulating. For an acute survey of modern opinion, see J. A. Mazzeo, "A Critique of Some Modern Theories of Metaphysical Poetry," *Modern Philology*, L (1952), reprinted in *Seventeenth-Century English Poetry* (1962), ed. William R. Keast, and in *Discussions of John Donne* (1962), ed. Frank Kermode. For the important early influence of Italy, consult Baxter Hathaway, *The Age of Criticism: The Late Renaissance in Italy* (1962) and Bernard Weinberg, *A History of Literary Criticism in the Italian Renaissance* (2 vols., 1961). The later but equally important contributions of the French are discussed by A. F. B. Clark, *Boileau and the French Classical Critics in England, 1660–1830* (1925). More specialized studies include René Wellek, *The Rise of English Literary History* (1941); H. T. Swedenberg, *The Theory of the Epic in England, 1650–1800* (1944); R. S. Crane,

"Neo-Classical Criticism," *Dictionary of World Literature* (1943); and George Williamson's indispensable "Strong Lines," *English Studies,* XVIII (1936), reprinted in *Seventeenth Century Contexts* (1961). Although seventeenth-century theories of versification have only rarely been the subject of historical inquiry, there is much that is useful in George Saintsbury's *History of English Prosody* (3 vols., 1906–10); in John Thompson, *The Founding of English Metre* (1961); in G. Willcock, "Passing Pitiful Hexameters: A Study of Quantity and Accent in English Renaissance Criticism," *Modern Language Review,* XXIX (1934); in A. Clark, "Milton and the Renaissance Revolt Against Rhyme," *Studies in Literary Modes* (1946); and George Williamson manages to touch on prosodic theory as well as practice from Puttenham to Bysshe in "The Rhetorical Pattern of Neo-Classical Wit," *Modern Philology,* XXXIII (1935), reprinted in *Seventeenth Century Contexts* (1961).

POETIC, RHETORIC, AND LOGIC

Although the standard treatment is Wilbur S. Howell, *Rhetoric and Logic in England, 1500–1700* (1956), Sister Miriam Joseph's *Shakespeare's Use of the Arts of Language* (1947) is perhaps a more useful introduction to the subject because it offers concise summaries of the rhetorical terms and illustrates some of the hazards involved in their literary application. In *The Enduring Monument* (1962) O. B. Hardison, Jr. examines the rhetorical (and cultural) "Idea of Praise in Renaissance Literary Theory and Practice." Rosemond Tuve's brilliant if murky *Elizabethan and Metaphysical Imagery* (1947) attempts to disentangle Renaissance poetic, especially insofar as it may be understood in terms of Renaissance logic and rhetoric, from the presuppositions of twentieth-century critics. *Ramus, Method, and the Decay of Dialogue* (1958), by Father Walter J. Ong, S.J., is the most thorough of the many works that explore the controversial subject of Ramist logic and rhetoric; and see, in this connection, the demurrals of Norman E. Nelson, "Peter Ramus and the Confusion of Logic, Rhetoric and Poetry," *University of Michigan Contributions in Modern Philology,* II (1947).

POETIC, WORDS, AND IDEAS

Ruth C. Wallerstein's *Studies in Seventeenth-Century Poetic* (1950) is the most ambitious effort to derive poetic "theory" from the background of ideas, but there are a number of shorter items that in their own way contribute as much or more to an understanding of the *forma mentis* and critical vocabulary of the period. Even a brief list should include George Williamson, *The Proper Wit of Poetry* (1961), and "The Restoration Revolt against Enthusiasm," *Studies in Philology*, XXX (1933), reprinted in *Seventeenth Century Contexts* (1961); S. L. Bethell, "Gracián, Tesauro, and the Nature of Metaphysical Wit," *Northern Miscellany of Literary Criticism*, I (1953), reprinted in *Discussions of John Donne* (1962), ed. Frank Kermode; Edward N. Hooker, "Pope on Wit—The Essay on Criticism," *The Seventeenth Century* (1951), ed. R. F. Jones *et al.*; Hoyt H. Hudson and W. L. Astick, "Wit, 'Mixt Wit,' and the Bee in Amber," *Huntington Library Bulletin*, V (1935); Richard E. Hughes, " 'Wit': The Genealogy of a Theory," *College Language Association Journal*, V (1961); C. S. Lewis, "Nature," "Wit," and "Sense," *Studies in Words* (1960); A. O. Lovejoy, "The Parallel of Deism and Classicism" and " 'Nature' as Aesthetic Norm," *Essays in the History of Ideas* (1948); Harold S. Wilson, "Some Meanings of 'Nature' in Renaissance Literary Theory," *Journal of the History of Ideas*, II (1941); Murray W. Bundy, " 'Invention' and 'Imagination' in the Renaissance," *Journal of English and Germanic Philology*, XXIX (1930); D. F. Bond, "Distrust of the Imagination in English Neo-Classicism," *Philological Quarterly*, XIV (1935), and "The Neo-Classical Psychology of the Imagination," *ELH: A Journal of English Literary History*, IV (1937); J. A. Mazzeo, "Metaphysical Poetry and the Poetic of Correspondence," *Journal of the History of Ideas*, XIV (1953), and "A Seventeenth-Century Theory of Metaphysical Poetry," *Romanic Review*, XLII (1951), reprinted in *Renaissance and Seventeenth-Century Studies* (1964); Rosalie L. Colie, *Paradoxia Epidemica* (1966).

Index

ABOUT THE EDITOR

*EDWARD W. TAYLER received his B.A. in
1954 from Amherst and his Ph.D. in 1960 from
Stanford. He is presently an associate professor of
Renaissance and seventeenth-century literature at
Columbia University where he has taught since
1960. Professor Tayler has received fellowships
from The Huntington Library and from the Council for Research in the Humanities at Columbia.
In 1964 he published* Nature and Art in Renaissance Literature.

A NOTE ON THE TYPE

The text of this book was set on the Linotype in a new face called Primer, designed by Rudolph Ruzicka, earlier responsible for the design of Fairfield and Fairfield Medium, Linotype faces whose virtues have for some time now been accorded wide recognition.

The complete range of sizes of Primer was first made available in 1954, although the pilot size of 12 point was ready as early as 1951. The design of the face makes general reference to Linotype Century (long a serviceable type, totally lacking in manner or frills of any kind) but brilliantly corrects the characterless quality of that face.

The book was designed by Betty Anderson and was composed, printed, and bound by H. Wolff, New York.